Butterworths Stu

EC La

Butterworths Student Statutes

# EC Law

**Sarah Gale**, LLB, London, Solicitor
Lecturer in Law
City University

**Butterworths**
London, Edinburgh, Dublin
1998

| United Kingdom | Butterworths, a Division of Reed Elsevier (UK) Ltd, Halsbury House, 35 Chancery Lane, LONDON WC2A 1EL and 4 Hill Street, EDINBURGH EH2 3JZ |
| --- | --- |
| Australia | Butterworths, a Division of Reed International Books Australia Pty Ltd, CHATSWOOD, New South Wales |
| Canada | Butterworths Canada Ltd, MARKHAM, Ontario |
| Hong Kong | Butterworths Asia (Hong Kong), HONG KONG |
| India | Butterworths India, NEW DELHI |
| Ireland | Butterworth (Ireland) Ltd, DUBLIN |
| Malaysia | Malayan Law Journal Sdn Bhd, KUALA LUMPUR |
| New Zealand | Butterworths of New Zealand Ltd, WELLINGTON |
| Singapore | Butterworths Asia, SINGAPORE |
| South Africa | Butterworths Publishers (Pty) Ltd, DURBAN |
| USA | Lexis Law Publishing, CHARLOTTESVILLE, Virginia |

A CIP Catalogue record for this book is available from the British Library.

ISBN  0 406 98169 8

Typeset by Doyle & Co, Colchester
Printed and bound in Great Britain by Butler and Tanner, Frome

# Preface

The signing of the Amsterdam Treaty made the Second Edition of this collection of EC materials inevitable. EC lawyers approach this Treaty with a feeling of dread because of the fact that much of the numbering of the key Treaty Articles has been changed. This will make the teaching and studying of EC Law far harder.

The Competition Section of the Second Edition has been amended to reflect the continuing importance of the enforcement of article 85 (new article 81) and 86 (new article 82) by domestic courts and competition authorities. This Section also contains the recent Commission Notices on Market Definition, Fines and the latest version of the De Minimis Notice.

I would like to thank the publishers, and in particular academic publishing, European Information Services and the Statutory Materials Departments for their help in the preparation of the Second Edition. This book could not have been published without their contribution.

The Law Librarian at City University, Dawn Patrick, played a vital role in the compilation of these materials. She kindly gave me very valuable tuition in the use of The Internet.

Thanks should also go to my mother and father for all the help and encouragement. This text is correct as at August 1998.


Sarah Gale
August 1998

# Contents

## SECONDARY LEGISLATION

# Contents

Contents

## UK LEGISLATION

# PRIMARY LEGISLATION

# CONSOLIDATED VERSION OF THE TREATY ESTABLISHING THE EUROPEAN COMMUNITY

NOTES

Consolidated version of the EC Treaty as amended by the Treaty of Amsterdam. Date of publication in the OJ: OJ C340, 10.11.97, p1.

## PART ONE
## PRINCIPLES

**Article 1** (ex Article 1)

By this Treaty, the High Contracting Parties establish among themselves a European Community.

**Article 2** (ex Article 2)

The Community shall have as its task, by establishing a common market and an economic and monetary union and by implementing common policies or activities referred to in Articles 3 and 4, to promote throughout the Community a harmonious, balanced and sustainable development of economic activities, a high level of employment and of social protection, equality between men and women, sustainable and non-inflationary growth, a high degree of competitiveness and convergence of economic performance, a high level of protection and improvement of the quality of the environment, the raising of the standard of living and quality of life, and economic and social cohesion and solidarity among Member States.

**Article 3** (ex Article 3)

1.    For the purposes set out in Article 2, the activities of the Community shall include, as provided in this Treaty and in accordance with the timetable set out therein:
   (a)  the prohibition, as between Member States, of customs duties and quantitative restrictions on the import and export of goods, and of all other measures having equivalent effect;
   (b)  a common commercial policy;
   (c)  an internal market characterised by the abolition, as between Member States, of obstacles to the free movement of goods, persons, services and capital;
   (d)  measures concerning the entry and movement of persons as provided for in Title IV;
   (e)  a common policy in the sphere of agriculture and fisheries;
   (f)  a common policy in the sphere of transport;
   (g)  a system ensuring that competition in the internal market is not distorted;
   (h)  the approximation of the laws of Member States to the extent required for the functioning of the common market;
   (i)  the promotion of co-ordination between employment policies of the Member States with a view to enhancing their effectiveness by developing a co-ordinated strategy for employment;

(j)  a policy in the social sphere comprising a European Social Fund;
(k)  the strengthening of economic and social cohesion;
(l)  a policy in the sphere of the environment;
(m) the strengthening of the competitiveness of Community industry;
(n)  the promotion of research and technological development;
(o)  encouragement for the establishment and development of trans-European networks;
(p)  a contribution to the attainment of a high level of health protection;
(q)  a contribution to education and training of quality and to the flowering of the cultures of the Member States;
(r)  a policy in the sphere of development co-operation;
(s)  the association of the overseas countries and territories in order to increase trade and promote jointly economic and social development;
(t)  a contribution to the strengthening of consumer protection;
(u)  measures in the spheres of energy, civil protection and tourism.

2.    In all the activities referred to in this Article, the Community shall aim to eliminate inequalities, and to promote equality, between men and women.

**Article 4** (ex Article 3a)

1.    For the purposes set out in Article 2, the activities of the Member States and the Community shall include, as provided in this Treaty and in accordance with the timetable set out therein, the adoption of an economic policy which is based on the close co-ordination of Member States' economic policies, on the internal market and on the definition of common objectives, and conducted in accordance with the principle of an open market economy with free competition.

2.    Concurrently with the foregoing, and as provided in this Treaty and in accordance with the timetable and the procedures set out therein, these activities shall include the irrevocable fixing of exchange rates leading to the introduction of a single currency, the ECU, and the definition and conduct of a single monetary policy and exchange-rate policy the primary objective of both of which shall be to maintain price stability and, without prejudice to this objective, to support the general economic policies in the Community, in accordance with the principle of an open market economy with free competition.

3.    These activities of the Member States and the Community shall entail compliance with the following guiding principles: stable prices, sound public finances and monetary conditions and a sustainable balance of payments.

**Article 5** (ex Article 3b)

The Community shall act within the limits of the powers conferred upon it by this Treaty and of the objectives assigned to it therein.

In areas which do not fall within its exclusive competence, the Community shall take action, in accordance with the principle of subsidiarity, only if and insofar as the objectives of the proposed action cannot be sufficiently achieved by the Member States and can therefore, by reason of the scale or effects of the proposed action, be better achieved by the Community.

Any action by the Community shall not go beyond what is necessary to achieve the objectives of this Treaty.

**Article 6** (ex Article 3c)

Environmental protection requirements must be integrated into the definition and implementation of the Community policies and activities referred to in Article 3, in particular with a view to promoting sustainable development.

**Article 7** (ex Article 4)

1.     The tasks entrusted to the Community shall be carried out by the following institutions :
   — a European Parliament,
   — a Council,
   — a Commission,
   — a Court of Justice,
   — a Court of Auditors.

Each institution shall act within the limits of the powers conferred upon it by this Treaty.

2.     The Council and the Commission shall be assisted by an Economic and Social Committee and a Committee of the Regions acting in an advisory capacity.

**Article 8** (ex Article 4a)

A European System of Central Banks (hereinafter referred to as 'ESCB') and a European Central Bank (hereinafter referred to as 'ECB') shall be established in accordance with the procedures laid down in this Treaty; they shall act within the limits of the powers conferred upon them by this Treaty and by the Statute of the ESCB and of the ECB (hereinafter referred to as 'Statute of the ESCB') annexed thereto.

**Article 9** (ex Article 4b)

A European Investment Bank is hereby established, which shall act within the limits of the powers conferred upon it by this Treaty and the Statute annexed thereto.

**Article 10** (ex Article 5)

Member States shall take all appropriate measures, whether general or particular, to ensure fulfilment of the obligations arising out of this Treaty or resulting from action taken by the institutions of the Community. They shall facilitate the achievement of the Community's tasks.

They shall abstain from any measure which could jeopardise the attainment of the objectives of this Treaty.

**Article 11** (ex Article 5a)

1.     Member States which intend to establish closer co-operation between themselves may be authorised, subject to Articles 43 and 44 of the Treaty on European Union, to make use of the institutions, procedures and mechanisms laid down by this Treaty, provided that the co-operation proposed:
   (a)  does not concern areas which fall within the exclusive competence of the Community;
   (b)  does not affect Community policies, actions or programmes;

   (c)  does not concern the citizenship of the Union or discriminate between nationals of Member States;

   (d)  remains within the limits of the powers conferred upon the Community by this Treaty; and

   (e)  does not constitute a discrimination or a restriction of trade between Member States and does not distort the conditions of competition between the latter.

2.    The authorisation referred to in paragraph 1 shall be granted by the Council, acting by a qualified majority on a proposal from the Commission and after consulting the European Parliament.

If a member of the Council declares that, for important and stated reasons of national policy, it intends to oppose the granting of an authorisation by qualified majority, a vote shall not be taken. The Council may, acting by a qualified majority, request that the matter be referred to the Council, meeting in the composition of the Heads of State or Government, for decision by unanimity.

Member States which intend to establish closer co-operation as referred to in paragraph 1 may address a request to the Commission, which may submit a proposal to the Council to that effect. In the event of the Commission not submitting a proposal, it shall inform the Member States concerned of the reasons for not doing so.

3.    Any Member State which wishes to become a party to co-operation set up in accordance with this Article shall notify its intention to the Council and to the Commission, which shall give an opinion to the Council within three months of receipt of that notification. Within four months of the date of that notification, the Commission shall decide on it and on such specific arrangements as it may deem necessary.

4.    The acts and decisions necessary for the implementation of co-operation activities shall be subject to all the relevant provisions of this Treaty, save as otherwise provided for in this Article and in Articles 43 and 44 of the Treaty on European Union.

5.    This Article is without prejudice to the provisions of the Protocol integrating the Schengen acquis into the framework of the European Union.

## Article 12 (ex Article 6)

Within the scope of application of this Treaty, and without prejudice to any special provisions contained therein, any discrimination on grounds of nationality shall be prohibited.

The Council, acting in accordance with the procedure referred to in Article 251, may adopt rules designed to prohibit such discrimination.

## Article 13 (ex Article 6a)

Without prejudice to the other provisions of this Treaty and within the limits of the powers conferred by it upon the Community, the Council, acting unanimously on a proposal from the Commission and after consulting the European Parliament, may take appropriate action to combat discrimination based on sex, racial or ethnic origin, religion or belief, disability, age or sexual orientation.

**Article 14** (ex Article 7a)

1.      The Community shall adopt measures with the aim of progressively establishing the internal market over a period expiring on 31 December 1992, in accordance with the provisions of this Article and of Articles 15, 26, 47(2), 49, 80, 93 and 95 and without prejudice to the other provisions of this Treaty.

2.      The internal market shall comprise an area without internal frontiers in which the free movement of goods, persons, services and capital is ensured in accordance with the provisions of this Treaty.

3.      The Council, acting by a qualified majority on a proposal from the Commission, shall determine the guidelines and conditions necessary to ensure balanced progress in all the sectors concerned.

**Article 15** (ex Article 7c)

When drawing up its proposals with a view to achieving the objectives set out in Article 14, the Commission shall take into account the extent of the effort that certain economies showing differences in development will have to sustain during the period of establishment of the internal market and it may propose appropriate provisions.

If these provisions take the form of derogations, they must be of a temporary nature and must cause the least possible disturbance to the functioning of the common market.

**Article 16** (ex Article 7d)

Without prejudice to Articles 73, 86 and 87, and given the place occupied by services of general economic interest in the shared values of the Union as well as their role in promoting social and territorial cohesion, the Community and the Member States, each within their respective powers and within the scope of application of this Treaty, shall take care that such services operate on the basis of principles and conditions which enable them to fulfil their missions.

# PART TWO
## CITIZENSHIP OF THE UNION

**Article 17** (ex Article 8)

1.      Citizenship of the Union is hereby established. Every person holding the nationality of a Member State shall be a citizen of the Union. Citizenship of the Union shall complement and not replace national citizenship.

2.      Citizens of the Union shall enjoy the rights conferred by this Treaty and shall be subject to the duties imposed thereby.

**Article 18** (ex Article 8a)

1.      Every citizen of the Union shall have the right to move and reside freely within the territory of the Member States, subject to the limitations and conditions laid down in this Treaty and by the measures adopted to give it effect.

2.      The Council may adopt provisions with a view to facilitating the exercise of the rights referred to in paragraph 1; save as otherwise provided in this Treaty, the Council

shall act in accordance with the procedure referred to in Article 251. The Council shall act unanimously throughout this procedure.

**Article 19** (ex Article 8b)

1.     Every citizen of the Union residing in a Member State of which he is not a national shall have the right to vote and to stand as a candidate at municipal elections in the Member State in which he resides, under the same conditions as nationals of that State. This right shall be exercised subject to detailed arrangements adopted by the Council, acting unanimously on a proposal from the Commission and after consulting the European Parliament; these arrangements may provide for derogations where warranted by problems specific to a Member State.

2.     Without prejudice to Article 190(4) and to the provisions adopted for its implementation, every citizen of the Union residing in a Member State of which he is not a national shall have the right to vote and to stand as a candidate in elections to the European Parliament in the Member State in which he resides, under the same conditions as nationals of that State. This right shall be exercised subject to detailed arrangements adopted by the Council, acting unanimously on a proposal from the Commission and after consulting the European Parliament; these arrangements may provide for derogations where warranted by problems specific to a Member State.

**Article 20** (ex Article 8c)

Every citizen of the Union shall, in the territory of a third country in which the Member State of which he is a national is not represented, be entitled to protection by the diplomatic or consular authorities of any Member State, on the same conditions as the nationals of that State. Member States shall establish the necessary rules among themselves and start the international negotiations required to secure this protection.

**Article 21** (ex Article 8d)

Every citizen of the Union shall have the right to petition the European Parliament in accordance with Article 194.

Every citizen of the Union may apply to the Ombudsman established in accordance with Article 195.

Every citizen of the Union may write to any of the institutions or bodies referred to in this Article or in Article 7 in one of the languages mentioned in Article 314 and have an answer in the same language.

**Article 22** (ex Article 8e)

The Commission shall report to the European Parliament, to the Council and to the Economic and Social Committee every three years on the application of the provisions of this Part. This report shall take account of the development of the Union.

On this basis, and without prejudice to the other provisions of this Treaty, the Council, acting unanimously on a proposal from the Commission and after consulting the European Parliament, may adopt provisions to strengthen or to add to the rights laid down in this Part, which it shall recommend to the Member States for adoption in accordance with their respective constitutional requirements.

# PART THREE
# COMMUNITY POLICIES

## TITLE I
## FREE MOVEMENT OF GOODS

**Article 23** (ex Article 9)

1.     The Community shall be based upon a customs union which shall cover all trade in goods and which shall involve the prohibition between Member States of customs duties on imports and exports and of all charges having equivalent effect, and the adoption of a common customs tariff in their relations with third countries.

2.     The provisions of Article 25 and of Chapter 2 of this Title shall apply to products originating in Member States and to products coming from third countries which are in free circulation in Member States.

**Article 24** (ex Article 10)

Products coming from a third country shall be considered to be in free circulation in a Member State if the import formalities have been complied with and any customs duties or charges having equivalent effect which are payable have been levied in that Member State, and if they have not benefited from a total or partial drawback of such duties or charges.

## CHAPTER 1
## THE CUSTOMS UNION

**Article 25** (ex Article 12)

Customs duties on imports and exports and charges having equivalent effect shall be prohibited between Member States.   This prohibition shall also apply to customs duties of a fiscal nature.

**Article 26** (ex Article 28)

Common Customs Tariff duties shall be fixed by the Council acting by a qualified majority on a proposal from the Commission.

**Article 27** (ex Article 29)

In carrying out the tasks entrusted to it under this Chapter the Commission shall be guided by:
- (a)  the need to promote trade between Member States and third countries;
- (b)  developments in conditions of competition within the Community insofar as they lead to an improvement in the competitive capacity of undertakings;
- (c)  the requirements of the Community as regards the supply of raw materials and semi-finished goods; in this connection the Commission shall take care to avoid distorting conditions of competition between Member States in respect of finished goods;
- (d)  the need to avoid serious disturbances in the economies of Member States and to ensure rational development of production and an expansion of consumption within the Community.

# CHAPTER 2
# PROHIBITION OF QUANTITATIVE RESTRICTIONS
# BETWEEN MEMBER STATES

**Article 28** (ex Article 30)

Quantitative restrictions on imports and all measures having equivalent effect shall be prohibited between Member States.

**Article 29** (ex Article 34)

Quantitative restrictions on exports, and all measures having equivalent effect, shall be prohibited between Member States.

**Article 30** (ex Article 36)

The provisions of Articles 28 and 29 shall not preclude prohibitions or restrictions on imports, exports or goods in transit justified on grounds of public morality, public policy or public security; the protection of health and life of humans, animals or plants; the protection of national treasures possessing artistic, historic or archaeological value; or the protection of industrial and commercial property. Such prohibitions or restrictions shall not, however, constitute a means of arbitrary discrimination or a disguised restriction on trade between Member States.

**Article 31** (ex Article 37)

1.      Member States shall adjust any State monopolies of a commercial character so as to ensure that no discrimination regarding the conditions under which goods are procured and marketed exists between nationals of Member States.

The provisions of this Article shall apply to any body through which a Member State, in law or in fact, either directly or indirectly supervises, determines or appreciably influences imports or exports between Member States. These provisions shall likewise apply to monopolies delegated by the State to others.

2.      Member States shall refrain from introducing any new measure which is contrary to the principles laid down in paragraph 1 or which restricts the scope of the Articles dealing with the prohibition of customs duties and quantitative restrictions between Member States.

3.      If a State monopoly of a commercial character has rules which are designed to make it easier to dispose of agricultural products or obtain for them the best return, steps should be taken in applying the rules contained in this Article to ensure equivalent safeguards for the employment and standard of living of the producers concerned.

# TITLE II
# AGRICULTURE

**Article 32** (ex Article 38)

1.      The common market shall extend to agriculture and trade in agricultural products. 'Agricultural products' means the products of the soil, of stockfarming and of fisheries and products of first-stage processing directly related to these products.

2.      Save as otherwise provided in Articles 33 to 38, the rules laid down for the establishment of the common market shall apply to agricultural products.

3.      The products subject to the provisions of Articles 33 to 38 are listed in Annex I to this Treaty.

4.      The operation and development of the common market for agricultural products must be accompanied by the establishment of a common agricultural policy.

## Article 33 (ex Article 39)

1.      The objectives of the common agricultural policy shall be:
   (a)  to increase agricultural productivity by promoting technical progress and by ensuring the rational development of agricultural production and the optimum utilisation of the factors of production, in particular labour;
   (b)  thus to ensure a fair standard of living for the agricultural community, in particular by increasing the individual earnings of persons engaged in agriculture;
   (c)  to stabilise markets;
   (d)  to assure the availability of supplies;
   (e)  to ensure that supplies reach consumers at reasonable prices.

2.      In working out the common agricultural policy and the special methods for its application, account shall be taken of:
   (a)  the particular nature of agricultural activity, which results from the social structure of agriculture and from structural and natural disparities between the various agricultural regions;
   (b)  the need to effect the appropriate adjustments by degrees;
   (c)  the fact that in the Member States agriculture constitutes a sector closely linked with the economy as a whole.

## Article 34 (ex Article 40)

1.      In order to attain the objectives set out in Article 33, a common organisation of agricultural markets shall be established.

This organisation shall take one of the following forms, depending on the product concerned:
   (a)  common rules on competition;
   (b)  compulsory co-ordination of the various national market organisations;
   (c)  a European market organisation.

2.      The common organisation established in accordance with paragraph 1 may include all measures required to attain the objectives set out in Article 33, in particular regulation of prices, aids for the production and marketing of the various products, storage and carryover arrangements and common machinery for stabilising imports or exports.

The common organisation shall be limited to pursuit of the objectives set out in Article 33 and shall exclude any discrimination between producers or consumers within the Community.

Any common price policy shall be based on common criteria and uniform methods of calculation.

3.     In order to enable the common organisation referred to in paragraph 1 to attain its objectives, one or more agricultural guidance and guarantee funds may be set up.

**Article 35** (ex Article 41)

To enable the objectives set out in Article 33 to be attained, provision may be made within the framework of the common agricultural policy for measures such as:
> (a) an effective co-ordination of efforts in the spheres of vocational training, of research and of the dissemination of agricultural knowledge; this may include joint financing of projects or institutions;
> (b) joint measures to promote consumption of certain products.

**Article 36** (ex Article 42)

The provisions of the Chapter relating to rules on competition shall apply to production of and trade in agricultural products only to the extent determined by the Council within the framework of Article 37(2) and (3) and in accordance with the procedure laid down therein, account being taken of the objectives set out in Article 33.

The Council may, in particular, authorise the granting of aid:
> (a) for the protection of enterprises handicapped by structural or natural conditions;
> (b) within the framework of economic development programmes.

**Article 37** (ex Article 43)

1.     In order to evolve the broad lines of a common agricultural policy, the Commission shall, immediately this Treaty enters into force, convene a conference of the Member States with a view to making a comparison of their agricultural policies, in particular by producing a statement of their resources and needs.

2.     Having taken into account the work of the Conference provided for in paragraph 1, after consulting the Economic and Social Committee and within two years of the entry into force of this Treaty, the Commission shall submit proposals for working out and implementing the common agricultural policy, including the replacement of the national organisations by one of the forms of common organisation provided for in Article 34(1), and for implementing the measures specified in this Title.

These proposals shall take account of the interdependence of the agricultural matters mentioned in this Title.

The Council shall, on a proposal from the Commission and after consulting the European Parliament, acting by a qualified majority, make regulations, issue directives, or take decisions, without prejudice to any recommendations it may also make.

3.     The Council may, acting by a qualified majority and in accordance with paragraph 2, replace the national market organisations by the common organisation provided for in Article 34(1) if:
> (a) the common organisation offers Member States which are opposed to this measure and which have an organisation of their own for the production in question equivalent safeguards for the employment and standard of living of the producers concerned, account being taken of the adjustments

that will be possible and the specialisation that will be needed with the passage of time;

(b) such an organisation ensures conditions for trade within the Community similar to those existing in a national market.

4.     If a common organisation for certain raw materials is established before a common organisation exists for the corresponding processed products, such raw materials as are used for processed products intended for export to third countries may be imported from outside the Community.

**Article 38** (ex Article 46)

Where in a Member State a product is subject to a national market organisation or to internal rules having equivalent effect which affect the competitive position of similar production in another Member State, a countervailing charge shall be applied by Member States to imports of this product coming from the Member State where such organisation or rules exist, unless that State applies a countervailing charge on export.

The Commission shall fix the amount of these charges at the level required to redress the balance; it may also authorise other measures, the conditions and details of which it shall determine.

# TITLE III
# FREE MOVEMENT OF PERSONS, SERVICES AND CAPITAL

## CHAPTER 1
## WORKERS

**Article 39** (ex Article 48)

1.     Freedom of movement for workers shall be secured within the Community.

2.     Such freedom of movement shall entail the abolition of any discrimination based on nationality between workers of the Member States as regards employment, remuneration and other conditions of work and employment.

3.     It shall entail the right, subject to limitations justified on grounds of public policy, public security or public health:
(a) to accept offers of employment actually made;
(b) to move freely within the territory of Member States for this purpose;
(c) to stay in a Member State for the purpose of employment in accordance with the provisions governing the employment of nationals of that State laid down by law, regulation or administrative action;
(d) to remain in the territory of a Member State after having been employed in that State, subject to conditions which shall be embodied in implementing regulations to be drawn up by the Commission.

4.     The provisions of this Article shall not apply to employment in the public service.

**Article 40** (ex Article 49)

The Council shall, acting in accordance with the procedure referred to in Article 251 and after consulting the Economic and Social Committee, issue directives or make regulations setting out the measures required to bring about freedom of movement for workers, as defined in Article 39, in particular:

> (a) by ensuring close co-operation between national employment services;
>
> (b) by abolishing those administrative procedures and practices and those qualifying periods in respect of eligibility for available employment, whether resulting from national legislation or from agreements previously concluded between Member States, the maintenance of which would form an obstacle to liberalisation of the movement of workers;
>
> (c) by abolishing all such qualifying periods and other restrictions provided for either under national legislation or under agreements previously concluded between Member States as imposed on workers of other Member States conditions regarding the free choice of employment other than those imposed on workers of the State concerned;
>
> (d) by setting up appropriate machinery to bring offers of employment into touch with applications for employment and to facilitate the achievement of a balance between supply and demand in the employment market in such a way as to avoid serious threats to the standard of living and level of employment in the various regions and industries.

### Article 41 (ex Article 50)

Member States shall, within the framework of a joint programme, encourage the exchange of young workers.

### Article 42 (ex Article 51)

The Council shall, acting in accordance with the procedure referred to in Article 251, adopt such measures in the field of social security as are necessary to provide freedom of movement for workers; to this end, it shall make arrangements to secure for migrant workers and their dependants:

> (a) aggregation, for the purpose of acquiring and retaining the right to benefit and of calculating the amount of benefit, of all periods taken into account under the laws of the several countries;
>
> (b) payment of benefits to persons resident in the territories of Member States.

The Council shall act unanimously throughout the procedure referred to in Article 251.

## CHAPTER 2
## RIGHT OF ESTABLISHMENT

### Article 43 (ex Article 52)

Within the framework of the provisions set out below, restrictions on the freedom of establishment of nationals of a Member State in the territory of another Member State shall be prohibited. Such prohibition shall also apply to restrictions on the setting-up of agencies, branches or subsidiaries by nationals of any Member State established in the territory of any Member State.

Freedom of establishment shall include the right to take up and pursue activities as self-employed persons and to set up and manage undertakings, in particular companies or firms within the meaning of the second paragraph of Article 48, under the conditions laid down for its own nationals by the law of the country where such establishment is effected, subject to the provisions of the Chapter relating to capital.

**Article 44** (ex Article 54)

1.    In order to attain freedom of establishment as regards a particular activity, the Council, acting in accordance with the procedure referred to in Article 251 and after consulting the Economic and Social Committee, shall act by means of directives.

2.    The Council and the Commission shall carry out the duties devolving upon them under the preceding provisions, in particular:

    (a)  by according, as a general rule, priority treatment to activities where freedom of establishment makes a particularly valuable contribution to the development of production and trade;

    (b)  by ensuring close co-operation between the competent authorities in the Member States in order to ascertain the particular situation within the Community of the various activities concerned;

    (c)  by abolishing those administrative procedures and practices, whether resulting from national legislation or from agreements previously concluded between Member States, the maintenance of which would form an obstacle to freedom of establishment;

    (d)  by ensuring that workers of one Member State employed in the territory of another Member State may remain in that territory for the purpose of taking up activities therein as self-employed persons, where they satisfy the conditions which they would be required to satisfy if they were entering that State at the time when they intended to take up such activities;

    (e)  by enabling a national of one Member State to acquire and use land and buildings situated in the territory of another Member State, insofar as this does not conflict with the principles laid down in Article 33(2);

    (f)  by effecting the progressive abolition of restrictions on freedom of establishment in every branch of activity under consideration, both as regards the conditions for setting up agencies, branches or subsidiaries in the territory of a Member State and as regards the subsidiaries in the territory of a Member State and as regards the conditions governing the entry of personnel belonging to the main establishment into managerial or supervisory posts in such agencies, branches or subsidiaries;

    (g)  by co-ordinating to the necessary extent the safeguards which, for the protection of the interests of members and other, are required by Member States of companies or firms within the meaning of the second paragraph of Article 48 with a view to making such safeguards equivalent throughout the Community;

    (h)  by satisfying themselves that the conditions of establishment are not distorted by aids granted by Member States.

**Article 45** (ex Article 55)

The provisions of this Chapter shall not apply, so far as any given Member State is concerned, to activities which in that State are connected, even occasionally, with the exercise of official authority.

The Council may, acting by a qualified majority on a proposal from the Commission, rule that the provisions of this Chapter shall not apply to certain activities.

**Article 46** (ex Article 56)

1.    The provisions of this Chapter and measures taken in pursuance thereof shall not prejudice the applicability of provisions laid down by law, regulation or administrative

action providing for special treatment for foreign nationals on grounds of public policy, public security or public health.

2.     The Council shall, acting in accordance with the procedure referred to in Article 251, issue directives for the co-ordination of the abovementioned provisions.

### Article 47 (ex Article 57)

1.     In order to make it easier for persons to take up and pursue activities as self-employed persons, the Council shall, acting in accordance with the procedure referred to in Article 251, issue directives for the mutual recognition of diplomas, certificates and other evidence of formal qualifications.

2.     For the same purpose, the Council shall, acting in accordance with the procedure referred to in Article 251, issue directives for the co-ordination of the provisions laid down by law, regulation or administrative action in Member States concerning the taking-up and pursuit of activities as self-employed persons. The Council, acting unanimously throughout the procedure referred to in Article 251, shall decide on directives the implementation of which involves in at least one Member State amendment of the existing principles laid down by law governing the professions with respect to training and conditions of access for natural persons. In other cases the Council shall act by qualified majority.

3.     In the case of the medical and allied and pharmaceutical professions, the progressive abolition of restrictions shall be dependent upon co-ordination of the conditions for their exercise in the various Member States.

### Article 48 (ex Article 58)

Companies or firms formed in accordance with the law of a Member State and having their registered office, central administration or principal place of business within the Community shall, for the purposes of this Chapter, be treated in the same way as natural persons who are nationals of Member States.

"Companies or firms" means companies or firms constituted under civil or commercial law, including co-operative societies, and other legal persons governed by public or private law, save for those which are non-profit-making.

## CHAPTER 3
## SERVICES

### Article 49 (ex Article 59)

Within the framework of the provisions set out below, restrictions on freedom to provide services within the Community shall be prohibited in respect of nationals of Member States who are established in a State of the Community other than that of the person for whom the services are intended.

The Council may, acting by a qualified majority on a proposal from the Commission, extend the provisions of the Chapter to nationals of a third country who provide services and who are established within the Community.

**Article 50** (ex Article 60)

Services shall be considered to be 'services' within the meaning of this Treaty where they are normally provided for remuneration, insofar as they are not governed by the provisions relating to freedom of movement for goods, capital and persons.

'Services' shall in particular include:
- (a) activities of an industrial character;
- (b) activities of a commercial character;
- (c) activities of craftsmen;
- (d) activities of the professions.

Without prejudice to the provisions of the Chapter relating to the right of establishment, the person providing a service may, in order to do so, temporarily pursue his activity in the State where the service is provided, under the same conditions as are imposed by that State on its own nationals.

**Article 51** (ex Article 61)

1.      Freedom to provide services in the field of transport shall be governed by the provisions of the Title relating to transport.

2.      The liberalisation of banking and insurance services connected with movements of capital shall be effected in step with the liberalisation of movement of capital.

**Article 52** (ex Article 63)

1.      In order to achieve the liberalisation of a specific service, the Council shall, on a proposal from the Commission and after consulting the Economic and Social Committee and the European Parliament, issue directives acting by a qualified majority.

2.      As regards the directives referred to in paragraph 1, priority shall as a general rule be given to those services which directly affect production costs or the liberalisation of which helps to promote trade in goods.

**Article 53** (ex Article 64)

The Member States declare their readiness to undertake the liberalisation of services beyond the extent required by the directives issued pursuant to Article 52(1), if their general economic situation and the situation of the economic sector concerned so permit.

To this end, the Commission shall make recommendations to the Member States concerned.

**Article 54** (ex Article 65)

As long as restrictions on freedom to provide services have not been abolished, each Member State shall apply such restrictions without distinction on grounds of nationality or residence to all persons providing services within the meaning of the first paragraph of Article 49.

**Article 55** (ex Article 66)

The provisions of Articles 45 to 48 shall apply to the matters covered by this Chapter.

# CHAPTER 4
# CAPITAL AND PAYMENTS

**Article 56** (ex Article 73b)

1.     Within the framework of the provisions set out in this Chapter, all restrictions on the movement of capital between Member States and between Member States and third countries shall be prohibited.

2.     Within the framework of the provisions set out in this Chapter, all restrictions on payments between Member States and between Member States and third countries shall be prohibited.

**Article 57** (ex Article 73c)

1.     The provisions of Article 56 shall be without prejudice to the application to third countries of any restrictions which exist on 31 December 1993 under national or Community law adopted in respect of the movement of capital to or from third countries involving direct investment — including in real estate — establishment, the provision of financial services or the admission of securities to capital markets.

2.     Whilst endeavouring to achieve the objective of free movement of capital between Member States and third countries to the greatest extent possible and without prejudice to the other Chapters of this Treaty, the Council may, acting by a qualified majority on a proposal from the Commission, adopt measures on the movement of capital to or from third countries involving direct investment — including investment in real estate — establishment, the provision of financial services or the admission of securities to capital markets. Unanimity shall be required for measures under this paragraph which constitute a step back in Community law as regards the liberalisation of the movement of capital to or from third countries.

**Article 58** (ex Article 73d)

1.     The provisions of Article 56 shall be without prejudice to the right of Member States:
    (a) to apply the relevant provisions of their tax law which distinguish between taxpayers who are not in the same situation with regard to their place of residence or with regard to the place where their capital is invested;
    (b) to take all requisite measures to prevent infringements of national law and regulations, in particular in the field of taxation and the prudential supervision of financial institutions, or to lay down procedures for the declaration of capital movements for purposes of administrative or statistical information, or to take measures which are justified on grounds of public policy or public security.

2.     The provisions of this Chapter shall be without prejudice to the applicability of restrictions on the right of establishment which are compatible with this Treaty.

3.     The measures and procedures referred to in paragraphs 1 and 2 shall not constitute a means of arbitrary discrimination or a disguised restriction on the free movement of capital and payments as defined in Article 56.

**Article 59** (ex Article 73f)

Where, in exceptional circumstances, movements of capital to or from third countries cause, or threaten to cause, serious difficulties for the operation of economic and monetary union, the Council, acting by a qualified majority on a proposal from the Commission and after consulting the ECB, may take safeguard measures with regard to third countries for a period not exceeding six months if such measures are strictly necessary.

**Article 60** (ex Article 73g)

1.    If, in the cases envisaged in Article 301, action by the Community is deemed necessary, the Council may, in accordance with the procedure provided for in Article 301, take the necessary urgent measures on the movement of capital and on payments as regards the third countries concerned.

2.    Without prejudice to Article 297 and as long as the Council has not taken measures pursuant to paragraph 1, a Member State may, for serious political reasons and on grounds of urgency, take unilateral measures against a third country with regard to capital movements and payments. The Commission and the other Member States shall be informed of such measures by the date of their entry into force at the latest.

The Council may, acting by a qualified majority on a proposal from the Commission, decide that the Member State concerned shall amend or abolish such measures. The President of the Council shall inform the European Parliament of any such decision taken by the Council.

# TITLE IV (ex Title IIIa)
## VISAS, ASYLUM, IMMIGRATION AND OTHER POLICIES RELATED TO FREE MOVEMENT OF PERSONS

**Article 61** (ex Article 73i)

In order to establish progressively an area of freedom, security and justice, the Council shall adopt:
  (a) within a period of five years after the entry into force of the Treaty of Amsterdam, measures aimed at ensuring the free movement of persons in accordance with Article 14, in conjunction with directly related flanking measures with respect to external border controls, asylum and immigration, in accordance with the provisions of Article 62(2) and (3) and Article 63(1)(a) and (2)(a), and measures to prevent and combat crime in accordance with the provisions of Article 31(e) of the Treaty on European Union;
  (b) other measures in the fields of asylum, immigration and safeguarding the rights of nationals of third countries, in accordance with the provisions of Article 63;
  (c) measures in the field of judicial co-operation in civil matters as provided for in Article 65;
  (d) appropriate measures to encourage and strengthen administrative co-operation, as provided for in Article 66;
  (e) measures in the field of police and judicial co-operation in criminal matters aimed at a high level of security by preventing and combating crime within the Union in accordance with the provisions of the Treaty on European Union.

**Article 62** (ex Article 73j)

The Council, acting in accordance with the procedure referred to in Article 67, shall, within a period of five years after the entry into force of the Treaty of Amsterdam, adopt:

    (1) measures with a view to ensuring, in compliance with Article 14, the absence of any controls on persons, be they citizens of the Union or nationals of third countries, when crossing internal borders;

    (2) measures on the crossing of the external borders of the Member States which shall establish:

        (a) standards and procedures to be followed by Member States in carrying out checks on persons at such borders;

        (b) rules on visas for intended stays of no more than three months, including:

            (i) the list of third countries whose nationals must be in possession of visas when crossing the external borders and those whose nationals are exempt from that requirement;

            (ii) the procedures and conditions for issuing visas by Member States;

            (iii) a uniform format for visas;

            (iv) rules on a uniform visa;

(3)    measures setting out the conditions under which nationals of third countries shall have the freedom to travel within the territory of the Member States during a period of no more than three months.

**Article 63** (ex Article 73k)

The Council, acting in accordance with the procedure referred to in Article 67, shall, within a period of five years after the entry into force of the Treaty of Amsterdam, adopt:

    (1) measures on asylum, in accordance with the Geneva Convention of 28 July 1951 and the Protocol of 31 January 1967 relating to the status of refugees and other relevant treaties, within the following areas:

        (a) criteria and mechanisms for determining which Member State is responsible for considering an application for asylum submitted by a national of a third country in one of the Member States,

        (b) minimum standards on the reception of asylum seekers in Member States,

        (c) minimum standards with respect to the qualification of nationals of third countries as refugees,

        (d) minimum standards on procedures in Member States for granting or withdrawing refugee status;

    (2) measures on refugees and displaced persons within the following areas:

        (a) minimum standards for giving temporary protection to displaced persons from third countries who cannot return to their country of origin and for persons who otherwise need international protection,

        (b) promoting a balance of effort between Member States in receiving and bearing the consequences of receiving refugees and displaced persons;

    (3) measures on immigration policy within the following areas:

        (a) conditions of entry and residence, and standards on procedures for the issue by Member States of long term visas and residence permits, including those for the purpose of family reunion,

        (b) illegal immigration and illegal residence, including repatriation of illegal residents;

(4) measures defining the rights and conditions under which nationals of third countries who are legally resident in a Member State may reside in other Member States.

Measures adopted by the Council pursuant to points 3 and 4 shall not prevent any Member State from maintaining or introducing in the areas concerned national provisions which are compatible with this Treaty and with international agreements.

Measures to be adopted pursuant to points 2(b), 3(a) and 4 shall not be subject to the five year period referred to above.

### Article 64 (ex Article 73l)

1. This Title shall not affect the exercise of the responsibilities incumbent upon Member States with regard to the maintenance of law and order and the safeguarding of internal security.

2. In the event of one or more Member States being confronted with an emergency situation characterised by a sudden inflow of nationals of third countries and without prejudice to paragraph 1, the Council may, acting by qualified majority on a proposal from the Commission, adopt provisional measures of a duration not exceeding six months for the benefit of the Member States concerned.

### Article 65 (ex Article 73m)

Measures in the field of judicial co-operation in civil matters having cross-border implications, to be taken in accordance with Article 67 and insofar as necessary for the proper functioning of the internal market, shall include:
  (a) improving and simplifying:
      — the system for cross-border service of judicial and extrajudicial documents;
      — co-operation in the taking of evidence;
      — the recognition and enforcement of decisions in civil and commercial cases, including decisions in extrajudicial cases;
  (b) promoting the compatibility of the rules applicable in the Member States concerning the conflict of laws and of jurisdiction;
  (c) eliminating obstacles to the good functioning of civil proceedings, if necessary by promoting the compatibility of the rules on civil procedure applicable in the Member States.

### Article 66 (ex Article 73n)

The Council, acting in accordance with the procedure referred to in Article 67, shall take measures to ensure co-operation between the relevant departments of the administrations of the Member States in the areas covered by this Title, as well as between those departments and the Commission.

### Article 67 (ex Article 73o)

1. During a transitional period of five years following the entry into force of the Treaty of Amsterdam, the Council shall act unanimously on a proposal from the Commission or on the initiative of a Member State and after consulting the European Parliament.

2. After this period of five years:

— the Council shall act on proposals from the Commission; the Commission shall examine any request made by a Member State that it submit a proposal to the Council;

— the Council, acting unanimously after consulting the European Parliament, shall take a decision with a view to providing for all or parts of the areas covered by this Title to be governed by the procedure referred to in Article 251 and adapting the provisions relating to the powers of the Court of Justice.

3. By derogation from paragraphs 1 and 2, measures referred to in Article 62(2)(b) (i) and (iii) shall, from the entry into force of the Treaty of Amsterdam, be adopted by the Council acting by a qualified majority on a proposal from the Commission and after consulting the European Parliament.

4. By derogation from paragraph 2, measures referred to in Article 62(2)(b) (ii) and (iv) shall, after a period of five years following the entry into force of the Treaty of Amsterdam, be adopted by the Council acting in accordance with the procedure referred to in Article 251.

## Article 68 (ex Article 73p)

1. Article 234 shall apply to this Title under the following circumstances and conditions: where a question on the interpretation of this Title or on the validity or interpretation of acts of the institutions of the Community based on this Title is raised in a case pending before a court or a tribunal of a Member State against whose decisions there is no judicial remedy under national law, that court or tribunal shall, if it considers that a decision on the question is necessary to enable it to give judgment, request the Court of Justice to give a ruling thereon.

2. In any event, the Court of Justice shall not have jurisdiction to rule on any measure or decision taken pursuant to Article 62(1) relating to the maintenance of law and order and the safeguarding of internal security.

3. The Council, the Commission or a Member State may request the Court of Justice to give a ruling on a question of interpretation of this Title or of acts of the institutions of the Community based on this Title. The ruling given by the Court of Justice in response to such a request shall not apply to judgments of courts or tribunals of the Member States which have become res judicata.

## Article 69 (ex Article 73q)

The application of this Title shall be subject to the provisions of the Protocol on the position of the United Kingdom and Ireland and to the Protocol on the position of Denmark and without prejudice to the Protocol on the application of certain aspects of Article 14 of the Treaty establishing the European Community to the United Kingdom and to Ireland.

## TITLE V (ex Title IV)
## TRANSPORT

## Article 70 (ex Article 74)

The objectives of this Treaty shall, in matters governed by this Title, be pursued by Member States within the framework of a common transport policy.

## Article 71 (ex Article 75)

1.      For the purpose of implementing Article 70, and taking into account the distinctive features of transport, the Council shall, acting in accordance with the procedure referred to in Article 251 and after consulting the Economic and Social Committee and the Committee of the Regions, lay down:

(a) common rules applicable to international transport to or from the territory of a Member State or passing across the territory of one or more Member States;

(b) the conditions under which non-resident carriers may operate transport services within a Member State;

(c) measures to improve transport safety;

(d) any other appropriate provisions.

2.      By way of derogation from the procedure provided for in paragraph 1, where the application of provisions concerning the principles of the regulatory system for transport would be liable to have a serious effect on the standard of living and on employment in certain areas and on the operation of transport facilities, they shall be laid down by the Council acting unanimously on a proposal from the Commission, after consulting the European Parliament and the Economic and Social Committee. In so doing, the Council shall take into account the need for adaptation to the economic development which will result from establishing the common market.

## Article 72 (ex Article 76)

Until the provisions referred to in Article 71(1) have been laid down, no Member State may, without the unanimous approval of the Council, make the various provisions governing the subject on 1 January 1958 or, for acceding States, the date of their accession less favourable in their direct or indirect effect on carriers of other Member States as compared with carriers who are nationals of that State.

## Article 73 (ex Article 77)

Aids shall be compatible with this Treaty if they meet the needs of co-ordination of transport or if they represent reimbursement for the discharge of certain obligations inherent in the concept of a public service.

## Article 74 (ex Article 78)

Any measures taken within the framework of this Treaty in respect of transport rates and conditions shall take account of the economic circumstances of carriers.

## Article 75 (ex Article 79)

1.      In the case of transport within the Community, discrimination which takes the form of carriers charging different rates and imposing different conditions for the carriage of the same goods over the same transport links on grounds of the country of origin or of destination of the goods in question shall be abolished.

2.      Paragraph 1 shall not prevent the Council from adopting other measures in pursuance of Article 71(1).

3.     The Council shall, acting by a qualified majority on a proposal from the Commission and after consulting the Economic and Social Committee, lay down rules for implementing the provisions of paragraph 1.

The Council may in particular lay down the provisions needed to enable the institutions of the Community to secure compliance with the rule laid down in paragraph 1 and to ensure that users benefit from it to the full.

4.     The Commission shall, acting on its own initiative or on application by a Member State, investigate any cases of discrimination falling within paragraph 1 and, after consulting any Member State concerned, shall take the necessary decisions within the framework of the rules laid down in accordance with the provisions of paragraph 3.

## Article 76 (ex Article 80)

1.     The imposition by a Member State, in respect of transport operations carried out within the Community, of rates and conditions involving any element of support or protection in the interest of one or more particular undertakings or industries shall be prohibited, unless authorised by the Commission.

2.     The Commission shall, acting on its own initiative or on application by a Member State, examine the rates and conditions referred to in paragraph 1, taking account in particular of the requirements of an appropriate regional economic policy, the needs of underdeveloped areas and the problems of areas seriously affected by political circumstances on the one hand, and of the effects of such rates and conditions on competition between the different modes of transport on the other.

After consulting each Member State concerned, the Commission shall take the necessary decisions.

3.     The prohibition provided for in paragraph 1 shall not apply to tariffs fixed to meet competition.

## Article 77 (ex Article 81)

Charges or dues in respect of the crossing of frontiers which are charged by a carrier in addition to the transport rates shall not exceed a reasonable level after taking the costs actually incurred thereby into account.

Member States shall endeavour to reduce these costs progressively.

The Commission may make recommendations to Member States for the application of this Article.

## Article 78 (ex Article 82)

The provisions of this Title shall not form an obstacle to the application of measures taken in the Federal Republic of Germany to the extent that such measures are required in order to compensate for the economic disadvantages caused by the division of Germany to the economy of certain areas of the Federal Republic affected by that division.

## Article 79 (ex Article 83)

An Advisory Committee consisting of experts designated by the governments of Member States shall be attached to the Commission. The Commission, whenever it considers it desirable, shall consult the Committee on transport matters without prejudice to the powers of the Economic and Social Committee.

**Article 80** (ex Article 84)

1.    The provisions of this Title shall apply to transport by rail, road and inland waterway.

2.    The Council may, acting by a qualified majority, decide whether, to what extent and by what procedure appropriate provisions may be laid down for sea and air transport.

The procedural provisions of Article 71 shall apply.

## TITLE VI (ex Title V)
## COMMON RULES ON COMPETITION, TAXATION AND APPROXIMATION OF LAWS

## CHAPTER 1
## RULES ON COMPETITION

## SECTION 1
## RULES APPLYING TO UNDERTAKINGS

**Article 81** (ex Article 85)

1.    The following shall be prohibited as incompatible with the common market: all agreements between undertakings, decisions by associations of undertakings and concerted practices which may affect trade between Member States and which have as their object or effect the prevention, restriction or distortion of competition within the common market, and in particular those which:
- (a)  directly or indirectly fix purchase or selling prices or any other trading conditions;
- (b)  limit or control production, markets, technical development, or investment;
- (c)  share markets or sources of supply;
- (d)  apply dissimilar conditions to equivalent transactions with other trading parties, thereby placing them at a competitive disadvantage;
- (e)  make the conclusion of contracts subject to acceptance by the other parties of supplementary obligations which, by their nature or according to commercial usage, have no connection with the subject of such contracts.

2.    Any agreements or decisions prohibited pursuant to this Article shall be automatically void.

3.    The provisions of paragraph 1 may, however, be declared inapplicable in the case of:
- —  any agreement or category of agreements between undertakings;
- —  any decision or category of decisions by associations of undertakings;
- —  any concerted practice or category of concerted practices,

which contributes to improving the production or distribution of goods or to promoting technical or economic progress, while allowing consumers a fair share of the resulting benefit, and which does not:

(a) impose on the undertakings concerned restrictions which are not indispensable to the attainment of these objectives;

(b) afford such undertakings the possibility of eliminating competition in respect of a substantial part of the products in question.

## Article 82 (ex Article 86)

Any abuse by one or more undertakings of a dominant position within the common market or in a substantial part of it shall be prohibited as incompatible with the common market insofar as it may affect trade between Member States.

Such abuse may, in particular, consist in:

(a) directly or indirectly imposing unfair purchase or selling prices or other unfair trading conditions;

(b) limiting production, markets or technical development to the prejudice of consumers;

(c) applying dissimilar conditions to equivalent transactions with other trading parties, thereby placing them at a competitive disadvantage;

(d) making the conclusion of contracts subject to acceptance by the other parties of supplementary obligations which, by their nature or according to commercial usage, have no connection with the subject of such contracts.

## Article 83 (ex Article 87)

1. The appropriate regulations or directives to give effect to the principles set out in Articles 81 and 82 shall be laid down by the Council, acting by a qualified majority on a proposal from the Commission and after consulting the European Parliament.

2. The regulations or directives referred to in paragraph 1 shall be designed in particular:

(a) to ensure compliance with the prohibitions laid down in Article 81(1) and in Article 82 by making provision for fines and periodic penalty payments;

(b) to lay down detailed rules for the application of Article 81(3), taking into account the need to ensure effective supervision on the one hand, and to simplify administration to the greatest possible extent on the other;

(c) to define, if need be, in the various branches of the economy, the scope of the provisions of Articles 81 and 82;

(d) to define the respective functions of the Commission and of the Court of Justice in applying the provisions laid down in this paragraph;

(e) to determine the relationship between national laws and the provisions contained in this Section or adopted pursuant to this Article.

## Article 84 (ex Article 88)

Until the entry into force of the provisions adopted in pursuance of Article 83, the authorities in Member States shall rule on the admissibility of agreements, decisions and concerted practices and on abuse of a dominant position in the common market in accordance with the law of their country and with the provisions of Article 81, in particular paragraph 3, and of Article 82.

## Article 85 (ex Article 89)

1. Without prejudice to Article 84, the Commission shall ensure the application of the principles laid down in Articles 81 and 82. On application by a Member State or on

its own initiative, and in co-operation with the competent authorities in the Member States, who shall give it their assistance, the Commission shall investigate cases of suspected infringement of these principles. If it finds that there has been an infringement, it shall propose appropriate measures to bring it to an end.

2.　　If the infringement is not brought to an end, the Commission shall record such infringement of the principles in a reasoned decision. The Commission may publish its decision and authorise Member States to take the measures, the conditions and details of which it shall determine, needed to remedy the situation.

**Article 86** (ex Article 90)

1.　　In the case of public undertakings and undertakings to which Member States grant special or exclusive rights, Member States shall neither enact nor maintain in force any measure contrary to the rules contained in this Treaty, in particular to those rules provided for in Article 12 and Articles 81 to 89.

2.　　Undertakings entrusted with the operation of services of general economic interest or having the character of a revenue-producing monopoly shall be subject to the rules contained in this Treaty, in particular to the rules on competition, insofar as the application of such rules does not obstruct the performance, in law or in fact, of the particular tasks assigned to them. The development of trade must not be affected to such an extent as would be contrary to the interests of the Community.

3.　　The Commission shall ensure the application of the provisions of this Article and shall, where necessary, address appropriate directives or decisions to Member States.

## SECTION 2
## AIDS GRANTED BY STATES

**Article 87** (ex Article 92)

1.　　Save as otherwise provided in this Treaty, any aid granted by a Member State or through State resources in any form whatsoever which distorts or threatens to distort competition by favouring certain undertakings or the production of certain goods shall, insofar as it affects trade between Member States, be incompatible with the common market.

2.　　The following shall be compatible with the common market:
　　(a) aid having a social character, granted to individual consumers, provided that such aid is granted without discrimination related to the origin of the products concerned;
　　(b) aid to make good the damage caused by natural disasters or exceptional occurrences;
　　(c) aid granted to the economy of certain areas of the Federal Republic of Germany affected by the division of Germany, insofar as such aid is required in order to compensate for the economic disadvantages caused by that division.

3.　　The following may be considered to be compatible with the common market:
　　(a) aid to promote the economic development of areas where the standard of living is abnormally low or where there is serious underemployment;
　　(b) aid to promote the execution of an important project of common European interest or to remedy a serious disturbance in the economy of a Member State;

(c) aid to facilitate the development of certain economic activities or of certain economic areas, where such aid does not adversely affect trading conditions to an extent contrary to the common interest;

(d) aid to promote culture and heritage conservation where such aid does not affect trading conditions and competition in the Community to an extent that is contrary to the common interest;

(e) such other categories of aid as may be specified by decision of the Council acting by a qualified majority on a proposal from the Commission.

## Article 88 (ex Article 93)

1. The Commission shall, in co-operation with Member States, keep under constant review all systems of aid existing in those States. It shall propose to the latter any appropriate measures required by the progressive development or by the functioning of the common market.

2. If, after giving notice to the parties concerned to submit their comments, the Commission finds that aid granted by a State or through State resources is not compatible with the common market having regard to Article 87, or that such aid is being misused, it shall decide that the State concerned shall abolish or alter such aid within a period of time to be determined by the Commission.

If the State concerned does not comply with this decision within the prescribed time, the Commission or any other interested State may, in derogation from the provisions of Articles 226 and 227, refer the matter to the Court of Justice direct.

On application by a Member State, the Council may, acting unanimously, decide that aid which that State is granting or intends to grant shall be considered to be compatible with the common market, in derogation from the provisions of Article 87 or from the regulations provided for in Article 89, if such a decision is justified by exceptional circumstances. If, as regards the aid in question, the Commission has already initiated the procedure provided for in the first subparagraph of this paragraph, the fact that the State concerned has made its application to the Council shall have the effect of suspending that procedure until the Council has made its attitude known.

If, however, the Council has not made its attitude known within three months of the said application being made, the Commission shall give its decision on the case.

3. The Commission shall be informed, in sufficient time to enable it to submit its comments, of any plans to grant or alter aid. If it considers that any such plan is not compatible with the common market having regard to Article 87, it shall without delay initiate the procedure provided for in paragraph 2. The Member State concerned shall not put its proposed measures into effect until this procedure has resulted in a final decision.

## Article 89 (ex Article 94)

The Council, acting by a qualified majority on a proposal from the Commission and after consulting the European Parliament, may make any appropriate regulations for the application of Articles 87 and 88 and may in particular determine the conditions in which Article 88(3) shall apply and the categories of aid exempted from this procedure.

## CHAPTER 2
## TAX PROVISIONS

**Article 90** (ex Article 95)

No Member State shall impose, directly or indirectly, on the products of other Member States any internal taxation of any kind in excess of that imposed directly or indirectly on similar domestic products.

Furthermore, no Member State shall impose on the products of other Member States any internal taxation of such a nature as to afford indirect protection to other products.

**Article 91** (ex Article 96)

Where products are exported to the territory of any Member State, any repayment of internal taxation shall not exceed the internal taxation imposed on them whether directly or indirectly.

**Article 92** (ex Article 98)

In the case of charges other than turnover taxes, excise duties and other forms of indirect taxation, remissions and repayments in respect of exports to other Member States may not be granted and countervailing charges in respect of imports from Member States may not be imposed unless the measures contemplated have been previously approved for a limited period by the Council acting by a qualified majority on a proposal from the Commission.

**Article 93** (ex Article 99)

The Council shall, acting unanimously on a proposal from the Commission and after consulting the European Parliament and the Economic and Social Committee, adopt provisions for the harmonisation of legislation concerning turnover taxes, excise duties and other forms of indirect taxation to the extent that such harmonisation is necessary to ensure the establishment and the functioning of the internal market within the time-limit laid down in Article 14.

## CHAPTER 3
## APPROXIMATION OF LAWS

**Article 94** (ex Article 100)

The Council shall, acting unanimously on a proposal from the Commission and after consulting the European Parliament and the Economic and Social Committee, issue directives for the approximation of such laws, regulations or administrative provisions of the Member States as directly affect the establishment or functioning of the common market.

**Article 95** (ex Article 100a)

1. By way of derogation from Article 94 and save where otherwise provided in this Treaty, the following provisions shall apply for the achievement of the objectives set out in Article 14. The Council shall, acting in accordance with the procedure referred to in Article 251 and after consulting the Economic and Social Committee, adopt the measures for the approximation of the provisions laid down by law,

regulation or administrative action in Member States which have as their object the establishment and functioning of the internal market.

2.       Paragraph 1 shall not apply to fiscal provisions, to those relating to the free movement of persons nor to those relating to the rights and interests of employed persons.

3.       The Commission, in its proposals envisaged in paragraph 1 concerning health, safety, environmental protection and consumer protection, will take as a base a high level of protection, taking account in particular of any new development based on scientific facts. Within their respective powers, the European Parliament and the Council will also seek to achieve this objective.

4.       If, after the adoption by the Council or by the Commission of a harmonisation measure, a Member State deems it necessary to maintain national provisions on grounds of major needs referred to in Article 30, or relating to the protection of the environment or the working environment, it shall notify the Commission of these provisions as well as the grounds for maintaining them.

5.       Moreover, without prejudice to paragraph 4, if, after the adoption by the Council or by the Commission of a harmonisation measure, a Member State deems it necessary to introduce national provisions based on new scientific evidence relating to the protection of the environment or the working environment on grounds of a problem specific to that Member State arising after the adoption of the harmonisation measure, it shall notify the Commission of the envisaged provisions as well as the grounds for introducing them.

6.       The Commission shall, within six months of the notifications as referred to in paragraphs 4 and 5, approve or reject the national provisions involved after having verified whether or not they are a means of arbitrary discrimination or a disguised restriction on trade between Member States and whether or not they shall constitute an obstacle to the functioning of the internal market.

In the absence of a decision by the Commission within this period the national provisions referred to in paragraphs 4 and 5 shall be deemed to have been approved.

When justified by the complexity of the matter and in the absence of danger for human health, the Commission may notify the Member State concerned that the period referred to in this paragraph may be extended for a further period of up to six months.

7.       When, pursuant to paragraph 6, a Member State is authorised to maintain or introduce national provisions derogating from a harmonisation measure, the Commission shall immediately examine whether to propose an adaptation to that measure.

8.       When a Member State raises a specific problem on public health in a field which has been the subject of prior harmonisation measures, it shall bring it to the attention of the Commission which shall immediately examine whether to propose appropriate measures to the Council.

9.       By way of derogation from the procedure laid down in Articles 226 and 227, the Commission and any Member State may bring the matter directly before the Court of Justice if it considers that another Member State is making improper use of the powers provided for in this Article.

10.      The harmonisation measures referred to above shall, in appropriate cases, include a safeguard clause authorising the Member States to take, for one or more of

the non-economic reasons referred to in Article 30, provisional measures subject to a Community control procedure.

**Article 96** (ex Article 101)

Where the Commission finds that a difference between the provisions laid down by law, regulation or administrative action in Member States is distorting the conditions of competition in the common market and that the resultant distortion needs to be eliminated, it shall consult the Member States concerned.

If such consultation does not result in an agreement eliminating the distortion in question, the Council shall, on a proposal from the Commission, acting by a qualified majority, issue the necessary directives. The Commission and the Council may take any other appropriate measures provided for in this Treaty.

**Article 97** (ex Article 102)

1.     Where there is a reason to fear that the adoption or amendment of a provision laid down by law, regulation or administrative action may cause distortion within the meaning of Article 96, a Member State desiring to proceed therewith shall consult the Commission. After consulting the Member States, the Commission shall recommend to the States concerned such measures as may be appropriate to avoid the distortion in question.

2.     If a State desiring to introduce or amend its own provisions does not comply with the recommendation addressed to it by the Commission, other Member States shall not be required, in pursuance of Article 96, to amend their own provisions in order to eliminate such distortion. If the Member State which has ignored the recommendation of the Commission causes distortion detrimental only to itself, the provisions of Article 96 shall not apply.

# TITLE VII (ex Title VI)
## ECONOMIC AND MONETARY POLICY

## CHAPTER 1
### ECONOMIC POLICY

**Article 98** (ex Article 102a)

Member States shall conduct their economic policies with a view to contributing to the achievement of the objectives of the Community, as defined in Article 2, and in the context of the broad guidelines referred to in Article 99(2). The Member States and the Community shall act in accordance with the principle of an open market economy with free competition, favouring an efficient allocation of resources, and in compliance with the principles set out in Article 4.

**Article 99** (ex Article 103)

1.     Member States shall regard their economic policies as a matter of common concern and shall co-ordinate them within the Council, in accordance with the provisions of Article 98.

2.     The Council shall, acting by a qualified majority on a recommendation from the Commission, formulate a draft for the broad guidelines of the economic policies

of the Member States and of the Community, and shall report its findings to the European Council.

The European Council shall, acting on the basis of the report from the Council, discuss a conclusion on the broad guidelines of the economic policies of the Member States and of the Community.

On the basis of this conclusion, the Council shall, acting by a qualified majority, adopt a recommendation setting out these broad guidelines. The Council shall inform the European Parliament of its recommendation.

3.    In order to ensure closer co-ordination of economic policies and sustained convergence of the economic performances of the Member States, the Council shall, on the basis of reports submitted by the Commission, monitor economic developments in each of the Member States and in the Community as well as the consistency of economic policies with the broad guidelines referred to in paragraph 2, and regularly carry out an overall assessment.

For the purpose of this multilateral surveillance, Member States shall forward information to the Commission about important measures taken by them in the field of their economic policy and such other information as they deem necessary.

4.    Where it is established, under the procedure referred to in paragraph 3, that the economic policies of a Member State are not consistent with the broad guidelines referred to in paragraph 2 or that they risk jeopardising the proper functioning of economic and monetary union, the Council may, acting by a qualified majority on a recommendation from the Commission, make the necessary recommendations to the Member State concerned. The Council may, acting by a qualified majority on a proposal from the Commission, decide to make its recommendations public.

The President of the Council and the Commission shall report to the European Parliament on the results of multilateral surveillance. The President of the Council may be invited to appear before the competent committee of the European Parliament if the Council has made its recommendations public.

5.    The Council, acting in accordance with the procedure referred to in Article 252, may adopt detailed rules for the multilateral surveillance procedure referred to in paragraphs 3 and 4 of this Article.

**Article 100** (ex Article 103a)

1.    Without prejudice to any other procedures provided for in this Treaty, the Council may, acting unanimously on a proposal from the Commission, decide upon the measures appropriate to the economic situation, in particular if severe difficulties arise in the supply of certain products.

2.    Where a Member State is in difficulties or is seriously threatened with severe difficulties caused by exceptional occurrences beyond its control, the Council may, acting unanimously on a proposal from the Commission, grant, under certain conditions, Community financial assistance to the Member State concerned. Where the severe difficulties are caused by natural disasters, the Council shall act by qualified majority. The President of the Council shall inform the European Parliament of the decision taken.

**Article 101** (ex Article 104)

1.      Overdraft facilities or any other type of credit facility with the ECB or with the central banks of the Member States (hereinafter referred to as 'national central banks') in favour of Community institutions or bodies, central governments, regional, local or other public authorities, other bodies governed by public law, or public undertakings of Member States shall be prohibited, as shall the purchase directly from them by the ECB or national central banks of debt instruments.

2.      Paragraph 1 shall not apply to publicly owned credit institutions which, in the context of the supply of reserves by central banks, shall be given the same treatment by national central banks and the ECB as private credit institutions.

**Article 102** (ex Article 104a)

1.      Any measure, not based on prudential considerations, establishing privileged access by Community institutions or bodies, central governments, regional, local or other public authorities, other bodies governed by public law, or public undertakings of Member States to financial institutions, shall be prohibited.

2.      The Council, acting in accordance with the procedure referred to in Article 252, shall, before 1 January 1994, specify definitions for the application of the prohibition referred to in paragraph 1.

**Article 103** (ex Article 104b)

1.      The Community shall not be liable for or assume the commitments of central governments, regional, local or other public authorities, other bodies governed by public law, or public undertakings of any Member State, without prejudice to mutual financial guarantees for the joint execution of a specific project. A Member State shall not be liable for or assume the commitments of central governments, regional, local or other public authorities, other bodies governed by public law, or public undertakings of another Member State, without prejudice to mutual financial guarantees for the joint execution of a specific project.

2.      If necessary, the Council, acting in accordance with the procedure referred to in Article 252, may specify definitions for the application of the prohibition referred to in Article 101 and in this Article.

**Article 104** (ex Article 104c)

1.      Member States shall avoid excessive government deficits.

2.      The Commission shall monitor the development of the budgetary situation and of the stock of government debt in the Member States with a view to identifying gross errors. In particular it shall examine compliance with budgetary discipline on the basis of the following two criteria:
  (a)  whether the ratio of the planned or actual government deficit to gross domestic product exceeds a reference value, unless:
      — either the ratio has declined substantially and continuously and reached a level that comes close to the reference value;
      — or, alternatively, the excess over the reference value is only exceptional and temporary and the ratio remains close to the reference value;

     (b) whether the ratio of government debt to gross domestic product exceeds a reference value, unless the ratio is sufficiently diminishing and approaching the reference value at a satisfactory pace.

The reference values are specified in the Protocol on the excessive deficit procedure annexed to this Treaty.

3.     If a Member State does not fulfil the requirements under one or both of these criteria, the Commission shall prepare a report. The report of the Commission shall also take into account whether the government deficit exceeds government investment expenditure and take into account all other relevant factors, including the medium-term economic and budgetary position of the Member State.

The Commission may also prepare a report if, notwithstanding the fulfilment of the requirements under the criteria, it is of the opinion that there is a risk of an excessive deficit in a Member State.

4.     The Committee provided for in Article 114 shall formulate an opinion on the report of the Commission.

5.     If the Commission considers that an excessive deficit in a Member State exists or may occur, the Commission shall address an opinion to the Council.

6.     The Council shall, acting by a qualified majority on a recommendation from the Commission, and having considered any observations which the Member State concerned may wish to make, decide after an overall assessment whether an excessive deficit exists.

7.     Where the existence of an excessive deficit is decided according to paragraph 6, the Council shall make recommendations to the Member State concerned with a view to bringing that situation to an end within a given period. Subject to the provisions of paragraph 8, these recommendations shall not be made public.

8.     Where it establishes that there has been no effective action in response to its recommendations within the period laid down, the Council may make its recommendations public.

9.     If a Member State persists in failing to put into practice the recommendations of the Council, the Council may decide to give notice to the Member State to take, within a specified time-limit, measures for the deficit reduction which is judged necessary by the Council in order to remedy the situation.

In such a case, the Council may request the Member State concerned to submit reports in accordance with a specific timetable in order to examine the adjustment efforts of that Member State.

10.     The rights to bring actions provided for in Articles 226 and 227 may not be exercised within the framework of paragraphs 1 to 9 of this Article.

11.     As long as a Member State fails to comply with a decision taken in accordance with paragraph 9, the Council may decide to apply or, as the case may be, intensify one or more of the following measures:

     — to require the Member State concerned to publish additional information, to be specified by the Council, before issuing bonds and securities;

     — to invite the European Investment Bank to reconsider its lending policy towards the Member State concerned;

> — to require the Member State concerned to make a non-interest-bearing deposit of an appropriate size with the Community until the excessive deficit has, in the view of the Council, been corrected;
> — to impose fines of an appropriate size.

The President of the Council shall inform the European Parliament of the decisions taken.

12.      The Council shall abrogate some or all of its decisions referred to in paragraphs 6 to 9 and 11 to the extent that the excessive deficit in the Member State concerned has, in the view of the Council, been corrected. If the Council has previously made public recommendations, it shall, as soon as the decision under paragraph 8 has been abrogated, make a public statement that an excessive deficit in the Member State concerned no longer exists.

13.      When taking the decisions referred to in paragraphs 7 to 9, 11 and 12, the Council shall act on a recommendation from the Commission by a majority of two-thirds of the votes of its members weighted in accordance with Article 205(2), excluding the votes of the representative of the Member State concerned.

14.      Further provisions relating to the implementation of the procedure described in this Article are set out in the Protocol on the excessive deficit procedure annexed to this Treaty.

The Council shall, acting unanimously on a proposal from the Commission and after consulting the European Parliament and the ECB, adopt the appropriate provisions which shall then replace the said Protocol.

Subject to the other provisions of this paragraph, the Council shall, before 1 January 1994, acting by a qualified majority on a proposal from the Commission and after consulting the European Parliament, lay down detailed rules and definitions for the application of the provisions of the said Protocol.

## CHAPTER 2
## MONETARY POLICY

**Article 105** (ex Article 105)

1.      The primary objective of the ESCB shall be to maintain price stability. Without prejudice to the objective of price stability, the ESCB shall support the general economic policies in the Community with a view to contributing to the achievement of the objectives of the Community as laid down in Article 2. The ESCB shall act in accordance with the principle of an open market economy with free competition, favouring an efficient allocation of resources, and in compliance with the principles set out in Article 4.

2.      The basic tasks to be carried out through the ESCB shall be:
> — to define and implement the monetary policy of the Community;
> — to conduct foreign exchange operations consistent with the provisions of Article 111;
> — to hold and manage the official foreign reserves of the Member States;
> — to promote the smooth operation of payment systems.

3.      The third indent of paragraph 2 shall be without prejudice to the holding and management by the governments of Member States of foreign-exchange working balances.

4. The ECB shall be consulted:
    — on any proposed Community act in its fields of competence;
    — by national authorities regarding any draft legislative provision in its fields of competence, but within the limits and under the conditions set out by the Council in accordance with the procedure laid down in Article 107(6).

The ECB may submit opinions to the appropriate Community institutions or bodies or to national authorities on matters in its fields of competence.

5. The ESCB shall contribute to the smooth conduct of policies pursued by the competent authorities relating to the prudential supervision of credit institutions and the stability of the financial system.

6. The Council may, acting unanimously on a proposal from the Commission and after consulting the ECB and after receiving the assent of the European Parliament, confer upon the ECB specific tasks concerning policies relating to the prudential supervision of credit institutions and other financial institutions with the exception of insurance undertakings.

### Article 106 (ex Article 105a)

1. The ECB shall have the exclusive right to authorise the issue of banknotes within the Community. The ECB and the national central banks may issue such notes. The banknotes issued by the ECB and the national central banks shall be the only such notes to have the status of legal tender within the Community.

2. Member States may issue coins subject to approval by the ECB of the volume of the issue. The Council may, acting in accordance with the procedure referred to in Article 252 and after consulting the ECB, adopt measures to harmonise the denominations and technical specifications of all coins intended for circulation to the extent necessary to permit their smooth circulation within the Community.

### Article 107 (ex Article 106)

1. The ESCB shall be composed of the ECB and of the national central banks.

2. The ECB shall have legal personality.

3. The ESCB shall be governed by the decision-making bodies of the ECB which shall be the Governing Council and the Executive Board.

4. The Statute of the ESCB is laid down in a Protocol annexed to this Treaty.

5. Articles 5.1, 5.2, 5.3, 17, 18, 19.1, 22, 23, 24, 26, 32.2, 32.3, 32.4, 32.6, 33.1(a) and 36 of the Statute of the ESCB may be amended by the Council, acting either by a qualified majority on a recommendation from the ECB and after consulting the Commission or unanimously on a proposal from the Commission and after consulting the ECB. In either case, the assent of the European Parliament shall be required.

6. The Council, acting by a qualified majority either on a proposal from the Commission and after consulting the European Parliament and the ECB or on a recommendation from the ECB and after consulting the European Parliament and the Commission, shall adopt the provisions referred to in Articles 4, 5.4, 19.2, 20, 28.1, 29.2, 30.4 and 34.3 of the Statute of the ESCB.

**Article 108** (ex Article 107)

When exercising the powers and carrying out the tasks and duties conferred upon them by this Treaty and the Statute of the ESCB, neither the ECB, nor a national central bank, nor any member of their decision-making bodies shall seek or take instructions from Community institutions or bodies, from any government of a Member State or from any other body. The Community institutions and bodies and the governments of the Member States undertake to respect this principle and not to seek to influence the members of the decision-making bodies of the ECB or of the national central banks in the performance of their tasks.

**Article 109** (ex Article 108)

Each Member State shall ensure, at the latest at the date of the establishment of the ESCB, that its national legislation including the statutes of its national central bank is compatible with this Treaty and the Statute of the ESCB.

**Article 110** (ex Article 108a)

1.    In order to carry out the tasks entrusted to the ESCB, the ECB shall, in accordance with the provisions of this Treaty and under the conditions laid down in the Statute of the ESCB:
— make regulations to the extent necessary to implement the tasks defined in Article 3.1, first indent, Articles 19.1, 22 and 25.2 of the Statute of the ESCB and in cases which shall be laid down in the acts of the Council referred to in Article 107(6);
— take decisions necessary for carrying out the tasks entrusted to the ESCB under this Treaty and the Statute of the ESCB;
— make recommendations and deliver opinions.

2.    A regulation shall have general application. It shall be binding in its entirety and directly applicable in all Member States.

Recommendations and opinions shall have no binding force.

A decision shall be binding in its entirety upon those to whom it is addressed.

Articles 253 to 256 shall apply to regulations and decisions adopted by the ECB.

The ECB may decide to publish its decisions, recommendations and opinions.

3.    Within the limits and under the conditions adopted by the Council under the procedure laid down in Article 107(6), the ECB shall be entitled to impose fines or periodic penalty payments on undertakings for failure to comply with obligations under its regulations and decisions.

**Article 111** (ex Article 109)

1.    By way of derogation from Article 300, the Council may, acting unanimously on a recommendation from the ECB or from the Commission, and after consulting the ECB in an endeavour to reach a consensus consistent with the objective of price stability, after consulting the European Parliament, in accordance with the procedure in paragraph 3 for determining the arrangements, conclude formal agreements on an exchange-rate system for the ECU in relation to non-Community currencies. The Council may, acting by a qualified majority on a recommendation from the ECB or from the Commission, and after consulting the ECB in an endeavour to reach a

consensus consistent with the objective of price stability, adopt, adjust or abandon the central rates of the ECU within the exchange-rate system. The President of the Council shall inform the European Parliament of the adoption, adjustment or abandonment of the ECU central rates.

2.     In the absence of an exchange-rate system in relation to one or more non-Community currencies as referred to in paragraph 1, the Council, acting by a qualified majority either on a recommendation from the Commission and after consulting the ECB or on a recommendation from the ECB, may formulate general orientations for exchange-rate policy in relation to these currencies. These general orientations shall be without prejudice to the primary objective of the ESCB to maintain price stability.

3.     By way of derogation from Article 300, where agreements concerning monetary or foreign exchange regime matters need to be negotiated by the Community with one or more States or international organisations, the Council, acting by a qualified majority on a recommendation from the Commission and after consulting the ECB, shall decide the arrangements for the negotiation and for the conclusion of such agreements. These arrangements shall ensure that the Community expresses a single position. The Commission shall be fully associated with the negotiations.

Agreements concluded in accordance with this paragraph shall be binding on the institutions of the Community, on the ECB and on Member States.

4.     Subject to paragraph 1, the Council shall, on a proposal from the Commission and after consulting the ECB, acting by a qualified majority decide on the position of the Community at international level as regards issues of particular relevance to economic and monetary union and, acting unanimously, decide its representation in compliance with the allocation of powers laid down in Articles 99 and 105.

5.     Without prejudice to Community competence and Community agreements as regards economic and monetary union, Member States may negotiate in international bodies and conclude international agreements.

# CHAPTER 3
## INSTITUTIONAL PROVISIONS

### Article 112 (ex Article 109a)

1.     The Governing Council of the ECB shall comprise the members of the Executive Board of the ECB and the Governors of the national central banks.

    2.  (a)   The Executive Board shall comprise the President, the Vice-President and four other members.

          (b)   The President, the Vice-President and the other members of the Executive Board shall be appointed from among persons of recognised standing and professional experience in monetary or banking matters by common accord of the governments of the Member States at the level of Heads of State or Government, on a recommendation from the Council, after it has consulted the European Parliament and the Governing Council of the ECB.

Their term of office shall be eight years and shall not be renewable.

Only nationals of Member States may be members of the Executive Board.

## Article 113 (ex Article 109b)

1.     The President of the Council and a member of the Commission may participate, without having the right to vote, in meetings of the Governing Council of the ECB.

The President of the Council may submit a motion for deliberation to the Governing Council of the ECB.

2.     The President of the ECB shall be invited to participate in Council meetings when the Council is discussing matters relating to the objectives and tasks of the ESCB.

3.     The ECB shall address an annual report on the activities of the ESCB and on the monetary policy of both the previous and current year to the European Parliament, the Council and the Commission, and also to the European Council. The President of the ECB shall present this report to the Council and to the European Parliament, which may hold a general debate on that basis.

The President of the ECB and the other members of the Executive Board may, at the request of the European Parliament or on their own initiative, be heard by the competent committees of the European Parliament.

## Article 114 (ex Article 109c)

1.     In order to promote co-ordination of the policies of Member States to the full extent needed for the functioning of the internal market, a Monetary Committee with advisory status is hereby set up.

It shall have the following tasks:
— to keep under review the monetary and financial situation of the Member States and of the Community and the general payments system of the Member States and to report regularly thereon to the Council and to the Commission;
— to deliver opinions at the request of the Council or of the Commission, or on its own initiative for submission to those institutions;
— without prejudice to Article 207, to contribute to the preparation of the work of the Council referred to in Articles 59, 60, 99(2), (3), (4) and (5), 100, 102, 103, 104, 116(2), 117(6), 119, 120, 121(2) and 122(1);
— to examine, at least once a year, the situation regarding the movement of capital and the freedom of payments, as they result from the application of this Treaty and of measures adopted by the Council; the examination shall cover all measures relating to capital movements and payments; the Committee shall report to the Commission and to the Council on the outcome of this examination.

The Member States and the Commission shall each appoint two members of the Monetary Committee.

2.     At the start of the third stage, an Economic and Financial Committee shall be set up. The Monetary Committee provided for in paragraph 1 shall be dissolved.

The Economic and Financial Committee shall have the following tasks:
— to deliver opinions at the request of the Council or of the Commission, or on its own initiative for submission to those institutions;
— to keep under review the economic and financial situation of the Member States and of the Community and to report regularly thereon to the

Council and to the Commission, in particular on financial relations with third countries and international institutions;

— without prejudice to Article 207, to contribute to the preparation of the work of the Council referred to in Articles 59, 60, 99(2), (3), (4) and (5), 100, 102, 103, 104, 105(6), 106(2), 107(5) and (6), 111, 119, 120(2) and (3), 122(2), 123(4) and (5), and to carry out other advisory and preparatory tasks assigned to it by the Council;

— to examine, at least once a year, the situation regarding the movement of capital and the freedom of payments, as they result from the application of this Treaty and of measures adopted by the Council; the examination shall cover all measures relating to capital movements and payments; the Committee shall report to the Commission and to the Council on the outcome of this examination.

The Member States, the Commission and the ECB shall each appoint no more than two members of the Committee.

3. The Council shall, acting by a qualified majority on a proposal from the Commission and after consulting the ECB and the Committee referred to in this Article, lay down detailed provisions concerning the composition of the Economic and Financial Committee. The President of the Council shall inform the European Parliament of such a decision.

4. In addition to the tasks set out in paragraph 2, if and as long as there are Member States with a derogation as referred to in Articles 122 and 123, the Committee shall keep under review the monetary and financial situation and the general payments system of those Member States and report regularly thereon to the Council and to the Commission.

**Article 115** (ex Article 109d)

For matters within the scope of Articles 99(4), 104 with the exception of paragraph 14, 111, 121, 122 and 123(4) and (5), the Council or a Member State may request the Commission to make a recommendation or a proposal, as appropriate. The Commission shall examine this request and submit its conclusions to the Council without delay.

# CHAPTER 4
## TRANSITIONAL PROVISIONS

**Article 116** (ex Article 109e)

1. The second stage for achieving economic and monetary union shall begin on 1 January 1994.

2. Before that date:
   (a) each Member State shall:
       — adopt, where necessary, appropriate measures to comply with the prohibitions laid down in Article 56 and in Articles 101 and 102(1);
       — adopt, if necessary, with a view to permitting the assessment provided for in subparagraph (b), multiannual programmes intended to ensure the lasting convergence necessary for the achievement of economic and monetary union, in particular with regard to price stability and sound public finances;

(b) the Council shall, on the basis of a report from the Commission, assess the progress made with regard to economic and monetary convergence, in particular with regard to price stability and sound public finances, and the progress made with the implementation of Community law concerning the internal market.

3.      The provisions of Articles 101, 102(1), 103(1) and 104 with the exception of paragraphs 1, 9, 11 and 14 shall apply from the beginning of the second stage.

The provisions of Articles 100(2), 104(1), (9) and (11), 105, 106, 108, 111, 112, 113 and 114(2) and (4) shall apply from the beginning of the third stage.

4.      In the second stage, Member States shall endeavour to avoid excessive government deficits.

5.      During the second stage, each Member State shall, as appropriate, start the process leading to the independence of its central bank, in accordance with Article 109.

**Article 117** (ex Article 109f)

1.      At the start of the second stage, a European Monetary Institute (hereinafter referred to as 'EMI') shall be established and take up its duties; it shall have legal personality and be directed and managed by a Council, consisting of a President and the Governors of the national central banks, one of whom shall be Vice-President.

The President shall be appointed by common accord of the governments of the Member States at the level of Heads of State or Government, on a recommendation from the Council of the EMI, and after consulting the European Parliament and the Council. The President shall be selected from among persons of recognised standing and professional experience in monetary or banking matters. Only nationals of Member States may be President of the EMI. The Council of the EMI shall appoint the Vice-President.

The Statute of the EMI is laid down in a Protocol annexed to this Treaty.

2.      The EMI shall:
   — strengthen co-operation between the national central banks;
   — strengthen the co-ordination of the monetary policies of the Member States, with the aim of ensuring price stability;
   — monitor the functioning of the European Monetary System;
   — hold consultations concerning issues falling within the competence of the national central banks and affecting the stability of financial institutions and markets;
   — take over the tasks of the European Monetary Co-operation Fund, which shall be dissolved; the modalities of dissolution are laid down in the Statute of the EMI;
   — facilitate the use of the ECU and oversee its development, including the smooth functioning of the ECU clearing system.

3.      For the preparation of the third stage, the EMI shall:
   — prepare the instruments and the procedures necessary for carrying out a single monetary policy in the third stage;
   — promote the harmonisation, where necessary, of the rules and practices governing the collection, compilation and distribution of statistics in the areas within its field of competence;

— prepare the rules for operations to be undertaken by the national central banks within the framework of the ESCB;
— promote the efficiency of cross-border payments;
— supervise the technical preparation of ECU banknotes.

At the latest by 31 December 1996, the EMI shall specify the regulatory, organisational and logistical framework necessary for the ESCB to perform its tasks in the third stage. This framework shall be submitted for decision to the ECB at the date of its establishment.

4.      The EMI, acting by a majority of two thirds of the members of its Council, may:
— formulate opinions or recommendations on the overall orientation of monetary policy and exchange-rate policy as well as on related measures introduced in each Member State;
— submit opinions or recommendations to governments and to the Council on policies which might affect the internal or external monetary situation in the Community and, in particular, the functioning of the European Monetary System;
— make recommendations to the monetary authorities of the Member States concerning the conduct of their monetary policy.

5.      The EMI, acting unanimously, may decide to publish its opinions and its recommendations.

6.      The EMI shall be consulted by the Council regarding any proposed Community act within its field of competence.

Within the limits and under the conditions set out by the Council, acting by a qualified majority on a proposal from the Commission and after consulting the European Parliament and the EMI, the EMI shall be consulted by the authorities of the Member States on any draft legislative provision within its field of competence.

7.      The Council may, acting unanimously on a proposal from the Commission and after consulting the European Parliament and the EMI, confer upon the EMI other tasks for the preparation of the third stage.

8.      Where this Treaty provides for a consultative role for the ECB, references to the ECB shall be read as referring to the EMI before the establishment of the ECB.

9.      During the second stage, the term 'ECB' used in Articles 230, 232, 233, 234, 237 and 288 shall be read as referring to the EMI.

**Article 118** (ex Article 109g)

The currency composition of the ECU basket shall not be changed.

From the start of the third stage, the value of the ECU shall be irrevocably fixed in accordance with Article 123(4).

**Article 119** (ex Article 109h)

1.      Where a Member State is in difficulties or is seriously threatened with difficulties as regards its balance of payments either as a result of an overall disequilibrium in its balance of payments, or as a result of the type of currency at its disposal, and where such difficulties are liable in particular to jeopardise the functioning of the common market or the progressive implementation of the common commercial policy, the

Commission shall immediately investigate the position of the State in question and the action which, making use of all the means at its disposal, that State has taken or may take in accordance with the provisions of this Treaty. The Commission shall state what measures it recommends the State concerned to take.

If the action taken by a Member State and the measures suggested by the Commission do not prove sufficient to overcome the difficulties which have arisen or which threaten, the Commission shall, after consulting the Committee referred to in Article 114, recommend to the Council the granting of mutual assistance and appropriate methods therefor.

The Commission shall keep the Council regularly informed of the situation and of how it is developing.

2.      The Council, acting by a qualified majority, shall grant such mutual assistance; it shall adopt directives or decisions laying down the conditions and details of such assistance, which may take such forms as:
   (a)   a concerted approach to or within any other international organisations to which Member States may have recourse;
   (b)   measures needed to avoid deflection of trade where the State which is in difficulties maintains or reintroduces quantitative restrictions against third countries;
   (c)   the granting of limited credits by other Member States, subject to their agreement.

3.      If the mutual assistance recommended by the Commission is not granted by the Council or if the mutual assistance granted and the measures taken are insufficient, the Commission shall authorise the State which is in difficulties to take protective measures, the conditions and details of which the Commission shall determine.

Such authorisation may be revoked and such conditions and details may be changed by the Council acting by a qualified majority.

4.      Subject to Article 122(6), this Article shall cease to apply from the beginning of the third stage.

## Article 120 (ex Article 109i)

1.      Where a sudden crisis in the balance of payments occurs and a decision within the meaning of Article 119(2) is not immediately taken, the Member State concerned may, as a precaution, take the necessary protective measures. Such measures must cause the least possible disturbance in the functioning of the common market and must not be wider in scope than is strictly necessary to remedy the sudden difficulties which have arisen.

2.      The Commission and the other Member States shall be informed of such protective measures not later than when they enter into force. The Commission may recommend to the Council the granting of mutual assistance under Article 119.

3.      After the Commission has delivered an opinion and the Committee referred to in Article 114 has been consulted, the Council may, acting by a qualified majority, decide that the State concerned shall amend, suspend or abolish the protective measures referred to above.

4.      Subject to Article 122(6), this Article shall cease to apply from the beginning of the third stage.

**Article 121** (ex Article 109j)

1.      The Commission and the EMI shall report to the Council on the progress made in the fulfilment by the Member States of their obligations regarding the achievement of economic and monetary union. These reports shall include an examination of the compatibility between each Member State's national legislation, including the statutes of its national central bank, and Articles 108 and 109 of this Treaty and the Statute of the ESCB. The reports shall also examine the achievement of a high degree of sustainable convergence by reference to the fulfilment by each Member State of the following criteria:

— the achievement of a high degree of price stability; this will be apparent from a rate of inflation which is close to that of, at most, the three best performing Member States in terms of price stability;

— the sustainability of the government financial position; this will be apparent from having achieved a government budgetary position without a deficit that is excessive as determined in accordance with Article 104(6);

— the observance of the normal fluctuation margins provided for by the exchange-rate mechanism of the European Monetary System, for at least two years, without devaluing against the currency of any other Member State;

— the durability of convergence achieved by the Member State and of its participation in the exchange-rate mechanism of the European Monetary System being reflected in the long-term interest-rate levels.

The four criteria mentioned in this paragraph and the relevant periods over which they are to be respected are developed further in a Protocol annexed to this Treaty. The reports of the Commission and the EMI shall also take account of the development of the ECU, the results of the integration of markets, the situation and development of the balances of payments on current account and an examination of the development of unit labour costs and other price indices.

2.      On the basis of these reports, the Council, acting by a qualified majority on a recommendation from the Commission, shall assess:

— for each Member State, whether it fulfils the necessary conditions for the adoption of a single currency;

— whether a majority of the Member States fulfil the necessary conditions for the adoption of a single currency,

and recommend its findings to the Council, meeting in the composition of the Heads of State or Government. The European Parliament shall be consulted and forward its opinion to the Council, meeting in the composition of the Heads of State or Government.

3.      Taking due account of the reports referred to in paragraph 1 and the opinion of the European Parliament referred to in paragraph 2, the Council, meeting in the composition of the Heads of State or Government, shall, acting by a qualified majority, not later than 31 December 1996:

— decide, on the basis of the recommendations of the Council referred to in paragraph 2, whether a majority of the Member States fulfil the necessary conditions for the adoption of a single currency;

— decide whether it is appropriate for the Community to enter the third stage, and if so:

— set the date for the beginning of the third stage.

4.     If by the end of 1997 the date for the beginning of the third stage has not been set, the third stage shall start on 1 January 1999.  Before 1 July 1998, the Council, meeting in the composition of the Heads of State or Government, after a repetition of the procedure provided for in paragraphs 1 and 2, with the exception of the second indent of paragraph 2, taking into account the reports referred to in paragraph 1 and the opinion of the European Parliament, shall, acting by a qualified majority and on the basis of the recommendations of the Council referred to in paragraph 2, confirm which Member States fulfil the necessary conditions for the adoption of a single currency.

**Article 122** (ex Article 109k)

1.     If the decision has been taken to set the date in accordance with Article 121(3), the Council shall, on the basis of its recommendations referred to in Article 121(2), acting by a qualified majority on a recommendation from the Commission, decide whether any, and if so which, Member States shall have a derogation as defined in paragraph 3 of this Article.  Such Member States shall in this Treaty be referred to as 'Member States with a derogation'.

If the Council has confirmed which Member States fulfil the necessary conditions for the adoption of a single currency, in accordance with Article 121(4), those Member States which do not fulfil the conditions shall have a derogation as defined in paragraph 3 of this Article.  Such Member States shall in this Treaty be referred to as 'Member States with a derogation'.

2.     At least once every two years, or at the request of a Member State with a derogation, the Commission and the ECB shall report to the Council in accordance with the procedure laid down in Article 121(1).  After consulting the European Parliament and after discussion in the Council, meeting in the composition of the Heads of State or Government, the Council shall, acting by a qualified majority on a proposal from the Commission, decide which Member States with a derogation fulfil the necessary conditions on the basis of the criteria set out in Article 121(1), and abrogate the derogations of the Member States concerned.

3.     A derogation referred to in paragraph 1 shall entail that the following Articles do not apply to the Member State concerned: Articles 104(9) and (11), 105(1), (2), (3) and (5), 106, 110, 111, and 112(2)(b).  The exclusion of such a Member State and its national central bank from rights and obligations within the ESCB is laid down in Chapter IX of the Statute of the ESCB.

4.     In Articles 105(1), (2) and (3), 106, 110, 111 and 112(2)(b), 'Member States' shall be read as 'Member States without a derogation'.

5.     The voting rights of Member States with a derogation shall be suspended for the Council decisions referred to in the Articles of this Treaty mentioned in paragraph 3.  In that case, by way of derogation from Articles 205 and 250(1), a qualified majority shall be defined as two-thirds of the votes of the representatives of the Member States without a derogation weighted in accordance with Article 205(2), and unanimity of those Member States shall be required for an act requiring unanimity.

6.     Articles 119 and 120 shall continue to apply to a Member State with a derogation.

**Article 123** (ex Article 109l)

1.      Immediately after the decision on the date for the beginning of the third stage has been taken in accordance with Article 121(3), or, as the case may be, immediately after 1 July 1998:
— the Council shall adopt the provisions referred to in Article 107(6);
— the governments of the Member States without a derogation shall appoint, in accordance with the procedure set out in Article 50 of the Statute of the ESCB, the President, the Vice-President and the other members of the Executive Board of the ECB. If there are Member States with a derogation, the number of members of the Executive Board may be smaller than provided for in Article 11.1 of the Statute of the ESCB, but in no circumstances shall it be less than four.

As soon as the Executive Board is appointed, the ESCB and the ECB shall be established and shall prepare for their full operation as described in this Treaty and the Statute of the ESCB. The full exercise of their powers shall start from the first day of the third stage.

2.      As soon as the ECB is established, it shall, if necessary, take over tasks of the EMI. The EMI shall go into liquidation upon the establishment of the ECB; the modalities of liquidation are laid down in the Statute of the EMI.

3.      If and as long as there are Member States with a derogation, and without prejudice to Article 107(3) of this Treaty, the General Council of the ECB referred to in Article 45 of the Statute of the ESCB shall be constituted as a third decision-making body of the ECB.

4.      At the starting date of the third stage, the Council shall, acting with the unanimity of the Member States without a derogation, on a proposal from the Commission and after consulting the ECB, adopt the conversion rates at which their currencies shall be irrevocably fixed and at which irrevocably fixed rate the ECU shall be substituted for these currencies, and the ECU will become a currency in its own right. This measure shall by itself not modify the external value of the ECU. The Council shall, acting according to the same procedure, also take the other measures necessary for the rapid introduction of the ECU as the single currency of those Member States.

5.      If it is decided, according to the procedure set out in Article 122(2), to abrogate a derogation, the Council shall, acting with the unanimity of the Member States without a derogation and the Member State concerned, on a proposal from the Commission and after consulting the ECB, adopt the rate at which the ECU shall be substituted for the currency of the Member State concerned, and take the other measures necessary for the introduction of the ECU as the single currency in the Member State concerned.

**Article 124** (ex Article 109m)

1.      Until the beginning of the third stage, each Member State shall treat its exchange-rate policy as a matter of common interest. In so doing, Member States shall take account of the experience acquired in co-operation within the framework of the European Monetary System (EMS) and in developing the ECU, and shall respect existing powers in this field.

2.      From the beginning of the third stage and for as long as a Member State has a derogation, paragraph 1 shall apply by analogy to the exchange-rate policy of that Member State.

# TITLE VIII (ex Title VIa)

# EMPLOYMENT

**Article 125** (ex Article 109n)

Member States and the Community shall, in accordance with this Title, work towards developing a co-ordinated strategy for employment and particularly for promoting a skilled, trained and adaptable workforce and labour markets responsive to economic change with a view to achieving the objectives defined in Article 2 of the Treaty on European Union and in Article 2 of this Treaty.

**Article 126** (ex Article 109o)

1.    Member States, through their employment policies, shall contribute to the achievement of the objectives referred to in Article 125 in a way consistent with the broad guidelines of the economic policies of the Member States and of the Community adopted pursuant to Article 99(2).

2.    Member States, having regard to national practices related to the responsibilities of management and labour, shall regard promoting employment as a matter of common concern and shall co-ordinate their action in this respect within the Council, in accordance with the provisions of Article 128.

**Article 127** (ex Article 109p)

1.    The Community shall contribute to a high level of employment by encouraging co-operation between Member States and by supporting and, if necessary, complementing their action. In doing so, the competences of the Member States shall be respected.

2.    The objective of a high level of employment shall be taken into consideration in the formulation and implementation of Community policies and activities.

**Article 128** (ex Article 109q)

1.    The European Council shall each year consider the employment situation in the Community and adopt conclusions thereon, on the basis of a joint annual report by the Council and the Commission.

2.    On the basis of the conclusions of the European Council, the Council, acting by a qualified majority on a proposal from the Commission and after consulting the European Parliament, the Economic and Social Committee, the Committee of the Regions and the Employment Committee referred to in Article 130, shall each year draw up guidelines which the Member States shall take into account in their employment policies. These guidelines shall be consistent with the broad guidelines adopted pursuant to Article 99(2).

3.    Each Member State shall provide the Council and the Commission with an annual report on the principal measures taken to implement its employment policy in the light of the guidelines for employment as referred to in paragraph 2.

4.    The Council, on the basis of the reports referred to in paragraph 3 and having received the views of the Employment Committee, shall each year carry out an examination of the implementation of the employment policies of the Member States

in the light of the guidelines for employment. The Council, acting by a qualified majority on a recommendation from the Commission, may, if it considers it appropriate in the light of that examination, make recommendations to Member States.

5.      On the basis of the results of that examination, the Council and the Commission shall make a joint annual report to the European Council on the employment situation in the Community and on the implementation of the guidelines for employment.

**Article 129** (ex Article 109r)

The Council, acting in accordance with the procedure referred to in Article 251 and after consulting the Economic and Social Committee and the Committee of the Regions, may adopt incentive measures designed to encourage co-operation between Member States and to support their action in the field of employment through initiatives aimed at developing exchanges of information and best practices, providing comparative analysis and advice as well as promoting innovative approaches and evaluating experiences, in particular by recourse to pilot projects.

Those measures shall not include harmonisation of the laws and regulations of the Member States.

**Article 130** (ex Article 109s)

The Council, after consulting the European Parliament, shall establish an Employment Committee with advisory status to promote co-ordination between Member States on employment and labour market policies.  The tasks of the Committee shall be:
  — to monitor the employment situation and employment policies in the Member States and the Community;
  — without prejudice to Article 207, to formulate opinions at the request of either the Council or the Commission or on its own initiative, and to contribute to the preparation of the Council proceedings referred to in Article 128.

In fulfilling its mandate, the Committee shall consult management and labour.

Each Member State and the Commission shall appoint two members of the Committee.

# TITLE  IX (ex Title VII)
## COMMON COMMERCIAL POLICY

**Article 131** (ex Article 110)

By establishing a customs union between themselves Member States aim to contribute, in the common interest, to the harmonious development of world trade, the progressive abolition of restrictions on international trade and the lowering of customs barriers.

The common commercial policy shall take into account the favourable effect which the abolition of customs duties between Member States may have on the increase in the competitive strength of undertakings in those States.

**Article 132** (ex Article 112)

1.      Without prejudice to obligations undertaken by them within the framework of other international organisations, Member States shall progressively harmonise the

systems whereby they grant aid for exports to third countries, to the extent necessary to ensure that competition between undertakings of the Community is not distorted.

On a proposal from the Commission, the Council shall, acting by a qualified majority, issue any directives needed for this purpose.

2.     The preceding provisions shall not apply to such a drawback of customs duties or charges having equivalent effect nor to such a repayment of indirect taxation including turnover taxes, excise duties and other indirect taxes as is allowed when goods are exported from a Member State to a third country, insofar as such a drawback or repayment does not exceed the amount imposed, directly or indirectly, on the products exported.

### Article 133 (ex Article 113)

1.     The common commercial policy shall be based on uniform principles, particularly in regard to changes in tariff rates, the conclusion of tariff and trade agreements, the achievement of uniformity in measures of liberalisation, export policy and measures to protect trade such as those to be taken in the event of dumping or subsidies.

2.     The Commission shall submit proposals to the Council for implementing the common commercial policy.

3.     Where agreements with one or more States or international organisations need to be negotiated, the Commission shall make recommendations to the Council, which shall authorise the Commission to open the necessary negotiations.

The Commission shall conduct these negotiations in consultation with a special committee appointed by the Council to assist the Commission in this task and within the framework of such directives as the Council may issue to it.

The relevant provisions of Article 300 shall apply.

4.     In exercising the powers conferred upon it by this Article, the Council shall act by a qualified majority.

5.     The Council, acting unanimously on a proposal from the Commission and after consulting the European Parliament, may extend the application of paragraphs 1 to 4 to international negotiations and agreements on services and intellectual property insofar as they are not covered by these paragraphs.

### Article 134 (ex Article 115)

In order to ensure that the execution of measures of commercial policy taken in accordance with this Treaty by any Member State is not obstructed by deflection of trade, or where differences between such measures lead to economic difficulties in one or more Member States, the Commission shall recommend the methods for the requisite co-operation between Member States. Failing this, the Commission may authorise Member States to take the necessary protective measures, the conditions and details of which it shall determine.

In case of urgency, Member States shall request authorisation to take the necessary measures themselves from the Commission, which shall take a decision as soon as possible; the Member States concerned shall then notify the measures to the other Member States. The Commission may decide at any time that the Member States concerned shall amend or abolish the measures in question.

In the selection of such measures, priority shall be given to those which cause the least disturbance of the functioning of the common market.

# TITLE X (ex Title VIIa)
# CUSTOMS CO-OPERATION

**Article 135** (ex Article 116)

Within the scope of application of this Treaty, the Council, acting in accordance with the procedure referred to in Article 251, shall take measures in order to strengthen customs co-operation between Member States and between the latter and the Commission. These measures shall not concern the application of national criminal law or the national administration of justice.

# TITLE XI (ex Title VIII)
# SOCIAL POLICY, EDUCATION,
# VOCATIONAL TRAINING AND YOUTH

# CHAPTER 1
# SOCIAL PROVISIONS

**Article 136** (ex Article 117)

The Community and the Member States, having in mind fundamental social rights such as those set out in the European Social Charter signed at Turin on 18 October 1961 and in the 1989 Community Charter of the Fundamental Social Rights of Workers, shall have as their objectives the promotion of employment, improved living and working conditions, so as to make possible their harmonisation while the improvement is being maintained, proper social protection, dialogue between management and labour, the development of human resources with a view to lasting high employment and the combating of exclusion.

To this end the Community and the Member States shall implement measures which take account of the diverse forms of national practices, in particular in the field of contractual relations, and the need to maintain the competitiveness of the Community economy.

They believe that such a development will ensue not only from the functioning of the common market, which will favour the harmonisation of social systems, but also from the procedures provided for in this Treaty and from the approximation of provisions laid down by law, regulation or administrative action.

**Article 137** (ex Article 118)

1. With a view to achieving the objectives of Article 136, the Community shall support and complement the activities of the Member States in the following fields:
    — improvement in particular of the working environment to protect workers' health and safety;
    — working conditions;
    — the information and consultation of workers;
    — the integration of persons excluded from the labour market, without prejudice to Article 150;
    — equality between men and women with regard to labour market opportunities and treatment at work.

2. To this end, the Council may adopt, by means of directives, minimum requirements for gradual implementation, having regard to the conditions and technical rules obtaining in each of the Member States. Such directives shall avoid imposing administrative, financial and legal constraints in a way which would hold back the creation and development of small and medium-sized undertakings.

The Council shall act in accordance with the procedure referred to in Article 251 after consulting the Economic and Social Committee and the Committee of the Regions.

The Council, acting in accordance with the same procedure, may adopt measures designed to encourage co-operation between Member States through initiatives aimed at improving knowledge, developing exchanges of information and best practices, promoting innovative approaches and evaluating experiences in order to combat social exclusion.

3. However, the Council shall act unanimously on a proposal from the Commission, after consulting the European Parliament, the Economic and Social Committee and the Committee of the Regions in the following areas:
— social security and social protection of workers;
— protection of workers where their employment contract is terminated;
— representation and collective defence of the interests of workers and employers, including co-determination, subject to paragraph 6;
— conditions of employment for third-country nationals legally residing in Community territory;
— financial contributions for promotion of employment and job-creation, without prejudice to the provisions relating to the Social Fund.

4. A Member State may entrust management and labour, at their joint request, with the implementation of directives adopted pursuant to paragraphs 2 and 3.

In this case, it shall ensure that, no later than the date on which a directive must be transposed in accordance with Article 249, management and labour have introduced the necessary measures by agreement, the Member State concerned being required to take any necessary measure enabling it at any time to be in a position to guarantee the results imposed by that directive.

5. The provisions adopted pursuant to this Article shall not prevent any Member State from maintaining or introducing more stringent protective measures compatible with this Treaty.

6. The provisions of this Article shall not apply to pay, the right of association, the right to strike or the right to impose lock-outs.

## Article 138 (ex Article 118a)

1. The Commission shall have the task of promoting the consultation of management and labour at Community level and shall take any relevant measure to facilitate their dialogue by ensuring balanced support for the parties.

2. To this end, before submitting proposals in the social policy field, the Commission shall consult management and labour on the possible direction of Community action.

3. If, after such consultation, the Commission considers Community action advisable, it shall consult management and labour on the content of the envisaged

proposal. Management and labour shall forward to the Commission an opinion or, where appropriate, a recommendation.

4.    On the occasion of such consultation, management and labour may inform the Commission of their wish to initiate the process provided for in Article 139. The duration of the procedure shall not exceed nine months, unless the management and labour concerned and the Commission decide jointly to extend it.

### Article 139 (ex Article 118b)

1.    Should management and labour so desire, the dialogue between them at Community level may lead to contractual relations, including agreements.

2.    Agreements concluded at Community level shall be implemented either in accordance with the procedures and practices specific to management and labour and the Member States or, in matters covered by Article 137, at the joint request of the signatory parties, by a Council decision on a proposal from the Commission.

The Council shall act by qualified majority, except where the agreement in question contains one or more provisions relating to one of the areas referred to in Article 137(3), in which case it shall act unanimously.

### Article 140 (ex Article 118c)

With a view to achieving the objectives of Article 136 and without prejudice to the other provisions of this Treaty, the Commission shall encourage co-operation between the Member States and facilitate the co-ordination of their action in all social policy fields under this chapter, particularly in matters relating to:
— employment;
— labour law and working conditions;
— basic and advanced vocational training;
— social security;
— prevention of occupational accidents and diseases;
— occupational hygiene;
— the right of association and collective bargaining between employers and workers.

To this end, the Commission shall act in close contact with Member States by making studies, delivering opinions and arranging consultations both on problems arising at national level and on those of concern to international organisations.

Before delivering the opinions provided for in this Article, the Commission shall consult the Economic and Social Committee.

### Article 141 (ex Article 119)

1.    Each Member State shall ensure that the principle of equal pay for male and female workers for equal work or work of equal value is applied.

2.    For the purpose of this Article, 'pay' means the ordinary basic or minimum wage or salary and any other consideration, whether in cash or in kind, which the worker receives directly or indirectly, in respect of his employment, from his employer.

Equal pay without discrimination based on sex means:

> (a) that pay for the same work at piece rates shall be calculated on the basis of the same unit of measurement;
>
> (b) that pay for work at time rates shall be the same for the same job.

3.    The Council, acting in accordance with the procedure referred to in Article 251, and after consulting the Economic and Social Committee, shall adopt measures to ensure the application of the principle of equal opportunities and equal treatment of men and women in matters of employment and occupation, including the principle of equal pay for equal work or work of equal value.

4.    With a view to ensuring full equality in practice between men and women in working life, the principle of equal treatment shall not prevent any Member State from maintaining or adopting measures providing for specific advantages in order to make it easier for the under-represented sex to pursue a vocational activity or to prevent or compensate for disadvantages in professional careers.

**Article 142** (ex Article 119a)

Member States shall endeavour to maintain the existing equivalence between paid holiday schemes.

**Article 143** (ex Article 120)

The Commission shall draw up a report each year on progress in achieving the objectives of Article 136, including the demographic situation in the Community. It shall forward the report to the European Parliament, the Council and the Economic and Social Committee.

The European Parliament may invite the Commission to draw up reports on particular problems concerning the social situation.

**Article 144** (ex Article 121)

The Council may, acting unanimously and after consulting the Economic and Social Committee, assign to the Commission tasks in connection with the implementation of common measures, particularly as regards social security for the migrant workers referred to in Articles 39 to 42.

**Article 145** (ex Article 122)

The Commission shall include a separate chapter on social developments within the Community in its annual report to the European Parliament.

The European Parliament may invite the Commission to draw up reports on any particular problems concerning social conditions.

## CHAPTER 2
## THE EUROPEAN SOCIAL FUND

**Article 146** (ex Article 123)

In order to improve employment opportunities for workers in the internal market and to contribute thereby to raising the standard of living, a European Social Fund is hereby established in accordance with the provisions set out below; it shall aim to render the employment of workers easier and to increase their geographical and occupational mobility within the Community, and to facilitate their adaptation to industrial changes and to changes in production systems, in particular through vocational training and retraining.

**Article 147** (ex Article 124)

The Fund shall be administered by the Commission.

The Commission shall be assisted in this task by a Committee presided over by a Member of the Commission and composed of representatives of governments, trade unions and employers' organisations.

**Article 148** (ex Article 125)

The Council, acting in accordance with the procedure referred to in Article 251 and after consulting the Economic and Social Committee and the Committee of the Regions, shall adopt implementing decisions relating to the European Social Fund.

## CHAPTER 3
## EDUCATION, VOCATIONAL TRAINING AND YOUTH

**Article 149** (ex Article 126)

1.     The Community shall contribute to the development of quality education by encouraging co-operation between Member States and, if necessary, by supporting and supplementing their action, while fully respecting the responsibility of the Member States for the content of teaching and the organisation of education systems and their cultural and linguistic diversity.

2.     Community action shall be aimed at:
   — developing the European dimension in education, particularly through the teaching and dissemination of the languages of the Member States;
   — encouraging mobility of students and teachers, inter alia by encouraging the academic recognition of diplomas and periods of study;
   — promoting co-operation between educational establishments;
   — developing exchanges of information and experience on issues common to the education systems of the Member States;
   — encouraging the development of youth exchanges and of exchanges of socio-educational instructors;
   — encouraging the development of distance education.

3.     The Community and the Member States shall foster co-operation with third countries and the competent international organisations in the field of education, in particular the Council of Europe.

4.     In order to contribute to the achievement of the objectives referred to in this Article, the Council:
   — acting in accordance with the procedure referred to in Article 251, after consulting the Economic and Social Committee and the Committee of the Regions, shall adopt incentive measures, excluding any harmonisation of the laws and regulations of the Member States;
   — acting by a qualified majority on a proposal from the Commission, shall adopt recommendations.

**Article 150** (ex Article 127)

1.    The Community shall implement a vocational training policy which shall support and supplement the action of the Member States, while fully respecting the responsibility of the Member States for the content and organisation of vocational training.

2.    Community action shall aim to:
— facilitate adaptation to industrial changes, in particular through vocational training and retraining;
— improve initial and continuing vocational training in order to facilitate vocational integration and reintegration into the labour market;
— facilitate access to vocational training and encourage mobility of instructors and trainees and particularly young people;
— stimulate co-operation on training between educational or training establishments and firms;
— develop exchanges of information and experience on issues common to the training systems of the Member States.

3.    The Community and the Member States shall foster co-operation with third countries and the competent international organisations in the sphere of vocational training.

4.    The Council, acting in accordance with the procedure referred to in Article 251 and after consulting the Economic and Social Committee and the Committee of the Regions, shall adopt measures to contribute to the achievement of the objectives referred to in this Article, excluding any harmonisation of the laws and regulations of the Member States.

# TITLE  XII (ex Title IX)
## CULTURE

**Article 151** (ex Article 128)

1.    The Community shall contribute to the flowering of the cultures of the Member States, while respecting their national and regional diversity and at the same time bringing the common cultural heritage to the fore.

2.    Action by the Community shall be aimed at encouraging co-operation between Member States and, if necessary, supporting and supplementing their action in the following areas:
— improvement of the knowledge and dissemination of the culture and history of the European peoples;
— conservation and safeguarding of cultural heritage of European significance;
— non-commercial cultural exchanges;
— artistic and literary creation, including in the audiovisual sector.

3.    The Community and the Member States shall foster co-operation with third countries and the competent international organisations in the sphere of culture, in particular the Council of Europe.

4.    The Community shall take cultural aspects into account in its action under other provisions of this Treaty, in particular in order to respect and to promote the diversity of its cultures.

5.    In order to contribute to the achievement of the objectives referred to in this Article, the Council:
—    acting in accordance with the procedure referred to in Article 251 and after consulting the Committee of the Regions, shall adopt incentive measures, excluding any harmonisation of the laws and regulations of the Member States.  The Council shall act unanimously throughout the procedure referred to in Article 251;
—    acting unanimously on a proposal from the Commission, shall adopt recommendations.

# TITLE  XIII (ex Title X)
# PUBLIC HEALTH

**Article 152** (ex Article 129)

1.    A high level of human health protection shall be ensured in the definition and implementation of all Community policies and activities.

Community action, which shall complement national policies, shall be directed towards improving public health, preventing human illness and diseases, and obviating sources of danger to human health.  Such action shall cover the fight against the major health scourges, by promoting research into their causes, their transmission and their prevention, as well as health information and education.

The Community shall complement the Member States' action in reducing drugs-related health damage, including information and prevention.

2.    The Community shall encourage co-operation between the Member States in the areas referred to in this Article and, if necessary, lend support to their action.

Member States shall, in liaison with the Commission, co-ordinate among themselves their policies and programmes in the areas referred to in paragraph 1.  The Commission may, in close contact with the Member States, take any useful initiative to promote such co-ordination.

3.    The Community and the Member States shall foster co-operation with third countries and the competent international organisations in the sphere of public health.

4.    The Council, acting in accordance with the procedure referred to in Article 251 and after consulting the Economic and Social Committee and the Committee of the Regions, shall contribute to the achievement of the objectives referred to in this Article through adopting:
(a)   measures setting high standards of quality and safety of organs and substances of human origin, blood and blood derivatives; these measures shall not prevent any Member State from maintaining or introducing more stringent protective measures;
(b)   by way of derogation from Article 37, measures in the veterinary and phytosanitary fields which have as their direct objective the protection of public health;
(c)   incentive measures designed to protect and improve human health, excluding any harmonisation of the laws and regulations of the Member States.

The Council, acting by a qualified majority on a proposal from the Commission, may also adopt recommendations for the purposes set out in this Article.

5.     Community action in the field of public health shall fully respect the responsibilities of the Member States for the organisation and delivery of health services and medical care.  In particular, measures referred to in paragraph 4(a) shall not affect national provisions on the donation or medical use of organs and blood.

# TITLE  XIV  (ex Title XI)
# CONSUMER PROTECTION

**Article 153** (ex Article 129a)

1.     In order to promote the interests of consumers and to ensure a high level of consumer protection, the Community shall contribute to protecting the health, safety and economic interests of consumers, as well as to promoting their right to information, education and to organise themselves in order to safeguard their interests.

2.     Consumer protection requirements shall be taken into account in defining and implementing other Community policies and activities.

3.     The Community shall contribute to the attainment of the objectives referred to in paragraph 1 through:
  (a)  measures adopted pursuant to Article 95 in the context of the completion of the internal market;
  (b)  measures which support, supplement and monitor the policy pursued by the Member States.

4.     The Council, acting in accordance with the procedure referred to in Article 251 and after consulting the Economic and Social Committee, shall adopt the measures referred to in paragraph 3(b).

5.     Measures adopted pursuant to paragraph 4 shall not prevent any Member State from maintaining or introducing more stringent protective measures.  Such measures must be compatible with this Treaty.  The Commission shall be notified of them.

# TITLE  XV  (ex Title XII)
# TRANS-EUROPEAN NETWORKS

**Article 154** (ex Article 129b)

1.     To help achieve the objectives referred to in Articles 14 and 158 and to enable citizens of the Union, economic operators and regional and local communities to derive full benefit from the setting-up of an area without internal frontiers, the Community shall contribute to the establishment and development of trans-European networks in the areas of transport, telecommunications and energy infrastructures.

2.     Within the framework of a system of open and competitive markets, action by the Community shall aim at promoting the interconnection and interoperability of national networks as well as access to such networks.  It shall take account in particular of the need to link island, landlocked and peripheral regions with the central regions of the Community.

**Article 155** (ex Article 129c)

1.     In order to achieve the objectives referred to in Article 154, the Community:

— shall establish a series of guidelines covering the objectives, priorities and broad lines of measures envisaged in the sphere of trans-European networks; these guidelines shall identify projects of common interest;

— shall implement any measures that may prove necessary to ensure the interoperability of the networks, in particular in the field of technical standardisation;

— may support projects of common interest supported by Member States, which are identified in the framework of the guidelines referred to in the first indent, particularly through feasibility studies, loan guarantees or interest-rate subsidies; the Community may also contribute, through the Cohesion Fund set up pursuant to Article 161, to the financing of specific projects in Member States in the area of transport infrastructure.

The Community's activities shall take into account the potential economic viability of the projects.

2. Member States shall, in liaison with the Commission, co-ordinate among themselves the policies pursued at national level which may have a significant impact on the achievement of the objectives referred to in Article 154. The Commission may, in close co-operation with the Member State, take any useful initiative to promote such co-ordination.

3. The Community may decide to co-operate with third countries to promote projects of mutual interest and to ensure the interoperability of networks.

### Article 156 (ex Article 129d)

The guidelines and other measures referred to in Article 155(1) shall be adopted by the Council, acting in accordance with the procedure referred to in Article 251 and after consulting the Economic and Social Committee and the Committee of the Regions.

Guidelines and projects of common interest which relate to the territory of a Member State shall require the approval of the Member State concerned.

## TITLE XVI (ex Title XIII)
## INDUSTRY

### Article 157 (ex Article 130)

1. The Community and the Member States shall ensure that the conditions necessary for the competitiveness of the Community's industry exist.

For that purpose, in accordance with a system of open and competitive markets, their action shall be aimed at:

— speeding up the adjustment of industry to structural changes;

— encouraging an environment favourable to initiative and to the development of undertakings throughout the Community, particularly small and medium-sized undertakings;

— encouraging an environment favourable to co-operation between undertakings;

— fostering better exploitation of the industrial potential of policies of innovation, research and technological development.

2.     The Member States shall consult each other in liaison with the Commission and, where necessary, shall co-ordinate their action. The Commission may take any useful initiative to promote such co-ordination.

3.     The Community shall contribute to the achievement of the objectives set out in paragraph 1 through the policies and activities it pursues under other provisions of this Treaty. The Council, acting unanimously on a proposal from the Commission, after consulting the European Parliament and the Economic and Social Committee, may decide on specific measures in support of action taken in the Member States to achieve the objectives set out in paragraph 1.

This Title shall not provide a basis for the introduction by the Community of any measure which could lead to a distortion of competition.

## TITLE XVII (ex Title XIV)
## ECONOMIC AND SOCIAL COHESION

**Article 158** (ex Article 130a)

In order to promote its overall harmonious development, the Community shall develop and pursue its actions leading to the strengthening of its economic and social cohesion.

In particular, the Community shall aim at reducing disparities between the levels of development of the various regions and the backwardness of the least favoured regions or islands, including rural areas.

**Article 159** (ex Article 130b)

Member States shall conduct their economic policies and shall co-ordinate them in such a way as, in addition, to attain the objectives set out in Article 158. The formulation and implementation of the Community's policies and actions and the implementation of the internal market shall take into account the objectives set out in Article 158 and shall contribute to their achievement. The Community shall also support the achievement of these objectives by the action it takes through the Structural Funds (European Agricultural Guidance and Guarantee Fund, Guidance Section; European Social Fund; European Regional Development Fund), the European Investment Bank and the other existing financial instruments.

The Commission shall submit a report to the European Parliament, the Council, the Economic and Social Committee and the Committee of the Regions every three years on the progress made towards achieving economic and social cohesion and on the manner in which the various means provided for in this Article have contributed to it. This report shall, if necessary, be accompanied by appropriate proposals.

If specific actions prove necessary outside the Funds and without prejudice to the measures decided upon within the framework of the other Community policies, such actions may be adopted by the Council acting unanimously on a proposal from the Commission and after consulting the European Parliament, the Economic and Social Committee and the Committee of the Regions.

**Article 160** (ex Article 130c)

The European Regional Development Fund is intended to help to redress the main regional imbalances in the Community through participation in the development and structural adjustment of regions whose development is lagging behind and in the conversion of declining industrial regions.

**Article 161** (ex Article 130d)

Without prejudice to Article 162, the Council, acting unanimously on a proposal from the Commission and after obtaining the assent of the European Parliament and consulting the Economic and Social Committee and the Committee of the Regions, shall define the tasks, priority objectives and the organisation of the Structural Funds, which may involve grouping the Funds. The Council, acting by the same procedure, shall also define the general rules applicable to them and the provisions necessary to ensure their effectiveness and the co-ordination of the Funds with one another and with the other existing financial instruments.

A Cohesion Fund set up by the Council in accordance with the same procedure shall provide a financial contribution to projects in the fields of environment and trans-European networks in the area of transport infrastructure.

**Article 162** (ex Article 130e)

Implementing decisions relating to the European Regional Development Fund shall be taken by the Council, acting in accordance with the procedure referred to in Article 251 and after consulting the Economic and Social Committee and the Committee of the Regions.

With regard to the European Agricultural Guidance and Guarantee Fund, Guidance Section, and the European Social Fund, Articles 37 and 148 respectively shall continue to apply.

# TITLE XVIII (ex Title XV)
# RESEARCH AND TECHNOLOGICAL DEVELOPMENT

**Article 163** (ex Article 130f)

1.    The Community shall have the objective of strengthening the scientific and technological bases of Community industry and encouraging it to become more competitive at international level, while promoting all the research activities deemed necessary by virtue of other Chapters of this Treaty.

2.    For this purpose the Community shall, throughout the Community, encourage undertakings, including small and medium-sized underta-kings, research centres and universities in their research and technological development activities of high quality; it shall support their efforts to co-operate with one another, aiming, notably, at enabling undertakings to exploit the internal market potential to the full, in particular through the opening-up of national public contracts, the definition of common standards and the removal of legal and fiscal obstacles to that co-operation.

3.    All Community activities under this Treaty in the area of research and technological development, including demonstration projects, shall be decided on and implemented in accordance with the provisions of this Title.

**Article 164** (ex Article 130g)

In pursuing these objectives, the Community shall carry out the following activities, complementing the activities carried out in the Member States:

(a) implementation of research, technological development and demonstration programmes, by promoting co-operation with and between undertakings, research centres and universities;

(b) promotion of co-operation in the field of Community research, technological development and demonstration with third countries and international organisations;

(c) dissemination and optimisation of the results of activities in Community research, technological development and demonstration;

(d) stimulation of the training and mobility of researchers in the Community.

## Article 165 (ex Article 130h)

1.     The Community and the Member States shall co-ordinate their research and technological development activities so as to ensure that national policies and Community policy are mutually consistent.

2.     In close co-operation with the Member State, the Commission may take any useful initiative to promote the co-ordination referred to in paragraph 1.

## Article 166 (ex Article 130i)

1.     A multiannual framework programme, setting out all the activities of the Community, shall be adopted by the Council, acting in accordance with the procedure referred to in Article 251 after consulting the Economic and Social Committee.

The framework programme shall:
— establish the scientific and technological objectives to be achieved by the activities provided for in Article 164 and fix the relevant priorities;
— indicate the broad lines of such activities;
— fix the maximum overall amount and the detailed rules for Community financial participation in the framework programme and the respective shares in each of the activities provided for.

2.     The framework programme shall be adapted or supplemented as the situation changes.

3.     The framework programme shall be implemented through specific programmes developed within each activity. Each specific programme shall define the detailed rules for implementing it, fix its duration and provide for the means deemed necessary. The sum of the amounts deemed necessary, fixed in the specific programmes, may not exceed the overall maximum amount fixed for the framework programme and each activity.

4.     The Council, acting by a qualified majority on a proposal from the Commission and after consulting the European Parliament and the Economic and Social Committee, shall adopt the specific programmes.

## Article 167 (ex Article 130j)

For the implementation of the multiannual framework programme the Council shall:
— determine the rules for the participation of undertakings, research centres and universities;
— lay down the rules governing the dissemination of research results.

**Article 168** (ex Article 130k)

In implementing the multiannual framework programme, supplementary programmes may be decided on involving the participation of certain Member States only, which shall finance them subject to possible Community participation.

The Council shall adopt the rules applicable to supplementary programmes, particularly as regards the dissemination of knowledge and access by other Member States.

**Article 169** (ex Article 130l)

In implementing the multiannual framework programme the Community may make provision, in agreement with the Member States concerned, for participation in research and development programmes undertaken by several Member States, including participation in the structures created for the execution of those programmes.

**Article 170** (ex Article 130m)

In implementing the multiannual framework programme the Community may make provision for co-operation in Community research, technological development and demonstration with third countries or international organisations.

The detailed arrangements for such co-operation may be the subject of agreements between the Community and the third parties concerned, which shall be negotiated and concluded in accordance with Article 300.

**Article 171** (ex Article 130n)

The Community may set up joint undertakings or any other structure necessary for the efficient execution of Community research, technological development and demonstration programmes.

**Article 172** (ex Article 130o)

The Council, acting by qualified majority on a proposal from the Commission and after consulting the European Parliament and the Economic and Social Committee, shall adopt the provisions referred to in Article 171.

The Council, acting in accordance with the procedure referred to in Article 251 and after consulting the Economic and Social Committee, shall adopt the provisions referred to in Articles 167, 168 and 169. Adoption of the supplementary programmes shall require the agreement of the Member States concerned.

**Article 173** (ex Article 130p)

At the beginning of each year the Commission shall send a report to the European Parliament and the Council. The report shall include information on research and technological development activities and the dissemination of results during the previous year, and the work programme for the current year.

# TITLE XIX (ex Title XVI)
# ENVIRONMENT

## Article 174 (ex Article 130r)

1.    Community policy on the environment shall contribute to pursuit of the following objectives:
— preserving, protecting and improving the quality of the environment;
— protecting human health;
— prudent and rational utilisation of natural resources;
— promoting measures at international level to deal with regional or worldwide environmental problems.

2.    Community policy on the environment shall aim at a high level of protection taking into account the diversity of situations in the various regions of the Community. It shall be based on the precautionary principle and on the principles that preventive action should be taken, that environmental damage should as a priority be rectified at source and that the polluter should pay.

In this context, harmonisation measures answering environmental protection requirements shall include, where appropriate, a safeguard clause allowing Member States to take provisional measures, for non-economic environmental reasons, subject to a Community inspection procedure.

3.    In preparing its policy on the environment, the Community shall take account of:
— available scientific and technical data;
— environmental conditions in the various regions of the Community;
— the potential benefits and costs of action or lack of action;
— the economic and social development of the Community as a whole and the balanced development of its regions.

4.    Within their respective spheres of competence, the Community and the Member States shall co-operate with third countries and with the competent international organisations. The arrangements for Community co-operation may be the subject of agreements between the Community and the third parties concerned, which shall be negotiated and concluded in accordance with Article 300.

The previous subparagraph shall be without prejudice to Member States' competence to negotiate in international bodies and to conclude international agreements.

## Article 175 (ex Article 130s)

1.    The Council, acting in accordance with the procedure referred to in Article 251 and after consulting the Economic and Social Committee and the Committee of the Regions, shall decide what action is to be taken by the Community in order to achieve the objectives referred to in Article 174.

2.    By way of derogation from the decision-making procedure provided for in paragraph 1 and without prejudice to Article 95, the Council, acting unanimously on a proposal from the Commission and after consulting the European Parliament, the Economic and Social Committee and the Committee of the Regions, shall adopt:
— provisions primarily of a fiscal nature;
— measures concerning town and country planning, land use with the exception of waste management and measures of a general nature, and management of water resources;

— measures significantly affecting a Member State's choice between different energy sources and the general structure of its energy supply.

The Council may, under the conditions laid down in the preceding subparagraph, define those matters referred to in this paragraph on which decisions are to be taken by a qualified majority.

3.     In other areas, general action programmes setting out priority objectives to be attained shall be adopted by the Council, acting in accordance with the procedure referred to in Article 251 and after consulting the Economic and Social Committee and the Committee of the Regions.

The Council, acting under the terms of paragraph 1 or paragraph 2 according to the case, shall adopt the measures necessary for the implementation of these programmes.

4.     Without prejudice to certain measures of a Community nature, the Member States shall finance and implement the environment policy.

5.     Without prejudice to the principle that the polluter should pay, if a measure based on the provisions of paragraph 1 involves costs deemed disproportionate for the public authorities of a Member State, the Council shall, in the act adopting that measure, lay down appropriate provisions in the form of:
— temporary derogations, and/or;
— financial support from the Cohesion Fund set up pursuant to Article 161.

**Article 176** (ex Article 130t)

The protective measures adopted pursuant to Article 175 shall not prevent any Member State from maintaining or introducing more stringent protective measures.    Such measures must be compatible with this Treaty.  They shall be notified to the Commission.

# TITLE  XX (ex Title XVII)
# DEVELOPMENT CO-OPERATION

**Article 177** (ex Article 130u)

1.     Community policy in the sphere of development co-operation, which shall be complementary to the policies pursued by the Member States, shall foster:
— the sustainable economic and social development of the developing countries, and more particularly the most disadvantaged among them;
— the smooth and gradual integration of the developing countries into the world economy;
— the campaign against poverty in the developing countries.

2.     Community policy in this area shall contribute to the general objective of developing and consolidating democracy and the rule of law, and to that of respecting human rights and fundamental freedoms.

3.     The Community and the Member States shall comply with the commitments and take account of the objectives they have approved in the context of the United Nations and other competent international organisations.

**Article 178** (ex Article 130v)

The Community shall take account of the objectives referred to in Article 177 in the policies that it implements which are likely to affect developing countries.

**Article 179** (ex Article 130w)

1.    Without prejudice to the other provisions of this Treaty, the Council, acting in accordance with the procedure referred to in Article 251, shall adopt the measures necessary to further the objectives referred to in Article 177. Such measures may take the form of multiannual program-mes.

2.    The European Investment Bank shall contribute, under the terms laid down in its Statute, to the implementation of the measures referred to in paragraph 1.

3.    The provisions of this Article shall not affect co-operation with the African, Caribbean and Pacific countries in the framework of the ACP-EC Convention.

**Article 180** (ex Article 130x)

1.    The Community and the Member States shall co-ordinate their policies on development co-operation and shall consult each other on their aid programmes, including in international organisations and during international conferences. They may undertake joint action. Member States shall contribute if necessary to the implementation of Community aid programmes.

2.    The Commission may take any useful initiative to promote the co-ordination referred to in paragraph 1.

**Article 181** (ex Article 130y)

Within their respective spheres of competence, the Community and the Member States shall co-operate with third countries and with the competent international organisations. The arrangements for Community co-operation may be the subject of agreements between the Community and the third parties concerned, which shall be negotiated and concluded in accordance with Article 300.

The previous paragraph shall be without prejudice to Member States' competence to negotiate in international bodies and to conclude international agreements.

## PART FOUR
## ASSOCIATION OF THE OVERSEAS COUNTRIES AND TERRITORIES

**Article 182** (ex Article 131)

The Member States agree to associate with the Community the non-European countries and territories which have special relations with Denmark, France, the Netherlands and the United Kingdom. These countries and territories (hereinafter called the 'countries and territories') are listed in Annex II to this Treaty.

The purpose of association shall be to promote the economic and social development of the countries and territories and to establish close economic relations between them and the Community as a whole.

In accordance with the principles set out in the Preamble to this Treaty, association shall serve primarily to further the interests and prosperity of the inhabitants of these countries and territories in order to lead them to the economic, social and cultural development to which they aspire.

**Article 183** (ex Article 132)

Association shall have the following objectives.

    (1) Member States shall apply to their trade with the countries and territories the same treatment as they accord each other pursuant to this Treaty.

    (2) Each country or territory shall apply to its trade with Member States and with the other countries and territories the same treatment as that which it applies to the European State with which is has special relations.

    (3) The Member States shall contribute to the investments required for the progressive development of these countries and territories.

    (4) For investments financed by the Community, participation in tenders and supplies shall be open on equal terms to all natural and legal persons who are nationals of a Member State or of one of the countries and territories.

    (5) In relations between Member States and the countries and territories the right of establishment of nationals and companies or firms shall be regulated in accordance with the provisions and procedures laid down in the Chapter relating to the right of establishment and on a non-discriminatory basis, subject to any special provisions laid down pursuant to Article 187.

**Article 184** (ex Article 133)

1.    Customs duties on imports into the Member States of goods originating in the countries and territories shall be prohibited in conformity with the prohibition of customs duties between Member States in accordance with the provisions of this Treaty.

2.    Customs duties on imports into each country or territory from Member States or from the other countries or territories shall be prohibited in accordance with the provisions of Article 25.

3.    The countries and territories may, however, levy customs duties which meet the needs of their development and industrialisation or produce revenue for their budgets.

The duties referred to in the preceding subparagraph may not exceed the level of those imposed on imports of products from the Member State with which each country or territory has special relations.

4.    Paragraph 2 shall not apply to countries and territories which, by reason of the particular international obligations by which they are bound, already apply a non-discriminatory customs tariff.

5.    The introduction of or any change in customs duties imposed on goods imported into the countries and territories shall not, either in law or in fact, give rise to any direct or indirect discrimination between imports from the various Member States.

**Article 185** (ex Article 134)

If the level of the duties applicable to goods from a third country on entry into a country or territory is liable, when the provisions of Article 184(1) have been applied, to cause deflections of trade to the detriment of any Member State, the latter may request the Commission to propose to the other Member States the measures needed to remedy the situation.

**Article 186** (ex Article 135)

Subject to the provisions relating to public health, public security or public policy, freedom of movement within Member States for workers from the countries and territories, and within the countries and territories for workers from Member States, shall be governed by agreements to be concluded subsequently with the unanimous approval of Member States.

**Article 187** (ex Article 136)

The Council, acting unanimously, shall, on the basis of the experience acquired under the association of the countries and territories with the Community and of the principles set out in this Treaty, lay down provisions as regards the detailed rules and the procedure for the association of the countries and territories with the Community.

**Article 188** (ex Article 136a)

The provisions of Articles 182 to 187 shall apply to Greenland, subject to the specific provisions for Greenland set out in the Protocol on special arrangements for Greenland, annexed to this Treaty.

# PART FIVE
# INSTITUTIONS OF THE COMMUNITY

## TITLE I
## PROVISIONS GOVERNING THE INSTITUTIONS

### CHAPTER 1
### THE INSTITUTIONS

### SECTION 1
### THE EUROPEAN PARLIAMENT

**Article 189** (ex Article 137)

The European Parliament, which shall consist of representatives of the peoples of the States brought together in the Community, shall exercise the powers conferred upon it by this Treaty.

The number of Members of the European Parliament shall not exceed seven hundred.

**Article 190** (ex Article 138)

1.    The representatives in the European Parliament of the peoples of the States brought together in the Community shall be elected by direct universal suffrage.

2.    The number of representatives elected in each Member State shall be as follows:

| | |
|---|---|
| Belgium | 25 |
| Denmark | 16 |
| Germany | 99 |
| Greece | 25 |
| Spain | 64 |

| France | 87 |
| --- | --- |
| Ireland | 15 |
| Italy | 87 |
| Luxembourg | 6 |
| Netherlands | 31 |
| Austria | 21 |
| Portugal | 25 |
| Finland | 16 |
| Sweden | 22 |
| United Kingdom | 87. |

In the event of amendments to this paragraph, the number of representatives elected in each Member State must ensure appropriate representation of the peoples of the States brought together in the Community.

3.      Representatives shall be elected for a term of five years.

4.      The European Parliament shall draw up a proposal for elections by direct universal suffrage in accordance with a uniform procedure in all Member States or in accordance with principles common to all Member States.

The Council shall, acting unanimously after obtaining the assent of the European Parliament, which shall act by a majority of its component members, lay down the appropriate provisions, which it shall recommend to Member States for adoption in accordance with their respective constitutional requirements.

5.      The European Parliament shall, after seeking an opinion from the Commission and with the approval of the Council acting unanimously, lay down the regulations and general conditions governing the performance of the duties of its Members.

### Article 191 (ex Article 138a)

Political parties at European level are important as a factor for integration within the Union. They contribute to forming a European awareness and to expressing the political will of the citizens of the Union.

### Article 192 (ex Article 138b)

Insofar as provided in this Treaty, the European Parliament shall participate in the process leading up to the adoption of Community acts by exercising its powers under the procedures laid down in Articles 251 and 252 and by giving its assent or delivering advisory opinions.

The European Parliament may, acting by a majority of its Members, request the Commission to submit any appropriate proposal on matters on which it considers that a Community act is required for the purpose of implementing this Treaty.

### Article 193 (ex Article 138c)

In the course of its duties, the European Parliament may, at the request of a quarter of its Members, set up a temporary Committee of Inquiry to investigate, without prejudice to the powers conferred by this Treaty on other institutions or bodies, alleged contraventions or maladministration in the implementation of Community law, except where the alleged facts are being examined before a court and while the case is still subject to legal proceedings.

The temporary Committee of Inquiry shall cease to exist on the submission of its report.

The detailed provisions governing the exercise of the right of inquiry shall be determined by common accord of the European Parliament, the Council and the Commission.

**Article 194** (ex Article 138d)

Any citizen of the Union, and any natural or legal person residing or having its registered office in a Member State, shall have the right to address, individually or in association with other citizens or persons, a petition to the European Parliament on a matter which comes within the Community's fields of activity and which affects him, her or it directly.

**Article 195** (ex Article 138e)

1.      The European Parliament shall appoint an Ombudsman empowered to receive complaints from any citizen of the Union or any natural or legal person residing or having its registered office in a Member State concerning instances of maladministration in the activities of the Community institutions or bodies, with the exception of the Court of Justice and the Court of First Instance acting in their judicial role.

In accordance with his duties, the Ombudsman shall conduct inquiries for which he finds grounds, either on his own initiative or on the basis of complaints submitted to him direct or through a Member of the European Parliament, except where the alleged facts are or have been the subject of legal proceedings. Where the Ombudsman establishes an instance of maladministration, he shall refer the matter to the institution concerned, which shall have a period of three months in which to inform him of its views. The Ombudsman shall then forward a report to the European Parliament and the institution concerned. The person lodging the complaint shall be informed of the outcome of such inquiries.

The Ombudsman shall submit an annual report to the European Parliament on the outcome of his inquiries.

2.      The Ombudsman shall be appointed after each election of the European Parliament for the duration of its term of office. The Ombudsman shall be eligible for reappointment.

The Ombudsman may be dismissed by the Court of Justice at the request of the European Parliament if he no longer fulfils the conditions required for the performance of his duties or if he is guilty of serious misconduct.

3.      The Ombudsman shall be completely independent in the performance of his duties. In the performance of those duties he shall neither seek nor take instructions from any body. The Ombudsman may not, during his term of office, engage in any other occupation, whether gainful or not.

4.      The European Parliament shall, after seeking an opinion from the Commission and with the approval of the Council acting by a qualified majority, lay down the regulations and general conditions governing the performance of the Ombudsman's duties.

**Article 196** (ex Article 139)

The European Parliament shall hold an annual session. It shall meet, without requiring to be convened, on the second Tuesday in March.

The European Parliament may meet in extraordinary session at the request of a majority of its Members or at the request of the Council or of the Commission.

**Article 197** (ex Article 140)

The European Parliament shall elect its President and its officers from among its Members.

Members of the Commission may attend all meetings and shall, at their request, be heard on behalf of the Commission.

The Commission shall reply orally or in writing to questions put to it by the European Parliament or by its Members.

The Council shall be heard by the European Parliament in accordance with the conditions laid down by the Council in its Rules of Procedure.

**Article 198** (ex Article 141)

Save as otherwise provided in this Treaty, the European Parliament shall act by an absolute majority of the votes cast.

The Rules of Procedure shall determine the quorum.

**Article 199** (ex Article 142)

The European Parliament shall adopt its Rules of Procedure, acting by a majority of its Members.

The proceedings of the European Parliament shall be published in the manner laid down in its Rules of Procedure.

**Article 200** (ex Article 143)

The European Parliament shall discuss in open session the annual general report submitted to it by the Commission.

**Article 201** (ex Article 144)

If a motion of censure on the activities of the Commission is tabled before it, the European Parliament shall not vote thereon until at least three days after the motion has been tabled and only by open vote.

If the motion of censure is carried by a two-thirds majority of the votes cast, representing a majority of the Members of the European Parliament, the Members of the Commission shall resign as a body. They shall continue to deal with current business until they are replaced in accordance with Article 214. In this case, the term of office of the Members of the Commission appointed to replace them shall expire on the date on which the term of office of the Members of the Commission obliged to resign as a body would have expired.

## SECTION 2
## THE COUNCIL

**Article 202** (ex Article 145)

To ensure that the objectives set out in this Treaty are attained the Council shall, in accordance with the provisions of this Treaty:
— ensure co-ordination of the general economic policies of the Member States;
— have power to take decisions;
— confer on the Commission, in the acts which the Council adopts, powers for the implementation of the rules which the Council lays down. The Council may impose certain requirements in respect of the exercise of these powers. The Council may also reserve the right, in specific cases, to exercise directly implementing powers itself. The procedures referred to above must be consonant with principles and rules to be laid down in advance by the Council, acting unanimously on a proposal from the Commission and after obtaining the Opinion of the European Parliament.

**Article 203** (ex Article 146)

The Council shall consist of a representative of each Member State at ministerial level, authorised to commit the government of that Member State.

The office of President shall be held in turn by each Member State in the Council for a term of six months in the order decided by the Council acting unanimously.

**Article 204** (ex Article 147)

The Council shall meet when convened by its President on his own initiative or at the request of one of its members or of the Commission.

**Article 205** (ex Article 148)

1.    Save as otherwise provided in this Treaty, the Council shall act by a majority of its members.

2.    Where the Council is required to act by a qualified majority, the votes of its members shall be weighted as follows:

| | |
|---|---|
| Belgium | 5 |
| Denmark | 3 |
| Germany | 10 |
| Greece | 5 |
| Spain | 8 |
| France | 10 |
| Ireland | 3 |
| Italy | 10 |
| Luxembourg | 2 |
| Netherlands | 5 |
| Austria | 4 |

| Portugal        | 5   |
|-----------------|-----|
| Finland         | 3   |
| Sweden          | 4   |
| United Kingdom  | 10. |

For their adoption, acts of the Council shall require at least:
— 62 votes in favour where this Treaty requires them to be adopted on a proposal from the Commission,
— 62 votes in favour, cast by at least 10 members, in other cases.

3.     Abstentions by members present in person or represented shall not prevent the adoption by the Council of acts which require unanimity.

**Article 206** (ex Article 150)

Where a vote is taken, any member of the Council may also act on behalf of not more than one other member.

**Article 207** (ex Article 151)

1.     A committee consisting of the Permanent Representatives of the Member States shall be responsible for preparing the work of the Council and for carrying out the tasks assigned to it by the Council.  The Committee may adopt procedural decisions in cases provided for in the Council's Rules of Procedure.

2.     The Council shall be assisted by a General Secretariat, under the responsibility of a Secretary-General, High Representative for the common foreign and security policy, who shall be assisted by a Deputy Secretary-General responsible for the running of the General Secretariat.  The Secretary-General and the Deputy Secretary-General shall be appointed by the Council acting unanimously.

The Council shall decide on the organisation of the General Secretariat.

3.     The Council shall adopt its Rules of Procedure.

For the purpose of applying Article 255(3), the Council shall elaborate in these Rules the conditions under which the public shall have access to Council documents.  For the purpose of this paragraph, the Council shall define the cases in which it is to be regarded as acting in its legislative capacity, with a view to allowing greater access to documents in those cases, while at the same time preserving the effectiveness of its decision-making process.  In any event, when the Council acts in its legislative capacity, the results of votes and explanations of vote as well as statements in the minutes shall be made public.

**Article 208** (ex Article 152)

The Council may request the Commission to undertake any studies the Council considers desirable for the attainment of the common objectives, and to submit to it any appropriate proposals.

**Article 209** (ex Article 153)

The Council shall, after receiving an opinion from the Commission, determine the rules governing the committees provided for in this Treaty.

**Article 210** (ex Article 154)

The Council shall, acting by a qualified majority, determine the salaries, allowances and pensions of the President and Members of the Commission, and of the President, Judges, Advocates-General and Registrar of the Court of Justice. It shall also, again by a qualified majority, determine any payment to be made instead of remuneration.

## SECTION 3
## THE COMMISSION

**Article 211** (ex Article 155)

In order to ensure the proper functioning and development of the common market, the Commission shall:
— ensure that the provisions of this Treaty and the measures taken by the institutions pursuant thereto are applied;
— formulate recommendations or deliver opinions on matters dealt with in this Treaty, if it expressly so provides or if the Commission considers it necessary;
— have its own power of decision and participate in the shaping of measures taken by the Council and by the European Parliament in the manner provided for in this Treaty;
— exercise the powers conferred on it by the Council for the implementation of the rules laid down by the latter.

**Article 212** (ex Article 156)

The Commission shall publish annually, not later than one month before the opening of the session of the European Parliament, a general report on the activities of the Community.

**Article 213** (ex Article 157)

1.    The Commission shall consist of 20 Members, who shall be chosen on the grounds of their general competence and whose independence is beyond doubt.

The number of Members of the Commission may be altered by the Council, acting unanimously.

Only nationals of Member States may be Members of the Commission.

The Commission must include at least one national of each of the Member States, but may not include more than two Members having the nationality of the same State.

2.    The Members of the Commission shall, in the general interest of the Community, be completely independent in the performance of their duties.

In the performance of these duties, they shall neither seek nor take instructions from any government or from any other body. They shall refrain from any action incompatible with their duties. Each Member State undertakes to respect this principle and not to seek to influence the Members of the Commission in the performance of their tasks.

The Members of the Commission may not, during their term of office, engage in any other occupation, whether gainful or not. When entering upon their duties they shall give a solemn undertaking that, both during and after their term of office, they will respect the obligations arising therefrom and in particular their duty to behave with integrity and discretion as regards the acceptance, after they have ceased to hold office, of certain appointments or benefits. In the event of any breach of these obligations, the Court of Justice may, on application by the Council or the Commission, rule that the Member concerned be, according to the circumstances, either compulsorily retired in accordance with Article 216 or deprived of his right to a pension or other benefits in its stead.

**Article 214** (ex Article 158)

1.     The Members of the Commission shall be appointed, in accordance with the procedure referred to in paragraph 2, for a period of five years, subject, if need be, to Article 201.

Their term of office shall be renewable.

2.     The governments of the Member States shall nominate by common accord the person they intend to appoint as President of the Commission; the nomination shall be approved by the European Parliament.

The governments of the Member States shall, by common accord with the nominee for President, nominate the other persons whom they intend to appoint as Members of the Commission.

The President and the other Members of the Commission thus nominated shall be subject as a body to a vote of approval by the European Parliament. After approval by the European Parliament, the President and the other Members of the Commission shall be appointed by common accord of the governments of the Member States.

**Article 215** (ex Article 159)

Apart from normal replacement, or death, the duties of a Member of the Commission shall end when he resigns or is compulsorily retired.

The vacancy thus caused shall be filled for the remainder of the Member's term of office by a new Member appointed by common accord of the governments of the Member States. The Council may, acting unanimously, decide that such a vacancy need not be filled.

In the event of resignation, compulsory retirement or death, the President shall be replaced for the remainder of his term of office. The procedure laid down in Article 214(2) shall be applicable for the replacement of the President.

Save in the case of compulsory retirement under Article 216, Members of the Commission shall remain in office until they have been replaced.

**Article 216** (ex Article 160)

If any Member of the Commission no longer fulfils the conditions required for the performance of his duties or if he has been guilty of serious misconduct, the Court of Justice may, on application by the Council or the Commission, compulsorily retire him.

**Article 217** (ex Article 161)

The Commission may appoint a Vice-President or two Vice-Presidents from among its Members.

**Article 218** (ex Article 162)

1.    The Council and the Commission shall consult each other and shall settle by common accord their methods of co-operation.

2.    The Commission shall adopt its Rules of Procedure so as to ensure that both it and its departments operate in accordance with the provisions of this Treaty. It shall ensure that these rules are published.

**Article 219** (ex Article 163)

The Commission shall work under the political guidance of its President.

The Commission shall act by a majority of the number of Members provided for in Article 213.

A meeting of the Commission shall be valid only if the number of Members laid down in its Rules of Procedure is present.

# SECTION 4
# THE COURT OF JUSTICE

**Article 220** (ex Article 164)

The Court of Justice shall ensure that in the interpretation and application of this Treaty the law is observed.

**Article 221** (ex Article 165)

The Court of Justice shall consist of 15 Judges.

The Court of Justice shall sit in plenary session. It may, however, form chambers, each consisting of three, five or seven Judges, either to undertake certain preparatory inquiries or to adjudicate on particular categories of cases in accordance with rules laid down for these purposes.

The Court of Justice shall sit in plenary session when a Member State or a Community institution that is a party to the proceedings so requests.

Should the Court of Justice so request, the Council may, acting unanimously, increase the number of Judges and make the necessary adjustments to the second and third paragraphs of this Article and to the second paragraph of Article 223.

**Article 222** (ex Article 166)

The Court of Justice shall be assisted by eight Advocates-General. However, a ninth Advocate-General shall be appointed as from 1 January 1995 until 6 October 2000.

It shall be the duty of the Advocate-General, acting with complete impartiality and independence, to make, in open court, reasoned submissions on cases brought before the Court of Justice, in order to assist the Court in the performance of the task assigned to it in Article 220.

Should the Court of Justice so request, the Council may, acting unanimously, increase the number of Advocates-General and make the necessary adjustments to the third paragraph of Article 223.

## Article 223 (ex Article 167)

The Judges and Advocates-General shall be chosen from persons whose independence is beyond doubt and who possess the qualifications required for appointment to the highest judicial offices in their respective countries or who are jurisconsults of recognised competence; they shall be appointed by common accord of the governments of the Member States for a term of six years.

Every three years there shall be a partial replacement of the Judges. Eight and seven Judges shall be replaced alternately.

Every three years there shall be a partial replacement of the Advocates-General. Four Advocates-General shall be replaced on each occasion.

Retiring Judges and Advocates-General shall be eligible for reappointment.

The Judges shall elect the President of the Court of Justice from among their number for a term of three years. He may be re-elected.

## Article 224 (ex Article 168)

The Court of Justice shall appoint its Registrar and lay down the rules governing his service.

## Article 225 (ex Article 168a)

1. A Court of First Instance shall be attached to the Court of Justice with jurisdiction to hear and determine at first instance, subject to a right of appeal to the Court of Justice on points of law only and in accordance with the conditions laid down by the Statute, certain classes of action or proceeding defined in accordance with the conditions laid down in paragraph 2. The Court of First Instance shall not be competent to hear and determine questions referred for a preliminary ruling under Article 234.

2. At the request of the Court of Justice and after consulting the European Parliament and the Commission, the Council, acting unanimously, shall determine the classes of action or proceeding referred to in paragraph 1 and the composition of the Court of First Instance and shall adopt the necessary adjustments and additional provisions to the Statute of the Court of Justice. Unless the Council decides otherwise, the provisions of this Treaty relating to the Court of Justice, in particular the provisions of the Protocol on the Statute of the Court of Justice, shall apply to the Court of First Instance.

3. The members of the Court of First Instance shall be chosen from persons whose independence is beyond doubt and who possess the ability required for appointment to judicial office; they shall be appointed by common accord of the governments of the Member States for a term of six years. The membership shall be partially renewed every three years. Retiring members shall be eligible for reappointment.

4. The Court of First Instance shall establish its Rules of Procedure in agreement with the Court of Justice. Those rules shall require the unanimous approval of the Council.

## Article 226 (ex Article 169)

If the Commission considers that a Member State has failed to fulfil an obligation under this Treaty, it shall deliver a reasoned opinion on the matter after giving the State concerned the opportunity to submit its observations.

If the State concerned does not comply with the opinion within the period laid down by the Commission, the latter may bring the matter before the Court of Justice.

## Article 227 (ex Article 170)

A Member State which considers that another Member State has failed to fulfil an obligation under this Treaty may bring the matter before the Court of Justice.

Before a Member State brings an action against another Member State for an alleged infringement of an obligation under this Treaty, it shall bring the matter before the Commission.

The Commission shall deliver a reasoned opinion after each of the States concerned has been given the opportunity to submit its own case and its observations on the other party's case both orally and in writing.

If the Commission has not delivered an opinion within three months of the date on which the matter was brought before it, the absence of such opinion shall not prevent the matter from being brought before the Court of Justice.

## Article 228 (ex Article 171)

1.     If the Court of Justice finds that a Member State has failed to fulfil an obligation under this Treaty, the State shall be required to take the necessary measures to comply with the judgment of the Court of Justice.

2.     If the Commission considers that the Member State concerned has not taken such measures it shall, after giving that State the opportunity to submit its observations, issue a reasoned opinion specifying the points on which the Member State concerned has not complied with the judgment of the Court of Justice.

If the Member State concerned fails to take the necessary measures to comply with the Court's judgment within the time-limit laid down by the Commission, the latter may bring the case before the Court of Justice. In so doing it shall specify the amount of the lump sum or penalty payment to be paid by the Member State concerned which it considers appropriate in the circumstances.

If the Court of Justice finds that the Member State concerned has not complied with its judgment it may impose a lump sum or penalty payment on it.

This procedure shall be without prejudice to Article 227.

## Article 229 (ex Article 172)

Regulations adopted jointly by the European Parliament and the Council, and by the Council, pursuant to the provisions of this Treaty, may give the Court of Justice unlimited jurisdiction with regard to the penalties provided for in such regulations.

## Article 230 (ex Article 173)

The Court of Justice shall review the legality of acts adopted jointly by the European Parliament and the Council, of acts of the Council, of the Commission and of the ECB, other than recommendations and opinions, and of acts of the European Parliament intended to produce legal effects vis-à-vis third parties.

It shall for this purpose have jurisdiction in actions brought by a Member State, the Council or the Commission on grounds of lack of competence, infringement of an essential procedural requirement, infringement of this Treaty or of any rule of law relating to its application, or misuse of powers.

The Court of Justice shall have jurisdiction under the same conditions in actions brought by the European Parliament, by the Court of Auditors and by the ECB for the purpose of protecting their prerogatives.

Any natural or legal person may, under the same conditions, institute proceedings against a decision addressed to that person or against a decision which, although in the form of a regulation or a decision addressed to another person, is of direct and individual concern to the former.

The proceedings provided for in this Article shall be instituted within two months of the publication of the measure, or of its notification to the plaintiff, or, in the absence thereof, of the day on which it came to the knowledge of the latter, as the case may be.

**Article 231** (ex Article 174)

If the action is well founded, the Court of Justice shall declare the act concerned to be void.

In the case of a regulation, however, the Court of Justice shall, if it considers this necessary, state which of the effects of the regulation which it has declared void shall be considered as definitive.

**Article 232** (ex Article 175)

Should the European Parliament, the Council or the Commission, in infringement of this Treaty, fail to act, the Member States and the other institutions of the Community may bring an action before the Court of Justice to have the infringement established.

The action shall be admissible only if the institution concerned has first been called upon to act. If, within two months of being so called upon, the institution concerned has not defined its position, the action may be brought within a further period of two months.

Any natural or legal person may, under the conditions laid down in the preceding paragraphs, complain to the Court of Justice that an institution of the Community has failed to address to that person any act other than a recommendation or an opinion.

The Court of Justice shall have jurisdiction, under the same conditions, in actions or proceedings brought by the ECB in the areas falling within the latter's field of competence and in actions or proceedings brought against the latter.

**Article 233** (ex Article 176)

The institution or institutions whose act has been declared void or whose failure to act has been declared contrary to this Treaty shall be required to take the necessary measures to comply with the judgment of the Court of Justice.

This obligation shall not affect any obligation which may result from the application of the second paragraph of Article 288.

This Article shall also apply to the ECB.

**Article 234** (ex Article 177)

The Court of Justice shall have jurisdiction to give preliminary rulings concerning:

(a) the interpretation of this Treaty;
(b) the validity and interpretation of acts of the institutions of the Community and of the ECB;
(c) the interpretation of the statutes of bodies established by an act of the Council, where those statutes so provide.

Where such a question is raised before any court or tribunal of a Member State, that court or tribunal may, if it considers that a decision on the question is necessary to enable it to give judgment, request the Court of Justice to give a ruling thereon.

Where any such question is raised in a case pending before a court or tribunal of a Member State against whose decisions there is no judicial remedy under national law, that court or tribunal shall bring the matter before the Court of Justice.

**Article 235** (ex Article 178)

The Court of Justice shall have jurisdiction in disputes relating to compensation for damage provided for in the second paragraph of Article 288.

**Article 236** (ex Article 179)

The Court of Justice shall have jurisdiction in any dispute between the Community and its servants within the limits and under the conditions laid down in the Staff Regulations or the Conditions of Employment.

**Article 237** (ex Article 180)

The Court of Justice shall, within the limits hereinafter laid down, have jurisdiction in disputes concerning:
(a) the fulfilment by Member States of obligations under the Statute of the European Investment Bank. In this connection, the Board of Directors of the Bank shall enjoy the powers conferred upon the Commission by Article 226;
(b) measures adopted by the Board of Governors of the European Investment Bank. In this connection, any Member State, the Commission or the Board of Directors of the Bank may institute proceedings under the conditions laid down in Article 230;
(c) measures adopted by the Board of Directors of the European Investment Bank. Proceedings against such measures may be instituted only by Member States or by the Commission, under the conditions laid down in Article 230, and solely on the grounds of non-compliance with the procedure provided for in Article 21(2), (5), (6) and (7) of the Statute of the Bank;
(d) the fulfilment by national central banks of obligations under this Treaty and the Statute of the ESCB. In this connection the powers of the Council of the ECB in respect of national central banks shall be the same as those conferred upon the Commission in respect of Member States by Article 226. If the Court of Justice finds that a national central bank has failed to fulfil an obligation under this Treaty, that bank shall be required to take the necessary measures to comply with the judgment of the Court of Justice.

**Article 238** (ex Article 181)

The Court of Justice shall have jurisdiction to give judgment pursuant to any arbitration clause contained in a contract concluded by or on behalf of the Community, whether that contract be governed by public or private law.

**Article 239** (ex Article 182)

The Court of Justice shall have jurisdiction in any dispute between Member States which relates to the subject matter of this Treaty if the dispute is submitted to it under a special agreement between the parties.

**Article 240** (ex Article 183)

Save where jurisdiction is conferred on the Court of Justice by this Treaty, disputes to which the Community is a party shall not on that ground be excluded from the jurisdiction of the courts or tribunals of the Member States.

**Article 241** (ex Article 184)

Notwithstanding the expiry of the period laid down in the fifth paragraph of Article 230, any party may, in proceedings in which a regulation adopted jointly by the European Parliament and the Council, or a regulation of the Council, of the Commission, or of the ECB is at issue, plead the grounds specified in the second paragraph of Article 230 in order to invoke before the Court of Justice the inapplicability of that regulation.

**Article 242** (ex Article 185)

Actions brought before the Court of Justice shall not have suspensory effect. The Court of Justice may, however, if it considers that circumstances so require, order that application of the contested act be suspended.

**Article 243** (ex Article 186)

The Court of Justice may in any cases before it prescribe any necessary interim measures.

**Article 244** (ex Article 187)

The judgments of the Court of Justice shall be enforceable under the conditions laid down in Article 256.

**Article 245** (ex Article 188)

The Statute of the Court of Justice is laid down in a separate Protocol.

The Council may, acting unanimously at the request of the Court of Justice and after consulting the Commission and the European Parliament, amend the provisions of Title III of the Statute.

The Court of Justice shall adopt its Rules of Procedure. These shall require the unanimous approval of the Council.

## SECTION 5
## THE COURT OF AUDITORS

**Article 246** (ex Article 188a)

The Court of Auditors shall carry out the audit.

**Article 247** (ex Article 188b)

1.     The Court of Auditors shall consist of 15 Members.

2.     The Members of the Court of Auditors shall be chosen from among persons who belong or have belonged in their respective countries to external audit bodies or who are especially qualified for this office. Their independence must be beyond doubt.

3.     The Members of the Court of Auditors shall be appointed for a term of six years by the Council, acting unanimously after consulting the European Parliament.

The Members of the Court of Auditors shall be eligible for reappointment.

They shall elect the President of the Court of Auditors from among their number for a term of three years. The President may be re-elected.

4.     The Members of the Court of Auditors shall, in the general interest of the Community, be completely independent in the performance of their duties.

In the performance of these duties, they shall neither seek nor take instructions from any government or from any other body. They shall refrain from any action incompatible with their duties.

5.     The Members of the Court of Auditors may not, during their term of office, engage in any other occupation, whether gainful or not. When entering upon their duties they shall give a solemn undertaking that, both during and after their term of office, they will respect the obligations arising therefrom and in particular their duty to behave with integrity and discretion as regards the acceptance, after they have ceased to hold office, of certain appointments or benefits.

6.     Apart from normal replacement, or death, the duties of a Member of the Court of Auditors shall end when he resigns, or is compulsorily retired by a ruling of the Court of Justice pursuant to paragraph 7.

The vacancy thus caused shall be filled for the remainder of the Member's term of office.

Save in the case of compulsory retirement, Members of the Court of Auditors shall remain in office until they have been replaced.

7.     A Member of the Court of Auditors may be deprived of his office or of his right to a pension or other benefits in its stead only if the Court of Justice, at the request of the Court of Auditors, finds that he no longer fulfils the requisite conditions or meets the obligations arising from his office.

8.     The Council, acting by a qualified majority, shall determine the conditions of employment of the President and the Members of the Court of Auditors and in particular their salaries, allowances and pensions. It shall also, by the same majority, determine any payment to be made instead of remuneration.

9.     The provisions of the Protocol on the privileges and immunities of the European Communities applicable to the Judges of the Court of Justice shall also apply to the Members of the Court of Auditors.

### Article 248 (ex Article 188c)

1.     The Court of Auditors shall examine the accounts of all revenue and expenditure of the Community. It shall also examine the accounts of all revenue and expenditure of all bodies set up by the Community insofar as the relevant constituent instrument does not preclude such examination.

The Court of Auditors shall provide the European Parliament and the Council with a statement of assurance as to the reliability of the accounts and the legality and regularity of the underlying transactions which shall be published in the *Official Journal of the European Communities.*

2.     The Court of Auditors shall examine whether all revenue has been received and all expenditure incurred in a lawful and regular manner and whether the financial management has been sound.  In doing so, it shall report in particular on any cases of irregularity.

The audit of revenue shall be carried out on the basis both of the amounts established as due and the amounts actually paid to the Community.

The audit of expenditure shall be carried out on the basis both of commitments undertaken and payments made.

These audits may be carried out before the closure of accounts for the financial year in question.

3.     The audit shall be based on records and, if necessary, performed on the spot in the other institutions of the Community, on the premises of any body which manages revenue or expenditure on behalf of the Community and in the Member States, including on the premises of any natural or legal person in receipt of payments from the budget.  In the Member States the audit shall be carried out in liaison with national audit bodies or, if these do not have the necessary powers, with the competent national departments.  The Court of Auditors and the national audit bodies of the Member States shall co-operate in a spirit of trust while maintaining their independence. These bodies or departments shall inform the Court of Auditors whether they intend to take part in the audit.

The other institutions of the Community, any bodies managing revenue or expenditure on behalf of the Community, any natural or legal person in receipt of payments from the budget, and the national audit bodies or, if these do not have the necessary powers, the competent national departments, shall forward to the Court of Auditors, at its request,  any document or information necessary to carry out its task.

In respect of the European Investment Bank's activity in managing Community expenditure and revenue, the Court's rights of access to information held by the Bank shall be governed by an agreement between the Court, the Bank and the Commission.  In the absence of an agreement, the Court shall nevertheless have access to information necessary for the audit of Community expenditure and revenue managed by the Bank.

4.     The Court of Auditors shall draw up an annual report after the close of each financial year. It shall be forwarded to the other institutions of the Community and shall be published, together with the replies of these institutions to the observations of the Court of Auditors, in the *Official Journal of the European Communities.*

The Court of Auditors may also, at any time, submit observations, particularly in the form of special reports, on specific questions and deliver opinions at the request of one of the other institutions of the Community.

It shall adopt its annual reports, special reports or opinions by a majority of its Members.

It shall assist the European Parliament and the Council in exercising their powers of control over the implementation of the budget.

# CHAPTER 2
# PROVISIONS COMMON TO SEVERAL INSTITUTIONS

**Article 249** (ex Article 189)

In order to carry out their task and in accordance with the provisions of this Treaty, the European Parliament acting jointly with the Council, the Council and the Commission shall make regulations and issue directives, take decisions, make recommendations or deliver opinions.

A regulation shall have general application. It shall be binding in its entirety and directly applicable in all Member States.

A directive shall be binding, as to the result to be achieved, upon each Member State to which it is addressed, but shall leave to the national authorities the choice of form and methods.

A decision shall be binding in its entirety upon those to whom it is addressed.

Recommendations and opinions shall have no binding force.

**Article 250** (ex Article 189a)

1.      Where, in pursuance of this Treaty, the Council acts on a proposal from the Commission, unanimity shall be required for an act constituting an amendment to that proposal, subject to Article 251(4) and (5).

2.      As long as the Council has not acted, the Commission may alter its proposal at any time during the procedures leading to the adoption of a Community act.

**Article 251** (ex Article 189b)

1.      Where reference is made in this Treaty to this Article for the adoption of an act, the following procedure shall apply.

2.      The Commission shall submit a proposal to the European Parliament and the Council.

The Council, acting by a qualified majority after obtaining the opinion of the European Parliament,
— if it approves all the amendments contained in the European Parliament's opinion, may adopt the proposed act thus amended;
— if the European Parliament does not propose any amendments, may adopt the proposed act;
— shall otherwise adopt a common position and communicate it to the European Parliament. The Council shall inform the European Parliament fully of the reasons which led it to adopt its common position. The Commission shall inform the European Parliament fully of its position.

If, within three months of such communication, the European Parliament:
(a) approves the common position or has not taken a decision, the act in question shall be deemed to have been adopted in accordance with that common position;

    (b)  rejects, by an absolute majority of its component members, the common position, the proposed act shall be deemed not to have been adopted;

    (c)  proposes amendments to the common position by an absolute majority of its component members, the amended text shall be forwarded to the Council and to the Commission, which shall deliver an opinion on those amendments.

3.    If, within three months of the matter being referred to it, the Council, acting by a qualified majority, approves all the amendments of the European Parliament, the act in question shall be deemed to have been adopted in the form of the common position thus amended; however, the Council shall act unanimously on the amendments on which the Commission has delivered a negative opinion. If the Council does not approve all the amendments, the President of the Council, in agreement with the President of the European Parliament, shall within six weeks convene a meeting of the Conciliation Committee.

4.    The Conciliation Committee, which shall be composed of the members of the Council or their representatives and an equal number of representatives of the European Parliament, shall have the task of reaching agreement on a joint text, by a qualified majority of the members of the Council or their representatives and by a majority of the representatives of the European Parliament. The Commission shall take part in the Conciliation Committee's proceedings and shall take all the necessary initiatives with a view to reconciling the positions of the European Parliament and the Council. In fulfilling this task, the Conciliation Committee shall address the common position on the basis of the amendments proposed by the European Parliament.

5.    If, within six weeks of its being convened, the Conciliation Committee approves a joint text, the European Parliament, acting by an absolute majority of the votes cast, and the Council, acting by a qualified majority, shall each have a period of six weeks from that approval in which to adopt the act in question in accordance with the joint text. If either of the two institutions fails to approve the proposed act within that period, it shall be deemed not to have been adopted.

6.    Where the Conciliation Committee does not approve a joint text, the proposed act shall be deemed not to have been adopted.

7.    The periods of three months and six weeks referred to in this Article shall be extended by a maximum of one month and two weeks respectively at the initiative of the European Parliament or the Council.

**Article 252** (ex Article 189c)

Where reference is made in this Treaty to this Article for the adoption of an act, the following procedure shall apply:

    (a)  The Council, acting by a qualified majority on a proposal from the Commission and after obtaining the opinion of the European Parliament, shall adopt a common position.

    (b)  The Council's common position shall be communicated to the European Parliament. The Council and the Commission shall inform the European Parliament fully of the reasons which led the Council to adopt its common position and also of the Commission's position.

        If, within three months of such communication, the European Parliament approves this common position or has not taken a decision within that period, the Council shall definitively adopt the act in question in accordance with the common position.

(c) The European Parliament may, within the period of three months referred to in point (b), by an absolute majority of its component Members, propose amendments to the Council's common position. The European Parliament may also, by the same majority, reject the Council's common position. The result of the proceedings shall be transmitted to the Council and the Commission.

If the European Parliament has rejected the Council's common position, unanimity shall be required for the Council to act on a second reading.

(d) The Commission shall, within a period of one month, re-examine the proposal on the basis of which the Council adopted its common position, by taking into account the amendments proposed by the European Parliament.

The Commission shall forward to the Council, at the same time as its re-examined proposal, the amendments of the European Parliament which it has not accepted, and shall express its opinion on them. The Council may adopt these amendments unanimously.

(e) The Council, acting by a qualified majority, shall adopt the proposal as re-examined by the Commission.

Unanimity shall be required for the Council to amend the proposal as re-examined by the Commission.

(f) In the cases referred to in points (c), (d) and (e), the Council shall be required to act within a period of three months. If no decision is taken within this period, the Commission proposal shall be deemed not to have been adopted.

(g) The periods referred to in points (b) and (f) may be extended by a maximum of one month by common accord between the Council and the European Parliament.

## Article 253 (ex Article 190)

Regulations, directives and decisions adopted jointly by the European Parliament and the Council, and such acts adopted by the Council or the Commission, shall state the reasons on which they are based and shall refer to any proposals or opinions which were required to be obtained pursuant to this Treaty.

## Article 254 (ex Article 191)

1.      Regulations, directives and decisions adopted in accordance with the procedure referred to in Article 251 shall be signed by the President of the European Parliament and by the President of the Council and published in the *Official Journal of the European Communities*. They shall enter into force on the date specified in them or, in the absence thereof, on the twentieth day following that of their publication.

2.      Regulations of the Council and of the Commission, as well as directives of those institutions which are addressed to all Member States, shall be published in the *Official Journal of the European Communities*. They shall enter into force on the date specified in them or, in the absence thereof, on the twentieth day following that of their publication.

3.      Other directives, and decisions, shall be notified to those to whom they are addressed and shall take effect upon such notification.

**Article 255** (ex Article 191a)

1.      Any citizen of the Union, and any natural or legal person residing or having its registered office in a Member State, shall have a right of access to European Parliament, Council and Commission documents, subject to the principles and the conditions to be defined in accordance with paragraphs 2 and 3.

2.      General principles and limits on grounds of public or private interest governing this right of access to documents shall be determined by the Council, acting in accordance with the procedure referred to in Article 251 within two years of the entry into force of the Treaty of Amsterdam.

3.      Each institution referred to above shall elaborate in its own Rules of Procedure specific provisions regarding access to its documents.

**Article 256** (ex Article 192)

Decisions of the Council or of the Commission which impose a pecuniary obligation on persons other than States, shall be enforceable.

Enforcement shall be governed by the rules of civil procedure in force in the State in the territory of which it is carried out. The order for its enforcement shall be appended to the decision, without other formality than verification of the authenticity of the decision, by the national authority which the government of each Member State shall designate for this purpose and shall make known to the Commission and to the Court of Justice.

When these formalities have been completed on application by the party concerned, the latter may proceed to enforcement in accordance with the national law, by bringing the matter directly before the competent authority.

Enforcement may be suspended only by a decision of the Court of Justice. However, the courts of the country concerned shall have jurisdiction over complaints that enforcement is being carried out in an irregular manner.

# CHAPTER 3
## THE ECONOMIC AND SOCIAL COMMITTEE

**Article 257** (ex Article 193)

An Economic and Social Committee is hereby established. It shall have advisory status.

The Committee shall consist of representatives of the various categories of economic and social activity, in particular, representatives of producers, farmers, carriers, workers, dealers, craftsmen, professional occupations and representatives of the general public.

**Article 258** (ex Article 194)

The number of members of the Economic and Social Committee shall be as follows:

| | |
|---|---|
| Belgium | 12 |
| Denmark | 9 |
| Germany | 24 |
| Greece | 12 |
| Spain | 21 |

| | |
|---|---|
| France | 24 |
| Ireland | 9 |
| Italy | 24 |
| Luxembourg | 6 |
| Netherlands | 12 |
| Austria | 12 |
| Portugal | 12 |
| Finland | 9 |
| Sweden | 12 |
| United Kingdom | 24 |

The members of the Committee shall be appointed by the Council, acting unanimously, for four years. Their appointments shall be renewable.

The members of the Committee may not be bound by any mandatory instructions. They shall be completely independent in the performance of their duties, in the general interest of the Community.

The Council, acting by a qualified majority, shall determine the allowances of members of the Committee.

### Article 259 (ex Article 195)

1.	For the appointment of the members of the Committee, each Member State shall provide the Council with a list containing twice as many candidates as there are seats allotted to its nationals.

The composition of the Committee shall take account of the need to ensure adequate representation of the various categories of economic and social activity.

2.	The Council shall consult the Commission. It may obtain the opinion of European bodies which are representative of the various economic and social sectors to which the activities of the Community are of concern.

### Article 260 (ex Article 196)

The Committee shall elect its chairman and officers from among its members for a term of two years.

It shall adopt its Rules of Procedure.

The Committee shall be convened by its chairman at the request of the Council or of the Commission. It may also meet on its own initiative.

### Article 261 (ex Article 197)

The Committee shall include specialised sections for the principal fields covered by this Treaty.

These specialised sections shall operate within the general terms of reference of the Committee. They may not be consulted independently of the Committee.

Subcommittees may also be established within the Committee to prepare on specific questions or in specific fields, draft opinions to be submitted to the Committee for its consideration.

The Rules of Procedure shall lay down the methods of composition and the terms of reference of the specialised sections and of the subcommittees.

**Article 262** (ex Article 198)

The Committee must be consulted by the Council or by the Commission where this Treaty so provides. The Committee may be consulted by these institutions in all cases in which they consider it appropriate. It may issue an opinion on its own initiative in cases in which it considers such action appropriate.

The Council or the Commission shall, if it considers it necessary, set the Committee, for the submission of its opinion, a time-limit which may not be less than one month from the date on which the chairman receives notification to this effect. Upon expiry of the time-limit, the absence of an opinion shall not prevent further action.

The opinion of the Committee and that of the specialised section, together with a record of the proceedings, shall be forwarded to the Council and to the Commission.

The Committee may be consulted by the European Parliament.

# CHAPTER 4
# THE COMMITTEE OF THE REGIONS

**Article 263** (ex Article 198a)

A Committee consisting of representatives of regional and local bodies, hereinafter referred to as 'the Committee of the Regions', is hereby established with advisory status.

The number of members of the Committee of the Regions shall be as follows:

| | |
|---|---|
| Belgium | 12 |
| Denmark | 9 |
| Germany | 24 |
| Greece | 12 |
| Spain | 21 |
| France | 24 |
| Ireland | 9 |
| Italy | 24 |
| Luxembourg | 6 |
| Netherlands | 12 |
| Austria | 12 |
| Portugal | 12 |
| Finland | 9 |
| Sweden | 12 |
| United Kingdom | 24 |

The members of the Committee and an equal number of alternate members shall be appointed for four years by the Council acting unanimously on proposals from the respective Member States. Their term of office shall be renewable. No member of the Committee shall at the same time be a Member of the European Parliament.

The members of the Committee may not be bound by any mandatory instructions. They shall be completely independent in the performance of their duties, in the general interest of Community.

**Article 264** (ex Article 198b)

The Committee of the Regions shall elect its chairman and officers from among its members for a term of two years.

It shall adopt its Rules of Procedure.

The Committee shall be convened by its chairman at the request of the Council or of the Commission. It may also meet on its own initiative.

**Article 265** (ex Article 198c)

The Committee of the Regions shall be consulted by the Council or by the Commission where this Treaty so provides and in all other cases, in particular those which concern cross-border co-operation, in which one of these two institutions considers it appropriate.

The Council or the Commission shall, if it considers it necessary, set the Committee, for the submission of its opinion, a time-limit which may not be less than one month from the date on which the chairman receives notification to this effect. Upon expiry of the time-limit, the absence of an opinion shall not prevent further action.

Where the Economic and Social Committee is consulted pursuant to Article 262, the Committee of the Regions shall be informed by the Council or the Commission of the request for an opinion. Where it considers that specific regional interests are involved, the Committee of the Regions may issue an opinion on the matter.

The Committee of the Regions may be consulted by the European Parliament.

It may issue an opinion on its own initiative in cases in which it considers such action appropriate.

The opinion of the Committee, together with a record of the proceedings, shall be forwarded to the Council and to the Commission.

# CHAPTER 5
# THE EUROPEAN INVESTMENT BANK

**Article 266** (ex Article 198d)

The European Investment Bank shall have legal personality.

The members of the European Investment Bank shall be the Member States.

The Statute of the European Investment Bank is laid down in a Protocol annexed to this Treaty.

**Article 267** (ex Article 198e)

The task of the European Investment Bank shall be to contribute, by having recourse to the capital market and utilising its own resources, to the balanced and steady development of the common market in the interest of the Community. For this purpose the Bank shall, operating on a non-profit-making basis, grant loans and give guarantees which facilitate the financing of the following projects in all sectors of the economy:

(a) projects for developing less-developed regions;

(b) projects for modernising or converting undertakings or for developing fresh activities called for by the progressive establishment of the common market, where these projects are of such a size or nature that they cannot be entirely financed by the various means available in the individual Member States;

(c) projects of common interest to several Member States which are of such a size or nature that they cannot be entirely financed by the various means available in the individual Member States.

In carrying out its task, the Bank shall facilitate the financing of investment programmes in conjunction with assistance from the Structural Funds and other Community financial instruments.

# TITLE II
# FINANCIAL PROVISIONS

## Article 268 (ex Article 199)

All items of revenue and expenditure of the Community, including those relating to the European Social Fund, shall be included in estimates to be drawn up for each financial year and shall be shown in the budget.

Administrative expenditure occasioned for the institutions by the provisions of the Treaty on European Union relating to common foreign and security policy and to co-operation in the fields of justice and home affairs shall be charged to the budget. The operational expenditure occasioned by the implementation of the said provisions may, under the conditions referred to therein, be charged to the budget.

The revenue and expenditure shown in the budget shall be in balance.

## Article 269 (ex Article 201)

Without prejudice to other revenue, the budget shall be financed wholly from own resources.

The Council, acting unanimously on a proposal from the Commission and after consulting the European Parliament, shall lay down provisions relating to the system of own resources of the Community, which it shall recommend to the Member States for adoption in accordance with their respective constitutional requirements.

## Article 270 (ex Article 201a)

With a view to maintaining budgetary discipline, the Commission shall not make any proposal for a Community act, or alter its proposals, or adopt any implementing measure which is likely to have appreciable implications for the budget without providing the assurance that that proposal or that measure is capable of being financed within the limit of the Community's own resources arising under provisions laid down by the Council pursuant to Article 269.

**Article 271** (ex Article 202)

The expenditure shown in the budget shall be authorised for one financial year, unless the regulations made pursuant to Article 279 provide otherwise.

In accordance with conditions to be laid down pursuant to Article 279, any appropriations, other than those relating to staff expenditure, that are unexpended at the end of the financial year may be carried forward to the next financial year only.

Appropriations shall be classified under different chapters grouping items of expenditure according to their nature or purpose and subdivided, as far as may be necessary, in accordance with the regulations made pursuant to Article 279.

The expenditure of the European Parliament, the Council, the Commission and the Court of Justice shall be set out in separate parts of the budget, without prejudice to special arrangements for certain common items of expenditure.

**Article 272** (ex Article 203)

1.      The financial year shall run from 1 January to 31 December.

2.      Each institution of the Community shall, before 1 July, draw up estimates of its expenditure. The Commission shall consolidate these estimates in a preliminary draft budget. It shall attach thereto an opinion which may contain different estimates.

The preliminary draft budget shall contain an estimate of revenue and an estimate of expenditure.

3.      The Commission shall place the preliminary draft budget before the Council not later than 1 September of the year preceding that in which the budget is to be implemented.

The Council shall consult the Commission and, where appropriate, the other institutions concerned whenever it intends to depart from the preliminary draft budget.

The Council, acting by a qualified majority, shall establish the draft budget and forward it to the European Parliament.

4.      The draft budget shall be placed before the European Parliament not later than 5 October of the year preceding that in which the budget is to be implemented.

The European Parliament shall have the right to amend the draft budget, acting by a majority of its Members, and to propose to the Council, acting by an absolute majority of the votes cast, modifications to the draft budget relating to expenditure necessarily resulting from this Treaty or from acts adopted in accordance therewith.

If, within 45 days of the draft budget being placed before it, the European Parliament has given its approval, the budget shall stand as finally adopted. If within this period the European Parliament has not amended the draft budget nor proposed any modifications thereto, the budget shall be deemed to be finally adopted.

If within this period the European Parliament has adopted amendments or proposed modifications, the draft budget together with the amendments or proposed modifications shall be forwarded to the Council.

5.    After discussing the draft budget with the Commission and, where appropriate, with the other institutions concerned, the Council shall act under the following conditions:

  (a)  the Council may, acting by a qualified majority, modify any of the amendments adopted by the European Parliament;

  (b)  with regard to the proposed modifications:

  —  where a modification proposed by the European Parliament does not have the effect of increasing the total amount of the expenditure of an institution, owing in particular to the fact that the increase in expenditure which it would involve would be expressly compensated by one or more proposed modifications correspondingly reducing expenditure, the Council may, acting by a qualified majority, reject the proposed modification. In the absence of a decision to reject it, the proposed modification shall stand as accepted;

  —  where a modification proposed by the European Parliament has the effect of increasing the total amount of the expenditure of an institution, the Council may, acting by a qualified majority, accept this proposed modification. In the absence of a decision to accept it, the proposed modification shall stand as rejected;

  —  where, in pursuance of one of the two preceding subparagraphs, the Council has rejected a proposed modification, it may, acting by a qualified majority, either retain the amount shown in the draft budget or fix another amount.

The draft budget shall be modified on the basis of the proposed modifications accepted by the Council.

If, within 15 days of the draft being placed before it, the Council has not modified any of the amendments adopted by the European Parliament and if the modifications proposed by the latter have been accepted, the budget shall be deemed to be finally adopted. The Council shall inform the European Parliament that it has not modified any of the amendments and that the proposed modifications have been accepted.

If within this period the Council has modified one or more of the amendments adopted by the European Parliament or if the modifications proposed by the latter have been rejected or modified, the modified draft budget shall again be forwarded to the European Parliament. The Council shall inform the European Parliament of the results of its deliberations.

6.    Within 15 days of the draft budget being placed before it, the European Parliament, which shall have been notified of the action taken on its proposed modifications, may, acting by a majority of its Members and three-fifths of the votes cast, amend or reject the modifications to its amendments made by the Council and shall adopt the budget accordingly. If within this period the European Parliament has not acted, the budget shall be deemed to be finally adopted.

7.    When the procedure provided for in this Article has been completed, the President of the European Parliament shall declare that the budget has been finally adopted.

8.    However, the European Parliament, acting by a majority of its Members and two-thirds of the votes cast, may, if there are important reasons, reject the draft budget and ask for a new draft to be submitted to it.

9.     A maximum rate of increase in relation to the expenditure of the same type to be incurred during the current year shall be fixed annually for the total expenditure other than that necessarily resulting from this Treaty or from acts adopted in accordance therewith.

The Commission shall, after consulting the Economic Policy Committee, declare what this maximum rate is as it results from:
—  the trend, in terms of volume, of the gross national product within the Community;
—  the average variation in the budgets of the Member States;
and
—  the trend of the cost of living during the preceding financial year.

The maximum rate shall be communicated, before 1 May, to all the institutions of the Community.  The latter shall be required to conform to this during the budgetary procedure, subject to the provisions of the fourth and fifth subparagraphs of this paragraph.

If, in respect of expenditure other than that necessarily resulting from this Treaty or from acts adopted in accordance therewith, the actual rate of increase in the draft budget established by the Council is over half the maximum rate, the European Parliament may, exercising its right of amendment, further increase the total amount of that expenditure to a limit not exceeding half the maximum rate.

Where the European Parliament, the Council or the Commission consider that the activities of the Communities require that the rate determined according to the procedure laid down in this paragraph should be exceeded, another rate may be fixed by agreement between the Council, acting by a qualified majority, and the European Parliament, acting by a majority of its Members and three-fifths of the votes cast.

10.     Each institution shall exercise the powers conferred upon it by this Article, with due regard for the provisions of the Treaty and for acts adopted in accordance therewith, in particular those relating to the Communities' own resources and to the balance between revenue and expenditure.

## Article 273 (ex Article 204)

If, at the beginning of a financial year, the budget has not yet been voted, a sum equivalent to not more than one-twelfth of the budget appropriations for the preceding financial year may be spent each month in respect of any chapter or other subdivision of the budget in accordance with the provisions of the Regulations made pursuant to Article 279; this arrangement shall not, however, have the effect of placing at the disposal of the Commission appropriations in excess of one-twelfth of those provided for in the draft budget in course of preparation.

The Council may, acting by a qualified majority, provided that the other conditions laid down in the first subparagraph are observed, authorise expenditure in excess of one-twelfth.

If the decision relates to expenditure which does not necessarily result from this Treaty or from acts adopted in accordance therewith, the Council shall forward it immediately to the European Parliament; within 30 days the European Parliament, acting by a majority of its Members and three-fifths of the votes cast, may adopt a different decision on the expenditure in excess of the one-twelfth referred to in the first subparagraph.

This part of the decision of the Council shall be suspended until the European Parliament has taken its decision. If within the said period the European Parliament has not taken a decision which differs from the decision of the Council, the latter shall be deemed to be finally adopted.

The decisions referred to in the second and third subparagraphs shall lay down the necessary measures relating to resources to ensure application of this Article.

### Article 274 (ex Article 205)

The Commission shall implement the budget, in accordance with the provisions of the regulations made pursuant to Article 279, on its own responsibility and within the limits of the appropriations, having regard to the principles of sound financial management. Member States shall co-operate with the Commission to ensure that the appropriations are used in accordance with the principles of sound financial management.

The regulations shall lay down detailed rules for each institution concerning its part in effecting its own expenditure.

Within the budget, the Commission may, subject to the limits and conditions laid down in the regulations made pursuant to Article 279, transfer appropriations from one chapter to another or from one subdivision to another.

### Article 275 (ex Article 205a)

The Commission shall submit annually to the Council and to the European Parliament the accounts of the preceding financial year relating to the implementation of the budget. The Commission shall also forward to them a financial statement of the assets and liabilities of the Community.

### Article 276 (ex Article 206)

1.     The European Parliament, acting on a recommendation from the Council which shall act by a qualified majority, shall give a discharge to the Commission in respect of the implementation of the budget. To this end, the Council and the European Parliament in turn shall examine the accounts and the financial statement referred to in Article 275, the annual report by the Court of Auditors together with the replies of the institutions under audit to the observations of the Court of Auditors, the statement of assurance referred to in Article 248(1), second subparagraph and any relevant special reports by the Court of Auditors.

2.     Before giving a discharge to the Commission, or for any other purpose in connection with the exercise of its powers over the implementation of the budget, the European Parliament may ask to hear the Commission give evidence with regard to the execution of expenditure or the operation of financial control systems. The Commission shall submit any necessary information to the European Parliament at the latter's request.

3.     The Commission shall take all appropriate steps to act on the observations in the decisions giving discharge and on other observations by the European Parliament relating to the execution of expenditure, as well as on comments accompanying the recommendations on discharge adopted by the Council.

At the request of the European Parliament or the Council, the Commission shall report on the measures taken in the light of these observations and comments and in particular on the instructions given to the departments which are responsible for the implementation of the budget. These reports shall also be forwarded to the Court of Auditors.

## Article 277 (ex Article 207)

The budget shall be drawn up in the unit of account determined in accordance with the provisions of the regulations made pursuant to Article 279.

## Article 278 (ex Article 208)

The Commission may, provided it notifies the competent authorities of the Member States concerned, transfer into the currency of one of the Member States its holdings in the currency of another Member State, to the extent necessary to enable them to be used for purposes which come within the scope of this Treaty. The Commission shall as far as possible avoid making such transfers if it possesses cash or liquid assets in the currencies which it needs.

The Commission shall deal with each Member State through the authority designated by the State concerned. In carrying out financial operations the Commission shall employ the services of the bank of issue of the Member State concerned or of any other financial institution approved by that State.

## Article 279 (ex Article 209)

The Council, acting unanimously on a proposal from the Commission and after consulting the European Parliament and obtaining the opinion of the Court of Auditors, shall:
   (a) make Financial Regulations specifying in particular the procedure to be adopted for establishing and implementing the budget and for presenting and auditing accounts;
   (b) determine the methods and procedure whereby the budget revenue provided under the arrangements relating to the Community's own resources shall be made available to the Commission, and determine the measures to be applied, if need be, to meet cash requirements;
   (c) lay down rules concerning the responsibility of financial controllers, authorising officers and accounting officers, and concerning appropriate arrangements for inspection.

## Article 280 (ex Article 209a)

1.    The Community and the Member States shall counter fraud and any other illegal activities affecting the financial interests of the Community through measures to be taken in accordance with this Article, which shall act as a deterrent and be such as to afford effective protection in the Member States.

2.    Member States shall take the same measures to counter fraud affecting the financial interests of the Community as they take to counter fraud affecting their own financial interests.

3.    Without prejudice to other provisions of this Treaty, the Member States shall co-ordinate their action aimed at protecting the financial interests of the Community against fraud. To this end they shall organise, together with the Commission, close and regular co-operation between the competent authorities.

4.    The Council, acting in accordance with the procedure referred to in Article 251, after consulting the Court of Auditors, shall adopt the necessary measures in the fields of

the prevention of and fight against fraud affecting the financial interests of the Community with a view to affording effective and equivalent protection in the Member States. These measures shall not concern the application of national criminal law or the national administration of justice.

5.     The Commission, in co-operation with Member States, shall each year submit to the European Parliament and to the Council a report on the measures taken for the implementation of this Article.

## PART SIX
## GENERAL AND FINAL PROVISIONS

**Article 281** (ex Article 210)

The Community shall have legal personality.

**Article 282** (ex Article 211)

In each of the Member States, the Community shall enjoy the most extensive legal capacity accorded to legal persons under their laws; it may, in particular, acquire or dispose of movable and immovable property and may be a party to legal proceedings. To this end, the Community shall be represented by the Commission.

**Article 283** (ex Article 212)

The Council shall, acting by a qualified majority on a proposal from the Commission and after consulting the other institutions concerned, lay down the Staff Regulations of officials of the European Communities and the Conditions of Employment of other servants of those Communities.

**Article 284** (ex Article 213)

The Commission may, within the limits and under conditions laid down by the Council in accordance with the provisions of this Treaty, collect any information and carry out any checks required for the performance of the tasks entrusted to it.

**Article 285** (ex Article 213a)

1.     Without prejudice to Article 5 of the Protocol on the Statute of the European System of Central Banks and of the European Central Bank, the Council, acting in accordance with the procedure referred to in Article 251, shall adopt measures for the production of statistics where necessary for the performance of the activities of the Community.

2.     The production of Community statistics shall conform to impartiality, reliability, objectivity, scientific independence, cost-effectiveness and statistical confidentiality; it shall not entail excessive burdens on economic operators.

**Article 286** (ex Article 213b)

1.     From 1 January 1999, Community acts on the protection of individuals with regard to the processing of personal data and the free movement of such data shall apply to the institutions and bodies set up by, or on the basis of, this Treaty.

2.    Before the date referred to in paragraph 1, the Council, acting in accordance with the procedure referred to in Article 251, shall establish an independent supervisory body responsible for monitoring the application of such Community acts to Community institutions and bodies and shall adopt any other relevant provisions as appropriate.

## Article 287 (ex Article 214)

The members of the institutions of the Community, the members of committees, and the officials and other servants of the Community shall be required, even after their duties have ceased, not to disclose information of the kind covered by the obligation of professional secrecy, in particular information about undertakings, their business relations or their cost components.

## Article 288 (ex Article 215)

The contractual liability of the Community shall be governed by the law applicable to the contract in question.

In the case of non-contractual liability, the Community shall, in accordance with the general principles common to the laws of the Member States, make good any damage caused by its institutions or by its servants in the performance of their duties.

The preceding paragraph shall apply under the same conditions to damage caused by the ECB or by its servants in the performance of their duties.

The personal liability of its servants towards the Community shall be governed by the provisions laid down in their Staff Regulations or in the Conditions of Employment applicable to them.

## Article 289 (ex Article 216)

The seat of the institutions of the Community shall be determined by common accord of the Governments of the Member States.

## Article 290 (ex Article 217)

The rules governing the languages of the institutions of the Community shall, without prejudice to the provisions contained in the Rules of Procedure of the Court of Justice, be determined by the Council, acting unanimously.

## Article 291 (ex Article 218)

The Community shall enjoy in the territories of the Member States such privileges and immunities as are necessary for the performance of its tasks, under the conditions laid down in the Protocol of 8 April 1965 on the privileges and immunities of the European Communities. The same shall apply to the European Central Bank, the European Monetary Institute, and the European Investment Bank.

## Article 292 (ex Article 219)

Member States undertake not to submit a dispute concerning the interpretation or application of this Treaty to any method of settlement other than those provided for therein.

**Article 293** (ex Article 220)

Member States shall, so far as is necessary, enter into negotiations with each other with a view to securing for the benefit of their nationals:
— the protection of persons and the enjoyment and protection of rights under the same conditions as those accorded by each State to its own nationals;
— the abolition of double taxation within the Community;
— the mutual recognition of companies or firms within the meaning of the second paragraph of Article 48, the retention of legal personality in the event of transfer of their seat from one country to another, and the possibility of mergers between companies or firms governed by the laws of different countries;
— the simplification of formalities governing the reciprocal recognition and enforcement of judgments of courts or tribunals and of arbitration awards.

**Article 294** (ex Article 221)

Member States shall accord nationals of the other Member States the same treatment as their own nationals as regards participation in the capital of companies or firms within the meaning of Article 48, without prejudice to the application of the other provisions of this Treaty.

**Article 295** (ex Article 222)

This Treaty shall in no way prejudice the rules in Member States governing the system of property ownership.

**Article 296** (ex Article 223)

1.    The provisions of this Treaty shall not preclude the application of the following rules:
(a)  no Member State shall be obliged to supply information the disclosure of which it considers contrary to the essential interests of its security;
(b)  any Member State may take such measures as it considers necessary for the protection of the essential interests of its security which are connected with the production of or trade in arms, munitions and war material; such measures shall not adversely affect the conditions of competition in the common market regarding products which are not intended for specifically military purposes.

2.    The Council may, acting unanimously on a proposal from the Commission, make changes to the list, which it drew up on 15 April 1958, of the products to which the provisions of paragraph 1(b) apply.

**Article 297** (ex Article 224)

Member States shall consult each other with a view to taking together the steps needed to prevent the functioning of the common market being affected by measures which a Member State may be called upon to take in the event of serious internal disturbances affecting the maintenance of law and order, in the event of war, serious international tension constituting a threat of war, or in order to carry out obligations it has accepted for the purpose of maintaining peace and international security.

**Article 298** (ex Article 225)

If measures taken in the circumstances referred to in Articles 296 and 297 have the effect of distorting the conditions of competition in the common market, the Commission shall, together with the State concerned, examine how these measures can be adjusted to the rules laid down in the Treaty.

By way of derogation from the procedure laid down in Articles 226 and 227, the Commission or any Member State may bring the matter directly before the Court of Justice if it considers that another Member State is making improper use of the powers provided for in Articles 296 and 297. The Court of Justice shall give its ruling in camera.

**Article 299** (ex Article 227)

1.     This Treaty shall apply to the Kingdom of Belgium, the Kingdom of Denmark, the Federal Republic of Germany, the Hellenic Republic, the Kingdom of Spain, the French Republic, Ireland, the Italian Republic, the Grand Duchy of Luxembourg, the Kingdom of the Netherlands, the Republic of Austria, the Portuguese Republic, the Republic of Finland, the Kingdom of Sweden and the United Kingdom of Great Britain and Northern Ireland.

2.     The provisions of this Treaty shall apply to the French overseas departments, the Azores, Madeira and the Canary Islands.

However, taking account of the structural social and economic situation of the French overseas departments, the Azores, Madeira and the Canary Islands, which is compounded by their remoteness, insularity, small size, difficult topography and climate, economic dependence on a few products, the permanence and combination of which severely restrain their development, the Council, acting by a qualified majority on a proposal from the Commission and after consulting the European Parliament, shall adopt specific measures aimed, in particular, at laying down the conditions of application of the present Treaty to those regions, including common policies.

The Council shall, when adopting the relevant measures referred to in the second subparagraph, take into account areas such as customs and trade policies, fiscal policy, free zones, agriculture and fisheries policies, conditions for supply of raw materials and essential consumer goods, State aids and conditions of access to structural funds and to horizontal Community programmes.

The Council shall adopt the measures referred to in the second subparagraph taking into account the special characteristics and constraints of the outermost regions without undermining the integrity and the coherence of the Community legal order, including the internal market and common policies.

3.     The special arrangements for association set out in Part Four of this Treaty shall apply to the overseas countries and territories listed in Annex II to this Treaty.

This Treaty shall not apply to those overseas countries and territories having special relations with the United Kingdom of Great Britain and Northern Ireland which are not included in the aforementioned list.

4.     The provisions of this Treaty shall apply to the European territories for whose external relations a Member State is responsible.

5.      The provisions of this Treaty shall apply to the Åland Islands in accordance with the provisions set out in Protocol No 2 to the Act concerning the conditions of accession of the Republic of Austria, the Republic of Finland and the Kingdom of Sweden.

6.      Notwithstanding the preceding paragraphs:
   (a)  this Treaty shall not apply to the Faeroe Islands;
   (b)  this Treaty shall not apply to the Sovereign Base Areas of the United Kingdom of Great Britain and Northern Ireland in Cyprus;
   (c)  this Treaty shall apply to the Channel Islands and the Isle of Man only to the extent necessary to ensure the implementation of the arrangements for those islands set out in the Treaty concerning the accession of new Member States to the European Economic Community and to the European Atomic Energy Community signed on 22 January 1972.

**Article 300** (ex Article 228)

1.      Where this Treaty provides for the conclusion of agreements between the Community and one or more States or international organisations, the Commission shall make recommendations to the Council, which shall authorise the Commission to open the necessary negotiations. The Commission shall conduct these negotiations in consultation with special committees appointed by the Council to assist it in this task and within the framework of such directives as the Council may issue to it.

In exercising the powers conferred upon it by this paragraph, the Council shall act by a qualified majority, except in the cases where the first subparagraph of paragraph 2 provides that the Council shall act unanimously.

2.      Subject to the powers vested in the Commission in this field, the signing, which may be accompanied by a decision on provisional application before entry into force, and the conclusion of the agreements shall be decided on by the Council, acting by a qualified majority on a proposal from the Commission. The Council shall act unanimously when the agreement covers a field for which unanimity is required for the adoption of internal rules and for the agreements referred to in Article 310.

By way of derogation from the rules laid down in paragraph 3, the same procedures shall apply for a decision to suspend the application of an agreement, and for the purpose of establishing the positions to be adopted on behalf of the Community in a body set up by an agreement based on Article 310, when that body is called upon to adopt decisions having legal effects, with the exception of decisions supplementing or amending the institutional framework of the agreement.

The European Parliament shall be immediately and fully informed on any decision under this paragraph concerning the provisional application or the suspension of agreements, or the establishment of the Community position in a body set up by an agreement based on Article 310.

3.      The Council shall conclude agreements after consulting the European Parliament, except for the agreements referred to in Article 133(3), including cases where the agreement covers a field for which the procedure referred to in Article 251 or that referred to in Article 252 is required for the adoption of internal rules. The European Parliament shall deliver its opinion within a time-limit which the Council may lay down according to the urgency of the matter. In the absence of an opinion within that time-limit, the Council may act.

By way of derogation from the previous subparagraph, agreements referred to in Article 310, other agreements establishing a specific institutional framework by organising co-operation procedures, agreements having important budgetary implications for the Community and agreements entailing amendment of an act adopted under the procedure referred to in Article 251 shall be concluded after the assent of the European Parliament has been obtained.

The Council and the European Parliament may, in an urgent situation, agree upon a time-limit for the assent.

4.　　When concluding an agreement, the Council may, by way of derogation from paragraph 2, authorise the Commission to approve modifications on behalf of the Community where the agreement provides for them to be adopted by a simplified procedure or by a body set up by the agreement; it may attach specific conditions to such authorisation.

5.　　When the Council envisages concluding an agreement which calls for amendments to this Treaty, the amendments must first be adopted in accordance with the procedure laid down in Article 48 of the Treaty on European Union.

6.　　The Council, the Commission or a Member State may obtain the opinion of the Court of Justice as to whether an agreement envisaged is compatible with the provisions of this Treaty. Where the opinion of the Court of Justice is adverse, the agreement may enter into force only in accordance with Article 48 of the Treaty on European Union.

7.　　Agreements concluded under the conditions set out in this Article shall be binding on the institutions of the Community and on Member States.

### Article 301 (ex Article 228a)

Where it is provided, in a common position or in a joint action adopted according to the provisions of the Treaty on European Union relating to the common foreign and security policy, for an action by the Community to interrupt or to reduce, in part or completely, economic relations with one or more third countries, the Council shall take the necessary urgent measures. The Council shall act by a qualified majority on a proposal from the Commission.

### Article 302 (ex Article 229)

It shall be for the Commission to ensure the maintenance of all appropriate relations with the organs of the United Nations and of its specialised agencies.

The Commission shall also maintain such relations as are appropriate with all international organisations.

### Article 303 (ex Article 230)

The Community shall establish all appropriate forms of co-operation with the Council of Europe.

### Article 304 (ex Article 231)

The Community shall establish close co-operation with the Organisation for Economic Co-operation and Development, the details of which shall be determined by common accord.

**Article 305** (ex Article 232)

1.     The provisions of this Treaty shall not affect the provisions of the Treaty establishing the European Coal and Steel Community, in particular as regards the rights and obligations of Member States, the powers of the institutions of that Community and the rules laid down by that Treaty for the functioning of the common market in coal and steel.

2.     The provisions of this Treaty shall not derogate from those of the Treaty establishing the European Atomic Energy Community.

**Article 306** (ex Article 233)

The provisions of this Treaty shall not preclude the existence or completion of regional unions between Belgium and Luxembourg, or between Belgium, Luxembourg and the Netherlands, to the extent that the objectives of these regional unions are not attained by application of this Treaty.

**Article 307** (ex Article 234)

The rights and obligations arising from agreements concluded before 1 January 1958 or, for acceding States, before the date of their accession, between one or more Member States on the one hand, and one or more third countries on the other, shall not be affected by the provisions of this Treaty.

To the extent that such agreements are not compatible with this Treaty, the Member State or States concerned shall take all appropriate steps to eliminate the incompatibilities established. Member States shall, where necessary, assist each other to this end and shall, where appropriate, adopt a common attitude.

In applying the agreements referred to in the first paragraph, Member States shall take into account the fact that the advantages accorded under this Treaty by each Member State form an integral part of the establishment of the Community and are thereby inseparably linked with the creation of common institutions, the conferring of powers upon them and the granting of the same advantages by all the other Member States.

**Article 308** (ex Article 235)

If action by the Community should prove necessary to attain, in the course of the operation of the common market, one of the objectives of the Community and this Treaty has not provided the necessary powers, the Council shall, acting unanimously on a proposal from the Commission and after consulting the European Parliament, take the appropriate measures.

**Article 309** (ex Article 236)

1.     Where a decision has been taken to suspend the voting rights of the representative of the government of a Member State in accordance with Article 7(2) of the Treaty on European Union, these voting rights shall also be suspended with regard to this Treaty.

2.     Moreover, where the existence of a serious and persistent breach by a Member State of principles mentioned in Article 6(1) of the Treaty on European Union has been determined in accordance with Article 7(1) of that Treaty, the

Council, acting by a qualified majority, may decide to suspend certain of the rights deriving from the application of this Treaty to the Member State in question. In doing so, the Council shall take into account the possible consequences of such a suspension on the rights and obligations of natural and legal persons.

The obligations of the Member State in question under this Treaty shall in any case continue to be binding on that State.

3.      The Council, acting by a qualified majority, may decide subsequently to vary or revoke measures taken in accordance with paragraph 2 in response to changes in the situation which led to their being imposed.

4.      When taking decisions referred to in paragraphs 2 and 3, the Council shall act without taking into account the votes of the representative of the government of the Member State in question. By way of derogation from Article 205(2) a qualified majority shall be defined as the same proportion of the weighted votes of the members of the Council concerned as laid down in Article 205(2).

This paragraph shall also apply in the event of voting rights being suspended in accordance with paragraph 1. In such cases, a decision requiring unanimity shall be taken without the vote of the representative of the government of the Member State in question.

## Article 310 (ex Article 238)

The Community may conclude with one or more States or international organisations agreements establishing an association involving reciprocal rights and obligations, common action and special procedure.

## Article 311 (ex Article 239)

The protocols annexed to this Treaty by common accord of the Member States shall form an integral part thereof.

## Article 312 (ex Article 240)

This Treaty is concluded for an unlimited period.

# FINAL PROVISIONS

## Article 313 (ex Article 247)

This Treaty shall be ratified by the High Contracting Parties in accordance with their respective constitutional requirements. The instruments of ratification shall be deposited with the Government of the Italian Republic.

This Treaty shall enter into force on the first day of the month following the deposit of the instrument of ratification by the last signatory State to take this step. If, however, such deposit is made less than 15 days before the beginning of the following month, this Treaty shall not enter into force until the first day of the second month after the date of such deposit.

## Article 314 (ex Article 248)

This Treaty, drawn up in a single original in the Dutch, French, German, and Italian languages, all four texts being equally authentic, shall be deposited in the archives of the Government of the Italian Republic, which shall transmit a certified copy to each of the Governments of the other signatory States.

Pursuant to the Accession Treaties, the Danish, English, Finnish, Greek, Irish, Portuguese, Spanish and Swedish versions of this Treaty shall also be authentic.

# CONSOLIDATED VERSION OF THE TREATY ON EUROPEAN UNION

## TITLE I
## COMMON PROVISIONS

NOTES

Consolidated version of the Treaty on European Union as amended by the Treaty of Amsterdam. Date of publication in the OJ: OJ C340, 10.11.97, p1.

### Article 1 (ex Article A)

By this Treaty, the High Contracting Parties establish among themselves a European Union, hereinafter called 'the Union'.

This Treaty marks a new stage in the process of creating an ever closer union among the peoples of Europe, in which decisions are taken as openly as possible and as closely as possible to the citizen.

The Union shall be founded on the European Communities, supplemented by the policies and forms of co-operation established by this Treaty. Its task shall be to organise, in a manner demonstrating consistency and solidarity, relations between the Member States and between their peoples.

### Article 2 (ex Article B)

The Union shall set itself the following objectives:

— to promote economic and social progress and a high level of employment and to achieve balanced and sustainable development, in particular through the creation of an area without internal frontiers, through the strengthening of economic and social cohesion and through the establishment of economic and monetary union, ultimately including a single currency in accordance with the provisions of this Treaty;

— to assert its identity on the international scene, in particular through the implementation of a common foreign and security policy including the progressive framing of a common defence policy, which might lead to a common defence, in accordance with the provisions of Article 17;

— to strengthen the protection of the rights and interests of the nationals of its Member States through the introduction of a citizenship of the Union;

— to maintain and develop the Union as an area of freedom, security and justice, in which the free movement of persons is assured in conjunction with appropriate measures with respect to external border controls, asylum, immigration and the prevention and combating of crime;

— to maintain in full the acquis communautaire and build on it with a view to considering to what extent the policies and forms of co-operation introduced by this Treaty may need to be revised with the aim of ensuring the effectiveness of the mechanisms and the institutions of the Community.

The objectives of the Union shall be achieved as provided in this Treaty and in accordance with the conditions and the timetable set out therein while respecting the principle of subsidiarity as defined in Article 5 of the Treaty establishing the European Community.

## Article 3 (ex Article C)

The Union shall be served by a single institutional framework which shall ensure the consistency and the continuity of the activities carried out in order to attain its objectives while respecting and building upon the acquis communautaire.

The Union shall in particular ensure the consistency of its external activities as a whole in the context of its external relations, security, economic and development policies. The Council and the Commission shall be responsible for ensuring such consistency and shall co-operate to this end. They shall ensure the implementation of these policies, each in accordance with its respective powers.

## Article 4 (ex Article D)

The European Council shall provide the Union with the necessary impetus for its development and shall define the general political guidelines thereof.

The European Council shall bring together the Heads of State or Government of the Member States and the President of the Commission. They shall be assisted by the Ministers for Foreign Affairs of the Member States and by a Member of the Commission. The European Council shall meet at least twice a year, under the chairmanship of the Head of State or Government of the Member State which holds the Presidency of the Council.

The European Council shall submit to the European Parliament a report after each of its meetings and a yearly written report on the progress achieved by the Union.

## Article 5 (ex Article E)

The European Parliament, the Council, the Commission, the Court of Justice and the Court of Auditors shall exercise their powers under the conditions and for the purposes provided for, on the one hand, by the provisions of the Treaties establishing the European Communities and of the subsequent Treaties and Acts modifying and supplementing them and, on the other hand, by the other provisions of this Treaty.

## Article 6 (ex Article F)

1.      The Union is founded on the principles of liberty, democracy, respect for human rights and fundamental freedoms, and the rule of law, principles which are common to the Member States.

2.      The Union shall respect fundamental rights, as guaranteed by the European Convention for the Protection of Human Rights and Fundamental Freedoms signed in Rome on 4 November 1950 and as they result from the constitutional traditions common to the Member States, as general principles of Community law.

3.      The Union shall respect the national identities of its Member States.

4.      The Union shall provide itself with the means necessary to attain its objectives and carry through its policies.

## Article 7 (ex Article F.1)

1.      The Council, meeting in the composition of the Heads of State or Government and acting by unanimity on a proposal by one third of the Member

States or by the Commission and after obtaining the assent of the European Parliament, may determine the existence of a serious and persistent breach by a Member State of principles mentioned in Article 6(1), after inviting the government of the Member State in question to submit its observations.

2.     Where such a determination has been made, the Council, acting by a qualified majority, may decide to suspend certain of the rights deriving from the application of this Treaty to the Member State in question, including the voting rights of the representative of the government of that Member State in the Council. In doing so, the Council shall take into account the possible consequences of such a suspension on the rights and obligations of natural and legal persons.

The obligations of the Member State in question under this Treaty shall in any case continue to be binding on that State.

3.     The Council, acting by a qualified majority, may decide subsequently to vary or revoke measures taken under paragraph 2 in response to changes in the situation which led to their being imposed.

4.     For the purposes of this Article, the Council shall act without taking into account the vote of the representative of the government of the Member State in question. Abstentions by members present in person or represented shall not prevent the adoption of decisions referred to in paragraph 1. A qualified majority shall be defined as the same proportion of the weighted votes of the members of the Council concerned as laid down in Article 205(2) of the Treaty establishing the European Community.

This paragraph shall also apply in the event of voting rights being suspended pursuant to paragraph 2.

5.     For the purposes of this Article, the European Parliament shall act by a two-thirds majority of the votes cast, representing a majority of its members.

# TITLE V
# PROVISIONS ON A COMMON FOREIGN AND SECURITY POLICY

**Article 11** (ex Article J.1)

1.     The Union shall define and implement a common foreign and security policy covering all areas of foreign and security policy, the objectives of which shall be:
— to safeguard the common values, fundamental interests, independence and integrity of the Union in conformity with the principles of the United Nations Charter;
— to strengthen the security of the Union in all ways;
— to preserve peace and strengthen international security, in accordance with the principles of the United Nations Charter, as well as the principles of the Helsinki Final Act and the objectives of the Paris Charter, including those on external borders;
— to promote international co-operation;
— to develop and consolidate democracy and the rule of law, and respect for human rights and fundamental freedoms.

2.     The Member States shall support the Union's external and security policy actively and unreservedly in a spirit of loyalty and mutual solidarity.

The Member States shall work together to enhance and develop their mutual political solidarity. They shall refrain from any action which is contrary to the interests of the Union or likely to impair its effectiveness as a cohesive force in international relations.

The Council shall ensure that these principles are complied with.

## Article 12 (ex Article J.2)

The Union shall pursue the objectives set out in Article 11 by:
— defining the principles of and general guidelines for the common foreign and security policy;
— deciding on common strategies;
— adopting joint actions;
— adopting common positions;
— strengthening systematic co-operation between Member States in the conduct of policy.

## Article 13 (ex Article J.3)

1.     The European Council shall define the principles of and general guidelines for the common foreign and security policy, including for matters with defence implications.

2.     The European Council shall decide on common strategies to be implemented by the Union in areas where the Member States have important interests in common.

Common strategies shall set out their objectives, duration and the means to be made available by the Union and the Member States.

3.     The Council shall take the decisions necessary for defining and implementing the common foreign and security policy on the basis of the general guidelines defined by the European Council.

The Council shall recommend common strategies to the European Council and shall implement them, in particular by adopting joint actions and common positions.

The Council shall ensure the unity, consistency and effectiveness of action by the Union.

## Article 14 (ex Article J.4)

1.     The Council shall adopt joint actions. Joint actions shall address specific situations where operational action by the Union is deemed to be required. They shall lay down their objectives, scope, the means to be made available to the Union, if necessary their duration, and the conditions for their implementation.

2.     If there is a change in circumstances having a substantial effect on a question subject to joint action, the Council shall review the principles and objectives of that action and take the necessary decisions. As long as the Council has not acted, the joint action shall stand.

3.     Joint actions shall commit the Member States in the positions they adopt and in the conduct of their activity.

4.     The Council may request the Commission to submit to it any appropriate proposals relating  to the common foreign and security policy to ensure the implementation of a joint action.

5.      Whenever there is any plan to adopt a national position or take national action pursuant to a joint action, information shall be provided in time to allow, if necessary, for prior consultations within the Council. The obligation to provide prior information shall not apply to measures which are merely a national transposition of Council decisions.

6.      In cases of imperative need arising from changes in the situation and failing a Council decision, Member States may take the necessary measures as a matter of urgency having regard to the general objectives of the joint action. The Member State concerned shall inform the Council immediately of any such measures.

7.      Should there be any major difficulties in implementing a joint action, a Member State shall refer them to the Council which shall discuss them and seek appropriate solutions. Such solutions shall not run counter to the objectives of the joint action or impair its effectiveness.

## Article 15 (ex Article J.5)

The Council shall adopt common positions. Common positions shall define the approach of the Union to a particular matter of a geographical or thematic nature. Member States shall ensure that their national policies conform to the common positions.

## Article 16 (ex Article J.6)

Member States shall inform and consult one another within the Council on any matter of foreign and security policy of general interest in order to ensure that the Union's influence is exerted as effectively as possible by means of concerted and convergent action.

## Article 17 (ex Article J.7)

1.      The common foreign and security policy shall include all questions relating to the security of the Union, including the progressive framing of a common defence policy, in accordance with the second subparagraph, which might lead to a common defence, should the European Council so decide. It shall in that case recommend to the Member States the adoption of such a decision in accordance with their respective constitutional requirements.

The Western European Union (WEU) is an integral part of the development of the Union providing the Union with access to an operational capability notably in the context of paragraph 2. It supports the Union in framing the defence aspects of the common foreign and security policy as set out in this Article. The Union shall accordingly foster closer institutional relations with the WEU with a view to the possibility of the integration of the WEU into the Union, should the European Council so decide. It shall in that case recommend to the Member States the adoption of such a decision in accordance with their respective constitutional requirements.

The policy of the Union in accordance with this Article shall not prejudice the specific character of the security and defence policy of certain Member States and shall respect the obligations of certain Member States, which see their common defence realised in the North Atlantic Treaty Organisation (NATO), under the North Atlantic Treaty and be compatible with the common security and defence policy established within that framework.

The progressive framing of a common defence policy will be supported, as Member States consider appropriate, by co-operation between them in the field of armaments.

2.    Questions referred to in this Article shall include humanitarian and rescue tasks, peacekeeping tasks and tasks of combat forces in crisis management, including peacemaking.

3.    The Union will avail itself of the WEU to elaborate and implement decisions and actions of the Union which have defence implications.

The competence of the European Council to establish guidelines in accordance with Article 13 shall also obtain in respect of the WEU for those matters for which the Union avails itself of the WEU.

When the Union avails itself of the WEU to elaborate and implement decisions of the Union on the tasks referred to in paragraph 2 all Member States of the Union shall be entitled to participate fully in the tasks in question. The Council, in agreement with the institutions of the WEU, shall adopt the necessary practical arrangements to allow all Member States contributing to the tasks in question to participate fully and on an equal footing in planning and decision-taking in the WEU.

Decisions having defence implications dealt with under this paragraph shall be taken without prejudice to the policies and obligations referred to in paragraph 1, third subparagraph.

4.    The provisions of this Article shall not prevent the development of closer co-operation between two or more Member States on a bilateral level, in the framework of the WEU and the Atlantic Alliance, provided such co-operation does not run counter to or impede that provided for in this Title.

5.    With a view to furthering the objectives of this Article, the provisions of this Article will be reviewed in accordance with Article 48.

**Article 18** (ex Article J.8)

1.    The Presidency shall represent the Union in matters coming within the common foreign and security policy.

2.    The Presidency shall be responsible for the implementation of decisions taken under this Title; in that capacity it shall in principle express the position of the Union in international organisations and international conferences.

3.    The Presidency shall be assisted by the Secretary-General of the Council who shall exercise the function of High Representative for the common foreign and security policy.

4.    The Commission shall be fully associated in the tasks referred to in paragraphs 1 and 2. The Presidency shall be assisted in those tasks if need be by the next Member State to hold the Presidency.

5.    The Council may, whenever it deems it necessary, appoint a special representative with a mandate in relation to particular policy issues.

**Article 19** (ex Article J.9)

1.    Member States shall co-ordinate their action in international organisations and at international conferences. They shall uphold the common positions in such fora.

In international organisations and at international conferences where not all the Member States participate, those which do take part shall uphold the common positions.

2.     Without prejudice to paragraph 1 and Article 14(3), Member States represented in international organisations or international conferences where not all the Member States participate shall keep the latter informed of any matter of common interest.

Member States which are also members of the United Nations Security Council will concert and keep the other Member States fully informed. Member States which are permanent members of the Security Council will, in the execution of their functions, ensure the defence of the positions and the interests of the Union, without prejudice to their responsibilities under the provisions of the United Nations Charter.

### Article 20 (ex Article J.10)

The diplomatic and consular missions of the Member States and the Commission Delegations in third countries and international conferences, and their representations to international organisations, shall co-operate in ensuring that the common positions and joint actions adopted by the Council are complied with and implemented.

They shall step up co-operation by exchanging information, carrying out joint assessments and contributing to the implementation of the provisions referred to in Article 20 of the Treaty establishing the European Community.

### Article 21 (ex Article J.11)

The Presidency shall consult the European Parliament on the main aspects and the basic choices of the common foreign and security policy and shall ensure that the views of the European Parliament are duly taken into consideration. The European Parliament shall be kept regularly informed by the Presidency and the Commission of the development of the Union's foreign and security policy.

The European Parliament may ask questions of the Council or make recommendations to it. It shall hold an annual debate on progress in implementing the common foreign and security policy.

### Article 22 (ex Article J.12)

1.     Any Member State or the Commission may refer to the Council any question relating to the common foreign and security policy and may submit proposals to the Council.

2.     In cases requiring a rapid decision, the Presidency, of its own motion, or at the request of the Commission or a Member State, shall convene an extraordinary Council meeting within forty-eight hours or, in an emergency, within a shorter period.

### Article 23 (ex Article J.13)

1.     Decisions under this Title shall be taken by the Council acting unanimously. Abstentions by members present in person or represented shall not prevent the adoption of such decisions.

When abstaining in a vote, any member of the Council may qualify its abstention by making a formal declaration under the present subparagraph. In that case, it shall not be obliged to apply the decision, but shall accept that the decision commits the Union. In a spirit of mutual solidarity, the Member State concerned shall refrain from any action likely to conflict with or impede Union action based on that decision and the other Member States shall respect its position. If the members of the Council qualifying their abstention in this way represent more than one third of the votes weighted in accordance with Article 205(2) of the Treaty establishing the European Community, the decision shall not be adopted.

2.     By derogation from the provisions of paragraph 1, the Council shall act by qualified majority:
   — when adopting joint actions, common positions or taking any other decision on the basis of a common strategy;
   — when adopting any decision implementing a joint action or a common position.

If a member of the Council declares that, for important and stated reasons of national policy, it intends to oppose the adoption of a decision to be taken by qualified majority, a vote shall not be taken. The Council may, acting by a qualified majority, request that the matter be referred to the European Council for decision by unanimity.

The votes of the members of the Council shall be weighted in accordance with Article 205(2) of the Treaty establishing the European Community. For their adoption, decisions shall require at least 62 votes in favour, cast by at least 10 members.

This paragraph shall not apply to decisions having military or defence implications.

3.     For procedural questions, the Council shall act by a majority of its members.

### Article 24 (ex Article J.14)

When it is necessary to conclude an agreement with one or more States or international organisations in implementation of this Title, the Council, acting unanimously, may authorise the Presidency, assisted by the Commission as appropriate, to open negotiations to that effect. Such agreements shall be concluded by the Council acting unanimously on a recommendation from the Presidency. No agreement shall be binding on a Member State whose representative in the Council states that it has to comply with the requirements of its own constitutional procedure; the other members of the Council may agree that the agreement shall apply provisionally to them.

The provisions of this Article shall also apply to matters falling under Title VI.

### Article 25 (ex Article J.15)

Without prejudice to Article 207 of the Treaty establishing the European Community, a Political Committee shall monitor the international situation in the areas covered by the common foreign and security policy and contribute to the definition of policies by delivering opinions to the Council at the request of the Council or on its own initiative. It shall also monitor the implementation of agreed policies, without prejudice to the responsibility of the Presidency and the Commission.

### Article 26 (ex Article J.16)

The Secretary-General of the Council, High Representative for the common foreign and security policy, shall assist the Council in matters coming within the scope of the common foreign and security policy, in particular through contributing to the formulation, preparation and implementation of policy decisions, and, when appropriate and acting on behalf of the Council at the request of the Presidency, through conducting political dialogue with third parties.

**Article 27** (ex Article J.17)

The Commission shall be fully associated with the work carried out in the common foreign and security policy field.

**Article 28** (ex Article J.18)

1.     Articles 189, 190, 196 to 199, 203, 204, 206 to 209, 213 to 219, 255 and 290 of the Treaty establishing the European Community shall apply to the provisions relating to the areas referred to in this Title.

2.     Administrative expenditure which the provisions relating to the areas referred to in this Title entail for the institutions shall be charged to the budget of the European Communities.

3.     Operational expenditure to which the implementation of those provisions gives rise shall also be charged to the budget of the European Communities, except for such expenditure arising from operations having military or defence implications and cases where the Council acting unanimously decides otherwise.

In cases where expenditure is not charged to the budget of the European Communities it shall be charged to the Member States in accordance with the gross national product scale, unless the Council acting unanimously decides otherwise. As for expenditure arising from operations having military or defence implications, Member States whose representatives in the Council have made a formal declaration under Article 23(1), second subparagraph, shall not be obliged to contribute to  the financing thereof.

4.     The budgetary procedure laid down in the Treaty establishing the European Community shall apply to the expenditure charged to the budget of the European Communities.

# TITLE VI
## PROVISIONS ON POLICE AND JUDICIAL CO-OPERATION IN CRIMINAL MATTERS

**Article 29** (ex Article K.1)

Without prejudice to the powers of the European Community, the Union's objective shall be to provide citizens with a high level of safety within an area of freedom, security and justice by developing common action among the Member States in the fields of police and judicial co-operation in criminal matters and by preventing and combating racism and xenophobia.

That objective shall be achieved by preventing and combating crime, organised or otherwise, in particular terrorism, trafficking in persons and offences against children, illicit drug trafficking and illicit arms trafficking, corruption and fraud, through:
— closer co-operation between police forces, customs authorities and other competent authorities in the Member States, both directly and through

the European Police Office (Europol), in accordance with the provisions of Articles 30 and 32;
— closer co-operation between judicial and other competent authorities of the Member States in accordance with the provisions of Articles 31(a) to (d) and 32;
— approximation, where necessary, of rules on criminal matters in the Member States, in accordance with the provisions of Article 31(e).

**Article 30** (ex Article K.2)

1.  Common action in the field of police co-operation shall include:
(a) operational co-operation between the competent authorities, including the police, customs and other specialised law enforcement services of the Member States in relation to the prevention, detection and investigation of criminal offences;
(b) the collection, storage, processing, analysis and exchange of relevant information, including information held by law enforcement services on reports on suspicious financial transactions, in particular through Europol, subject to appropriate provisions on the protection of personal data;
(c) co-operation and joint initiatives in training, the exchange of liaison officers, secondments, the use of equipment, and forensic research;
(d) the common evaluation of particular investigative techniques in relation to the detection of serious forms of organised crime.

2.  The Council shall promote co-operation through Europol and shall in particular, within a period of five years after the date of entry into force of the Treaty of Amsterdam:
(a) enable Europol to facilitate and support the preparation, and to encourage the co-ordination and carrying out, of specific investigative actions by the competent authorities of the Member States, including operational actions of joint teams comprising representatives of Europol in a support capacity;
(b) adopt measures allowing Europol to ask the competent authorities of the Member States to conduct and co-ordinate their investigations in specific cases and to develop specific expertise which may be put at the disposal of Member States to assist them in investigating cases of organised crime;
(c) promote liaison arrangements between prosecuting/investigating officials specialising in the fight against organised crime in close co-operation with Europol;
(d) establish a research, documentation and statistical network on cross-border crime.

**Article 31** (ex Article K.3)

Common action on judicial co-operation in criminal matters shall include:
(a) facilitating and accelerating co-operation between competent ministries and judicial or equivalent authorities of the Member States in relation to proceedings and the enforcement of decisions;
(b) facilitating extradition between Member States;
(c) ensuring compatibility in rules applicable in the Member States, as may be necessary to improve such co-operation;
(d) preventing conflicts of jurisdiction between Member States;

(e) progressively adopting measures establishing minimum rules relating to the constituent elements of criminal acts and to penalties in the fields of organised crime, terrorism and illicit drug trafficking.

**Article 32** (ex Article K.4)

The Council shall lay down the conditions and limitations under which the competent authorities referred to in Articles 30 and 31 may operate in the territory of another Member State in liaison and in agreement with the authorities of that State.

**Article 33** (ex Article K.5)

This Title shall not affect the exercise of the responsibilities incumbent upon Member States with regard to the maintenance of law and order and the safeguarding of internal security.

**Article 34** (ex Article K.6)

1.     In the areas referred to in this Title, Member States shall inform and consult one another within the Council with a view to co-ordinating their action. To that end, they shall establish collaboration between the relevant departments of their administrations.

2.     The Council shall take measures and promote co-operation, using the appropriate form and procedures as set out in this Title, contributing to the pursuit of the objectives of the Union. To that end, acting unanimously on the initiative of any Member State or of the Commission, the Council may:
   (a) adopt common positions defining the approach of the Union to a particular matter;
   (b) adopt framework decisions for the purpose of approximation of the laws and regulations of the Member States. Framework decisions shall be binding upon the Member States as to the result to be achieved but shall leave to the national authorities the choice of form and methods. They shall not entail direct effect;
   (c) adopt decisions for any other purpose consistent with the objectives of this Title, excluding any approximation of the laws and regulations of the Member States. These decisions shall be binding and shall not entail direct effect; the Council, acting by a qualified majority, shall adopt measures necessary to implement those decisions at the level of the Union;
   (d) establish conventions which it shall recommend to the Member States for adoption in accordance with their respective constitutional requirements. Member States shall begin the procedures applicable within a time limit to be set by the Council.

Unless they provide otherwise, conventions shall, once adopted by at least half of the Member States, enter into force for those Member States. Measures implementing conventions shall be adopted within the Council by a majority of two-thirds of the Contracting Parties.

3.     Where the Council is required to act by a qualified majority, the votes of its members shall be weighted as laid down in Article 205(2) of the Treaty establishing the European Community, and for their adoption acts of the Council shall require at least 62 votes in favour, cast by at least 10 members.

4.     For procedural questions, the Council shall act by a majority of its members.

**Article 35** (ex Article K.7)

1.    The Court of Justice of the European Communities shall have jurisdiction, subject to the conditions laid down in this Article, to give preliminary rulings on the validity and interpretation of framework decisions and decisions, on the interpretation of conventions established under this Title and on the validity and interpretation of the measures implementing them.

2.    By a declaration made at the time of signature of the Treaty of Amsterdam or at any time thereafter, any Member State shall be able to accept the jurisdiction of the Court of Justice to give preliminary rulings as specified in paragraph 1.

3.    A Member State making a declaration pursuant to paragraph 2 shall specify that either:

  (a)  any court or tribunal of that State against whose decisions there is no judicial remedy under national law may request the Court of Justice to give a preliminary ruling on a question raised in a case pending before it and concerning the validity or interpretation of an act referred to in paragraph 1 if that court or tribunal considers that a decision on the question is necessary to enable it to give judgment, or

  (b)  any court or tribunal of that State may request the Court of Justice to give a preliminary ruling on a question raised in a case pending before it and concerning the validity or interpretation of an act referred to in paragraph 1 if that court or tribunal considers that a decision on the question is necessary to enable it to give judgment.

4.    Any Member State, whether or not it has made a declaration pursuant to paragraph 2, shall be entitled to submit statements of case or written observations to the Court in cases which arise under paragraph 1.

5.    The Court of Justice shall have no jurisdiction to review the validity or proportionality of operations carried out by the police or other law enforcement services of a Member State or the exercise of the responsibilities incumbent upon Member States with regard to the maintenance of law and order and the safeguarding of internal security.

6.    The Court of Justice shall have jurisdiction to review the legality of framework decisions and decisions in actions brought by a Member State or the Commission on grounds of lack of competence, infringement of an essential procedural requirement, infringement of this Treaty or of any rule of law relating to its application, or misuse of powers. The proceedings provided for in this paragraph shall be instituted within two months of the publication of the measure.

7.    The Court of Justice shall have jurisdiction to rule on any dispute between Member States regarding the interpretation or the application of acts adopted under Article 34(2) whenever such dispute cannot be settled by the Council within six months of its being referred to the Council by one of its members. The Court shall also have jurisdiction to rule on any dispute between Member States and the Commission regarding the interpretation or the application of conventions established under Article 34(2)(d).

**Article 36** (ex Article K.8)

1.    A Co-ordinating Committee shall be set up consisting of senior officials. In addition to its co-ordinating role, it shall be the task of the Committee to:

— give opinions for the attention of the Council, either at the Council's request or on its own initiative;
— contribute, without prejudice to Article 207 of the Treaty establishing the European Community, to the preparation of the Council's discussions in the areas referred to in Article 29.

2.    The Commission shall be fully associated with the work in the areas referred to in this Title.

**Article 37** (ex Article K.9)

Within international organisations and at international conferences in which they take part, Member States shall defend the common positions adopted under the provisions of this Title.

Articles 18 and 19 shall apply as appropriate to matters falling under this Title.

**Article 38** (ex Article K.10)

Agreements referred to in Article 24 may cover matters falling under this Title.

**Article 39** (ex Article K.11)

1.    The Council shall consult the European Parliament before adopting any measure referred to in Article 34(2)(b), (c) and (d). The European Parliament shall deliver its opinion within a time-limit which the Council may lay down, which shall not be less than three months. In the absence of an opinion within that time-limit, the Council may act.

2.    The Presidency and the Commission shall regularly inform the European Parliament of discussions in the areas covered by this Title.

3.    The European Parliament may ask questions of the Council or make recommendations to it. Each year, it shall hold a debate on the progress made in the areas referred to in this Title.

**Article 40** (ex Article K.12)

1.    Member States which intend to establish closer co-operation between themselves may be authorised, subject to Articles 43 and 44, to make use of the institutions, procedures and mechanisms laid down by the Treaties provided that the co-operation proposed:
(a) respects the powers of the European Community, and the objectives laid down by this Title;
(b) has the aim of enabling the Union to develop more rapidly into an area of freedom, security and justice.

2.    The authorisation referred to in paragraph 1 shall be granted by the Council, acting by a qualified majority at the request of the Member States concerned and after inviting the Commission to present its opinion; the request shall also be forwarded to the European Parliament.

If a member of the Council declares that, for important and stated reasons of national policy, it intends to oppose the granting of an authorisation by qualified majority, a vote shall not be taken. The Council may, acting by a qualified majority, request that the matter be referred to the European Council for decision by unanimity.

The votes of the members of the Council shall be weighted in accordance with Article 205(2) of the Treaty establishing the European Community. For their adoption, decisions shall require at least 62 votes in favour, cast by at least 10 members.

3.	Any Member State which wishes to become a party to co-operation set up in accordance with this Article shall notify its intention to the Council and to the Commission, which shall give an opinion to the Council within three months of receipt of that notification, possibly accompanied by a recommendation for such specific arrangements as it may deem necessary for that Member State to become a party to the co-operation in question. Within four months of the date of that notification, the Council shall decide on the request and on such specific arrangements as it may deem necessary. The decision shall be deemed to be taken unless the Council, acting by a qualified majority, decides to hold it in abeyance; in this case, the Council shall state the reasons for its decision and set a deadline for reexamining it. For the purposes of this paragraph, the Council shall act under the conditions set out in Article 44.

4.	The provisions of Articles 29 to 41 shall apply to the closer co-operation provided for by this Article, save as otherwise provided for in this Article and in Articles 43 and 44.

The provisions of the Treaty establishing the European Community concerning the powers of the Court of Justice of the European Communities and the exercise of those powers shall apply to paragraphs 1, 2 and 3.

5.	This Article is without prejudice to the provisions of the Protocol integrating the Schengen acquis into the framework of the European Union.

### Article 41 (ex Article K.13)

1.	Articles 189, 190, 195, 196 to 199, 203, 204, 205(3), 206 to 209, 213 to 219, 255 and 290 of the Treaty establishing the European Community shall apply to the provisions relating to the areas referred to in this Title.

2.	Administrative expenditure which the provisions relating to the areas referred to in this Title entail for the institutions shall be charged to the budget of the European Communities.

3.	Operational expenditure to which the implementation of those provisions gives rise shall also be charged to the budget of the European Communities, except where the Council acting unanimously decides otherwise. In cases where expenditure is not charged to the budget of the European Communities it shall be charged to the Member States in accordance with the gross national product scale, unless the Council acting unanimously decides otherwise.

4.	The budgetary procedure laid down in the Treaty establishing the European Community shall apply to the expenditure charged to the budget of the European Communities.

### Article 42 (ex Article K.14)

The Council, acting unanimously on the initiative of the Commission or a Member State, and after consulting the European Parliament, may decide that action in areas referred to in Article 29 shall fall under Title IV of the Treaty establishing the European Community, and at the same time determine the relevant voting conditions relating to it. It shall recommend the Member States to adopt that decision in accordance with their respective constitutional requirements.

# TITLE VII (ex Title VIa)
# PROVISIONS ON CLOSER CO-OPERATION

## Article 43 (ex Article K.15)

1.     Member States which intend to establish closer co-operation between themselves may make use of the institutions, procedures and mechanisms laid down by this Treaty and the Treaty establishing the European Community provided that the co-operation:

(a)  is aimed at furthering the objectives of the Union and at protecting and serving its interests;

(b)  respects the principles of the said Treaties and the single institutional framework of the Union;

(c)  is only used as a last resort, where the objectives of the said Treaties could not be attained by applying the relevant procedures laid down therein;

(d)  concerns at least a majority of Member States;

(e)  does not affect the 'acquis communautaire' and the measures adopted under the other provisions of the said Treaties;

(f)  does not affect the competences, rights, obligations and interests of those Member States which do not participate therein;

(g)  is open to all Member States and allows them to become parties to the co-operation at any time, provided that they comply with the basic decision and with the decisions taken within that framework;

(h)  complies with the specific additional criteria laid down in Article 11 of the Treaty establishing the European Community and Article 40 of this Treaty, depending on the area concerned, and is authorised by the Council in accordance with the procedures laid down therein.

2.     Member States shall apply, as far as they are concerned, the acts and decisions adopted for the implementation of the co-operation in which they participate. Member States not participating in such co-operation shall not impede the implementation thereof by the participating Member States.

## Article 44 (ex Article K.16)

1.     For the purposes of the adoption of the acts and decisions necessary for the implementation of the co-operation referred to in Article 43, the relevant institutional provisions of this Treaty and of the Treaty establishing the European Community shall apply. However, while all members of the Council shall be able to take part in the deliberations, only those representing participating Member States shall take part in the adoption of decisions. The qualified majority shall be defined as the same proportion of the weighted votes of the members of the Council concerned as laid down in Article 205(2) of the Treaty establishing the European Community. Unanimity shall be constituted by only those Council members concerned.

2.     Expenditure resulting from implementation of the co-operation, other than administrative costs entailed for the institutions, shall be borne by the participating Member States, unless the Council, acting unanimously, decides otherwise.

**Article 45** (ex Article K.17)

The Council and the Commission shall regularly inform the European Parliament of the development of closer co-operation established on the basis of this Title.

# TITLE VIII (ex Title VII)
# FINAL PROVISIONS

**Article 46** (ex Article L)

The provisions of the Treaty establishing the European Community, the Treaty establishing the European Coal and Steel Community and the Treaty establishing the European Atomic Energy Community concerning the powers of the Court of Justice of the European Communities and the exercise of those powers shall apply only to the following provisions of this Treaty:

(a) provisions amending the Treaty establishing the European Economic Community with a view to establishing the European Community, the Treaty establishing the European Coal and Steel Community and the Treaty establishing the European Atomic Energy Community;

(b) provisions of Title VI, under the conditions provided for by Article 35;

(c) provisions of Title VII, under the conditions provided for by Article 11 of the Treaty establishing the European Community and Article 40 of this Treaty;

(d) Article 6(2) with regard to action of the institutions, insofar as the Court has jurisdiction under the Treaties establishing the European Communities and under this Treaty;

(e) Articles 46 to 53.

**Article 47** (ex Article M)

Subject to the provisions amending the Treaty establishing the European Economic Community with a view to establishing the European Community, the Treaty establishing the European Coal and Steel Community and the Treaty establishing the European Atomic Energy Community, and to these final provisions, nothing in this Treaty shall affect the Treaties establishing the European Communities or the subsequent Treaties and Acts modifying or supplementing them.

**Article 48** (ex Article N)

The government of any Member State or the Commission may submit to the Council proposals for the amendment of the Treaties on which the Union is founded.

If the Council, after consulting the European Parliament and, where appropriate, the Commission, delivers an opinion in favour of calling a conference of representatives of the governments of the Member States, the conference shall be convened by the President of the Council for the purpose of determining by common accord the amendments to be made to those Treaties. The European Central Bank shall also be consulted in the case of institutional changes in the monetary area.

The amendments shall enter into force after being ratified by all the Member States in accordance with their respective constitutional requirements.

**Article 49** (ex Article O)

Any European State which respects the principles set out in Article 6(1) may apply to become a member of the Union. It shall address its application to the Council, which shall act unanimously after consulting the Commission and after receiving the assent of the European Parliament, which shall act by an absolute majority of its component members.

The conditions of admission and the adjustments to the Treaties on which the Union is founded which such admission entails shall be the subject of an agreement between the Member States and the applicant State. This agreement shall be submitted for ratification by all the contracting States in accordance with their respective constitutional requirements.

**Article 50** (ex Article P)

1.     Articles 2 to 7 and 10 to 19 of the Treaty establishing a Single Council and a Single Commission of the European Communities, signed in Brussels on 8 April 1965, are hereby repealed.

2.     Article 2, Article 3(2) and Title III of the Single European Act signed in Luxembourg on 17 February 1986 and in The Hague on 28 February 1986 are hereby repealed.

**Article 51** (ex Article Q)

This Treaty is concluded for an unlimited period.

**Article 52** (ex Article R)

1.     This Treaty shall be ratified by the High Contracting Parties in accordance with their respective constitutional requirements. The instruments of ratification shall be deposited with the Government of the Italian Republic.

2.     This Treaty shall enter into force on 1 January 1993, provided that all the instruments of ratification have been deposited, or, failing that, on the first day of the month following the deposit of the instrument of ratification by the last signatory State to take this step.

**Article 53** (ex Article S)

This Treaty, drawn up in a single original in the Danish, Dutch, English, French, German, Greek, Irish, Italian, Portuguese and Spanish languages, the texts in each of these languages being equally authentic, shall be deposited in the archives of the government of the Italian Republic, which will transmit a certified copy to each of the governments of the other signatory States.

Pursuant to the Accession Treaty of 1994, the Finnish and Swedish versions of this Treaty shall also be authentic.

# TABLES OF EQUIVALENCES REFERRED TO IN ARTICLE 12 OF THE TREATY OF AMSTERDAM

## A. Treaty on European Union

| Previous numbering | New numbering | Previous numbering | New numbering |
|---|---|---|---|
| TITLE I | TITLE I | TITLE VI★★★ | TITLE VI |
| Article A | Article 1 | Article K.1 | Article 29 |
| Article B | Article 2 | Article K.2 | Article 30 |
| Article C | Article 3 | Article K.3 | Article 31 |
| Article D | Article 4 | Article K.4 | Article 32 |
| Article E | Article 5 | Article K.5 | Article 33 |
| Article F | Article 6 | Article K.6 | Article 34 |
| Article F.1★ | Article 7 | Article K.7 | Article 35 |
| | | Article K.8 | Article 36 |
| TITLE II | TITLE II | Article K.9 | Article 37 |
| Article G | Article 8 | Article K.10 | Article 38 |
| | | Article K.11 | Article 39 |
| TITLE III | TITLE III | Article K.12 | Article 40 |
| Article H | Article 9 | Article K.13 | Article 41 |
| | | Article K.14 | Article 42 |
| TITLE IV | TITLE IV | | |
| Article I | Article 10 | TITLE VIa★★ | TITLE VII |
| | | Article K.15★ | Article 43 |
| TITLE V★★★ | TITLE V | Article K.16★ | Article 44 |
| Article J.1 | Article 11 | Article K.17★ | Article 45 |
| Article J.2 | Article 12 | | |
| Article J.3 | Article 13 | TITLE VII | TITLE VIII |
| Article J.4 | Article 14 | Article L | Article 46 |
| Article J.5 | Article 15 | Article M | Article 47 |
| Article J.6 | Article 16 | Article N | Article 48 |
| Article J.7 | Article 17 | Article O | Article 49 |
| Article J.8 | Article 18 | Article P | Article 50 |
| Article J.9 | Article 19 | Article Q | Article 51 |
| Article J.10 | Article 20 | Article R | Article 52 |
| Article J.11 | Article 21 | Article S | Article 53 |
| Article J.12 | Article 22 | | |
| Article J.13 | Article 23 | | |
| Article J.14 | Article 24 | | |
| Article J.15 | Article 25 | | |
| Article J.16 | Article 26 | | |
| Article J.17 | Article 27 | | |
| Article J.18 | Article 28 | | |

NOTES
   ★   New Article introduced by the Treaty of Amsterdam.
  ★★  New Title introduced by the Treaty of Amsterdam.
★★★ Title restructured by the Treaty of Amsterdam.

# B. Treaty establishing the European Community

| Previous numbering | New numbering | Previous numbering | New numbering |
|---|---|---|---|
| **PART ONE** | **PART ONE** | Article 16 (repealed | — |
| | | Article 17 (repealed) | — |
| Article 1 | Article 1 | | |
| Article 2 | Article 2 | SECTION 2 (deleted) | — |
| Article 3 | Article 3 | Article 18 (repealed) | — |
| Article 3a | Article 4 | Article 19 (repealed) | — |
| Article 3b | Article 5 | Article 20 (repealed) | — |
| Article 3c★ | Article 6 | Article 21 (repealed) | — |
| Article 4 | Article 7 | Article 22 (repealed) | — |
| Article 4a | Article 8 | Article 23 (repealed) | — |
| Article 4b | Article 9 | Article 24 (repealed) | — |
| Article 5 | Article 10 | Article 25 (repealed) | — |
| Article 5a★ | Article 11 | Article 26 (repealed) | — |
| Article 6 | Article 12 | Article 27 (repealed) | — |
| Article 6a★ | Article 13 | Article 28 | Article 26 |
| Article 7 (repealed) | — | Article 29 | Article 27 |
| Article 7a | Article 14 | | |
| Article 7b (repealed) | — | CHAPTER 2 | CHAPTER 2 |
| Article 7c | Article 15 | Article 30 | Article 28 |
| Article 7d★ | Article 16 | Article 31 (repealed) | — |
| | | Article 32 (repealed) | — |
| **PART TWO** | **PART TWO** | Article 33 (repealed) | — |
| | | Article 34 | Article 29 |
| Article 8 | Article 17 | Article 35 (repealed) | — |
| Article 8a | Article 18 | Article 36 | Article 30 |
| Article 8b | Article 19 | Article 37 | Article 31 |
| Article 8c | Article 20 | | |
| Article 8d | Article 21 | TITLE II | TITLE II |
| Article 8e | Article 22 | Article 38 | Article 32 |
| | | Article 39 | Article 33 |
| **PART THREE** | **PART THREE** | Article 40 | Article 34 |
| | | Article 41 | Article 35 |
| TITLE I | TITLE I | Article 42 | Article 36 |
| Article 9 | Article 23 | Article 43 | Article 37 |
| Article 10 | Article 24 | Article 44 (repealed) | — |
| Article 11 (repealed) | — | Article 45 (repealed) | — |
| | | Article 46 | Article 38 |
| CHAPTER 1 | CHAPTER 1 | Article 47 (repealed) | — |
| SECTION 1 (deleted) | — | | |
| Article 12 | Article 25 | TITLE III | TITLE III |
| Article 13 (repealed) | — | CHAPTER 1 | CHAPTER 1 |
| Article 14 (repealed) | — | Article 48 | Article 39 |
| Article 15 (repealed) | — | Article 49 | Article 40 |

NOTES
★New article introduced by the Treaty of Amsterdam.

| Previous numbering | New numbering | Previous numbering | New numbering |
|---|---|---|---|
| Article 50 | Article 41 | Article 73l ★ | Article 64 |
| Article 51 | Article 42 | Article 73m ★ | Article 65 |
| | | Article 73n ★ | Article 66 |
| CHAPTER 2 | CHAPTER 2 | Article 73o ★ | Article 67 |
| Article 52 | Article 43 | Article 73p ★ | Article 68 |
| Article 53 (repealed) | — | Article 73q ★ | Article 69 |
| Article 54 | Article 44 | | |
| Article 55 | Article 45 | TITLE IV | TITLE V |
| Article 56 | Article 46 | Article 74 | Article 70 |
| Article 57 | Article 47 | Article 75 | Article 71 |
| Article 58 | Article 48 | Article 76 | Article 72 |
| | | Article 77 | Article 73 |
| CHAPTER 3 | CHAPTER 3 | Article 78 | Article 74 |
| Article 59 | Article 49 | Article 79 | Article 75 |
| Article 60 | Article 50 | Article 80 | Article 76 |
| Article 61 | Article 51 | Article 81 | Article 77 |
| Article 62 (repealed) | — | Article 82 | Article 78 |
| Article 63 | Article 52 | Article 83 | Article 79 |
| Article 64 | Article 53 | Article 84 | Article 80 |
| Article 65 | Article 54 | | |
| Article 66 | Article 55 | TITLE V | TITLE VI |
| | | CHAPTER 1 | CHAPTER 1 |
| CHAPTER 4 | CHAPTER 4 | SECTION 1 | SECTION 1 |
| Article 67 (repealed) | — | Article 85 | Article 81 |
| Article 68 (repealed) | — | Article 86 | Article 82 |
| Article 69 (repealed) | — | Article 87 | Article 83 |
| Article 70 (repealed) | — | Article 88 | Article 84 |
| Article 71 (repealed) | — | Article 89 | Article 85 |
| Article 72 (repealed) | — | Article 90 | Article 86 |
| Article 73 (repealed) | — | | |
| Article 73a (repealed) | — | SECTION 2 | |
| Article 73b | Article 56 | (deleted) | — |
| Article 73c | Article 57 | Article 91 (repealed) | — |
| Article 73d | Article 58 | | |
| Article 73e (repealed) | — | SECTION 3 | SECTION 2 |
| Article 73f | Article 59 | Article 92 | Article 87 |
| Article 73g | Article 60 | Article 93 | Article 88 |
| Article 73h (repealed) | — | Article 94 | Article 89 |
| | | | |
| TITLE IIIa ★★ | TITLE IV | CHAPTER 2 | CHAPTER 2 |
| Article 73i ★ | Article 61 | Article 95 | Article 90 |
| Article 73j ★ | Article 62 | Article 96 | Article 91 |
| Article 73k ★ | Article 63 | Article 97 (repealed) | — |

NOTES
★   New Article introduced by the Treaty of Amsterdam.
★★  New Title introduced by the Treaty of Amsterdam.

| Previous numbering | New numbering | Previous numbering | New numbering |
|---|---|---|---|
| Article 98 | Article 92 | Article 109i | Article 120 |
| Article 99 | Article 93 | Article 109j | Article 121 |
| | | Article 109k | Article 122 |
| CHAPTER 3 | CHAPTER 3 | Article 109l | Article 123 |
| Article 100 | Article 94 | Article 109m | Article 124 |
| Article 100a | Article 95 | | |
| Article 100b (repealed) | — | TITLE VIa ★★ | TITLE VIII |
| Article 100c (repealed) | — | Article 109n ★ | Article 125 |
| Article 100d (repealed) | — | Article 109o ★ | Article 126 |
| Article 101 | Article 96 | Article 109p ★ | Article 127 |
| Article 102 | Article 97 | Article 109q ★ | Article 128 |
| | | Article 109r ★ | Article 129 |
| TITLE VI | TITLE VII | Article 109s ★ | Article 130 |
| CHAPTER 1 | CHAPTER 1 | | |
| Article 102a | Article 98 | TITLE VII | TITLE IX |
| Article 103 | Article 99 | Article 110 | Article 131 |
| Article 103a | Article 100 | Article 111 (repealed) | — |
| Article 104 | Article 101 | Article 112 | Article 132 |
| Article 104a | Article 102 | Article 113 | Article 133 |
| Article 104b | Article 103 | Article 114 (repealed) | — |
| Article 104c | Article 104 | Article 115 | Article 134 |
| | | | |
| CHAPTER 2 | CHAPTER 2 | TITLE VIIa ★★ | TITLE X |
| Article 105 | Article 105 | Article 116 ★ | Article 135 |
| Article 105a | Article 106 | | |
| Article 106 | Article 107 | TITLE VIII | TITLE XI |
| Article 107 | Article 108 | CHAPTER 1 ★★★ | CHAPTER 1 |
| Article 108 | Article 109 | Article 117 | Article 136 |
| Article 108a | Article 110 | Article 118 | Article 137 |
| Article 109 | Article 111 | Article 118a | Article 138 |
| | | Article 118b | Article 139 |
| CHAPTER 3 | CHAPTER 3 | Article 118c | Article 140 |
| Article 109a | Article 112 | Article 119 | Article 141 |
| Article 109b | Article 113 | Article 119a | Article 142 |
| Article 109c | Article 114 | Article 120 | Article 143 |
| Article 109d | Article 115 | Article 121 | Article 144 |
| | | Article 122 | Article 145 |
| CHAPTER 4 | CHAPTER 4 | | |
| Article 109e | Article 116 | CHAPTER 2 | CHAPTER 2 |
| Article 109f | Article 117 | Article 123 | Article 146 |
| Article 109g | Article 118 | Article 124 | Article 147 |
| Article 109h | Article 119 | Article 125 | Article 148 |

NOTES
★ New Article introduced by the Treaty of Amsterdam.
★★ New Title introduced by the Treaty of Amsterdam.
★★★ Title restructured by the Treaty of Amsterdam.

| Previous numbering | New numbering | Previous numbering | New numbering |
| --- | --- | --- | --- |
| CHAPTER 3 | CHAPTER 3 | TITLE XVII | TITLE XX |
| Article 126 | Article 149 | Article 130u | Article 177 |
| Article 127 | Article 150 | Article 130v | Article 178 |
| | | Article 130w | Article 179 |
| TITLE IX | TITLE XII | Article 130x | Article 180 |
| Article 128 | Article 151 | Article 130y | Article 181 |
| TITLE X | TITLE XIII | **PART FOUR** | **PART FOUR** |
| Article 129 | Article 152 | | |
| | | Article 131 | Article 182 |
| TITLE XI | TITLE XIV | Article 132 | Article 183 |
| Article 129a | Article 153 | Article 133 | Article 184 |
| | | Article 134 | Article 185 |
| TITLE XII | TITLE XV | Article 135 | Article 186 |
| Article 129b | Article 154 | Article 136 | Article 187 |
| Article 129c | Article 155 | Article 136a | Article 188 |
| Article 129d | Article 156 | | |
| | | **PART FIVE** | **PART FIVE** |
| TITLE XIII | TITLE XVI | | |
| Article 130 | Article 157 | TITLE I | TITLE I |
| | | CHAPTER 1 | CHAPTER 1 |
| TITLE XIV | TITLE XVII | SECTION 1 | SECTION 1 |
| Article 130a | Article 158 | Article 137 | Article 189 |
| Article 130b | Article 159 | Article 138 | Article 190 |
| Article 130c | Article 160 | Article 138a | Article 191 |
| Article 130d | Article 161 | Article 138b | Article 192 |
| Article 130e | Article 162 | Article 138c | Article 193 |
| | | Article 138d | Article 194 |
| TITLE XV | TITLE XVIII | Article 138e | Article 195 |
| Article 130f | Article 163 | Article 139 | Article 196 |
| Article 130g | Article 164 | Article 140 | Article 197 |
| Article 130h | Article 165 | Article 141 | Article 198 |
| Article 130i | Article 166 | Article 142 | Article 199 |
| Article 130j | Article 167 | Article 143 | Article 200 |
| Article 130k | Article 168 | Article 144 | Article 201 |
| Article 130l | Article 169 | | |
| Article 130m | Article 170 | SECTION 2 | SECTION 2 |
| Article 130n | Article 171 | Article 145 | Article 202 |
| Article 130o | Article 172 | Article 146 | Article 203 |
| Article 130p | Article 173 | Article 147 | Article 204 |
| Article 130q (repealed) | — | Article 148 | Article 205 |
| | | Article 149 (repealed) | — |
| TITLE XVI | TITLE XIX | Article 150 | Article 206 |
| Article 130r | Article 174 | Article 151 | Article 207 |
| Article 130s | Article 175 | Article 152 | Article 208 |
| Article 130t | Article 176 | Article 153 | Article 209 |

| Previous numbering | New numbering | Previous numbering | New numbering |
|---|---|---|---|
| Article 154 | Article 210 | CHAPTER 2 | CHAPTER 2 |
| | | Article 189 | Article 249 |
| SECTION 3 | SECTION 3 | Article 189a | Article 250 |
| Article 155 | Article 211 | Article 189b | Article 251 |
| Article 156 | Article 212 | Article 189c | Article 252 |
| Article 157 | Article 213 | Article 190 | Article 253 |
| Article 158 | Article 214 | Article 191 | Article 254 |
| Article 159 | Article 215 | Article 191a ★ | Article 255 |
| Article 160 | Article 216 | Article 192 | Article 256 |
| Article 161 | Article 217 | | |
| Article 162 | Article 218 | CHAPTER 3 | CHAPTER 3 |
| Article 163 | Article 219 | Article 193 | Article 257 |
| | | Article 194 | Article 258 |
| SECTION 4 | SECTION 4 | Article 195 | Article 259 |
| Article 164 | Article 220 | Article 196 | Article 260 |
| Article 165 | Article 221 | Article 197 | Article 261 |
| Article 166 | Article 222 | Article 198 | Article 262 |
| Article 167 | Article 223 | | |
| Article 168 | Article 224 | CHAPTER 4 | CHAPTER 4 |
| Article 168a | Article 225 | Article 198a | Article 263 |
| Article 169 | Article 226 | Article 198b | Article 264 |
| Article 170 | Article 227 | Article 198c | Article 265 |
| Article 171 | Article 228 | | |
| Article 172 | Article 229 | CHAPTER 5 | CHAPTER 5 |
| Article 173 | Article 230 | Article 198d | Article 266 |
| Article 174 | Article 231 | Article 198e | Article 267 |
| Article 175 | Article 232 | | |
| Article 176 | Article 233 | TITLE II | TITLE II |
| Article 177 | Article 234 | Article 199 | Article 268 |
| Article 178 | Article 235 | Article 200 (repealed) | — |
| Article 179 | Article 236 | Article 201 | Article 269 |
| Article 180 | Article 237 | Article 201a | Article 270 |
| Article 181 | Article 238 | Article 202 | Article 272 |
| Article 182 | Article 239 | Article 203 | Article 272 |
| Article 183 | Article 240 | Article 204 | Article 273 |
| Article 184 | Article 241 | Article 205 | Article 274 |
| Article 185 | Article 242 | Article 205a | Article 275 |
| Article 186 | Article 243 | Article 206 | Article 276 |
| Article 187 | Article 244 | Article 206a (repealed) | — |
| Article 188 | Article 245 | Article 207 | Article 277 |
| | | Article 208 | Article 278 |
| SECTION 5 | SECTION 5 | Article 209 | Article 279 |
| Article 188a | Article 246 | Article 209a | Article 280 |
| Article 188b | Article 247 | | |
| Article 188c | Article 248 | | |

NOTES
★   New Article introduced by the Treaty of Amsterdam.

| Previous numbering | New numbering | Previous numbering | New numbering |
|---|---|---|---|
| **PART SIX** | **PART SIX** | Article 229 | Article 302 |
| | | Article 230 | Article 303 |
| Article 210 | Article 281 | Article 231 | Article 304 |
| Article 211 | Article 282 | Article 232 | Article 305 |
| Article 212 ★ | Article 283 | Article 233 | Article 306 |
| Article 213 | Article 284 | Article 234 | Article 307 |
| Article 213a ★ | Article 285 | Article 235 | Article 308 |
| Article 213b ★ | Article 286 | Article 236 ★ | Article 309 |
| Article 214 | Article 287 | Article 237 (repealed) | — |
| Article 215 | Article 288 | Article 238 | Article 310 |
| Article 216 | Article 289 | Article 239 | Article 311 |
| Article 217 | Article 290 | Article 240 | Article 312 |
| Article 218 ★ | Article 291 | Article 241 (repealed) | — |
| Article 219 | Article 292 | Article 242 (repealed) | — |
| Article 220 | Article 293 | Article 243 (repealed) | — |
| Article 221 | Article 294 | Article 244 (repealed) | — |
| Article 222 | Article 295 | Article 245 (repealed) | — |
| Article 223 | Article 296 | Article 246 (repealed) | — |
| Article 224 | Article 297 | | |
| Article 225 | Article 298 | **FINAL PROVISIONS** | **FINAL PROVISIONS** |
| Article 226 (repealed) | — | Article 247 | Article 313 |
| Article 227 | Article 299 | Article 248 | Article 314 |
| Article 228 | Article 300 | | |
| Article 228a | Article 301 | | |

NOTES
★ New Article introduced by the Treaty of Amsterdam.

# SECONDARY LEGISLATION

# COMMISSION REGULATION

of 22 June 1983

## on the application of Article 85(3) of the Treaty to categories of exclusive distribution agreements

### (1983/83/EEC)

NOTES

Date of Publication in OJ: OJ L173, 30.6.83, p 1. The text of this Regulation incorporates the corrigenda published by the Commission in OJ L281, 13.10.83, p 24.

THE COMMISSION OF THE EUROPEAN COMMUNITIES,

Having regard to the Treaty establishing the European Economic Community,

Having regard to Council Regulation No 19/65/EEC of 2 March 1965 on the application of Article 85(3) of the Treaty to certain categories of agreements and concerted practices, as last amended by the Act of Accession of Greece, and in particular Article 1 thereof,

Having published a draft of this Regulation,

Having consulted the Advisory Committee on Restrictive Practices and Dominant Positions,

(1)    Whereas Regulation No 19/65/EEC empowers the Commission to apply Article 85(3) of the Treaty by regulation to certain categories of bilateral exclusive distribution agreements and analogous concerted practices falling within Article 85(1);

(2)    Whereas experience to date makes it possible to define a category of agreements and concerted practices which can be regarded as normally satisfying the conditions laid down in Article 85(3);

(3)    Whereas exclusive distribution agreements of the category defined in Article 1 of this Regulation may fall within the prohibition contained in Article 85(1) of the Treaty; whereas this will apply only in exceptional cases to exclusive agreements of this kind to which only undertakings from one Member State are party and which concern the resale of goods within that Member State; whereas, however, to the extent that such agreements may affect trade between Member States and also satisfy all the requirements set out in this Regulation there is no reason to withhold from them the benefit of the exemption by category;

(4)    Whereas it is not necessary expressly to exclude from the defined category those agreements which do not fulfil the conditions of Article 85(1) of the Treaty;

(5)    Whereas exclusive distribution agreements lead in general to an improvement in distribution because the undertaking is able to concentrate its sales activities, does not need to maintain numerous business relations with a larger number of dealers and is able, by dealing with only one dealer, to overcome more easily distribution difficulties in international trade resulting from linguistic, legal and other differences;

(6)    Whereas exclusive distribution agreements facilitate the promotion of sales of a product and lead to intensive marketing and to continuity of supplies while at the same time rationalising distribution; whereas they stimulate competition between the products of different manufacturers; whereas the appointment of an exclusive distributor who will take over sales promotion, customer services and carrying of stocks is often the most effective way, and sometimes indeed the only way, for the manufacturer to enter a market and compete with other manufacturers already present; whereas this is particularly so in the case of small and medium-sized undertakings; whereas it must be left to the contracting parties to decide whether and to what extent they consider it desirable to incorporate in the agreements terms providing for the promotion of sales;

(7)    Whereas, as a rule, such exclusive distribution agreements also allow consumers a fair share of the resulting benefit as they gain directly from the improvement in distribution, and

their economic and supply position is improved as they can obtain products manufactured in particular in other countries more quickly and more easily;

(8)    Whereas this Regulation must define the obligations restricting competition which may be included in exclusive distribution agreements; whereas the other restrictions on competition allowed under this Regulation in addition to the exclusive supply obligation produce a clear division of functions between the parties and compel the exclusive distributor to concentrate his sales efforts on the contract goods and the contract territory; whereas they are, where they are agreed only for the duration of the agreement, generally necessary in order to attain the improvement in the distribution of goods sought through exclusive distribution; whereas it may be left to the contracting parties to decide which of these obligations they include in their agreements; whereas further restrictive obligations and in particular those which limit the exclusive distributor's choice of customers or his freedom to determine his prices and conditions of sale cannot be exempted under this Regulation;

(9)    Whereas the exemption by category should be reserved for agreements for which it can be assumed with sufficient certainty that they satisfy the conditions of Article 85(3) of the Treaty;

(10)    Whereas it is not possible, in the absence of a case-by-case examination, to consider that adequate improvements in distribution occur where a manufacturer entrusts the distribution of his goods to another manufacturer with whom he is in competition; whereas such agreements should, therefore, be excluded from the exemption by category; whereas certain derogations from this rule in favour of small and medium-sized undertakings can be allowed;

(11)    Whereas consumers will be assured of a fair share of the benefits resulting from exclusive distribution only if parallel imports remain possible; whereas agreements relating to goods which the user can obtain only from the exclusive distributor should therefore be excluded from the exemption by category; whereas the parties cannot be allowed to abuse industrial property rights or other rights in order to create absolute territorial protection; whereas this does not prejudice the relationship between competition law and industrial property rights, since the sole object here is to determine the conditions for exemption by category;

(12)    Whereas, since competition at the distribution stage is ensured by the possibility of parallel imports, the exclusive distribution agreements covered by this Regulation will not normally afford any possibility of eliminating competition in respect of a substantial part of the products in question; whereas this is also true of agreements that allot to the exclusive distributor a contract territory covering the whole of the common market;

(13)    Whereas, in particular cases in which agreements or concerted practices satisfying the requirements of this Regulation nevertheless have effects incompatible with Article 85(3) of the Treaty, the Commission may withdraw the benefit of the exemption by category from the undertakings party to them;

(14)    Whereas agreements and concerted practices which satisfy the conditions set out in this Regulation need not be notified; whereas an undertaking may nonetheless in a particular case where real doubt exists, request the Commission to declare whether its agreements comply with this Regulation;

(15)    Whereas this Regulation does not affect the applicability of Commission Regulation (EEC) No 3604/82 of 23 December 1982 on the application of Article 85(3) of the Treaty to categories of specialisation agreements; whereas it does not exclude the application of Article 86 of the Treaty,

## HAS ADOPTED THIS REGULATION—

### Article 1

Pursuant to Article 85(3) of the Treaty and subject to the provisions of this Regulation, it is hereby declared that Article 85(1) of the Treaty shall not apply to agreements to which only two undertakings are party and whereby one party agrees with the other to supply certain goods for resale within the whole or a defined area of the common market only to that other.

**Article 2**

1.      Apart from the obligation referred to in Article 1 no restriction on competition shall be imposed on the supplier other than the obligation not to supply the contract goods to users in the contract territory.

2.      No restriction on competition shall be imposed on the exclusive distributor other than—
- (a) the obligation not to manufacture or distribute goods which compete with the contract goods;
- (b) the obligation to obtain the contract goods for resale only from the other party;
- (c) the obligation to refrain, outside the contract territory and in relation to the contract goods, from seeking customers, from establishing any branch and from maintaining any distribution depot.

3.      Article 1 shall apply notwithstanding that the exclusive distributor undertakes all or any of the following obligations—
- (a) to purchase complete ranges of goods or minimum quantities;
- (b) to sell the contract goods under trade marks or packed and presented as specified by the other party;
- (c) to take measures for promotion of sales, in particular—
  - — to advertise,
  - — to maintain a sales network or stock of goods,
  - — to provide customer and guarantee services,
  - — to employ staff having specialised or technical training.

**Article 3**

Article 1 shall not apply where—
- (a) manufacturers of identical goods or of goods which are considered by users as equivalent in view of their characteristics, price and intended use enter into reciprocal exclusive distribution agreements between themselves in respect of such goods;
- (b) manufacturers of identical goods or of goods which are considered by users as equivalent in view of their characteristics, price and intended use enter into a non-reciprocal exclusive distribution agreement between themselves in respect of such goods unless at least one of them has a total annual turnover of no more than 100 million ECU;
- (c) users can obtain the contract goods in the contract territory only from the exclusive distributor and have no alternative source of supply outside the contract territory;
- (d) one or both of the parties makes it difficult for intermediaries or users to obtain the contract goods from other dealers inside the common market or, in so far as no alternative source of supply is available there, from outside the common market, in particular where one or both of them—
  1. exercises industrial property rights so as to prevent dealers or users from obtaining outside, or from selling in, the contract territory properly marked or otherwise properly marketed contract goods;
  2. exercises other rights or takes other measures so as to prevent dealers or users from obtaining outside, or from selling in, the contract territory contract goods.

**Article 4**

1.    Article 3(a) and (b) shall also apply where the goods there referred to are manufactured by an undertaking connected with a party to the agreement.

2.    Connected undertakings are—
  (a) undertakings in which a party to the agreement, directly or indirectly—
    — owns more than half the capital or business assets, or
    — has the power to exercise more than half the voting rights, or
    — has the power to appoint more than half the members of the supervisory board, board of directors or bodies legally representing the undertaking, or
    — has the right to manage the affairs;
  (b) undertakings which directly or indirectly have in or over a party to the agreement the rights or powers listed in (a);
  (c) undertakings in which an undertaking referred to in (b) directly or indirectly has the rights or powers listed in (a).

3.    Undertakings in which the parties to the agreement or undertakings connected with them jointly have the rights or powers set out in paragraph 2(a) shall be considered to be connected with each of the parties to the agreement.

**Article 5**

1.    For the purpose of Article 3(b), the ECU is the unit of account used for drawing up the budget of the Community pursuant to Articles 207 and 209 of the Treaty.

2.    Article 1 shall remain applicable where during any period of two consecutive financial years the total turnover referred to in Article 3(b) is exceeded by no more than 10%.

3.    For the purpose of calculating total turnover within the meaning of Article 3(b), the turnovers achieved during the last financial year by the party to the agreement and connected undertakings in respect of all goods and services, excluding all taxes and other duties, shall be added together. For this purpose no account shall be taken of dealings between the party to the agreement and its connected undertakings or between its connected undertakings.

**Article 6**

The Commission may withdraw the benefit of this Regulation, pursuant to Article 7 of Regulation No 19/65/EEC, when it finds in a particular case that an agreement which is exempted by this Regulation nevertheless has certain effects which are incompatible with the conditions set out in Article 85(3) of the Treaty, and in particular where—
  (a) the contract goods are not subject, in the contract territory, to effective competition from identical goods or goods considered by users as equivalent in view of their characteristics, price and intended use;
  (b) access by other suppliers to the different stages of distribution within the contract territory is made difficult to a significant extent;
  (c) for reasons other than those referred to in Article 3(c) and (d) it is not possible for intermediaries or users to obtain supplies of the contract goods from dealers outside the contract territory on the terms there customary;
  (d) the exclusive distributor—

1.  without any objectively justified reason refuses to supply in the contract territory categories of purchasers who cannot obtain contract goods elsewhere on suitable terms or applies to them differing prices or conditions of sale;
2.  sells the contract goods at excessively high prices.

## Article 7

In the period 1 July 1983 to 31 December 1986, the prohibition in Article 85(1) of the Treaty shall not apply to agreements which were in force on 1 July 1983 or entered into force between 1 July and 31 December 1983 and which satisfy the exemption conditions of Regulation No 67/67/EEC.

[The provisions of the preceding paragraph shall apply in the same way to agreements which were in force on the date of accession of the Kingdom of Spain and of the Portuguese Republic and which, as a result of accession, fall within the scope of Article 85(1) of the Treaty.]

NOTES

Words in square brackets added by the 1985 Act of Accession of the Kingdom of Spain and the Portuguese Republic, Annex I(IV)(10).

## [Article 7a

The prohibition in Article 85(1) of the Treaty shall not apply to agreements which were in existence at the date of accession of Austria, Finland and Sweden and which, by reason of this accession, fall within the scope of Article 85(1) if, within six months from the date of accession, they are so amended that they comply with the conditions laid down in this Regulation. However, this Article shall not apply to agreements which at the date of accession already fall under Article 53 of the EEA Agreement.]

NOTES

Inserted by the 1994 Act of Accession of the Kingdom of Norway, the Republic of Austria, the Republic of Finland and the Kingdom of Sweden, Annex I(III)(D)(1), as adjusted by Council Decision 95/1/EC, Annex I(III)(D)(1).

## Article 8

This Regulation shall not apply to agreements entered into for the resale of drinks in premises used for the sale and consumption of drinks or for the resale of petroleum products in service stations.

## Article 9

This Regulation shall apply *mutatis mutandis* to concerted practices of the type defined in Article 1.

## Article 10

This Regulation shall enter into force on 1 July 1983.

It shall expire on [31 December 1999].

This Regulation shall be binding in its entirety and directly applicable in all Member States.

NOTES

Words in square brackets substituted by Commission Regulation 1582/97/EC, Art 1.

# COMMISSION REGULATION

of 22 June 1983

## on the application of Article 85(3) of the Treaty to categories of exclusive purchasing agreements

### (1984/83/EEC)

NOTES

Date of publication in OJ: OJ L173, 30.6.83, p 5. The text of this Regulation incorporates the corrigenda published by the Commission in OJ L281, 13.10.83. pp 24–25.

THE COMMISSION OF THE EUROPEAN COMMUNITIES,

Having regard to the Treaty establishing the European Economic Community,

Having regard to Council Regulation No 19/65/EEC of 2 March 1965 on the application of Article 85(3) of the Treaty to certain categories of agreements and concerted practices, as last amended by the Act of Accession of Greece, and in particular Article 1 thereof,

Having published a draft of this Regulation,

Having consulted the Advisory Committee on Restrictive Practices and Dominant Positions,

(1) Whereas Regulation No 19/65/EEC empowers the Commission to apply Article 85(3) of the Treaty by regulation to certain categories of bilateral exclusive purchasing agreements entered into for the purpose of the resale of goods and corresponding concerted practices falling within Article 85(1);

(2) Whereas experience to date makes it possible to define three categories of agreements and concerted practices which can be regarded as normally satisfying the conditions laid down in Article 85(3); whereas the first category comprises exclusive purchasing agreements of short and medium duration in all sectors of the economy; whereas the other two categories comprise long-term exclusive purchasing agreements entered into for the resale of beer in premises used for the sale and consumption of drinks (beer supply agreements) and of petroleum products in service stations (service station agreements);

(3) Whereas exclusive purchasing agreements of the categories defined in this Regulation may fall within the prohibition contained in Article 85(1) of the Treaty; whereas this will often be the case with agreements concluded between undertakings from different Member States; whereas an exclusive purchasing agreement to which undertakings from only one Member State are party and which concerns the resale of goods within that Member State may also be caught by the prohibition; whereas this is in particular the case where it is one of a number of similar agreements which together may affect trade between Member States;

(4) Whereas it is not necessary expressly to exclude from the defined categories those agreements which do not fulfil the conditions of Article 85(1) of the Treaty;

(5) Whereas the exclusive purchasing agreements defined in this Regulation lead in general to an improvement in distribution; whereas they enable the supplier to plan the sales of his goods with greater precision and for a longer period and ensure that the reseller's requirements will be met on a regular basis for the duration of the agreement; whereas this allows the parties to limit the risk to them of variations in market conditions and to lower distribution costs;

(6) Whereas such agreements also facilitate the promotion of the sales of a product and lead to Intensive marketing because the supplier, in consideration for the exclusive purchasing obligation, is as a rule under an obligation to contribute to the improvement of the structure of the distribution network, the quality of the promotional effort or the sales success; whereas, at the same time, they stimulate competition between the products of different manufacturers; whereas the appointment of several resellers, who are bound to purchase exclusively from the manufacturer and who take over sales promotion, customer services and carrying of stock, is often the most effective way, and sometimes the only way, for the manufacturer to penetrate a market and compete with other manufacturers already present; whereas this is particularly so in the case of small and medium-size undertakings; whereas it must be left to the contracting

parties to decide whether and to what extent they consider it desirable to incorporate in their agreements terms concerning the promotion of sales;

(7)   Whereas, as a rule, exclusive purchasing agreements between suppliers and resellers also allow consumers a fair share of the resulting benefit as they gain the advantages of regular supply and are able to obtain the contract goods more quickly and more easily;

(8)   Whereas this Regulation must define the obligations restricting competition which may be included in an exclusive purchasing agreement; whereas the other restrictions of competition allowed under this Regulation in addition to the exclusive purchasing obligation lead to a clear division of functions between the parties and compel the reseller to concentrate his sales efforts on the contract goods; whereas they are, where they are agreed only for the duration of the agreement, generally necessary in order to attain the improvement in the distribution of goods sought through exclusive purchasing; whereas further restrictive obligations and in particular those which limit the reseller's choice of customers or his freedom to determine his prices and conditions of sale cannot be exempted under this Regulation;

(9)   Whereas the exemption by categories should be reserved for agreements for which it can be assumed with sufficient certainty that they satisfy the conditions of Article 85(3) of the Treaty;

(10)   Whereas it is not possible, in the absence of a case-by-case examination, to consider that adequate improvements in distribution occur where a manufacturer imposes an exclusive purchasing obligation with respect to his goods on a manufacturer with whom he is in competition; whereas such agreements should, therefore, be excluded from the exemption by categories; whereas certain derogations from this rule in favour of small and medium-sized undertakings can be allowed;

(11)   Whereas certain conditions must be attached to the exemption by categories so that access by other undertakings to the different stages of distribution can be ensured; whereas, to this end, limits must be set to the scope and to the duration of the exclusive purchasing obligation; whereas it appears appropriate as a general rule to grant the benefit of a general exemption from the prohibition on restrictive agreements only to exclusive purchasing agreements which are concluded for a specified product or range of products and for not more than five years;

(12)   Whereas, in the case of beer supply agreements and service-station agreements, different rules should be laid down which take account of the particularities of the markets in question;

(13)   Whereas these agreements are generally distinguished by the fact that, on the one hand, the supplier confers on the reseller special commercial or financial advantages by contributing to his financing, granting him or obtaining for him a loan on favourable terms, equipping him with a site or premises for conducting his business, providing him with equipment or fittings, or undertaking other investments for his benefit and that, on the other hand, the reseller enters into a long-term exclusive purchasing obligation which in most cases is accompanied by a ban on dealing in competing products;

(14)   Whereas beer supply and service-station agreements, like the other exclusive purchasing agreements dealt with in this Regulation, normally produce an appreciable improvement in distribution in which consumers are allowed a fair share of the resulting benefit;

(15)   Whereas the commercial and financial advantages conferred by the supplier on the reseller make it significantly easier to establish, modernise, maintain and operate premises used for the sale and consumption of drinks and service stations; whereas the exclusive purchasing obligation and the ban on dealing in competing products imposed on the reseller incite the reseller to devote all the resources at his disposal to the sale of the contract goods; whereas such agreements lead to durable co-operation between the parties allowing them to improve or maintain the quality of the contract goods and of the services to the customer and sales efforts of the reseller; whereas they allow long-term planning of sales and consequently a cost effective organisation of production and distribution; whereas the pressure of competition between products of different makes obliges the undertakings involved to determine the number and character of premises used for the sale and consumption of drinks and service stations, in accordance with the wishes of customers;

(16)   Whereas consumers benefit from the improvements described, in particular because they are ensured supplies of goods of satisfactory quality at fair prices and conditions while being able to choose between the products of different manufacturers;

(17) Whereas the advantages produced by beer supply agreements and service-station agreements cannot otherwise be secured to the same extent and with the same degree of certainty; whereas the exclusive purchasing obligation on the reseller and the non-competition clause imposed on him are essential components of such agreements and thus usually indispensable for the attainment of these advantages; whereas, however, this is true only as long as the reseller's obligation to purchase from the supplier is confined in the case of premises used for the sale and consumption of drinks to beers and other drinks of the types offered by the supplier, and in the case of service stations to petroleum-based fuel for motor vehicles and other petroleum-based fuels; whereas the exclusive purchasing obligation for lubricants and related petroleum-based products can be accepted only on condition that the supplier provides for the reseller or finances the procurement of specific equipment for the carrying out of lubrication work; whereas this obligation should only relate to products intended for use within the service station;

(18) Whereas, in order to maintain the reseller's commercial freedom and to ensure access to the retail level of distribution on the part of other suppliers, not only the scope but also the duration of the exclusive purchasing obligation must be limited; whereas it appears appropriate to allow drinks suppliers a choice between a medium-term exclusive purchasing agreement covering a range of drinks and a long-term exclusive purchasing agreement for beer; whereas it is necessary to provide special rules for those premises used for the sale and consumption of drinks which the supplier lets to the reseller; whereas, in this case, the reseller must have the right to obtain from other undertakings, under the conditions specified in this Regulation, other drinks, except beer, supplied under the agreement or of the same type but bearing a different trademark; whereas a uniform maximum duration should be provided for service-station agreements, with the exception of tenancy agreements between the supplier and the reseller, which takes account of the long-term character of the relationship between the parties;

(19) Whereas to the extent that Member States provide, by law or administrative measures, for the same upper limit of duration for the exclusive purchasing obligation upon the reseller in service-station agreements as laid down in this Regulation but provide for a permissible duration which varies in proportion to the consideration provided by the supplier or generally provide for a shorter duration than that permitted by this Regulation, such laws or measures are not contrary to the objectives of this Regulation which, in this respect, merely sets an upper limit to the duration of service-station agreements; whereas the application and enforcement of such national laws or measures must therefore be regarded as compatible with the provisions of this Regulation;

(20) Whereas the limitations and conditions provided for in this Regulation are such as to guarantee effective competition on the markets in question; whereas, therefore, the agreements to which the exemption by category applies do not normally enable the participating undertakings to eliminate competition for a substantial part of the products in question;

(21) Whereas, in particular cases in which agreements or concerted practices satisfying the conditions of this Regulation nevertheless have effects incompatible with Article 85(3) of the Treaty, the Commission may withdraw the benefit of the exemption by category from the undertakings party thereto;

(22) Whereas agreements and concerted practices which satisfy the conditions set out in this Regulation need not be notified; whereas an undertaking may nonetheless, in a particular case where real doubt exists, request the Commission to declare whether its agreements comply with this Regulation;

(23) Whereas this Regulation does not affect the applicability of Commission Regulation (EEC) No 3604/82 of 23 December 1982 on the application of Article 85(3) of the Treaty to categories of specialisation agreements; whereas it does not exclude the application of Article 86 of the Treaty,

HAS ADOPTED THIS REGULATION—

# TITLE I
# GENERAL PROVISIONS

## Article 1

Pursuant to Article 85(3) of the Treaty, and subject to the conditions set out in Articles 2 to 5 of this Regulation, it is hereby declared that Article 85(1) of the Treaty shall not apply to agreements to which only two undertakings are party and whereby one party, the reseller, agrees with the other, the supplier, to purchase certain goods specified in the agreement for resale only from the supplier or from a connected undertaking or from another undertaking which the supplier has entrusted with the sale of his goods.

## Article 2

1.     No other restriction of competition shall be imposed on the supplier than the obligation not to distribute the contract goods or goods which compete with the contract goods in the reseller's principal sales area and at the reseller's level of distribution.

2.     Apart from the obligation described in Article 1, no other restriction of competition shall be imposed on the reseller than the obligation not to manufacture or distribute goods which compete with the contract goods.

3.     Article 1 shall apply notwithstanding that the reseller undertakes any or all of the following obligations—
     (a)  to purchase complete ranges of goods;
     (b)  to purchase minimum quantities of goods which are subject to the exclusive purchasing obligation;
     (c)  to sell the contract goods under trademarks, or packed and presented as specified by the supplier;
     (d)  to take measures for the promotion of sales, in particular—
       — to advertise,
       — to maintain a sales network or stock of goods,
       — to provide customer and guarantee services,
       — to employ staff having specialised or technical training.

## Article 3

Article 1 shall not apply where—
     (a)  manufacturers of identical goods or of goods which are considered by users as equivalent in view of their characteristics, price and intended use enter into reciprocal exclusive purchasing agreements between themselves in respect of such goods;
     (b)  manufacturers of identical goods or of goods which are considered by users as equivalent in view of their characteristics, price and intended use enter into a non-reciprocal exclusive purchasing agreement between themselves in respect of such goods, unless at least one of them has a total annual turnover of no more than 100 million ECU;
     (c)  the exclusive purchasing obligation is agreed for more than one type of goods where these are neither by their nature nor according to commercial usage connected to each other;
     (d)  the agreement is concluded for an indefinite duration or for a period of more than five years.

## Article 4

1.     Article 3(a) and (b) shall also apply where the goods there referred to are manufactured by an undertaking connected with a party to the agreement.

2.     Connected undertakings are—
     (a)  undertakings in which a party to the agreement, directly or indirectly—

- owns more than half the capital or business assets, or
- has the power to exercise more than half the voting rights, or
- has the power to appoint more than half the members of the supervisory board, board of directors or bodies legally representing the undertaking, or
- has the right to manage the affairs;

(b) undertakings which directly or indirectly have in or over a party to the agreement the rights or powers listed in (a);

(c) undertakings in which an undertaking referred to in (b) directly or indirectly has the rights or powers listed in (a).

3.     Undertakings in which the parties to the agreement or undertakings connected with them jointly have the rights or powers set out in paragraph 2(a) shall be considered to be connected with each of the parties to the agreement.

## Article 5

1.     For the purpose of Article 3(b), the ECU is the unit of account used for drawing up the budget of the Community pursuant to Articles 207 and 209 of the Treaty.

2.     Article 1 shall remain applicable where during any period of two consecutive financial years the total turnover referred to in Article 3(b) is exceeded by no more than 10%.

3.     For the purpose of calculating total turnover within the meaning of Article 3(b), the turnovers achieved during the last financial year by the party to the agreement and connected undertakings in respect of all goods and services, excluding all taxes and other duties, shall be added together. For this purpose, no account shall be taken of dealings between the party to the agreement and its connected undertakings or between its connected undertakings.

# TITLE II
## SPECIAL PROVISIONS FOR BEER SUPPLY AGREEMENTS

## Article 6

1.     Pursuant to Article 85(3) of the Treaty, and subject to Articles 7 to 9 of this Regulation, it is hereby declared that Article 85(1) of the Treaty shall not apply to agreements to which only two undertakings are party and whereby one party, the reseller, agrees with the other, the supplier, in consideration for the according of special commercial or financial advantages, to purchase only from the supplier, an undertaking connected with the supplier or another undertaking entrusted by the supplier with the distribution of his goods, certain beers, or certain beers and certain other drinks, specified in the agreement for resale in premises used for the sale and consumption of drinks and designated in the agreement.

2.     The declaration in paragraph 1 shall also apply where exclusive purchasing obligations of the kind described in paragraph 1 are imposed on the reseller in favour of the supplier by another undertaking which is itself not a supplier.

## Article 7

1.     Apart from the obligation referred to in Article 6, no restriction on competition shall be imposed on the reseller other than—

(a) the obligation not to sell beers and other drinks which are supplied by other undertakings and which are of the same type as the beers or other drinks supplied under the agreement in the premises designated in the agreement;

(b) the obligation, in the event that the reseller sells in the premises designated in the agreement beers which are supplied by other undertakings and which are of a different type from the beers supplied under the agreement, to sell such beers only in bottles, cans or other small packages, unless the sale of such beers in draught form is customary or is necessary to satisfy a sufficient demand from consumers;

(c) the obligation to advertise goods supplied by other undertakings within or outside the premises designated in the agreement only in proportion to the share of these goods in the total turnover realised in the premises.

2.    Beers or other drinks are of different types where they are clearly distinguishable by their composition, appearance or taste.

## Article 8

1.    Article 6 shall not apply where—

(a) the supplier or a connected undertaking imposes on the reseller exclusive purchasing obligations for goods other than drinks or for services;

(b) the supplier restricts the freedom of the reseller to obtain from an undertaking of his choice either services or goods for which neither an exclusive purchasing obligation nor a ban on dealing in competing products may be imposed;

(c) the agreement is concluded for an indefinite duration or for a period of more than five years and the exclusive purchasing obligation relates to specified beers and other drinks;

(d) the agreement is concluded for an indefinite duration or for a period of more than 10 years and the exclusive purchasing obligation relates only to specified beers;

(e) the supplier obliges the reseller to impose the exclusive purchasing obligation on his successor for a longer period than the reseller would himself remain tied to the supplier.

2.    Where the agreement relates to premises which the supplier lets to the reseller or allows the reseller to occupy on some other basis in law or in fact, the following provisions shall also apply—

(a) notwithstanding paragraphs (1)(c) and (d), the exclusive purchasing obligations and bans on dealing in competing products specified in this Title may be imposed on the reseller for the whole period for which the reseller in fact operates the premises;

(b) the agreement must provide for the reseller to have the right to obtain—
— drinks, except beer, supplied under the agreement from other undertakings where these undertakings offer them on more favourable conditions which the supplier does not meet,
— drinks, except beer, which are of the same type as those supplied under the agreement but which bear different trade marks, from other undertakings where the supplier does not offer them.

## Article 9

Articles 2(1) and (3), 3(a) and (b), 4 and 5 shall apply *mutatis mutandis.*

# TITLE III
## SPECIAL PROVISIONS FOR SERVICE-STATION AGREEMENTS

### Article 10

Pursuant to Article 85(3) of the Treaty and subject to Articles 11 to 13 of this Regulation, it is hereby declared that Article 85(1) of the Treaty shall not apply to agreements to which only two undertakings are party and whereby one party, the reseller, agrees with the other, the supplier, in consideration for the according of special commercial or financial advantages, to purchase only from the supplier, an undertaking connected with the supplier or another undertaking entrusted by the supplier with the distribution of his goods, certain petroleum-based motor-vehicle fuels or certain petroleum-based motor-vehicle and other fuels specified in the agreement for resale in a service station designated in the agreement.

### Article 11

Apart from the obligation referred to in Article 10, no restriction on competition shall be imposed on the reseller other than—

    (a) the obligation not to sell motor-vehicle fuel and other fuels which are supplied by other undertakings in the service station designated in the agreement;

    (b) the obligation not to use lubricants or related petroleum-based products which are supplied by other undertakings within the service station designated in the agreement where the supplier or a connected undertaking has made available to the reseller, or financed, a lubrication bay or other motor-vehicle lubrication equipment;

    (c) the obligation to advertise goods supplied by other undertakings within or outside the service station designated in the agreement only in proportion to the share of these goods in the total turnover realised in the service station;

    (d) the obligation to have equipment owned by the supplier or a connected undertaking or financed by the supplier or a connected undertaking serviced by the supplier or an undertaking designated by him.

### Article 12

1.    Article 10 shall not apply where—

    (a) the supplier or a connected undertaking imposes on the reseller exclusive purchasing obligations for goods other than motor-vehicle and other fuels or for services, except in the case of the obligations referred to in Article 11(b) and (d);

    (b) the supplier restricts the freedom of the reseller to obtain from an undertaking of his choice goods or services for which under the provisions of this Title neither an exclusive purchasing obligation nor a ban on dealing in competing products may be imposed;

    (c) the agreement is concluded for an indefinite duration or for a period of more than 10 years;

    (d) the supplier obliges the reseller to impose the exclusive purchasing obligation on his successor for a longer period than the reseller would himself remain tied to the supplier.

2.    Where the agreement relates to a service station which the supplier lets to the reseller, or allows the reseller to occupy on some other basis, in law or in fact, exclusive purchasing obligations or bans on dealing in competing products specified in this Title may, notwithstanding paragraph 1(c), be imposed on the reseller for the whole period for which the reseller in fact operates the premises.

**Article 13**

Articles 2(1) and (3), 3(a) and (b), 4 and 5 of this Regulation shall apply *mutatis mutandis*.

## TITLE IV
## MISCELLANEOUS PROVISIONS

**Article 14**

The Commission may withdraw the benefit of this Regulation, pursuant to Article 7 of Regulation No 19/65/EEC, when it finds in a particular case that an agreement which is exempted by this Regulation nevertheless has certain effects which are incompatible with the conditions set out in Article 85(3) of the Treaty, and in particular where—

(a) the contract goods are not subject, in a substantial part of the common market, to effective competition from identical goods or goods considered by users as equivalent in view of their characteristics, price and intended use;

(b) access by other suppliers to the different stages of distribution in a substantial part of the common market is made difficult to a significant extent;

(c) the supplier without any objectively justified reason—

1. refuses to supply categories of resellers who cannot obtain the contract goods elsewhere on suitable terms or applies to them differing prices or conditions of sale;

2. applies less favourable prices or conditions of sale to resellers bound by an exclusive purchasing obligation as compared with other resellers at the same level of distribution.

**Article 15**

1. In the period 1 July 1983 to 31 December 1986, the prohibition in Article 85(1) of the Treaty shall not apply to agreements of the kind described in Article 1 which either were in force on 1 July 1983 or entered into force between 1 July and 31 December 1983 and which satisfy the exemption conditions of Regulation No 67/67/EEC.

2. In the period 1 July 1983 to 31 December 1988, the prohibition in Article 85(1) of the Treaty shall not apply to agreements of the kinds described in Articles 6 and 10 which either were in force on 1 July 1983 or entered into force between 1 July and 31 December 1983 and which satisfy the exemption conditions of Regulation No 67/67/EEC.

3. In the case of agreements of the kinds described in Articles 6 and 10, which were in force on 1 July 1983 and which expire after 31 December 1988, the prohibition in Article 85(1) of the Treaty shall not apply in the period from 1 January 1989 to the expiry of the agreement but at the latest to the expiry of this Regulation to the extent that the supplier releases the reseller, before 1 January 1989, from all obligations which would prevent the application of the exemption under Titles II and III.

[4. The provisions of the preceding paragraphs shall apply in the same way to the agreements referred to respectively in those paragraphs, which were in force on the date of accession of the Kingdom of Spain and of the Portuguese Republic and which, as a result of accession, fall within the scope of Article 85(1) of the Treaty.]

NOTES
Para 4: added by the 1985 Act of Accession of the Kingdom of Spain and the Portuguese Republic, Annex l(IV)(11).

**[Article 15a**

The prohibition in Article 85(1) of the Treaty shall not apply to agreements which were in existence at the date of accession of Austria, Finland and Sweden and which, by reason of this accession, fall within the scope of Article 85(1) if, within six months from the date of accession, they are so amended that they comply with the conditions laid down in this Regulation. However, this Article shall not apply to agreements which at the date of accession already fall under Article 53(1) of the EEA Agreement.]

NOTES

Inserted by the 1994 Act of Accession of the Kingdom of Norway, the Republic of Austria, the Republic of Finland and the Kingdom of Sweden, Annex I(III)(D)(2), as adjusted by Council Decision 95/1/EC, Annex I(III)(D)(2).

**Article 16**

This Regulation shall not apply to agreements by which the supplier undertakes with the reseller to supply only to the reseller certain goods for resale, in the whole or in a defined part of the Community, and the reseller undertakes with the supplier to purchase these goods only from the supplier.

**Article 17**

This Regulation shall not apply where the parties or connected undertakings, for the purpose of resale in one and the same premises used for the sale and consumption of drinks or service station, enter into agreements both of the kind referred to in Title I and of a kind referred to in Title II or III.

**Article 18**

This Regulation shall apply *mutatis mutandis* to the categories of concerted practices defined in Articles 1, 6 and 10.

**Article 19**

This Regulation shall enter into force on 1 July 1983.

It shall expire on [31 December 1999].

This Regulation shall be binding in its entirety and directly applicable in all Member States.

NOTES

Words in square brackets substituted by Commission Regulation 1582/97/EC, Art 2.

# COMMISSION NOTICE

of 22 June 1983

**concerning Commission Regulations (EEC) No 1983/83 and (EEC) No 1984/83 of 22 June 1983 on the application of Article 85(3) of the Treaty to categories of exclusive distribution and exclusive purchasing agreements**

NOTES

Date of publication in OJ: OJ C101, 13.4.84, p 2.

# I   Introduction

1.      Commission Regulation No 67/67/EEC of 22 March 1967 on the application of Article 85(3) of the Treaty to certain categories of exclusive dealing agreements expired on 30 June 1983 after being in force for over 15 years. With Regulations (EEC) No 1983/83 and (EEC) No 1984/83, the Commission has adapted the block exemption of exclusive distribution agreements and exclusive purchasing agreements to the intervening developments in the common market and in Community law. Several of the provisions in the new Regulations are new. A certain amount of interpretative guidance is therefore called for. This will assist undertakings in bringing their agreements into line with the new legal requirements and will also help ensure that the Regulations are applied uniformly in all the Member States.

2.      In determining how a given provision is to be applied, one must take into account, in addition to the ordinary meaning of the words used, the intention of the provision, as this emerges from the preamble. For further guidance, reference should be made to the principles that have been involved in the case law of the Court of Justice of the European Communities and in the Commission's decisions on individual cases.

3.      This notice sets out the main considerations which will determine the Commission's view of whether or not an exclusive distribution or purchasing agreement is covered by the block exemption. The notice is without prejudice to the jurisdiction of national courts to apply the Regulations, although it may well be of persuasive authority in proceedings before such courts. Nor does the notice necessarily indicate the interpretation which might be given to the provisions by the Court of Justice.

## II   Exclusive distribution and exclusive purchasing agreements (Regulations (EEC) No 1983/83 and (EEC) No 1984/83)

*1.   Similarities and differences*

4.      Regulations (EEC) No 1983/83 and (EEC) No 1984/83 are both concerned with exclusive agreements between two undertakings for the purpose of the resale of goods. Each deals with a particular type of such agreements. Regulation (EEC) No 1983/83 applies to exclusive distribution agreements, Regulation (EEC) No 1984/83 to exclusive purchasing agreements. The distinguishing feature of exclusive distribution agreements is that one party, the supplier, allots to the other, the reseller, a defined territory (the contract territory) on which the reseller has to concentrate his sales effort, and in return undertakes not to supply any other reseller in that territory. In exclusive purchasing agreements, the reseller agrees to purchase the contract goods only from the other party and not from any other supplier. The supplier is entitled to supply other resellers in the same sales area and at the same level of distribution. Unlike an exclusive distributor, the tied reseller is not protected against competition from other resellers who, like himself, receive the contract goods direct from the supplier. On the other hand, he is free of restrictions as to the area over which he may make his sales effort.

5.      In keeping with their common starting point, the Regulations have many provisions that are the same or similar in both Regulations. This is true of the basic provision in Article 1, in which the respective subject-matters of the block exemption, the exclusive supply or purchasing obligation, are defined, and of the exhaustive list of restrictions of competition which may be agreed in addition to the exclusive supply or purchasing obligation (Article 2(1) and (2)), the non-exhaustive enumeration of other obligations which do not prejudice the block exemption (Article 2(3)), the inapplicability

of the block exemption in principle to exclusive agreements between competing manufacturers (Article 3(a) and (b), 4 and 5), the withdrawal of the block exemption in individual cases (Article 6 of Regulation (EEC) No 1983/83 and Article 14 of Regulation (EEC) No 1984/83), the transitional provisions (Article 7 of Regulation (EEC) No 1983/83 and Article 15(1) of Regulation (EEC) No 1984/83), and the inclusion of concerted practices within the scope of the Regulations (Article 9 of Regulation (EEC) No 1983/83 and Article 18 of Regulation (EEC) No 1984/83). In so far as their wording permits, these parallel provisions are to be interpreted in the same way.

6.     Different rules are laid down in the Regulations wherever they need to take account of matters which are peculiar to the exclusive distribution agreements or exclusive purchasing agreements respectively. This applies in Regulation (EEC) No 1983/83, to the provisions regarding the obligation on the exclusive distributor not actively to promote sales outside the contract territory (Article 2(2)(c)) and the inapplicability of the block exemption to agreements which give the exclusive distributor absolute territorial protection (Article 3(c) and (d)) and, in Regulation (EEC) No 1984/83, to the provisions limiting the scope and duration of the block exemption for exclusive purchasing agreements in general (Article 3(c) and (d) and for beer-supply and service-station agreements in particular (Titles II and III).

7.     The scope of the two Regulations has been defined so as to avoid any overlap (Article 16 of Regulation (EEC) No 1984/83).

2.     *Basic provision*

**(Article 1)**

8.     Both Regulations apply only to agreements entered into for the purpose of the resale of goods to which not more than two undertakings are party.

(a)     "For resale"

9.     The notion of resale requires that the goods concerned be disposed of by the purchasing party to others in return for consideration. Agreements on the supply or purchase of goods which the purchasing party transforms or processes into other goods or uses or consumes in manufacturing other goods are not agreements for resale. The same applies to the supply of components which are combined with other components into a different product. The criterion is that the goods distributed by the reseller are the same as those the other party has supplied to him for that purpose. The economic identity of the goods is not affected if the reseller merely breaks up and packages the goods in smaller quantities, or repackages them, before resale.

10.     Where the reseller performs additional operations to improve the quality, durability, appearance or taste of the goods (such as rust-proofing of metals, sterilisation of food or the addition of colouring matter or flavourings to drugs), the position will mainly depend on how much value the operation adds to the goods. Only a slight addition in value can be taken not to change the economic identity of the goods. In determining the precise dividing line in individual cases, trade usage in particular must be considered. The Commission applies the same principles to agreements under which the reseller is supplied with a concentrated extract for a drink which he has to dilute with water, pure alcohol or another liquid and to bottle before reselling.

(b)     "Goods"

11.     Exclusive agreements for the supply of services rather than the resale of goods are not covered by the Regulations. The block exemption still applies, however,

where the reseller provides customer or after-sales services incidentally to the resale of the goods. Nevertheless, a case where the charge for the service is higher than the price of the goods would fall outside the scope of the Regulations.

12.     The hiring out of goods in return for payment comes closer, economically speaking, to a resale of goods than to provision of services. The Commission therefore regards exclusive agreements under which the purchasing party hires out or leases to others the goods supplied to him as covered by the Regulations.

(c)     "Only two undertakings party"

13.     To be covered by the block exemption, the exclusive distribution or purchasing agreement must be between only one supplier and one reseller in each case. Several undertakings forming one economic unit count as one undertaking.

14.     This limitation on the number of undertakings that may be party relates solely to the individual agreement. A supplier does not lose the benefit of the block exemption if he enters into exclusive distribution or purchasing agreements covering the same goods with several resellers.

15.     The supplier may delegate the performance of his contractual obligations to a connected or independent undertaking which he has entrusted with the distribution of his goods, so that the reseller has to purchase the contract goods from the latter undertaking. This principle is expressly mentioned only in Regulation (EEC) No 1984/83 (Article 1, 6, and 10), because the question of delegation arises mainly in connection with exclusive purchasing agreements. It also applies, however, to exclusive distribution agreements under Regulation (EEC) No 1983/83.

16.     The involvement of undertakings other than the contracting parties must be confined to the execution of deliveries. The parties may accept exclusive supply or purchase obligations only for themselves, and not impose them on third parties, since otherwise more than two undertakings would be party to the agreement. The obligation of the parties to ensure that the obligations they have accepted are respected by connected undertakings is, however, covered by the block exemption.

3.     *Other restrictions on competition that are exempted*

## (Article 2(1) and (2))

17.     Apart from the exclusive supply obligation (Regulation (EEC) No 1983/83) or exclusive purchase obligation (Regulation (EEC) No 1984/83), obligations defined in Article 1 which must be present if the block exemption is to apply, the only other restrictions of competition that may be agreed by the parties are those set out in Article 2(1) and (2). If they agree on further obligations restrictive of competition, the agreement as a whole is no longer covered by the block exemption and requires individual exemption. For example, an agreement will exceed the bounds of the Regulations if the parties relinquish the possibility of independently determining their prices or conditions of business or undertake to refrain from, or even prevent, cross-border trade, which the Regulations expressly state must not be impeded. Among other clauses which in general are not permissible under the Regulations are those which impede the reseller in his free choice of customers.

18.     The obligations restrictive of competition that are exempted may be agreed only for the duration of the agreement. This also applies to restrictions accepted by the supplier or reseller on competing with the other party.

4.	*Obligations upon the reseller which do not prejudice the block exemption*

**(Article 2(3))**

19.	The obligations cited in this provision are examples of clauses which generally do not restrict competition. Undertakings are therefore free to include one, several or all of these obligations in their agreements. However, the obligations may not be formulated or applied in such a way as to take on the character of restrictions of competition that are not permitted. To forestall this danger, Article 2(3)(b) of Regulation (EEC) No 1984/83 expressly allows minimum purchase obligations only for goods that are subject to an exclusive purchasing obligation.

20.	As part of the obligation to take measures for promotion of sales and in particular to maintain a distribution network (Article 2(3)(c) of Regulation (EEC) No 1983/83 and Article 2(3)(d) of Regulation (EEC) No 1984/83), the reseller may be forbidden to supply the contract goods to unsuitable dealers. Such clauses are unobjectionable if admission to the distribution network is based on objective criteria of a qualitative nature relating to the professional qualifications of the owner of the business or his staff or the suitability of his business premises, if the criteria are the same for all potential dealers, and if the criteria are actually applied in a non-discriminatory manner. Distribution systems which do not fulfil these conditions are not covered by the block exemption.

5.	*Inapplicability of the block exemption to exclusive agreements between competing manufacturers*

**(Articles 3(a) and (b), 4 and 5)**

21.	The block exemption does not apply if either the parties themselves or undertakings connected with them are manufacturers, manufacture goods belonging to the same product market, and enter into exclusive distribution or purchasing agreements with one another in respect of those goods. Only identical or equivalent goods are regarded as belonging to the same product market. The goods in question must be interchangeable. Whether or not this is the case must be judged from the vantage point of the user, normally taking the characteristics, price and intended use of the goods together. In certain cases, however, goods can form a separate market on the basis of their characteristics, their price or their intended use alone. This is true especially where consumer preferences have developed. The above provisions are applicable regardless of whether or not the parties or the undertakings connected with them are based in the Community and whether or not they are already actually in competition with one another in the relevant goods inside or outside the Community.

22.	In principle, both reciprocal and non-reciprocal exclusive agreements between competing manufacturers are not covered by the block exemption and are therefore subject to individual scrutiny of their compatibility with Article 85 of the Treaty, but there is an exception for non-reciprocal agreements of the abovementioned kind where one or both of the parties are undertakings with a total annual turnover of no more than 100 million ECU (Article 3(b)). Annual turnover is used as a measure of the economic strength of the undertakings involved. Therefore, the aggregate turnover from goods and services of all types, and not only from the contract goods, is to be taken. Turnover taxes and other turnover-related levies are not included in turnover. Where a party belongs to a group of connected undertakings, the world-wide turnover of the group, excluding intragroup sales (Article 5(3)), is to be used.

23.    The total turnover limit can be exceeded during any period of two successive financial years by up to 10% without loss of the block exemption. The block exemption is lost if, at the end of the second financial year, the total turnover over the preceding two years has been over 220 million ECU (Article 5(2)).

6.    *Withdrawal of the block exemption in individual cases*

## (Article 6 of Regulation (EEC) No 1983/83 and Article 14 of Regulation (EEC) No 1984/83)

24.    The situations described are meant as illustrations of the sort of situations in which the Commission can exercise its powers under Article 7 of Council Regulation No 19/65/EEC to withdraw a block exemption. The benefit of the block exemption can only be withdrawn by a decision in an individual case following proceedings under Regulation No 17. Such a decision cannot have retroactive effect. It may be coupled with an individual exemption subject to conditions or obligations or, in an extreme case, with the finding of an infringement and an order to bring it to an end.

7.    *Transitional provisions*

## (Article 7 of Regulation (EEC) No 1983/83 and Article 15(1) of Regulation (EEC) No 1984/83)

25.    Exclusive distribution or exclusive purchasing agreements which were concluded and entered into force before 1 January 1984 continue to be exempted under the provisions of Regulation No 67/67/EEC until 31 December 1986. Should the parties wish to apply such agreements beyond 1 January 1987, they will either have to bring them into line with the provisions of the new Regulations or to notify them to the Commission. Special rules apply in the case of beer-supply and service-station agreements (see paragraphs 64 and 65 below).

8.    *Concerted practices*

## (Article 9 of Regulation (EEC) No 1983/83 and Article 18 of Regulation (EEC) No 1984/83)

26.    These provisions bring within the scope of the Regulations exclusive distribution and purchasing arrangements which are operated by undertakings but are not the subject of a legally-binding agreement.

## III    Exclusive distribution agreements (Regulation (EEC) No 1983/83)

1.    *Exclusive supply obligation*

## (Article 1)

27.    The exclusive supply obligation does not prevent the supplier from providing the contract goods to other resellers who afterwards sell them in the exclusive distributor's territory. It makes no difference whether the other dealers concerned are established outside or inside the territory. The supplier is not in breach of his obligation to the exclusive distributor provided that he supplies the resellers who wish to sell the contract goods in the territory only at their request and that the goods are handed over outside the territory. It does not matter whether the reseller takes delivery of the goods himself or through an intermediary, such as a freight forwarder. However, supplies of this nature are only permissible if the reseller and not the supplier pays the transport costs of the goods into the contract territory.

28.    The goods supplied to the exclusive distributor must be intended for resale in the contract territory. This basic requirement does not, however, mean that the exclusive distributor cannot sell the contract goods to customers outside his contract territory should he receive orders from them. Under Article 2(2)(c), the supplier can prohibit him only from seeking customers in other areas, but not from supplying them.

29.    It would also be incompatible with the Regulation for the exclusive distributor to be restricted to supplying only certain categories of customers (eg specialist retailers) in his contract territory and prohibited from supplying other categories (eg department stores), which are supplied by other resellers appointed by the supplier for that purpose.

2.    *Restriction on competition by the supplier*

**(Article 2(1))**

30.    The restriction on the supplier himself supplying the contract goods to final users in the exclusive distributor's contract territory need not be absolute. Clauses permitting the supplier to supply certain customers in the territory—with or without payment of compensation to the exclusive distributor—are compatible with the block exemption provided the customers in question are not resellers. The supplier remains free to supply the contract goods outside the contract territory to final users based in the territory. In this case the position is the same as for dealers (see paragraph 27 above).

3.    *Inapplicability of the block exemption in cases of absolute territorial protection*

**(Articles 3(c) and (d))**

31.    The block exemption cannot be claimed for agreements that give the exclusive distributor absolute territorial protection. If the situation described in Article 3(c) obtains, the parties must ensure either that the contract goods can be sold in the contract territory by parallel importers or that users have a real possibility of obtaining them from undertakings outside the contract territory, if necessary outside the Community, at the prices and on the terms there prevailing. The supplier can represent an alternative source of supply for the purposes of this provision if he is prepared to supply the contract goods on request to final users located in the contract territory.

32.    Article 3(d) is chiefly intended to safeguard the freedom of dealers and users to obtain the contract goods in other Member States. Action to impede imports into the Community from third countries will only lead to loss of the block exemption if there are no alternative sources of supply in the Community. This situation can arise especially where the exclusive distributor's contract territory covers the whole or the major part of the Community.

33.    The block exemption ceases to apply as from the moment that either of the parties takes measures to impede parallel imports into the contract territory. Agreements in which the supplier undertakes with the exclusive distributor to prevent his other customers from supplying into the contract territory are ineligible for the block exemption from the outset. This is true even if the parties agree only to prevent imports into the Community from third countries. In this case it is immaterial whether or not there are alternative sources of supply in the Community. The inapplicability of the block exemption follows from the mere fact that the agreement contains restrictions on competition which are not covered by Article 2(1).

## IV    Exclusive purchasing agreements (Regulation (EEC) No 1984/83)

### 1.    *Structure of the Regulation*

34.    Title I of the Regulation contains general provisions for exclusive purchasing agreements and Titles II and III special provisions for beer-supply and service-station agreements. The latter types of agreement are governed exclusively by the special provisions, some of which (Articles 9 and 13), however, refer to some of the general provisions, Article 17 also excludes the combination of agreements of the kind referred to in Title I with those of the kind referred to in Titles II or III to which the same undertakings or undertakings connected with them are party. To prevent any avoidance of the special provisions for beer-supply and service-station agreements, it is also made clear that the provisions governing the exclusive distribution of goods do not apply to agreements entered into for the resale of drinks on premises used for the sale or consumption of beer or for the resale of petroleum products in service stations (Article 8 of Regulation (EEC) No 1983/83).

### 2.    *Exclusive purchasing obligation*

### (Article 1)

35.    The Regulation only covers agreements whereby the reseller agrees to purchase all his requirements for the contract goods from the other party. If the purchasing obligation relates to only part of such requirements, the block exemption does not apply. Clauses which allow the reseller to obtain the contract goods from other suppliers, should these sell them more cheaply or on more favourable terms than the other party are still covered by the block exemption. The same applies to clauses releasing the reseller from his exclusive purchasing obligation should the other party be unable to supply.

36.    The contract goods must be specified by brand or denomination in the agreement. Only if this is done will it be possible to determine the precise scope of the reseller's exclusive purchasing obligation (Article 1) and of the ban on dealing in competing products (Article 2(2)).

### 3.    *Restriction on competition by the supplier*

### (Article 2(1))

37.    This provision allows the reseller to protect himself against direct competition from the supplier in his principal sales area. The reseller's principal sales area is determined by his normal business activity. It may be more closely defined in the agreement. However, the supplier cannot be forbidden to supply dealers who obtain the contract goods outside this area and afterwards resell them to customers inside it or to appoint other resellers in the area.

### 4.    *Limits of the block exemption*

### (Article 3(c) and (d))

38.    Article 3(c) provides that the exclusive purchasing obligation can be agreed for one or more products, but in the latter case the products must be so related as to be thought of as belonging to the same range of goods. The relationship can be founded on technical (eg, a machine, accessories and spare parts for it) or commercial grounds (eg several products used for the same purpose) or on usage in the trade (different goods that are customarily offered for sale together). In the latter case, regard must be

had to the usual practice at the reseller's level of distribution on the relevant market, taking into account all relevant dealers and not only particular forms of distribution. Exclusive purchasing agreements covering goods which do not belong together can only be exempted from the competition rules by an individual decision.

39.     Under Article 3(d), exclusive purchasing agreements concluded for an indefinite period are not covered by the block exemption. Agreements which specify a fixed term but are automatically renewable unless one of the parties gives notice to terminate are to be considered to have been concluded for an indefinite period.

## V     Beer-supply agreements (Title II of Regulation (EEC) No 1984/83)

[1.     *Agreements of minor importance*

40.     It is recalled that the Commission's notice on agreements of minor importance states that the Commission holds the view that agreements between undertakings do not fall under the prohibition of Article 85(1) of the EEC Treaty if certain conditions as regards market share and turnover are met by the undertakings concerned. Thus, it is evident that when an undertaking, brewery or wholesaler, surpasses the limits as laid down in the above notice, the agreements concluded by it may fall under Article 85(1) of the EEC Treaty. The notice, however, does not apply where in a relevant market competition is restricted by the cumulative effects of parallel networks of similar agreements which would not individually fall under Article 85(1) of the EEC Treaty if the notice was applicable. Since the markets for beer will frequently be characterised by the existence of cumulative effects, it seems appropriate to determine which agreements can nevertheless be considered *de minimis*.

The Commission is of the opinion that an exclusive beer supply agreement concluded by a brewery, in the sense of Article 6, and including Article 8(2) of Regulation (EEC) 1984/83 does not, in general, fall under Article 85(1) of the EEC Treaty if—

—     the market share of that brewery is not higher than 1% on the national market for the resale of beer in premises used for the sale and consumption of drinks, and

—     if that brewery does not produce more than 200,000 hl of beer per annum.

However, these principles do not apply if the agreement in question is concluded for more than 7 and a half years in as far as it covers beer and other drinks, and for 15 years if it covers only beer.

In order to establish the market share of the brewery and its annual production, the provisions of Article 4(2) of Regulation (EEC) 1984/83 apply.

As regards exclusive beer supply agreements in the sense of Article 6, and including Article 8(2) of Regulation (EEC) 1984/83 which are concluded by wholesalers, the above principles apply *mutatis mutandis* by taking account of the position of the brewery whose beer is the main subject of the agreement in question.

The present communication does not preclude that in individual cases even agreements between undertakings which do not fulfil the above criteria, in particular where the number of outlets tied to them is limited as compared to the number of outlets existing on the market, may still have only a negligible effect on trade between Member States or on competition, and would therefore not be caught by Article 85(1) of the EEC Treaty.

Neither does this communication in any way prejudice the application of national law to the agreements covered by it.]

NOTES

Sub-heading 1 and para 40 inserted, original sub-headings 1–3 renumbered as 2–4, and original paras 40–66 renumbered as paras 41–67, by the EEC Commission Notice of 13 May 1992. The modification was expressed to be undertaken consequent to the judgment of the Court of Justice in case C-234/89 *Delimitis v Henninger Bräu, AG.*

[2.]    *Exclusive purchasing obligation*

## (Article 6)

[41.]    The beers and other drinks covered by the exclusive purchasing obligation must be specified by brand or denomination in the agreement. An exclusive purchasing obligation can only be imposed on the reseller for drinks which the supplier carries at the time the contract takes effect and provided that they are supplied in the quantities required, at sufficiently regular intervals and at prices and on conditions allowing normal sales to the consumer. Any extension of the exclusive purchasing obligation to drinks not specified in the agreement requires an additional agreement, which must likewise satisfy the requirements of Title II of the Regulation. A change in the brand or denomination of a drink which in other respects remains unchanged does not constitute such an extension of the exclusive purchasing obligation.

[42.]    The exclusive purchasing obligation can be agreed in respect of one or more premises used for the sale and consumption of drinks which the reseller runs at the time the contract takes effect. The name and location of the premises must be stated in the agreement. Any extension of the exclusive purchasing obligation to other such premises requires an additional agreement, which must likewise satisfy the provisions of Title II of the Regulation.

[43.]    The concept of "premises used for the sale and consumption of drinks" covers any licensed premises used for this purpose. Private clubs are also included. Exclusive purchasing agreements between the supplier and the operator of an off-licence shop are governed by the provisions of Title I of the Regulation.

[44.]    Special commercial or financial advantages are those going beyond what the reseller could normally expect under an agreement. The explanations given in the 13th recital are illustrations. Whether or not the supplier is affording the reseller special advantages depends on the nature, extent and duration of the obligations undertaken by the parties. In doubtful cases usage in the trade is the decisive element.

[45.]    The reseller can enter into exclusive purchasing obligations both with a brewery in respect of beers of a certain type and with a drinks wholesaler in respect of beers of another type and/or other drinks. The two agreements can be combined into one document. Article 6 also covers cases where the drinks wholesaler performs several functions at once, signing the first agreement on the brewery's and the second on his own behalf and also undertaking delivery of all the drinks. The provision of Title II do not apply to the contractual relations between the brewery and the drinks wholesaler.

[46.]    Article 6(2) makes the block exemption also applicable to cases in which the supplier affords the owner of premises financial or other help in equipping them as a public house, restaurant, etc, and in return the owner imposes on the buyer or tenant of the premises an exclusive purchasing obligation in favour of the supplier. A similar situation, economically speaking, is the transmission of an exclusive purchasing obligation from the owner of a public house to his successor. Under Article 8(1)(e) this is also, in principle, permissible.

[3.]     *Other restrictions of competition that are exempted*

## (Article 7)

[47.]   The list of permitted obligations given in Article 7 is exhaustive. If any further obligations restricting competition are imposed on the reseller, the exclusive purchasing agreement as a whole is no longer covered by the block exemption.

[48.]   The obligation referred to in paragraph 1(a) applies only so long as the supplier is able to supply the beers or other drinks specified in the agreement and subject to the exclusive purchasing obligation in sufficient quantities to cover the demand the reseller anticipates for the products from his customers.

[49.]   Under paragraph 1(b), the reseller is entitled to sell beer of other types in draught form if the other party has tolerated this in the past. If this is not the case, the reseller must indicate that there is sufficient demand from his customers to warrant the sale of other draught beers. The demand must be deemed sufficient if it can be satisfied without a simultaneous drop in sales of the beers specified in the exclusive purchasing agreement. It is definitely not sufficient if sales of the additional draught beer turn out to be so slow that there is a danger of its quality deteriorating. It is for the reseller to assess the potential demand of his customers for other types of beer; after all, be bears the risk if his forecasts are wrong.

[50.]   The provision in paragraph 1(c) is not only intended to ensure the possibility of advertising products supplied by other undertakings to the minimum extent necessary in any given circumstances. The advertising of such products should also reflect their relative importance *vis-à-vis* the competing products of the supplier who is party to the exclusive purchasing agreement. Advertising for products which the public house has just begun to sell may not be excluded or unduly impeded.

[51.]   The Commission believes that the designations of types customary in inter-State trade and within the individual Member States may afford useful pointers to the interpretation of Article 7(2). Nevertheless the alternative criteria stated in the provision itself are decisive. In doubtful cases, whether or not two beers are clearly distinguishable by their composition, appearance or taste depends on custom at the place where the public house is situated. The parties may, if they wish, jointly appoint an expert to decide the matter.

[4.]     *Agreements excluded from the block exemption*

## (Article 8)

[52.]   The reseller's right to purchase drinks from third parties may be restricted only to the extent allowed by Articles 6 and 7. In his purchases of goods other than drinks and in his procurement of services which are not directly connected with the supply of drinks by the other party, the reseller must remain free to choose his supplier. Under Article 8(1)(a) and (b), any action by the other party or by an undertaking connected with or appointed by him or acting at his instigation or with his agreement to prevent the reseller exercising his rights in this regard will entail the loss of the block exemption. For the purposes of these provisions it makes no difference whether the reseller's freedom is restricted by contract, informal understanding, economic pressures or other practical measures.

[53.]   The installation of amusement machines in tenanted public houses may by agreement be made subject to the owner's permission. The owner may refuse permission on the ground that this would impair the character of the premises or he may restrict the tenant to particular types of machines. However, the practice of some owners of tenanted public houses to allow the tenant to conclude contracts for the installation of such machines only with certain undertakings which the owner recommends is, as a rule, incompatible with this Regulation, unless the undertakings are selected on the basis of objective criteria of a qualitative nature that are the same for all potential providers of such equipment and are applied in a non-discriminatory manner. Such criteria may refer to the reliability of the undertaking and its staff and the quality of the services it provides. The supplier may not prevent a public house tenant from purchasing amusement machines rather than renting them.

[54.] The limitation of the duration of the agreement in Article 8(1)(c) and (d) does not affect the parties' right to renew their agreement in accordance with the provisions of Title II of the Regulation.

[55.] Article 8(2)(b) must be interpreted in the light both of the aims of the Community competition rules and of the general legal principle whereby contracting parties must exercise their rights in good faith.

[56.] Whether or not a third undertaking offers certain drinks covered by the exclusive purchasing obligation on more favourable terms than the other party for the purposes of the first indent of Article 8(2)(b) is to be judged in the first instance on the basis of a comparison of prices. This should take into account the various factors that go to determine the prices. If a more favourable offer is available and the tenant wishes to accept it, he must inform the other party of his intentions without delay so that the other party has an opportunity of matching the terms offered by the third undertaking. If the other party refuses to do so or fails to let the tenant have his decision within a short period, the tenant is entitled to purchase the drinks from the other undertaking. The Commission will ensure that exercise of the brewery's or drinks wholesaler's right to match the prices quoted by another supplier does not make it significantly harder for other suppliers to enter the market.

[57.] The tenant's right provided for in the second indent of Article 8(2)(b) to purchase drinks of another brand or denomination from third undertakings obtains in cases where the other party does not offer them. Here the tenant is not under a duty to inform the other party of his intentions.

[58.] The tenant's rights arising from Article 8(2)(b) override any obligation to purchase minimum quantities imposed upon him under Article 9 in conjunction with Article 2(3)(b) to the extent that this is necessary to allow the tenant full exercise of those rights.

## VI  Service-station agreements (Title III of Regulation (EEC) No 1984/83)

1.  *Exclusive purchasing obligation*

**(Article 10)**

[59.] The exclusive purchasing obligation can cover either motor vehicle fuels (eg, petrol, diesel fuel, LPG, kerosene) alone or motor vehicle fuels and other fuels (eg, heating oil, bottled gas, paraffin). All the goods concerned must be petroleum-based products.

[60.] The motor vehicle fuels covered by the exclusive purchasing obligations must be for use in motor-powered land or water vehicles or aircraft. The term 'service station' is to be interpreted in a correspondingly wide sense.

[61.]   The Regulation applies to petrol stations adjoining public roads and fuelling installations on private property not open to public traffic.

2.      *Other restrictions on competition that are exempted*

**(Article 11)**

[62.]   Under Article 11(b) only the use of lubricants and related petroleum-based products supplied by other undertakings can be prohibited. This provision refers to the servicing and maintenance of motor vehicles, ie, to the reseller's activity in the field of provision of services. It does not affect the reseller's freedom to purchase the said products from other undertakings for resale in the service station. The petroleum-based products related to lubricants referred to in paragraph (b) are additives and brake fluids.

[63.]   For the interpretation of Article 11(c), the considerations stated in paragraph 49 above apply by analogy.

3.      *Agreements excluded from the block exemption*

**(Article 12)**

[64.]   These provisions are analogous to those of Article 8(1)(a),(b),(d) and (e) and 8(2)(a). Reference is therefore made to paragraphs 51 and 53 above.

## VII   Transitional provisions for beer-supply and service-station agreements (Article 15(2) and (3))

[65.]   Under Article 15(2), all beer-supply and service-station agreements which were concluded and entered into force before 1 January 1984 remain covered by the provisions of Regulation No 67/67/EEC until 31 December 1988. From 1 January 1989 they must comply with the provisions of Titles II and III of Regulation (EEC) No 1984/83. Under Article 15(3), in the case of agreements which were in force on 1 July 1983, the same principle applies except that the 10-year maximum duration for such agreements laid down in Article 8(1)(d) and Article 12(1)(c) may be exceeded.

[66.]   The sole requirement for the eligible beer-supply and service-station agreements to continue to enjoy the block exemption beyond 1 January 1989 is that they be brought into line with the new provisions. It is left to the undertakings concerned how they do so. One way is for the parties to agree to amend the original agreement, another for the supplier unilaterally to release the reseller from all obligations that would prevent the application of the block exemption after 1 January 1989. The latter method is only mentioned in Article 15(3) in relation to agreements in force on 1 July 1983. However, there is no reason why this possibility should not also be open to parties to agreements entered into between 1 July 1983 and 1 January 1984.

[67.]   Parties lose the benefit of application of the transitional provisions if they extend the scope of their agreement as regards persons, places or subject matter, or incorporate into it additional obligations restrictive of competition. The agreement then counts as a new agreement. The same applies if the parties substantially change the nature or extent of their obligations to one another. A substantial change in this sense includes a revision of the purchase price of the goods supplied to the reseller or of the rent for a public house or service station which goes beyond mere adjustment to the changing economic environment.

# COMMISSION REGULATION

of 19 December 1984

## on the application of Article 85(3) of the Treaty to categories of specialisation agreements

## (417/85/EEC)

NOTES

Date of publication in OJ: OJ L53, 22.2.85, p 1.

THE COMMISSION OF THE EUROPEAN COMMUNITIES,

Having regard to the Treaty establishing the European Economic Community,

Having regard to Council Regulation (EEC) No 2821/71 of 20 December 1971 on the application of Article 85(3) of the Treaty to categories of agreements, decisions and concerted practices, as last amended by the Act of Accession of Greece, and in particular Article 1 thereof,

Having published a draft of this Regulation,

Having consulted the Advisory Committee on Restrictive Practices and Dominant Positions,

Whereas—

(1) Regulation (EEC) No 2821/71 empowers the Commission to apply Article 85(3) of the Treaty by Regulation to certain categories of agreements, decisions and concerted practices falling within the scope of Article 85(1) which relate to specialisation, including agreements necessary for achieving it.

(2) Agreements on specialisation in present or future production may fall within the scope of Article 85(1).

(3) Agreements on specialisation in production generally contribute to improving the production or distribution of goods, because undertakings concerned can concentrate on the manufacture of certain products and thus operate more efficiently and supply the products more cheaply. It is likely that, given effective competition, consumers will receive a fair share of the resulting benefit.

(4) Such advantages can arise equally from agreements whereby each participant gives up the manufacture of certain products in favour of another participant and from agreements whereby the participants undertake to manufacture certain products or have them manufactured only jointly.

(5) The Regulation must specify what restrictions of competition may be included in specialisation agreements. The restrictions of competition that are permitted in the Regulation in addition to reciprocal obligations to give up manufacture are normally essential for the making and implementation of such agreements. These restrictions are therefore, in general, indispensable for the attainment of the desired advantages for the participating undertakings and consumers. It may be left to the parties to decide which of these provisions they include in their agreements.

(6) The exemption must be limited to agreements which do not give rise to the possibility of eliminating competition in respect of a substantial part of the products in question. The Regulation must therefore apply only as long as the market share and turnover of the participating undertakings do not exceed a certain limit.

(7) It is, however, appropriate to offer undertakings which exceed the turnover limit set in the Regulation a simplified means of obtaining the legal certainty provided by the block exemption. This must allow the Commission to exercise effective supervision as well as simplifying its administration of such agreements.

(8) In order to facilitate the conclusion of long-term specialisation agreements, which can have a bearing on the structure of the participating undertakings, it is appropriate to fix the period of validity of the Regulation at 13 years. If the circumstances on the basis of which the Regulation was adopted should change significantly within this period, the Commission will make the necessary amendments.

(9) Agreements, decisions and concerted practices which are automatically exempted pursuant to this Regulation need not be notified. Undertakings may none the less in an individual case request a decision pursuant to Council Regulation No 17, as last amended by the Act of Accession of Greece.

HAS ADOPTED THIS REGULATION—

## Article 1

Pursuant to Article 85(3) of the Treaty and subject to the provisions of this Regulation, it is hereby declared that Article 85(1) of the Treaty shall not apply to agreements on specialisation whereby, for the duration of the agreement, undertakings accept reciprocal obligations—

(a) not to manufacture certain products or to have them manufactured, but to leave it to other parties to manufacture the products or have them manufactured; or

(b) to manufacture certain products or have them manufactured only jointly.

## Article 2

1.  [Article 1 shall also apply to the following restrictions of competition—]

(a) an obligation not to conclude with third parties specialisation agreements relating to identical products or to products considered by users to be equivalent in view of their characteristics, price and intended use;

(b) an obligation to procure products which are the subject of the specialisation exclusively from another party, a joint undertaking or an undertaking jointly charged with their manufacture, except where they are obtainable on more favourable terms elsewhere and the other party, the joint undertaking or the undertaking charged with manufacture is not prepared to offer the same terms;

[(c) an obligation to grant other parties the exclusive right, within the whole or a defined area of the common market, to distribute products which are the subject of the specialisation, provided that intermediaries and users can also obtain the products from other suppliers and the parties do not render it difficult for intermediaries or users to thus obtain the products;]

[(d) an obligation to grant one of the parties the exclusive right to distribute products which are the subject of the specialisation provided that that party does not distribute products of a third undertaking which compete with the contract products;

(e) an obligation to grant the exclusive right to distribute products which are the subject of the specialisation to a joint undertaking or to a third undertaking, provided that the joint undertaking or third undertaking does not manufacture or distribute products which compete with the contract products;

(f) an obligation to grant the exclusive right to distribute within the whole or a defined area of the common market the products which are the subject of the specialisation to joint undertakings or third undertakings which do not manufacture or distribute products which compete with the contract products, provided that users and intermediaries can also obtain the contract products from other suppliers and that neither the parties nor the joint undertakings or third undertakings entrusted with the exclusive distribution of the contract products render it difficult for users and intermediaries to thus obtain the contract products.]

2.      Article 1 shall also apply where the parties undertake obligations of the types referred to in paragraph 1 but with a more limited scope than is permitted by that paragraph.

[2a.    Article 1 shall not apply if restrictions of competition other than those set out in paragraphs 1 and 2 are imposed upon the parties by agreement, decision or concerted practice.]

3.      Article 1 shall apply notwithstanding that any of the following obligations, in particular, are imposed—
> (a)  an obligation to supply other parties with products which are the subject of the specialisation and in so doing to observe minimum standards of quality;
> (b)  an obligation to maintain minimum stocks of products which are the subject of the specialisation and of replacement parts for them;
> (c)  an obligation to provide customer and guarantee services for products which are the subject of the specialisation.

NOTES
> Para 1: first words in square brackets substituted, sub-para (c) substituted, and sub-paras (d)–(f) inserted, by EEC Commission Regulation No 151/93, Art 1(1)–(3), with retroactive effect from the time at which the conditions for the application of the group exemption were fulfilled
> Para 2a: inserted by EEC Commission Regulation No 151/93, Art 1(4), with retroactive effect from the time at which the conditions for the application of the group exemption were fulfilled.

## [Article 3

1.      Article 1 shall apply only if—
> (a)  the products which are the subject of the specialisation together with the participating undertakings' other products which are considered by users to be equivalent in view of their characteristics, price and intended use do not represent more than 20% of the market for all such products in the common market or a substantial part thereof; and
> (b)  the aggregate turnover of all the participating undertakings does not exceed ECU 1 000 million.

2.      If pursuant to point (d), (e) or (f) of Article 2(1), one of the parties, a joint undertaking, a third undertaking or more than one joint undertaking or third undertaking are entrusted with the distribution of the products which are the subject of the specialisation, Article 1 shall apply only if—
> (a)  the products which are the subject of the specialisation together with the participating undertakings' other products which are considered by users to be equivalent in view of their characteristics, price and intended use do not represent more than 10% of the market for all such products in the common market or a substantial part thereof; and
> (b)  the aggregate annual turnover of all the participating undertakings does not exceed ECU 1 000 million.

3.      Article 1 shall continue to apply if the market shares and turnover referred to in paragraphs 1 and 2 are exceeded during any period of two consecutive years by not more than one-tenth.

4.      Where the limits laid down in paragraph 3 are also exceeded, Article 1 shall continue to apply for a period of six months following the end of the financial year during which they were exceeded.]

NOTES

Substituted by EEC Commission Regulation No 151/93, Art 1(5), with retroactive effect from the time at which the conditions for the application of the group exemption were fulfilled.

## Article 4

1.    The exemption provided for in Article 1 shall also apply to agreements involving participating undertakings whose aggregate turnover exceeds the limits laid down in [Article 3(1)(b), 2(b) and (3)], on condition that the agreements in question are notified to the Commission in accordance with the provisions of Commission Regulation No 27, and that the Commission does not oppose such exemption within a period of six months.

2.    The period of six months shall run from the date on which the notification is received by the Commission. Where, however, the notification is made by registered post, the period shall run from the date shown on the postmark of the place of posting.

3.    Paragraph 1 shall apply only if—
(a)  express reference is made to this Article in the notification or in a communication accompanying it; and
(b)  the information furnished with the notification is complete and in accordance with the facts.

4.    The benefit of paragraph 1 may be claimed for agreements notified before the entry into force of this Regulation by submitting a communication to the Commission referring expressly to this Article and to the notification. Paragraphs 2 and 3(b) shall apply *mutatis mutandis*.

5.    The Commission may oppose the exemption. It shall oppose exemption if it receives a request to do so from a Member State within three months of the forwarding to the Member State of the notification referred to in paragraph 1 or of the communication referred to in paragraph 4. This request must be justified on the basis of considerations relating to the competition rules of the Treaty.

6.    The Commission may withdraw the opposition to the exemption at any time. However, where the opposition was raised at the request of a Member State and this request is maintained, it may be withdrawn only after consultation of the Advisory Committee on Restrictive Practices and Dominant Positions.

7.    If the opposition is withdrawn because the undertakings concerned have shown that the conditions of Article 85(3) are fulfilled, the exemption shall apply from the date of notification.

8.    If the opposition is withdrawn because the undertakings concerned have amended the agreement so that the conditions of Article 85(3) are fulfilled, the exemption shall apply from the date on which the amendments take effect.

9.    If the Commission opposes exemption and the opposition is not withdrawn, the effects of the notification shall be governed by the provisions of Regulation No 17.

NOTES

Para 1: words in square brackets substituted by EEC Commission Regulation No 151/93, Art 1(6), with retroactive effect from the time at which the conditions for the application of the group exemption were fulfilled.

## Article 5

1.     Information acquired pursuant to Article 4 shall be used only for the purposes of this Regulation.

2.     The Commission and the authorities of the Member States, their officials and other servants shall not disclose information acquired by them pursuant to this Regulation of a kind that is covered by the obligation of professional secrecy.

3.     Paragraphs 1 and 2 shall not prevent publication of general information or surveys which do not contain information relating to particular undertakings or associations of undertakings.

## Article 6

For the purpose of calculating total annual turnover within the meaning of Article 3(1)(b) [and (2)(b)], the turnovers achieved during the last financial year by the participating undertakings in respect of all goods and services excluding tax shall be added together. For this purpose, no account shall be taken of dealings between the participating undertakings or between these undertakings and a third undertaking jointly charged with manufacture [or sale].

NOTES
   Words in square brackets inserted by EEC Commission Regulation No 151/93, Art 1(7), (8), with retroactive effect from the time at which the conditions for the application of the group exemption were fulfilled.

## Article 7

1.     [For the purposes of Article 3(1) and (2), and Article 6, participating undertakings are—]
   (a)   undertakings party to the agreement;
   (b)   undertakings in which a party to the agreement, directly or indirectly—
         —   owns more than half the capital or business assets,
         —   has the power to exercise more than half the voting rights,
         —   has the power to appoint at least half the members of the supervisory board, board of management or bodies legally representing the undertakings, or
         —   has the right to manage the affairs;
   (c)   undertakings which directly or indirectly have in or over a party to the agreement the rights or powers listed in (b);
   (d)   undertakings in or over which an undertaking referred to in (c) directly or indirectly has the rights or powers listed in (b).

2.     Undertakings in which the undertakings referred to in paragraph 1(a) to (d) directly or indirectly jointly have the rights or powers set out in paragraph 1(b) shall also be considered to be participating undertakings.

NOTES
   Para 1: words in square brackets substituted by EEC Commission Regulation No 151/93, Art 1(9), with retroactive effect from the time at which the conditions for the application of the group exemption were fulfilled.

## Article 8

The Commission may withdraw the benefit of this Regulation, pursuant to Article 7 of Regulation (EEC) No 2821/71, where it finds in a particular case that an agreement exempted by this Regulation nevertheless has effects which are incompatible with the conditions set out in Article 85(3) of the Treaty, and in particular where—

(a) the agreement is not yielding significant results in terms of rationalisation or consumers are not receiving a fair share of the resulting benefit; or

(b) the products which are the subject of the specialisation are not subject in the common market or a substantial part thereof to effective competition from identical products or products considered by users to be equivalent in view of their characteristics, price and intended use.

## Article 9

This Regulation shall apply *mutatis mutandis* to decisions of associations of undertakings and concerted practices.

## [Article 9A

The prohibition in Article 85(1) of the Treaty shall not apply to the specialisation agreements which were in existence at the date of the accession of the Kingdom of Spain and of the Portuguese Republic and which, by reason of this accession, fall within the scope of Article 85(1), if, before 1 July 1986, they are so amended that they comply with the conditions laid down in this Regulation.]

[As regards agreements to which Article 85 of the Treaty applies as a result of the accession of Austria, Finland and Sweden, the preceding paragraph shall apply *mutatis mutandis* on the understanding that the relevant dates shall be the date of accession of those countries and six months after the date of accession of those countries respectively. However, this paragraph shall not apply to agreements which at the date of accession already fall under Article 53(1) of the EEA Agreement.]

NOTES

Inserted by the 1985 Act of Accession of the Kingdom of Spain and the Portuguese Republic, Annex I(IV)(14). Second subparagraph added by the 1994 Act of Accession of the Kingdom of Norway, the Republic of Austria, the Republic of Finland and the Kingdom of Sweden, Annex I(III)(D)(5), as adjusted by Council Decision 95/1/EC, Annex I(III)(D)(5).

## Article 10

1. This Regulation shall enter into force on 1 March 1985. It shall apply until [31 December 2000].

2. Commission Regulation (EEC) No 3604/82 is hereby repealed.

This Regulation shall be binding in its entirety and directly applicable in all Member States.

NOTES

Words in square brackets substituted by Commission Regulation 2236/97, Art 1.

# COMMISSION REGULATION

of 19 December 1984

## on the application of Article 85(3) of the Treaty to categories of research and development agreements

### (418/85/EEC)

NOTES

Date of publication in OJ: OJ L53, 22.2.85, p 5.

# THE COMMISSION OF THE EUROPEAN COMMUNITIES,

Having regard to the Treaty establishing the European Economic Community,

Having regard to Council Regulation (EEC) No 2821/71 of 20 December 1971 on the application of Article 85(3) of the Treaty to categories of agreements, decisions and concerted practices, as last amended by the Act of Accession of Greece, and in particular Article 1 thereof,

Having published a draft of this Regulation,

Having consulted the Advisory Committee on Restrictive Practices and Dominant Positions, Whereas—

(1) Regulation (EEC) No 2821/71 empowers the Commission to apply Article 85(3) of the Treaty by Regulation to certain categories of agreements, decisions and concerted practices falling within the scope of Article 85(1) which have as their object the research and development of products or processes up to the stage of industrial application, and exploitation of the results, including provisions regarding industrial property rights and confidential technical knowledge.

(2) As stated in the Commission's 1968 notice concerning agreements, decisions and concerted practices in the field of co-operation between enterprises, agreements on the joint execution of research work or the joint development of the results of the research, up to but not including the stage of industrial application, generally do not fall within the scope of Article 85(1) of the Treaty. In certain circumstances, however, such as where the parties agree not to carry out other research and development in the same field, thereby forgoing the opportunity of gaining competitive advantages over the other parties, such agreements may fall within Article 85(1) and should therefore not be excluded from this Regulation.

(3) Agreements providing for both joint research and development and joint exploitation of the results may fall within Article 85(1) because the parties jointly determine how the products developed are manufactured or the processes developed are applied or how related intellectual property rights or know-how are exploited.

(4) Co-operation in research and development and in the exploitation of the results generally promotes technical and economic progress by increasing the dissemination of technical knowledge between the parties and avoiding duplication of research and development work, by stimulating new advances through the exchange of complementary technical knowledge, and by rationalising the manufacture of the products or application of the processes arising out of the research and development. These aims can be achieved only where the research and development programme and its objectives are clearly defined and each of the parties is given the opportunity of exploiting any of the results of the programme that interest it; where universities or research institutes participate and are not interested in the industrial exploitation of the results, however, it may be agreed that they may use the said results solely for the purpose of further research.

(5) Consumers can generally be expected to benefit from the increased volume and effectiveness of research and development through the introduction of new or improved products or services or the reduction of prices brought about by new or improved processes.

(6) This Regulation must specify the restrictions of competition which may be included in the exempted agreements. The purpose of the permitted restrictions is to concentrate the research activities of the parties in order to improve their chances of success, and to facilitate the introduction of new products and services onto the market. These restrictions are generally necessary to secure the desired benefits for the parties and consumers.

(7) The joint exploitation of results can be considered as the natural consequence of joint research and development. It can take different forms ranging from manufacture to the exploitation of intellectual property rights or know-how that substantially contributes to technical or economic progress. In order to attain the benefits and objectives described above and to justify the restrictions of competition which are exempted, the joint exploitation must relate to products or processes for which the use of the results of the research and development is decisive. Joint exploitation is not therefore justified where it relates to improvements which were not made within the framework of a joint research and development programme but under an agreement having some other principal objective, such as the licensing of intellectual property rights, joint manufacture or specialisation, and merely containing ancillary provisions on joint research and development.

(8) The exemption granted under the Regulation must be limited to agreements which do not afford the undertakings the possibility of eliminating competition in respect of a substantial

part of the products in question. In order to guarantee that several independent poles of research can exist in the common market in any economic sector, it is necessary to exclude from the block exemption agreements between competitors whose combined share of the market for products capable of being improved or replaced by the results of the research and development exceeds a certain level at the time the agreement is entered into.

(9)  In order to guarantee the maintenance of effective competition during joint exploitation of the results, it is necessary to provide that the block exemption will cease to apply if the parties' combined shares of the market for the products arising out of the joint research and development become too great. However, it should be provided that the exemption will continue to apply, irrespective of the parties' market shares, for a certain period after the commencement of joint exploitation, so as to await stabilisation of their market shares, particularly after the introduction of an entirely new product, and to guarantee a minimum period of return on the generally substantial investments involved.

(10)  Agreements between undertakings which do not fulfil the market share conditions laid down in the Regulation may, in appropriate cases, be granted an exemption by individual decision, which will in particular take account of world competition and the particular circumstances prevailing in the manufacture of high technology products.

(11)  It is desirable to list in the Regulation a number of obligations that are commonly found in research and development agreements but that are normally not restrictive of competition and to provide that, in the event that, because of the particular economic or legal circumstances, they should fall within Article 85(1), they also would be covered by the exemption. This list is not exhaustive.

(12)  The Regulation must specify what provisions may not be included in agreements if these are to benefit from the block exemption by virtue of the fact that such provisions are restrictions falling within Article 85(1) for which there can be no general presumption that they will lead to the positive effects required by Article 85(3).

(13)  Agreements which are not automatically covered by the exemption because they include provisions that are not expressly exempted by the Regulation and are not expressly excluded from exemption are none the less capable of benefiting from the general presumption of compatibility with Article 85(3) on which the block exemption is based. It will be possible for the Commission rapidly to establish whether this is the case for a particular agreement. Such an agreement should therefore be deemed to be covered by the exemption provided for in this Regulation where it is notified to the Commission and the Commission does not oppose the application of the exemption within a specified period of time.

(14)  Agreements covered by this Regulation may also take advantage of provisions contained in other block exemption Regulations of the Commission, and in particular Regulation (EEC) No 417/85 on specialisation agreements, Regulation (EEC) No 1983/83 on exclusive distribution agreements, Regulation (EEC) No 1984/83 on exclusive purchasing agreements and Regulation (EEC) No 2349/84 on patent licensing agreements, if they fulfil the conditions set out in these Regulations. The provisions of the aforementioned Regulations are, however, not applicable in so far as this Regulation contains specific rules.

(15)  If individual agreements exempted by this Regulation nevertheless have effects which are incompatible with Article 85(3), the Commission may withdraw the benefit of the block exemption.

(16)  The Regulation should apply with retroactive effect to agreements in existence when the Regulation comes into force where such agreements already fulfil its conditions or are modified to do so. The benefit of these provisions may not be claimed in actions pending at the date of entry into force of this Regulation, nor may it be relied on as grounds for claims for damages against third parties.

(17)  Since research and development co-operation agreements are often of a long-term nature, especially where the co-operation extends to the exploitation of the results, it is appropriate to fix the period of validity of the Regulation at 13 years. If the circumstances on the basis of which the Regulation was adopted should change significantly within this period, the Commission will make the necessary amendments.

(18)  Agreements which are automatically exempted pursuant to this Regulation need not be notified. Undertakings may nevertheless in a particular case request a decision pursuant to Council Regulation No 17 as last amended by the Act of Accession of Greece,

HAS ADOPTED THIS REGULATION—

## Article 1

1.    Pursuant to Article 85(3) of the Treaty and subject to the provisions of this Regulation, it is hereby declared that Article 85(1) of the Treaty shall not apply to agreements entered into between undertakings for the purpose of—
- (a) joint research and development of products or processes and joint exploitation of the results of that research and development;
- (b) joint exploitation of the results of research and development of products or processes jointly carried out pursuant to a prior agreement between the same undertakings; or
- (c) joint research and development of products or processes excluding joint exploitation of the results, in so far as such agreements fall within the scope of Article 85(1).

2.    For the purposes of this Regulation—
- (a) *research and development of products or processes* means the acquisition of technical knowledge and the carrying out of theoretical analysis, systematic study or experimentation, including experimental production, technical testing of products or processes, the establishment of the necessary facilities and the obtaining of intellectual property rights for the results;
- (b) *contract processes* means processes arising out of the research and development;
- (c) *contract products* means products or services arising out of the research and development or manufactured or provided applying the contract processes;
- (d) *exploitation of the results* means the manufacture of the contract products or the application of the contract processes or the assignment or licensing of intellectual property rights or the communication of know-how required for such manufacture or application;
- (e) *technical knowledge* means technical knowledge which is either protected by an intellectual property right or is secret (know-how).

3.    Research and development of the exploitation of the results are carried out *jointly* where—
- (a) the work involved is—
  - — carried out by a joint team, organisation or undertaking,
  - — jointly entrusted to a third party, or
  - — allocated between the parties by way of specialisation in research, development or production;
- (b) the parties collaborate in any way in the assignment or the licensing of intellectual property rights or the communication of know-how, within the meaning of paragraph 2(d), to third parties.

## Article 2

The exemption provided for in Article 1 shall apply on condition that—
- (a) the joint research and development work is carried out within the framework of a programme defining the objectives of the work and the field in which it is to be carried out;
- (b) all the parties have access to the results of the work;
- (c) where the agreement provides only for joint research and development, each party is free to exploit the results of the joint research and development and any pre-existing technical knowledge necessary therefor independently;

(d) the joint exploitation relates only to results which are protected by intellectual property rights or constitute know-how which substantially contributes to technical or economic progress and that the results are decisive for the manufacture of the contract products or the application of the contract processes;

(e) . . .

(f) undertakings charged with manufacture by way of specialisation in production are required to fulfil orders for supplies from all the parties.

NOTES

Para (e) deleted by Commission Regulation (EEC) 151/93, Art 2(1), with retroactive effect from the time at which the conditions for the application of the group exemption were fulfilled.

## Article 3

1. Where the parties are not competing manufacturers of products capable of being improved or replaced by the contract products, the exemption provided for in Article 1 shall apply for the duration of the research and development programme and, where the results are jointly exploited, for five years from the time the contract products are first put on the market within the common market.

2. Where two or more of the parties are competing manufacturers within the meaning of paragraph 1, the exemption provided for in Article 1 shall apply for the period specified in paragraph 1 only if, at the time the agreement is entered into, the parties' combined production of the products capable of being improved or replaced by the contract products does not exceed 20% of the market for such products in the common market or a substantial part thereof.

3. After the end of the period referred to in paragraph 1, the exemption provided for in Article 1 shall continue to apply as long as the production of the contract products together with the parties' combined production of other products which are considered by users to be equivalent in view of their characteristics, price and intended use does not exceed 20% of the total market for such products in the common market or a substantial part thereof. Where contract products are components used by the parties of the manufacture of other products, reference shall be made to the markets for such of those latter products for which the components represent a significant part.

[3a. Where one of the parties, a joint undertaking, a third undertaking or more than one joint undertaking or third undertaking are entrusted with the distribution of the products which are the subject of the agreement under Article 4(1)(fa), (fb) or (fc), the exemption provided for in Article 1 shall apply only if the parties production of the products referred to in paragraphs 2 and 3 does not exceed 10% of the market for all such products in the common market or a substantial part thereof.]

[4. The exemption provided for in Article 1 shall continue to apply where the market shares referred to in paragraphs 3 and 4 are exceeded during any period of two consecutive financial years by not more than one-tenth.

5. Where the limits laid down in paragraph 5 are also exceeded, the exemption provided for in Article 1 shall continue to apply for a period of six months following the end of the financial year during which they were exceeded.]

NOTES

Para 3a: inserted by Commission Regulation (EEC) 151/93, Art 2(2), with retroactive effect from the time at which the conditions for the application of the group exemption were fulfilled.

Paras 4, 5: substituted by Commission Regulation (EEC) 151/93, Art 2(3), with retroactive effect from the time at which the conditions for the application of the group exemption were fulfilled.

**Article 4**

1.     The exemption provided for in Article 1 shall also apply to the following restrictions of competition imposed on the parties—

    (a)  an obligation not to carry out independently research and development in the field to which the programme relates or in a closely connected field during the execution of the programme;

    (b)  an obligation not to enter into agreements with third parties on research and development in the field to which the programme relates or in a closely connected field during the execution of the programme;

    (c)  an obligation to procure the contract products exclusively from parties, joint organisations or undertakings or third parties, jointly charged with their manufacture;

    (d)  an obligation not to manufacture the contract products or apply the contract processes in territories reserved for other parties;

    (e)  an obligation to restrict the manufacture of the contract products or application of the contract processes to one or more technical fields of application, except where two or more of the parties are competitors within the meaning of Article 3 at the time the agreement is entered into;

    (f)  an obligation not to pursue, for a period of five years from the time the contract products are first put on the market within the common market, an active policy of putting the products on the market in territories reserved for other parties, and in particular not to engage in advertising specifically aimed at such territories or to establish any branch or maintain any distribution depot there for the distribution of the products, provided that users and intermediaries can obtain the contract products from other suppliers and the parties do not render it difficult for intermediaries and users to thus obtain the products;

   [(fa)  an obligation to grant one of the parties the exclusive right to distribute the contract products, provided that that party does not distribute products manufactured by a third producer which compete with the contract products;

    (fb)  an obligation to grant the exclusive right to distribute the contract products to a joint undertaking or a third undertaking, provided that the joint undertaking or third undertaking does not manufacture or distribute products which compete with the contract products;

    (fc)  an obligation to grant the exclusive right to distribute the contract products in the whole or a defined area of the common market to joint undertakings or third undertakings which do not manufacture or distribute products which compete with the contract products, provided that users and intermediaries are also able to obtain the contract products from other suppliers and neither the parties nor the joint undertakings or third undertakings entrusted with the exclusive distribution of the contract products render it difficult for users and intermediaries to thus obtain the contract products.]

    (g)  an obligation on the parties to communicate to each other any experience they may gain in exploiting the results and to grant each other non-exclusive licences for inventions relating to improvements or new applications.

2.     The exemption provided for in Article 1 shall also apply where in a particular agreement the parties undertake obligations of the types referred to in paragraph 1 but with a more limited scope than is permitted by that paragraph.

NOTES
Para 1: sub-paras (fa), (fb), (fc) inserted by Commission Regulation (EEC) 151/93, Art 2(4), with retroactive effect from the time at which the conditions for the application of the group exemption were fulfilled.

## Article 5

1.      Article 1 shall apply notwithstanding that any of the following obligations, in particular, are imposed on the parties during the currency of the agreement—
- (a) an obligation to communicate patented or non-patented technical knowledge necessary for the carrying out of the research and development programme for the exploitation of its results;
- (b) an obligation not to use any know-how received from another party for purposes other than carrying out the research and development programme and the exploitation of its results;
- (c) an obligation to obtain and maintain in force intellectual property rights for the contract products or processes;
- (d) an obligation to preserve the confidentiality of any know-how received or jointly developed under the research and development programme; this obligation may be imposed even after the expiry of the agreement;
- (e) an obligation—
  - (i) to inform other parties of infringements of their intellectual property rights,
  - (ii) to take legal action against infringers, and
  - (iii) to assist in any such legal action or share with the other parties in the cost thereof;
- (f) an obligation to pay royalties or render services to other parties to compensate for unequal contributions to the joint research and development or unequal exploitation of its results;
- (g) an obligation to share royalties received from third parties with other parties;
- (h) an obligation to supply other parties with minimum quantities of contract products and to observe minimum standards of quality.

2.      In the event that, because of particular circumstances, the obligations referred to in paragraph 1 fall within the scope of Article 85(1), they also shall be covered by the exemption. The exemption provided for in this paragraph shall also apply where in a particular agreement the parties undertake obligations of the types referred to in paragraph 1 but with a more limited scope than is permitted by that paragraph.

## Article 6

The exemption provided for in Article 1 shall not apply where the parties, by agreement, decision or concerted practice—
- (a) are restricted in their freedom to carry out research and development independently or in co-operation with third parties in a field unconnected with that to which the programme relates or, after its completion, in the field to which the programme relates or in a connected field;
- (b) are prohibited after completion of the research and development programme from challenging the validity of intellectual property rights which the parties hold in the common market and which are relevant to the programme or, after the expiry of the agreement, from challenging the

validity of intellectual property rights which the parties hold in the common market and which protect the results of the research and development;

(c) are restricted as to the quantity of the contract products they may manufacture or sell or as to the number of operations employing the contract process they may carry out;

(d) are restricted in their determination of prices, components of prices or discounts when selling the contract products to third parties;

(e) are restricted as to the customers they may serve, without prejudice to Article 4(1)(e);

(f) are prohibited from putting the contract products on the market or pursuing an active sales policy for them in territories within the common market that are reserved for other parties after the end of the period referred to in Article 4(1)(f);

[(g) are required not to grant licences to third parties to manufacture the contract products or to apply the contract processes even though the exploitation by the parties themselves of the results of the joint research and development is not provided for or does not take place.]

(h) are required—

— to refuse without any objectively justified reason to meet demand from users or dealers established in their respective territories who would market the contract products in other territories within the common market, or

— to make it difficult for users or dealers to obtain the contract products from other dealers within the common market, and in particular to exercise intellectual property rights or take measures so as to prevent users or dealers from obtaining, or from putting on the market within the common market, products which have been lawfully put on the market within the common market by another party or with its consent.

NOTES

Para (g) substituted by Commission Regulation (EEC) 151/93, Art 2(5), with retroactive effect from the time at which the conditions for the application of the group exemption were fulfilled.

## Article 7

1.  The exemption provided for in this Regulation shall also apply to agreements of the kinds described in Article 1 which fulfil the conditions laid down in Articles 2 and 3 and which contain obligations restrictive of competition which are not covered by Articles 4 and 5 and do not fall within the scope of Article 6, on condition that the agreements in question are notified to the Commission in accordance with the provisions of Commission Regulation No 27, and that the Commission does not oppose such exemption within a period of six months.

2.  The period of six months shall run from the date on which the notification is received by the Commission. Where, however, the notification is made by registered post, the period shall run from the date shown on the postmark of the place of posting.

3.  Paragraph 1 shall apply only if—

(a) express reference is made to this Article in the notification or in a communication accompanying it, and

(b) the information furnished with the notification is complete and in accordance with the facts.

4.    The benefit of paragraph 1 may be claimed for agreements notified before the entry into force of this Regulation by submitting a communication to the Commission referring expressly to this Article and to the notification. Paragraphs 2 and 3(b) shall apply *mutatis mutandis*.

5.    The Commission may oppose the exemption. It shall oppose exemption if it receives a request to do so from a Member State within three months of the forwarding to the Member State of the notification referred to in paragraph 1 or of the communication referred to in paragraph 4. This request must be justified on the basis of considerations relating to the competition rules of the Treaty.

6.    The Commission may withdraw the opposition to the exemption at any time. However, where the opposition was raised at the request of a Member State and this request is maintained, it may be withdrawn only after consultation of the Advisory Committee on Restrictive Practices and Dominant Positions.

7.    If the opposition is withdrawn because the undertakings concerned have shown that the conditions of Article 85(3) are fulfilled, the exemption shall apply from the date of notification.

8.    If the opposition is withdrawn because the undertakings concerned have amended the agreement so that the conditions of Article 85(3) are fulfilled, the exemption shall apply from the date on which the amendments take effect.

9.    If the Commission opposes exemption and the opposition is not withdrawn, the effects of the notification shall be governed by the provisions of Regulation No 17.

### Article 8

1.    Information acquired pursuant to Article 7 shall be used only for the purposes of this Regulation.

2.    The Commission and the authorities of the Member States, their officials and other servants shall not disclose information acquired by them pursuant to this Regulation of a kind that is covered by the obligation of professional secrecy.

3.    Paragraphs 1 and 2 shall not prevent publication of general information or surveys which do not contain information relating to particular undertakings or associations of undertakings.

### Article 9

1.    The provisions of this Regulation shall also apply to rights and obligations which the parties create for undertakings connected with them. The market shares held and the actions and measures taken by connected undertakings shall be treated as those of the parties themselves.

2.    Connected undertakings for the purposes of this Regulation are—
  (a)  undertakings in which a party to the agreement, directly or indirectly—
    — owns more than half the capital or business assets,
    — has the power to exercise more than half the voting rights,
    — has the power to appoint more than half the members of the supervisory board, board of directors or bodies legally representing the undertakings, or
    — has the right to manage the affairs;

(b) undertakings which directly have in or over a party to the agreement the rights or powers listed in (a);

(c) undertakings in or over which an undertaking referred to in (b) directly or indirectly has the rights or powers listed in (a);

3.　Undertakings in which the parties to the agreement or undertakings connected with them jointly have, directly or indirectly, the rights or powers set out in paragraph 2(a) shall be considered to be connected with each of the parties to the agreement.

## Article 10

The Commission may withdraw the benefit of this Regulation, pursuant to Article 7 of Regulation (EEC) No 2821/71, where it finds in a particular case that an agreement exempted by this Regulation nevertheless has certain effects which are incompatible with the conditions laid down in Article 85(3) of the Treaty, and in particular where—

(a) the existence of the agreement substantially restricts the scope for third parties to carry out research and development in the relevant field because of the limited research capacity available elsewhere;

(b) because of the particular structure of supply, the existence of the agreement substantially restricts the access of third parties to the market for the contract products;

(c) without any objectively valid reason, the parties do not exploit the results of the joint research and development;

(d) the contract products are not subject in the whole or a substantial part of the common market to effective competition from identical products or products considered by users as equivalent in view of their characteristics, price and intended use.

## Article 11

1.　In the case of agreements notified to the Commission before 1 March 1985, the exemption provided for in Article 1 shall have retroactive effect from the time at which the conditions for application of this Regulation were fulfilled or, where the agreement does not fall within Article 4(2)(3)(b) of Regulation No 17, not earlier than the date of notification.

2.　In the case of agreements existing on 13 March 1962 and notified to the Commission before 1 February 1963, the exemption shall have retroactive effect from the time at which the conditions for application of this Regulation were fulfilled.

3.　Where agreements which were in existence on 13 March 1962 and which were notified to the Commission before 1 February 1963, or which are covered by Article 4(2)(3)(b) of Regulation No 17 and were notified to the Commission before 1 January 1967, are amended before 1 September 1985 so as to fulfil the conditions for application of this Regulation, such amendment being communicated to the Commission before 1 October 1985, the prohibition laid down in Article 85(1) of the Treaty shall not apply in respect of the period prior to the amendment. The communication of amendments shall take effect from the date of their receipt by the Commission. Where the communication is sent by registered post, it shall take effect from the date shown on the postmark of the place of posting.

4.　In the case of agreements to which Article 85 of the Treaty applies as a result of the accession of the United Kingdom, Ireland and Denmark, paragraphs 1 to 3 shall apply except that the relevant dates shall be 1 January 1973 instead of 13 March 1962 and 1 July 1973 instead of 1 February 1963 and 1 January 1967.

5.     In the case of agreements to which Article 85 of the Treaty applies as a result of the accession of Greece, paragraphs 1 to 3 shall apply except that the relevant dates shall be 1 January 1981 instead of 13 March 1962 and 1 July 1981 instead of 1 February 1963 and 1 January 1967.

[6.     As regards agreements to which Article 83 of the Treaty applies as a result of the accession of the Kingdom of Spain and of the Portuguese Republic, paragraphs 1 to 3 shall apply except that the relevant dates should be 1 January 1986 instead of 13 March 1962 and 1 July 1986 instead of 1 February 1963, 1 January 1967, 1 March 1985 and 1 September 1985. The amendment made to the agreements in accordance with the provisions of paragraph 3 need not be notified to the Commission.]

[7.     As regards agreements to which Article 85 of the Treaty applies as a result of the accession of Austria, Finland and Sweden, paragraphs 1 to 3 shall apply *mutatis mutandis* on the understanding that the relevant dates shall be the date of accession instead of 13 March 1962 and six months after the date of accession instead of 1 February 1963, 1 January 1967, 1 March 1985 and 1 September 1985. The amendment made to these agreements in accordance with the provisions of paragraph 3 need not be notified to the Commission. However, this paragraph shall not apply to agreements which at the date of accession already fall under Article 53(1) of the EEA Agreement.]

NOTES
Para 6: added by the 1985 Act of Accession of the Kingdom of Spain and the Portuguese Republic, Annex I(IV)(15).
Para 7: added by the 1994 Act of Accession of the Kingdom of Norway, the Republic of Austria, the Republic of Finland and the Kingdom of Sweden, Annex I(III)(D)(6), as adjusted by Council Decision 95/1/EC, Annex I(III)(D)(6).

### Article 12

This Regulation shall apply *mutatis mutandis* to decisions of associations of undertakings.

### Article 13

This Regulation shall enter into force on 1 March 1985.

It shall apply until [31 December 2000].

This Regulation shall be binding in its entirety and directly applicable in all Member States.

NOTES
Words in square brackets substituted by Commission Regulation 2236/97, Art 2.

# COMMISSION REGULATION

of 30 November 1988

## on the application of Article 85(3) of the Treaty to categories of franchise agreements

## (4087/88/EEC)

NOTES
Date of publication in OJ: OJ L359, 28.12.88, p 46.

## THE COMMISSION OF THE EUROPEAN COMMUNITIES,

Having regard to the Treaty establishing the European Economic Community,

Having regard to Council Regulation No 19/65/EEC of 2 March 1965 on the application of Article 85(3) of the Treaty to certain categories of agreements and concerted practices as last amended by the Act of Accession of Spain and Portugal, and in particular Article 1 thereof,

Having published a draft of this Regulation,

Having consulted the Advisory Committee on Restrictive Practices and Dominant Positions,

Whereas—

(1) Regulation No 19/65/EEC empowers the Commission to apply Article 85(3) of the Treaty by Regulation to certain categories of bilateral exclusive agreements falling within the scope of Article 85(1) which either have as their object the exclusive distribution or exclusive purchase of goods, or include restrictions imposed in relation to the assignment or use of industrial property rights.

(2) Franchise agreements consist essentially of licences of industrial or intellectual property rights relating to trade marks or signs and know-how, which can be combined with restrictions relating to supply or purchase of goods.

(3) Several types of franchise can be distinguished according to their object: industrial franchise concerns the manufacturing of goods, distribution franchise concerns the sale of goods, and service franchise concerns the supply of services.

(4) It is possible on the basis of the experience of the Commission to define categories of franchise agreements which fall under Article 85(1) but can normally by regarded as satisfying the conditions laid down in Article 85(3). This is the case for franchise agreements whereby one of the parties supplies goods or provides services to end users. On the other hand, industrial franchise agreements should not be covered by this Regulation. Such agreements, which usually govern relationships between producers, present different characteristics than the other types of franchise. They consist of manufacturing licences based on patents and/or technical know-how, combined with trade-mark licences. Some of them may benefit from other block exemptions if they fulfil the necessary conditions.

(5) This Regulation covers franchise agreements between two undertakings, the franchisor and the franchisee, for the retailing of goods or the provision of services to end users, or a combination of these activities, such as the processing or adaptation of goods to fit specific needs of their customers. It also covers cases where the relationship between franchisor and franchisees is made through a third undertaking, the master franchisee. It does not cover wholesale franchise agreements because of the lack of experience of the Commission in that field.

(6) Franchise agreements as defined in this Regulation can fall under Article 85(1). They may in particular affect intra-Community trade where they are concluded between undertakings from different Member States or where they form the basis of a network which extends beyond the boundaries of a single Member State.

(7) Franchise agreements as defined in this Regulation normally improve the distribution of goods and/or the provision of services as they give franchisors the possibility of establishing a uniform network with limited investments, which may assist the entry of new competitors on the market, particularly in the case of small and medium-sized undertakings, thus increasing interbrand competition. They also allow independent traders to set up outlets more rapidly and with higher chance of success than if they had to do so without the franchisor's experience and assistance. They have therefore the possibility of competing more efficiently with large distribution undertakings.

(8) As a rule, franchise agreements also allow consumers and other end users a fair share of the resulting benefit, as they combine the advantage of a uniform network with the existence of traders personally interested in the efficient operation of their business. The homogeneity of the network and the constant co-operation between the franchisor and the franchisees ensures a constant quality of the products and services. The favourable effect of franchising on interbrand competition and the fact that consumers are free to deal with any franchisee in the network guarantees that a reasonable part of the resulting benefits will be passed on to the consumers.

(9) This Regulation must define the obligations restrictive of competition which maybe included in franchise agreements. This is the case in particular for the granting of an exclusive territory to the franchisees combined with the prohibition on actively seeking customers outside that territory, which allows them to concentrate their efforts on their allotted territory.

The same applies to the granting of an exclusive territory to a master franchisee combined with the obligation not to conclude franchise agreements with third parties outside that territory. Where the franchisees sell or use in the process of providing services, goods manufactured by the franchisor or according to its instructions and or bearing its trade mark, an obligation on the franchisees not to sell, or use in the process of the provision of services, competing goods, makes it possible to establish a coherent network which is identified with the franchised goods. However, this obligation should only be accepted with respect to the goods which form the essential subject-matter of the franchise. It should notably not relate to accessories or spare parts for these goods.

(10) The obligations referred to above thus do not impose restrictions which are not necessary for the attainment of the abovementioned objectives. In particular, the limited territorial protection granted to the franchisees is indispensable to protect their investment.

(11) It is desirable to list in the Regulation a number of obligations that are commonly found in franchise agreements and are normally not restrictive of competition and to provide that if, because of the particular economic or legal circumstances, they fall under Article 85(1), they are also covered by the exemption. This list, which is not exhaustive, includes in particular clauses which are essential either to preserve the common identity and reputation of the network or to prevent the know-how made available and the assistance given by the franchisor from benefiting competitors.

(12) The Regulation must specify the conditions which must be satisfied for the exemption to apply. To guarantee that competition is not eliminated for a substantial part of the goods which are the subject of the franchise, it is necessary that parallel imports remain possible. Therefore, cross deliveries between franchisees should always be possible. Furthermore, where a franchise network is combined with another distribution system, franchisees should be free to obtain supplies from authorised distributors. To better inform consumers, thereby helping to ensure that they receive a fair share of the resulting benefits, it must be provided that the franchisee shall be obliged to indicate its status as an independent undertaking, by any appropriate means which does not jeopardise the common identity of the franchised network. Furthermore, where the franchisees have to honour guarantees for the franchisor's goods, this obligation should also apply to goods supplied by the franchisor, other franchisees or other agreed dealers.

(13) The Regulation must also specify restrictions which may not be included in franchise agreements if these are to benefit from the exemption granted by the Regulation, by virtue of the fact that such provisions are restrictions falling under Article 85(1) for which there is no general presumption that they will lead to the positive effects required by Article 85(3). This applies in particular to market sharing between competing manufacturers, to clauses unduly limiting the franchisee's choice of suppliers or customers, and to cases where the franchisee is restricted in determining its prices. However, the franchisor should be free to recommend prices to the franchisees, where it is not prohibited by national laws and to the extent that it does not lead to concerted practices for the effective application of these prices.

(14) Agreements which are not automatically covered by the exemption because they contain provisions that are not expressly exempted by the Regulation and not expressly excluded from exemption may nonetheless generally be presumed to be eligible for application of Article 85(3). It will be possible for the Commission rapidly to establish whether this is the case for a particular agreement. Such agreements should therefore be deemed to be covered by the exemption provided for in this Regulation where they are notified to the Commission and the Commission does not oppose the application of the exemption within a specified period of time.

(15) If individual agreements exempted by this Regulation nevertheless have effects which are incompatible with Article 85(3), in particular as interpreted by the administrative practice of the Commission and the case law of the Court of Justice, the Commission may withdraw the benefit of the block exemption. This applies in particular where competition is significantly restricted because of the structure of the relevant market.

(16) Agreements which are automatically exempted pursuant to this Regulation need not be notified. Undertakings may nevertheless in a particular case request a decision pursuant to Council Regulation No 17 as last amended by the Act of Accession of Spain and Portugal.

(17) Agreements may benefit from the provisions either of this Regulation or of another Regulation, according to their particular nature and provided that they fulfil the necessary

conditions of application. They may not benefit from a combination of the provisions of this Regulation with those of another block exemption Regulation,

HAS ADOPTED THIS REGULATION—

## Article 1

1.    Pursuant to Article 85(3) of the Treaty and subject to the provisions of this Regulation, it is hereby declared that Article 85(1) of the Treaty shall not apply to franchise agreements to which two undertakings are party, which include one or more of the restrictions listed in Article 2.

2.    The exemption provided for in paragraph 1 shall also apply to master franchise agreements to which two undertakings are party. Where applicable, the provisions of this Regulation concerning the relationship between franchisor and franchisee shall apply *mutatis mutandis* to the relationship between franchisor and master franchisee and between master franchisee and franchisee.

3.    For the purposes of this Regulation—
   (a) 'franchise' means a package of industrial or intellectual property rights relating to trade marks, trade names, shop signs, utility models, designs, copyrights, know-how or patents, to be exploited for the resale of goods or the provision of services to end users;
   (b) 'franchise agreement' means an agreement whereby one undertaking, the franchisor, grants the other, the franchisee, in exchange for direct or indirect financial consideration, the right to exploit a franchise for the purposes of marketing specified types of goods and/or services; it includes at least obligations relating to—
      — the use of a common name or shop sign and a uniform presentation of contract premises and/or means of transport,
      — the communication by the franchisor to the franchisee of know-how,
      — the continuing provision by the franchisor to the franchisee of commercial or technical assistance during the life of the agreement;
   (c) 'master franchise agreement' means an agreement whereby one undertaking, the franchisor, grants the other, the master franchisee, in exchange of direct or indirect financial consideration, the right to exploit a franchise for the purposes of concluding franchise agreements with third parties, the franchisees;
   (d) 'franchisor's goods' means goods produced by the franchisor or according to its instructions, and/or bearing the franchisor's name or trade mark;
   (e) 'contract premises' means the premises used for the exploitation of the franchise or, when the franchise is exploited outside those premises, the base from which the franchisee operates the means of transport used for the exploitation of the franchise (contract means of transport);
   (f) 'know-how' means a package of non-patented practical information, resulting from experience and testing by the franchisor, which is secret, substantial and identified;
   (g) 'secret' means that the know-how, as a body or in the precise configuration and assembly of its components, is not generally known or easily accessible; it is not limited in the narrow sense that each individual component of the know-how should be totally unknown or unobtainable outside the franchisor's business;
   (h) 'substantial' means that the know-how includes information which is of importance for the sale of goods or the provision of services to end users,

and in particular for the presentation of goods for sale, the processing of goods in connection which the provision of services, methods of dealing with customers, and administration and financial management; the know-how must be useful for the franchisee by being capable, at the date of conclusion of the agreement, of improving the competitive position of the franchisee, in particular by improving the franchisee's performance or helping it to enter a new market;

(i) 'identified' means that the know-how must be described in a sufficiently comprehensive manner so as to make it possible to verify that it fulfils the criteria of secrecy and substantiality; the description of the know-how can either be set out in the franchise agreement or in a separate document or recorded in any other appropriate form.

## Article 2

The exemption provided for in Article 1 shall apply to the following restrictions of competition—

(a) an obligation on the franchisor, in a defined area of the common market, the contract territory, not to—
— grant the right to exploit all or part of the franchise to third parties,
— itself exploit the franchise, or itself market the goods or services which are the subject-matter of the franchise under a similar formula.
— itself supply the franchisor's goods to third parties;

(b) an obligation on the master franchisee not to conclude a franchise agreement with third parties outside its contract territory;

(c) an obligation on the franchisee to exploit the franchise only from the contract premises;

(d) an obligation on the franchisee to refrain, outside the contract territory, from seeking customers for the goods or the services which are the subject-matter of the franchise;

(e) an obligation on the franchisee not to manufacture, sell or use in the course of the provision of services, goods competing with the franchisor's goods which are the subject-matter of the franchise; where the subject-matter of the franchise is the sale or use in the course of the provision of services both certain types of goods and spare parts or accessories therefor, that obligation may not be imposed in respect of these spare parts or accessories.

## Article 3

1.    Article 1 shall apply notwithstanding the presence of any of the following obligations on the franchisee, in so far as they are necessary to protect the franchisor's industrial or intellectual property rights or to maintain the common identity and reputation of the franchised network—

(a) to sell, or use in the course of the provision of services, exclusively goods matching minimum objective quality specifications laid down by the franchisor;

(b) to sell, or use in the course of the provision of services, goods which are manufactured only by the franchisor or by third parties designed by it, where it is impracticable, owing to the nature of the goods which are the subject-matter of the franchise, to apply objective quality specifications;

(c) not to engage, directly or indirectly, in any similar business in a territory where it would compete with a member of the franchised network, including the franchisor; the franchisee may be held to this obligation after termination of the agreement, for a reasonable period which may not exceed one year, in the territory where it has exploited the franchise;

(d) not to acquire financial interests in the capital of a competing undertaking, which would give the franchisee the power to influence the economic conduct of such undertaking;

(e) to sell the goods which are the subject-matter of the franchise only to end users, to other franchisees and to resellers within other channels of distribution supplied by the manufacturer of these goods or with its consent;

(f) to use its best endeavours to sell the goods or provide the services that are the subject-matter of the franchise; to offer for sale a minimum range of goods, achieve a minimum turnover, plan its orders in advance, keep minimum stocks and provide customer and warranty services;

(g) to pay to the franchisor a specified proportion of its revenue for advertising and itself carry out advertising for the nature of which it shall obtain the franchisor's approval.

2.    Article 1 shall apply notwithstanding the presence of any of the following obligations on the franchisee—

(a) not to disclose to third parties the know-how provided by the franchisor; the franchisee may be held to this obligation after termination of the agreement;

(b) to communicate to the franchisor any experience gained in exploiting the franchise and to grant it, and other franchisees, a non-exclusive licence for the know-how resulting from that experience;

(c) to inform the franchisor of infringements of licensed industrial or intellectual property rights, to take legal action against infringers or to assist the franchisor in any legal actions against infringers;

(d) not to use know-how licensed by the franchisor for purposes other than the exploitation of the franchise; the franchisee may be held to this obligation after termination of the agreement;

(e) to attend or have its staff attend training courses arranged by the franchisor;

(f) to apply the commercial methods devised by the franchisor, including any subsequent modification thereof, and use the licensed industrial or intellectual property rights;

(g) to comply with the franchisor's standards for the equipment and presentation of the contract premises and/or means of transport;

(h) to allow the franchisor to carry out checks of the contract premises and/ or means of transport, including the goods sold and the services provided, and the inventory and accounts of the franchisee;

(i) not without the franchisor's consent to change the location of the contract premises;

(j) not without the franchisor's consent to assign the rights and obligations under the franchise agreement.

3.    In the event that, because of particular circumstances, obligations referred to in paragraph 2 fall within the scope of Article 85(1), they shall also be exempted even if they are not accompanied by any of the obligations exempted by Article 1.

## Article 4

The exemption provided for in Article 1 shall apply on condition that—

(a) the franchisee is free to obtain the goods that are the subject-matter of the franchise from other franchisees; where such goods are also distributed through another network of authorised distributors, the franchisee must be free to obtain the goods from the latter;

(b) where the franchisor obliges the franchisee to honour guarantees for the franchisor's goods, that obligation shall apply in respect of such goods supplied by any member of the franchised network or other distributors which give a similar guarantee, in the common market;

(c) the franchisee is obliged to indicate its status as an independent undertaking; this indication shall however not interfere with the common identity of the franchised network resulting in particular from the common name or shop sign and uniform appearance of the contract premises and/or means of transport.

## Article 5

The exemption granted by Article 1 shall not apply where—

(a) undertakings producing goods or providing services which are identical or are considered by users as equivalent in view of their characteristics, price and intended use, enter into franchise agreements in respect of such goods or services;

(b) without prejudice to Article 2(e) and Article 3(1)(b), the franchisee is prevented from obtaining supplies of goods of a quality equivalent to those offered by the franchisor;

(c) without prejudice to Article 2(e), the franchisee is obliged to sell, or use in the process of providing services, goods manufactured by the franchisor or third parties designated by the franchisor and the franchisor refuses, for reasons other than protecting the franchisor's industrial or intellectual property rights, or maintaining the common identity and reputation of the franchised network, to designate as authorised manufacturers third parties proposed by the franchisee;

(d) the franchisee is prevented from continuing to use the licensed know-how after termination of the agreement where the know-how has become generally known or easily accessible, other than by breach of an obligation by the franchisee;

(e) the franchisee is restricted by the franchisor, directly or indirectly, in the determination of sale prices for the goods or services which are the subject-matter of the franchise, without prejudice to the possibility for the franchisor of recommending sale prices;

(f) the franchisor prohibits the franchisee from challenging the validity of the industrial or intellectual property rights which form part of the franchise, without prejudice to the possibility for the franchisor of terminating the agreement in such a case;

(g) franchisees are obliged not to supply within the common market the goods or services which are the subject-matter of the franchise to end users because of their place of residence.

## Article 6

1.    The exemption provided for in Article 1 shall also apply to franchise agreements which fulfil the conditions laid down in Article 4 and include obligations restrictive of competition which are not covered by Articles 2 and 3(3) and do not fall within the scope of Article 5, on condition that the agreements in question are notified to the Commission in accordance with the provisions of Commission Regulation No 27 and that the Commission does not oppose such exemption within a period of six months.

2.     The period of six months shall run from the date on which the notification is received by the Commission. Where, however, the notification is made by registered post, the period shall run from the date shown on the postmark of the place of posting.

3.     Paragraph 1 shall apply only if—
   (a) express reference is made to this Article in the notification or in a communication accompanying it; and
   (b) the information furnished with the notification is complete and in accordance with the facts.

4.     The benefit of paragraph 1 can be claimed for agreements notified before the entry into force of this Regulation by submitting a communication to the Commission referring expressly to this Article and to the notification. Paragraphs 2 and 3(b) shall apply *mutatis mutandis*.

5.     The Commission may oppose exemption. It shall oppose exemption if it receives a request to do so from a Member State within three months of the forwarding to the Member State of the notification referred to in paragraph 1 or the communication referred to in paragraph 4. This request must be justified on the basis of considerations relating to the competition rules of the Treaty.

6.     The Commission may withdraw its opposition to the exemption at any time. However, where that opposition was raised at the request of a Member State, it may be withdrawn only after consultation of the advisory Committee on Restrictive Practices and Dominant Positions.

7.     If the opposition is withdrawn because the undertakings concerned have shown that the conditions of Article 85(3) are fulfilled, the exemption shall apply from the date of the notification.

8.     If the opposition is withdrawn because the undertakings concerned have amended the agreement so that the conditions of Article 85(3) are fulfilled, the exemption shall apply from the date on which the amendments take effect.

9.     If the Commission opposes exemption and its opposition is not withdrawn, the effects of the notification shall be governed by the provisions of Regulation No 17.

## Article 7

1.     Information acquired pursuant to Article 6 shall be used only for the purposes of this Regulation.

2.     The Commission and the authorities of the Member States, their officials and other servants shall not disclose information acquired by them pursuant to this Regulation of a kind that is covered by the obligation of professional secrecy.

3.     Paragraphs 1 and 2 shall not prevent publication of general information or surveys which do not contain information relating to particular undertakings or associations of undertakings.

## Article 8

The Commission may withdraw the benefit of this Regulation, pursuant to Article 7 of Regulation No 19/65/EEC, where it finds in a particular case that an agreement exempted by this Regulation nevertheless has certain effects which are incompatible with the conditions laid down in Article 85(3) of the EEC Treaty, and in particular where territorial protection is awarded to the franchisee and—

(a)  access to the relevant market or competition therein is significantly restricted by the cumulative effect of parallel networks of similar agreements established by competing manufacturers or distributors;

(b)  the goods or services which are the subject-matter of the franchise do not face, in a substantial part of the common market, effective competition from goods or services which are identical or considered by users as equivalent in view of their characteristics, price and intended use;

(c)  the parties, or one of them, prevent end users, because of their place of residence, from obtaining, directly or through intermediaries, the goods or services which are the subject-matter of the franchise within the common market, or use differences in specifications concerning those goods or services in different Member States, to isolate markets;

(d)  franchisees engage in concerted practices relating to the sale prices of the goods or services which are the subject-matter of the franchise;

(e)  the franchisor uses its right to check the contract premises and means of transport, or refuses its agreement to requests by the franchisee to move the contract premises or assign its rights and obligations under the franchise agreement, for reasons other than protecting the franchisor's industrial or intellectual property rights, maintaining the common identity and reputation of the franchised network or verifying that the franchisee abides by its obligations under the agreement.

## [Article 8a

The prohibition in Article 85(1) of the Treaty shall not apply to the franchise agreements which were in existence at the date of accession of Austria, Finland and Sweden and which, by reason of this accession, fall within the scope of Article 85(1) if, within six mónths from the date of accession, they are so amended that they comply with the conditions laid down in this Regulation. However, this Article shall not apply to agreements which at the date of accession already fall under Article 53(1) of the EEA Agreement.]

---

NOTES

Inserted by the 1994 Act of Accession of the Kingdom of Norway, the Republic of Austria, the Republic of Finland and the Kingdom of Sweden, Annex I(III)(D)(7), as adjusted by Council Decision 95/1/EC, Annex I(III)(D)(7).

---

## Article 9

This Regulation shall enter into force on 1 February 1989.

It shall remain in force until 31 December 1999.

This Regulation shall be binding in its entirety and directly applicable in all Member States.

**COMPETITION**

# COUNCIL REGULATION

## First Regulation implementing Articles 85 and 86 of the Treaty

## (17/62/EEC)

NOTES

Date of publication in OJ: OJ L13, 21.2.62, p 204 (S edn, 1959–62, p 87).

THE COUNCIL OF THE EUROPEAN ECONOMIC COMMUNITY,

Having regard to the Treaty establishing the European Economic Community, and in particular Article 87 thereof;

Having regard to the proposal from the Commission;

Having regard to the Opinion of the Economic and Social Committee;

Having regard to the Opinion of the European Parliament;

Whereas, in order to establish a system ensuring that competition shall not be distorted in the common market, it is necessary to provide for balanced application of Articles 85 and 86 in a uniform manner in the Member States;

Whereas in establishing the rules for applying Article 85(3) account must be taken of the need to ensure effective supervision and to simplify administration to the greatest possible extent;

Whereas it is accordingly necessary to make it obligatory, as a general principle, for undertakings which seek application of Article 85(3) to notify to the Commission their agreements, decisions and concerted practices;

Whereas, on the one hand, such agreements, decisions and concerted practices are probably very numerous and cannot therefore all be examined at the same time and, on the other hand, some of them have special features which may make them less prejudicial to the development of the common market;

Whereas there is consequently a need to make more flexible arrangements for the time being in respect of certain categories of agreement, decision and concerted practice without prejudging their validity under Article 85;

Whereas it may be in the interest of undertakings to know whether any agreements, decisions or practices to which they are party, or propose to become party, may lead to action on the part of the Commission pursuant to Article 85(1) or Article 86;

Whereas, in order to secure uniform application of Articles 85 and 86 in the common market, rules must be made under which the Commission, acting in close and constant liaison with the competent authorities of the Member States, may take the requisite measures for applying those Articles;

Whereas for this purpose the Commission must have the co-operation of the competent authorities of the Member States and be empowered, throughout the common market, to require such information to be supplied and to undertake such investigations as are necessary to bring to light any agreement, decision or concerted practice prohibited by Article 85(1) or any abuse of a dominant position prohibited by Article 86;

Whereas, in order to carry out its duty of ensuring that the provisions of the Treaty are applied, the Commission must be empowered to address to undertakings or associations of undertakings recommendations and decisions for the purpose of bringing to an end infringements of Articles 85 and 86;

Whereas compliance with Articles 85 and 86 and the fulfilment of obligations imposed on undertakings and associations of undertakings under this Regulation must be enforceable by means of fines and periodic penalty payments;

Whereas undertakings concerned must be accorded the right to be heard by the Commission, third parties whose interests may be affected by a decision must be given the opportunity of submitting their comments beforehand, and it must be ensured that wide publicity is given to decisions taken;

Whereas all decisions taken by the Commission under this Regulation are subject to review by the Court of Justice under the conditions specified in the Treaty; whereas it is moreover desirable to confer upon the Court of Justice, pursuant to Article 172, unlimited jurisdiction in respect of decisions under which the Commission imposes fines or periodic penalty payments;

Whereas this Regulation may enter into force without prejudice to any other provisions that may hereafter be adopted pursuant to Article 87;

HAS ADOPTED THIS REGULATION—

## Article 1

### Basic provision

Without prejudice to Articles 6, 7 and 23 of this Regulation, agreements, decisions and concerted practices of the kind described in Article 85(1) of the Treaty and the abuse of a dominant position in the market, within the meaning of Article 86 of the Treaty, shall be prohibited, no prior decision to that effect being required.

## Article 2

### Negative clearance

Upon application by the undertakings or associations of undertakings concerned, the Commission may certify that, on the basis of the facts in its possession, there are no grounds under Article 85(1) or Article 86 of the Treaty for action on its part in respect of an agreement, decision or practice.

## Article 3

### Termination of infringements

1.      Where the Commission, upon application or upon its own initiative, finds that there is infringement of Article 85 or Article 86 of the Treaty, it may by decision require the undertakings or associations of undertakings concerned to bring such infringement to an end.

2.      Those entitled to make application are—
    (a) Member States;
    (b) natural or legal persons who claim a legitimate interest.

3.      Without prejudice to the other provisions of this Regulation, the Commission may, before taking a decision under paragraph 1, address to the undertakings or associations of undertakings concerned recommendations for termination of the infringement.

## Article 4

### Notification of new agreements, decisions and practices

1.      Agreements, decisions and concerted practices of the kind described in Article 85(1) of the Treaty which come into existence after the entry into force of this Regulation and in respect of which the parties seek application of Article 85(3) must be notified to the Commission. Until they have been notified, no decision in application of Article 85(3) may be taken.

2.      Paragraph 1 shall not apply to agreements, decisions or concerted practices where—
    (1) the only parties thereto are undertakings from one Member State and the agreements, decisions or practices do not relate either to imports or to exports between Member States;

(2) not more than two undertakings are party thereto, and the agreements only—

    (a) restrict the freedom of one party to the contract in determining the prices or conditions of business upon which the goods which he has obtained from the other party to the contract may be resold; or

    (b) impose restrictions on the exercise of the rights of the assignee or user of industrial property rights—in particular patents, utility models, designs or trade marks—or of the person entitled under a contract to the assignment, or grant, of the right to use a method of manufacture or knowledge relating to the use and to the application of industrial processes;

(3) they have as their sole object—

    (a) the development or uniform application of standards or types; or

    [(b) joint research and development;

    (c) specialisation in the manufacture of products, including agreements necessary for the achievement thereof;

       — where the products which are the subject of specialisation do not, in a substantial part of the common market, represent more than 15% of the volume of business done in identical products or those considered by consumers to be similar by reason of their characteristics, price and use, and

       — where the total annual turnover of the participating undertakings does not exceed 200 million units of account.

These agreements decisions and concerted practices may be notified to the Commission].

NOTES

Para 2: in sub-para (3), para (b) substituted, and para (c) and remaining words added, by Council Regulation 2822/71/EEC.

## Article 5

### Notification of existing agreements, decisions and practices

1.    Agreements, decisions and concerted practices of the kind described in Article 85(1) of the Treaty which are in existence at the date of entry into force of this Regulation and in respect of which the parties seek application of Article 85(3) shall be notified to the Commission [before 1 November 1962]. [However, notwithstanding the foregoing provisions, any agreements, decisions and concerted practices to which not more than two undertakings are party shall be notified before 1 February 1963].

2.    Paragraph 1 shall not apply to agreements, decisions or concerted practices falling within Article 4(2); these may be notified to the Commission.

NOTES

Para 1: first words in square brackets substituted, and second words in square brackets added, by Council Regulation 59/62/EEC, Art 1(1), (2).

## Article 6

### Decisions pursuant to Article 85(3)

1.    Whenever the Commission takes a decision pursuant to Article 85(3) of the Treaty, it shall specify therein the date from which the decision shall take effect. Such date shall not be earlier than the date of notification.

2.     The second sentence of paragraph 1 shall not apply to agreements, decisions or concerted practices falling within Article 4(2) and Article 5(2), nor to those falling within Article 5(1) which have been notified within the time limit specified in Article 5(1).

## Article 7

### Special provisions for existing agreements, decisions and practices

1.     Where agreements, decisions and concerted practices in existence at the date of entry into force of this Regulation and notified [within the limits specified in Article (1)] do not satisfy the requirements of Article 85(3) of the Treaty and the undertakings or associations of undertakings concerned cease to give effect to them or modify them in such manner that they no longer fall within the prohibition contained in Article 85(1) or that they satisfy the requirements of Article 85(3), the prohibition contained in Article 85(1) shall apply only for a period fixed by the Commission. A decision by the Commission pursuant to the foregoing sentence shall not apply as against undertakings and associations of undertakings which did not expressly consent to the notification.

2.     Paragraph 1 shall apply to agreements, decisions and concerted practices falling within Article 4(2) which are in existence at the date of entry into force of this Regulation if they are notified [before 1 January 1967].

---

NOTES

   Para 1: words in square brackets substituted by Council Regulation 59/62/EEC, Art 1(3).
   Para 2: words in square brackets substituted by Council Regulation 118/63/EEC, Art 1.

---

## Article 8

### Duration and revocation of decisions under Article 85(3)

1.     A decision in application of Article 85(3) of the Treaty shall be issued for a specified period and conditions and obligations may be attached thereto.

2.     A decision may on application be renewed if the requirements of Article 85(3) of the Treaty continue to be satisfied.

3.     The Commission may revoke or amend its decision or prohibit specified acts by the parties—
   (a) where there has been a change in any of the facts which were basic to the making of the decision;
   (b) where the parties commit a breach of any obligation attached to the decision;
   (c) where the decision is based on incorrect information or was induced by deceit;
   (d) where the parties abuse the exemption from the provisions of Article 85(1) of the Treaty granted to them by the decision.

   In cases to which subparagraphs (b), (c) or (d) apply, the decision may be revoked with retroactive effect.

## Article 9

### Powers

1.     Subject to review of its decision by the Court of Justice, the Commission shall have sole power to declare Article 85(1) inapplicable pursuant to Article 85(3) of the Treaty.

2.     The Commission shall have power to apply Article 85(1) and Article 86 of the Treaty; this power may be exercised notwithstanding that the time limits specified in Article 5(1) and in Article 7(2) relating to notification have not expired.

3.     As long as the Commission has not initiated any procedure under Articles 2, 3 or 6, the authorities of the Member States shall remain competent to apply Article 85(1) and Article 86 in accordance with Article 88 of the Treaty; they shall remain competent in this respect notwithstanding that the time limits specified in Article 5(1) and in Article 7(2) relating to notification have not expired.

## Article 10

### Liaison with the authorities of the Member States

1.     The Commission shall forthwith transmit to the competent authorities of the Member States a copy of the applications and notifications together with copies of the most important documents lodged with the Commission for the purpose of establishing the existence of infringements of Articles 85 or 86 of the Treaty or of obtaining negative clearance or a decision in application of Article 85(3).

2.     The Commission shall carry out the procedure set out in paragraph 1 in close and constant liaison with the competent authorities of the Member States; such authorities shall have the right to express their views upon that procedure.

3.     An Advisory Committee on Restrictive Practices and Monopolies shall be consulted prior to the taking of any decision following upon a procedure under paragraph 1, and of any decision concerning the renewal, amendment or revocation of a decision pursuant to Article 85(3) of the Treaty.

4.     The Advisory Committee shall be composed of officials competent in the matter of restrictive practices and monopolies. Each Member State shall appoint an official to represent it who, if prevented from attending, may be replaced by another official.

5.     The consultation shall take place at a joint meeting convened by the Commission; such meeting shall be held not earlier than fourteen days after dispatch of the notice convening it. The notice shall, in respect of each case to be examined, be accompanied by a summary of the case together with an indication of the most important documents, and a preliminary draft decision.

6.     The Advisory Committee may deliver an opinion notwithstanding that some of its members or their alternates are not present. A report of the outcome of the consultative proceedings shall be annexed to the draft decision. It shall not be made public.

## Article 11

### Requests for information

1.     In carrying out the duties assigned to it by Article 89 and by provisions adopted under Article 87 of the Treaty, the Commission may obtain all necessary information from the Governments and competent authorities of the Member States and from undertakings and associations of undertakings.

2.     When sending a request for information to an undertaking or association of undertakings, the Commission shall at the same time forward a copy of the request to the competent authority of the Member State in whose territory the seat of the undertaking or association of undertakings is situated.

3.     In its request the Commission shall state the legal basis and the purpose of the request and also the penalties provided for in Article 15(1)(b) for supplying incorrect information.

4.     The owners of the undertakings or their representatives and, in the case of legal persons, companies or firms, or of associations having no legal personality, the persons authorised to represent them by law or by their constitution shall supply the information requested.

5.     Where an undertaking or association of undertakings does not supply the information requested within the time limit fixed by the Commission, or supplies incomplete information, the Commission shall by decision require the information to be supplied. The decision shall specify what information is required, fix an appropriate time limit within which it is to be supplied and indicate the penalties provided for in Article 15(1)(b) and Article 16(1)(c) and the right to have the decision reviewed by the Court of Justice.

6.     The Commission shall at the same time forward a copy of its decision to the competent authority of the Member State in whose territory the seat of the undertaking or association of undertakings is situated.

### Article 12

### Inquiry into sectors of the economy

1.     If in any sector of the economy the trend of trade between Member States, price movements, inflexibility of prices or other circumstances suggest that in the economic sector concerned competition is being restricted or distorted within the common market, the Commission may decide to conduct a general inquiry into that economic sector and in the course thereof may request undertakings in the sector concerned to supply the information necessary for giving effect to the principles formulated in Articles 85 and 86 of the Treaty and for carrying out the duties entrusted to the Commission.

2.     The Commission may in particular request every undertaking or association of undertakings in the economic sector concerned to communicate to it all agreements, decisions and concerted practices which are exempt from notification by virtue of Article 4(2) and Article 5(2).

3.     When making inquiries pursuant to paragraph 2, the Commission shall also request undertakings or groups of undertakings whose size suggests that they occupy a dominant position within the common market or a substantial part thereof to supply to the Commission such particulars of the structure of the undertakings and of their behaviour as are requisite to an appraisal of their position in the light of Article 86 of the Treaty.

4.     Article 10(3) to (6) and Articles 11, 13 and 14 shall apply correspondingly.

### Article 13

### Investigations by the authorities of the Member States

1.     At the request of the Commission, the competent authorities of the Member States shall undertake the investigations which the Commission considers to be necessary under Article 14(1), or which it has ordered by decision pursuant to Article 14(3). The officials of the competent authorities of the Member States responsible for

conducting these investigations shall exercise their powers upon production of an authorisation in writing issued by the competent authority of the Member State in whose territory the investigation is to be made. Such authorisation shall specify the subject matter and purpose of the investigation.

2.    If so requested by the Commission or by the competent authority of the Member State in whose territory the investigation is to be made, the officials of the Commission may assist the officials of such authorities in carrying out their duties.

## Article 14

### Investigating powers of the Commission

1.    In carrying out the duties assigned to it by Article 89 and by provisions adopted under Article 87 of the Treaty, the Commission may undertake all necessary investigations into undertakings and associations of undertakings. To this end the officials authorised by the Commission are empowered—
   (a)  to examine the books and other business records;
   (b)  to take copies of or extracts from the books and business records;
   (c)  to ask for oral explanations on the spot;
   (d)  to enter any premises, land and means of transport of undertakings.

2.    The officials of the Commission authorised for the purpose of these investigations shall exercise their powers upon production of an authorisation in writing specifying the subject matter and purpose of the investigation and the penalties provided for in Article 15(1)(c) in cases where production of the required books or other business records is incomplete. In good time before the investigation, the Commission shall inform the competent authority of the Member State in whose territory the same is to be made of the investigation and of the identity of the authorised officials.

3.    Undertakings and associations of undertakings shall submit to investigations ordered by decision of the Commission. The decision shall specify the subject matter and purpose of the investigation, appoint the date on which it is to begin and indicate the penalties provided for in Article 15(1)(c) and Article 16(1)(d) and the right to have the decision reviewed by the Court of Justice.

4.    The Commission shall take decisions referred to in paragraph 3 after consultation with the competent authority of the Member State in whose territory the investigation is to be made.

5.    Officials of the competent authority of the Member State in whose territory the investigation is to be made may, at the request of such authority or of the Commission, assist the officials of the Commission in carrying out their duties.

6.    Where an undertaking opposes an investigation ordered pursuant to this Article, the Member State concerned shall afford the necessary assistance to the officials authorised by the Commission to enable them to make their investigation. Member States shall, after consultation with the Commission, take the necessary measures to this end before 1 October 1962.

## Article 15

### Fines

1.    The Commission may by decision impose on undertakings or associations of undertakings fines of from 100 to 5 000 units of account where, intentionally or negligently—

   (a) they supply incorrect or misleading information in an application pursuant to Article 2 or in a notification pursuant to Articles 4 or 5; or

   (b) they supply incorrect information in response to a request made pursuant to Article 11(3) or (5) or to Article 12, or do not supply information within the time limit fixed by a decision taken under Article 11(5); or

   (c) they produce the required books or other business records in incomplete form during investigations under Article 13 or 14, or refuse to submit to an investigation ordered by decision issued in implementation of Article 14(3).

2.    The Commission may by decision impose on undertakings or associations of undertakings fines of from 1 000 to 1 000 000 units of account, or a sum in excess thereof but not exceeding 10% of the turnover in the preceding business year of each of the undertakings participating in the infringement where, either intentionally or negligently—

   (a)  they infringe Article 85(1) or Article 86 of the Treaty; or

   (b)  they commit a breach of any obligation imposed pursuant to Article 8(1).

   In fixing the amount of the fine, regard shall be had both to the gravity and to the duration of the infringement.

3.    Article 10(3) to (6) shall apply.

4.    Decisions taken pursuant to paragraphs 1 and 2 shall not be of a criminal law nature.

5.    The fines provided for in paragraph 2(a) shall not be imposed in respect of acts taking place—

   (a)  after notification to the Commission and before its decision in application of Article 85(3) of the Treaty, provided they fall within the limits of the activity described in the notification;

   (b)  before notification and in the course of agreements, decisions or concerted practices in existence at the date of entry into force of this Regulation, provided that notification was effected within the time limits specified in Article 5(1) and Article 7(2).

6.    Paragraph 5 shall not have effect where the Commission has informed the undertakings concerned that after preliminary examination it is of opinion that Article 85(1) of the Treaty applies and that application of Article 85(3) is not justified.

## Article 16

### Periodic penalty payments

1.    The Commission may by decision impose on undertakings or associations of undertakings periodic penalty payments of from 50 to 1000 units of account per day, calculated from the date appointed by the decision, in order to compel them—

   (a)  to put an end to an infringement of Article 85 or 86 of the Treaty, in accordance with a decision taken pursuant to Article 3 of this Regulation;

   (b)  to refrain from any act prohibited under Article 8(3);

   (c)  to supply complete and correct information which it has requested by decision taken pursuant to Article 11(5);

   (d)  to submit to an investigation which it has ordered by decision taken pursuant to Article 14(3).

2.    Where the undertakings or associations of undertakings have satisfied the obligation which it was the purpose of the periodic penalty payment to enforce, the

Commission may fix the total amount of the periodic penalty payment at a lower figure than that which would arise under the original decision.

3.      Article 10(3) to (6) shall apply.

## Article 17

### Review by the Court of Justice

The Court of Justice shall have unlimited jurisdiction within the meaning of Article 172 of the Treaty to review decisions whereby the Commission has fixed a fine or periodic penalty payment; it may cancel, reduce or increase the fine or periodic penalty payment imposed.

## Article 18

### Unit of account

For the purposes of applying Articles 15 to 17 the unit of account shall be that adopted in drawing up the budget of the Community in accordance with Articles 207 and 209 of the Treaty.

## Article 19

### Hearing of the parties and of third persons

1.      Before taking decisions as provided for in Articles 2, 3, 6, 7, 8, 15 and 16, the Commission shall give the undertakings or associations of undertakings concerned the opportunity of being heard on the matters to which the Commission has taken objection.

2.      If the Commission or the competent authorities of the Member States consider it necessary, they may also hear other natural or legal persons. Applications to be heard on the part of such persons shall, where they show a sufficient interest, be granted.

3.      Where the Commission intends to give negative clearance pursuant to Article 2 or take a decision in application of Article 85(3) of the Treaty, it shall publish a summary of the relevant application or notification and invite all interested third parties to submit their observations within a time limit which it shall fix being not less than one month. Publication shall have regard to the legitimate interest of undertakings in the protection of their business secrets.

## Article 20

### Professional secrecy

1.      Information acquired as a result of the application of Articles 11, 12, 13 and 14 shall be used only for the purpose of the relevant request or investigation.

2.      Without prejudice to the provisions of Articles 19 and 21, the Commission and the competent authorities of the Member States, their officials and other servants shall not disclose information acquired by them as a result of the application of this Regulation and of the kind covered by the obligation of professional secrecy.

3.      The provisions of paragraphs 1 and 2 shall not prevent publication of general information or surveys which do not contain information relating to particular undertakings or associations of undertakings.

## Article 21

### Publication of decisions

1.     The Commission shall publish the decisions which it takes pursuant to Articles 2, 3, 6, 7 and 8.

2.     The publication shall state the names of the parties and the main content of the decision; it shall have regard to the legitimate interest of undertakings in the protection of their business secrets.

## Article 22

### Special provisions

1.     The Commission shall submit to the Council proposals for making certain categories of agreement, decision and concerted practice falling within Article 4(2) or Article 5(2) compulsorily notifiable under Article 4 or 5.

2.     Within one year from the date of entry into force of this Regulation, the Council shall examine, on a proposal from the Commission, what special provisions might be made for exempting from the provisions of this Regulation agreements, decisions and concerted practices falling within Article 4(2) or Article 5(2).

## Article 23

### Transitional provisions applicable to decisions of authorities of the Member States

1.     Agreements, decisions and concerted practices of the kind described in Article 85(1) of the Treaty to which, before the entry into force of this Regulation, the competent authority of a Member State has declared Article 85(1) to be inapplicable pursuant to Article 85(3) shall not be subject to compulsory notification under Article 5. The decision of the competent authority of the Member State shall be deemed to be a decision within the meaning of Article 6; it shall cease to be valid upon expiration of the period fixed by such authority but in any event not more than three years after the entry into force of this Regulation. Article 8(3) shall apply.

2.     Applications for renewal of decisions of the kind described in paragraph 1 shall be decided upon by the Commission in accordance with Article 8(2).

## Article 24

### Implementing provisions

The Commission shall have power to adopt implementing provisions concerning the form, content and other details of applications pursuant to Articles 2 and 3 and of notifications pursuant to Articles 4 and 5, and concerning hearings pursuant to Article 19(1) and (2).

## [Article 25

1.     As regards agreements, decisions and concerted practices to which Article 85 of the Treaty applies by virtue of accession, the date of accession shall be substituted for the date of entry into force of this regulation in every place where reference is made in this Regulation to this latter date.

2.      Agreements, decisions and concerted practices existing at the date of accession to which Article 85 of the Treaty applies by virtue of accession shall be notified pursuant to Article 5(1) or Article 7(1) and (2) within six months from the date of accession.

3.      Fines under Article 15(2)(a) shall not be imposed in respect of any act prior to notification of the agreements, decisions and practices to which paragraph 2 applies and which have been notified within the period therein specified.

4.      New Member States shall take the measures referred to in Article 14(6) within six months from the date of accession after consulting the Commission.]

[5.      The provisions of paragraphs (1) to (4) above still apply in the same way in the case of accession of the Hellenic Republic, the Kingdom of Spain and of the Portuguese Republic.]

[6.      The provisions of paragraphs 1 to 4 still apply in the same way in the case of the accession of Austria, Finland and Sweden. However, they do not apply to agreements, decisions and concerted practices which at the date of the accession already fall under Article 53 of the EEA Agreement.]

NOTES

Paras 1–4: added by the 1972 Act of Accession of Denmark, Ireland and the United Kingdom, Annex I(V)(1).

Para 5: originally added by the 1979 Act of Accession of the Hellenic Republic, Annex I(V)(1) and subsequently substituted by the 1985 Act of Accession of the Kingdom of Spain and the Portuguese Republic, Annex I(IV)(5).

Para 6: added by the 1994 Act of Accession of the Kingdom of Norway, the Republic of Austria, the Republic of Finland and the Kingdom of Sweden, Annex I(III)(B)(1), as adjusted by Council Decision 95/1/EC, Annex I(III)(B)(1).

This Regulation shall be binding in its entirety and directly applicable in all Member States.

# COMMISSION REGULATION

## of 25 July 1963

### on the hearings provided for in Article 19(1) and (2) of Council Regulation No 17

### (99/63/EEC)

NOTES

Date of publication in OJ: OJ L127, 20.8.63, p 2268 (S edn, 1963–64, p 47).

## THE COMMISSION OF THE EUROPEAN ECONOMIC COMMUNITY,

Having regard to the Treaty establishing the European Economic Community, and in particular Articles 87 and 155 thereof;

Having regard to Article 24 of Council Regulation No 17 of 6 February 1962 (First Regulation implementing Articles 85 and 86 of the Treaty);

Whereas the Commission has power under Article 24 of Council Regulation No 17 to lay down implementing provisions concerning the hearings provided for in Article 19(1) and (2) of that Regulation;

Whereas in most cases the Commission will in the course of its inquiries already be in close touch with the undertakings or associations of undertakings which are the subject thereof and they will accordingly have the opportunity of making known their views regarding the objections raised against them;

Whereas, however, in accordance with Article 19(1) of Regulation No 17 and with the rights of defence, the undertakings and associations of undertakings concerned must have the right on conclusion of the inquiry to submit their comments on the whole of the objections raised against them which the Commission proposes to deal with in its decisions;

Whereas persons other than the undertakings or associations of undertakings which are the subject of the inquiry may have an interest in being heard; whereas, by the second sentence of Article 19(2) of Regulation No 17, such persons must have the opportunity of being heard if they apply and show that they have a sufficient interest;

Whereas it is desirable to enable persons who, pursuant to Article 3(2) of Regulation No 17, have applied for an infringement to be terminated to submit their comments where the Commission considers that on the basis of the information in its possession there are insufficient grounds for granting the application;

Whereas the various persons entitled to submit comments must do so in writing, both in their own interest and in the interests of good administration, without prejudice to oral procedure where appropriate to supplement the written evidence;

Whereas it is necessary to define the rights of persons who are to be heard, and in particular the conditions upon which they may be represented or assisted and the setting and calculation of time limits;

Whereas the Advisory Committee on Restrictive Practices and Monopolies delivers its Opinion on the basis of a preliminary draft decision; whereas it must therefore be consulted concerning a case after the inquiry in respect thereof has been completed; whereas such consultation does not prevent the Commission from re-opening an inquiry if need be;

HAS ADOPTED THIS REGULATION—

## Article 1

Before consulting the Advisory Committee on Restrictive Practices and Monopolies, the Commission shall hold a hearing pursuant to Article 19(1) of Regulation No 17.

## Article 2

1. The Commission shall inform undertakings and associations of undertakings in writing of the objections raised against them. The communication shall be addressed to each of them or to a joint agent appointed by them.

2. The Commission may inform the parties by giving notice in the *Official Journal of the European Communities*, if from the circumstances of the case this appears appropriate, in particular where notice is to be given to a number of undertakings but no joint agent has been appointed. The notice shall have regard to the legitimate interest of the undertakings in the protection of their business secrets.

3. A fine or a periodic penalty payment may be imposed on an undertaking or association of undertakings only if the objections were notified in the manner provided for in paragraph 1.

4. The Commission shall when giving notice of objections fix a time limit up to which the undertakings and associations of undertakings may inform the Commission of their views.

## Article 3

1. Undertakings and associations of undertakings shall, within the appointed time limit, make known in writing their views concerning the objections raised against them.

2.      They may in their written comments set out all matters relevant to their defence.

3.      They may attach any relevant documents in proof of the facts set out. They may also propose that the Commission hear persons who may corroborate those facts.

### Article 4

The Commission shall in its decisions deal only with those objections raised against undertakings and associations of undertakings in respect of which they have been afforded the opportunity of making known their views.

### Article 5

If natural or legal persons showing a sufficient interest apply to be heard pursuant to Article 19(2) of Regulation No 17, the Commission shall afford them the opportunity of making known their views in writing within such time limit as it shall fix.

### Article 6

Where the Commission, having received an application pursuant to Article 3(2) of Regulation No 17, considers that on the basis of the information in its possession there are insufficient grounds for granting the application, it shall inform the applicants of its reasons and fix a time limit for them to submit any further comments in writing.

### Article 7

1.      The Commission shall afford to persons who have so requested in their written comments the opportunity to put forward their arguments orally, if those persons show a sufficient interest or if the Commission proposes to impose on them a fine or periodic penalty payment.

2.      The Commission may likewise afford to any other person the opportunity of orally expressing his views.

### Article 8

1.      The Commission shall summon the persons to be heard to attend on such date as it shall appoint.

2.      It shall forthwith transmit a copy of the summons to the competent authorities of the Member States, who may appoint an official to take part in the hearing.

### Article 9

1.      Hearings shall be conducted by the persons appointed by the Commission for that purpose.

2.      Persons summoned to attend shall appear either in person or be represented by legal representatives or by representatives authorised by their constitution. Undertakings and associations of undertakings may moreover be represented by a duly authorised agent appointed from among their permanent staff.

Persons heard by the Commission may be assisted by lawyers or university teachers who are entitled to plead before the Court of Justice of the European Communities in accordance with Article 17 of the Protocol on the Statute of the Court, or by other qualified persons.

3.     Hearings shall not be public. Persons shall be heard separately or in the presence of other persons summoned to attend. In the latter case, regard shall be had to the legitimate interest of the undertakings in the protection of their business secrets.

4.     The essential content of the statements made by each person heard shall be recorded in minutes which shall be read and approved by him.

## Article 10

Without prejudice to Article 2(2), information and summonses from the Commission shall be sent to the addressees by registered letter with acknowledgement of receipt, or shall be delivered by hand against receipt.

## Article 11

1.     In fixing the time limits provided for in Articles 2, 5 and 6, the Commission shall have regard both to the time required for preparation of comments and to the urgency of the case. The time limit shall be not less than two weeks; it may be extended.

2.     Time limits shall run from the day following receipt of a communication or delivery thereof by hand.

3.     Written comments must reach the Commission or be dispatched by registered letter before expiry of the time limit. Where the time limit would expire on a Sunday or public holiday, it shall be extended up to the end of the next following working day. For the purpose of calculating this extension, public holidays shall, in cases where the relevant date is the date of receipt of written comments, be those set out in the Annex to this Regulation, and in cases where the relevant date is the date of dispatch, those appointed by law in the country of dispatch.

   This Regulation shall be binding in its entirety and directly applicable in all Member States.

## ANNEX
## REFERRED TO IN THE THIRD SENTENCE OF ARTICLE 11(3)

(List of public holidays)

New Year ..................................... 1 Jan

Good Friday ...................................

Easter Saturday ...............................

Easter Monday ...............................

Labour Day ..................................... 1 May

Schuman Plan Day ......................... 9 May

Ascension Day ...............................

Whit Monday ................................

Belgian National Day ..................... 21 July

Assumption .................................... 15 Aug

All Saints .......................................... 1 Nov

All Souls ........................................... 2 Nov

Christmas Eve ................................ 24 Dec

Christmas Day ............................... 25 Dec

The day following Christmas Day, ... 26 Dec

New Year's Eve ............................. 31 Dec

# COUNCIL REGULATION

of 21 December 1989

## on the control of concentrations between undertakings

## (4064/89/EEC)

NOTES

Date of publication in OJ: OJ L257, 21.9.90, pp 14–25.

## THE COUNCIL OF THE EUROPEAN COMMUNITIES,

Having regard to the Treaty establishing the European Economic Community, and in particular Articles 87 and 235 thereof,

Having regard to the proposal from the Commission,

Having regard to the opinion of the European Parliament,

Having regard to the opinion of the Economic and Social Committee,

(1)    Whereas, for the achievement of the aims of the Treaty establishing the European Economic Community, Article 3(f) gives the Community the objective of instituting "a system ensuring that competition in the common market is not distorted";

(2)    Whereas this system is essential for the achievement of the internal market by 1992 and its further development;

(3)    Whereas the dismantling of internal frontiers is resulting and will continue to result in major corporate reorganisations in the Community, particularly in the form of concentrations;

(4)    Whereas such a development must be welcomed as being in line with the requirements of dynamic competition and capable of increasing the competitiveness of European industry, improving the conditions of growth and raising the standard of living in the Community;

(5)    Whereas, however, it must be ensured that the process of reorganisation does not result in lasting damage to competition; whereas Community law must therefore include provisions governing those concentrations which may significantly impede effective competition in the common market or in a substantial part of it;

(6)    Whereas Articles 85 and 86, while applicable, according to the case-law of the Court of Justice, to certain concentrations, are not, however, sufficient to control all operations which may prove to be incompatible with the system of undistorted competition envisaged in the Treaty;

(7)    Whereas a new legal instrument should therefore be created in the form of a Regulation to permit effective control of all concentrations from the point of view of their effect on the structure of competition in the Community and to be the only instrument applicable to such concentrations;

(8)    Whereas this Regulation should therefore be based not only on Article 87 but, principally, on Article 235 of the Treaty, under which the Community may give itself the additional powers of action necessary for the attainment of its objectives, including with regard to concentrations on the markets for agricultural products listed in Annex II to the Treaty;

(9) Whereas the provisions to be adopted in this Regulation should apply to significant structural changes the impact of which on the market goes beyond the national borders of any one Member State;

(10) Whereas the scope of application of this Regulation should therefore be defined according to the geographical area of activity of the undertakings concerned and be limited by quantitative thresholds in order to cover those concentrations which have a Community dimension; whereas, at the end of an initial phase of the application of this Regulation, these thresholds should be reviewed in the light of the experience gained;

(11) Whereas a concentration with a Community dimension exists where the combined aggregate turnover of the undertakings concerned exceeds given levels worldwide and within the Community and where at least two of the undertakings concerned have their sole or main fields of activities in different Member States or where, although the undertakings in question act mainly in one and the same Member State, at least one of them has substantial operations in at least one other Member State; whereas that is also the case where the concentrations are effected by undertakings which do not have their principal fields of activities in the Community but which have substantial operations there;

(12) Whereas the arrangements to be introduced for the control of concentrations should, without prejudice to Article 90(2) of the Treaty, respect the principle of non-discrimination between the public and the private sectors; whereas, in the public sector, calculation of the turnover of an undertaking concerned in a concentration needs, therefore, to take account of undertakings making up an economic unit with an independent power of decision, irrespective of the way in which their capital is held or of the rules of administrative supervision applicable to them;

(13) Whereas it is necessary to establish whether concentrations with a Community dimension are compatible or not with the common market from the point of view of the need to maintain and develop effective competition in the common market; whereas, in so doing, the Commission must place its appraisal within the general framework of the achievement of the fundamental objectives referred to in Article 2 of the Treaty, including that of strengthening the Community's economic and social cohesion, referred to in Article 130a;

(14) Whereas this Regulation should establish the principle that a concentration with a Community dimension which creates or strengthens a position as a result of which effective competition in the common market or in a substantial part of it is significantly impeded is to be declared incompatible with the common market;

(15) Whereas concentrations which, by reason of the limited market share of the undertakings concerned, are not liable to impede effective competition may be presumed to be compatible with the common market; whereas, without prejudice to Articles 85 and 86 of the Treaty, an indication to this effect exists, in particular, where the market share of the undertakings concerned does not exceed 25% either in the common market or in a substantial part of it;

(16) Whereas the Commission should have the task of taking all the decisions necessary to establish whether or not concentrations with a Community dimension are compatible with the common market, as well as decisions designed to restore effective competition;

(17) Whereas to ensure effective control undertakings should be obliged to give prior notification of concentrations with a Community dimension and provision should be made for the suspension of concentrations for a limited period, and for the possibility of extending or waiving a suspension where necessary; whereas in the interests of legal certainty the validity of transactions must nevertheless be protected as much as necessary;

(18) Whereas a period within which the Commission must initiate proceedings in respect of a notified concentration and periods within which it must give a final decision on the compatibility or incompatibility with the common market of a notified concentration should be laid down;

(19) Whereas the undertakings concerned must be afforded the right to be heard by the Commission when proceedings have been initiated; whereas the members of the management and supervisory bodies and the recognised representatives of the employees of the undertakings concerned, and third parties showing a legitimate interest, must also be given the opportunity to be heard;

(20) Whereas the Commission should act in close and constant liaison with the competent authorities of the Member States from which it obtains comments and information;

(21) Whereas, for the purposes of this Regulation, and in accordance with the case-law of the Court of Justice, the Commission must be afforded the assistance of the Member States and must also be empowered to require information to be given and to carry out the necessary investigations in order to appraise concentrations;

(22) Whereas compliance with this Regulation must be enforceable by means of fines and periodic penalty payments; whereas the Court of Justice should be given unlimited jurisdiction in that regard pursuant to Article 172 of the Treaty;

(23) Whereas it is appropriate to define the concept of concentration in such a manner as to cover only operations bringing about a lasting change in the structure of the undertakings concerned; whereas it is therefore necessary to exclude from the scope of this Regulation those operations which have as their object or effect the co-ordination of the competitive behaviour of undertakings which remain independent, since such operations fall to be examined under the appropriate provisions of the Regulations implementing Articles 85 and 86 of the Treaty; whereas it is appropriate to make this distinction specifically in the case of the creation of joint ventures;

(24) Whereas there is no co-ordination of competitive behaviour within the meaning of this Regulation where two or more undertakings agree to acquire jointly control of one or more other undertakings with the object and effect of sharing amongst themselves such undertakings or their assets;

(25) Whereas this Regulation should still apply where the undertakings concerned accept restrictions directly related and necessary to the implementation of the concentration;

(26) Whereas the Commission should be given exclusive competence to apply this Regulation, subject to review by the Court of Justice;

(27) Whereas the Member States may not apply their national legislation on competition to concentrations with a Community dimension, unless this Regulation makes provision therefor; whereas the relevant powers of national authorities should be limited to cases where, failing intervention by the Commission, effective competition is likely to be significantly impeded within the territory of a Member State and where the competition interests of that Member State cannot be sufficiently protected otherwise by this Regulation; whereas the Member States concerned must act promptly in such cases; whereas this Regulation cannot, because of the diversity of national law, fix a single deadline for the adoption of remedies;

(28) Whereas, furthermore, the exclusive application of this Regulation to concentrations with a Community dimension is without prejudice to Article 223 of the Treaty, and does not prevent the Member States from taking appropriate measures to protect legitimate interests other than those pursued by this Regulation, provided that such measures are compatible with the general principles and other provisions of Community law;

(29) Whereas concentrations not covered by this Regulation come, in principle, within the jurisdiction of the Member States; whereas, however, the Commission should have the power to act, at the request of a Member State concerned, in cases where effective competition could be significantly impeded within that Member State's territory;

(30) Whereas the conditions in which concentrations involving Community undertakings are carried out in non-member countries should be observed, and provision should be made for the possibility of the Council giving the Commission an appropriate mandate for negotiation with a view to obtaining non-discriminatory treatment for Community undertakings;

(31) Whereas this Regulation in no way detracts from the collective rights of employees as recognised in the undertakings concerned,

## HAS ADOPTED THIS REGULATION—

### Article 1

### Scope

[1.    Without prejudice to Article 22, this Regulation shall apply to all concentrations with a Community dimension as defined in paragraphs 2 and 3.]

2.    For the purposes of this Regulation, a concentration has a Community dimension where—

(a) the combined aggregate worldwide turnover of all the undertakings concerned is more than ECU 5 000 million; and

(b) the aggregate Community-wide turnover of each of at least two of the undertakings concerned is more than ECU 250 million,

unless each of the undertakings concerned achieves more than two-thirds of its aggregate Community-wide turnover within one and the same Member State.

3.        The thresholds laid down in paragraph 2 will be reviewed before the end of the fourth year following that of the adoption of this Regulation by the Council acting by a qualified majority on a proposal from the Commission .

[3.        For the purposes of this Regulation, a concentration that does not meet the thresholds laid down in paragraph 2 has a Community dimension where—

(a) the combined aggregate worldwide turnover of all the undertakings concerned is more than ECU 2 500 million;

(b) in each of at least three Member States, the combined aggregate turnover of all the undertakings concerned is more than ECU 100 million;

(c) in each of at least three Member States included for the purpose of point (b), the aggregate turnover of each of at least two of the undertakings concerned is more than ECU 25 million; and

(d) the aggregate Community-wide turnover of at least two of the undertakings concerned is more than ECU 100 million;

unless each of the undertakings concerned achieves more than two-thirds of its aggregate Community-wide turnover within one and the same Member State.]

[4.        Before 1 July 2000 the Commission shall report to the Council on the operation of the thresholds and criteria set out in paragraphs 2 and 3.]

[5.        Following the report referred to in paragraph 4 and on a proposal from the Commission, the Council, acting by a qualified majority, may revise the thresholds and criteria mentioned in paragraph 3.]

NOTES

Paras 1, 3 substituted, paras 4, 5 added : Council Regulation (EC) No 1310/97, Art 1(1),

## Article 2

### Appraisal of concentrations

1.        Concentrations within the scope of this Regulation shall be appraised in accordance with the following provisions with a view to establishing whether or not they are compatible with the common market.

In making this appraisal, the Commission shall take into account—

(a) the need to maintain and develop effective competition within the common market in view of, among other things, the structure of all the markets concerned and the actual or potential competition from undertakings located either within or out with the Community;

(b) the market position of the undertakings concerned and their economic and financial power, the alternatives available to suppliers and users, their access to supplies or markets, any legal or other barriers to entry, supply and demand trends for the relevant goods and services, the interests of the intermediate and ultimate consumers, and the development of technical and economic progress provided that it is to consumers' advantage and does not form an obstacle to competition.

2.    A concentration which does not create or strengthen a dominant position as a result of which effective competition would be significantly impeded in the common market or in a substantial part of it shall be declared compatible with the common market.

3.    A concentration which creates or strengthens a dominant position as a result of which effective competition would be significantly impeded in the common market or in a substantial part of it shall be declared incompatible with the common market.

[4.    To the extent that the creation of a joint venture constituting a concentration pursuant to Article 3 has as its object or effect the coordination of the competitive behaviour of undertakings that remain independent, such coordination shall be appraised in accordance with the criteria of Article 85(1) and (3) of the Treaty, with a view to establishing whether or not the operation is compatible with the common market.

In making this appraisal, the Commission shall take into account in particular—
— whether two or more parent companies retain to a significant extent activities in the same market as the joint venture or in a market which is downstream or upstream from that of the joint venture or in a neighbouring market closely related to this market,
— whether the coordination which is the direct consequence of the creation of the joint venture affords the undertakings concerned the possibility of eliminating competition in respect of a substantial part of the products or services in question.]

NOTES
Para 4: added by Council Regulation (EC) No 1310/97, Art 1(2).

## Article 3

### Definition of concentration

1.    A concentration shall be deemed to arise where—
(a) two or more previously independent undertakings merge, or
(b) — one or more persons already controlling at least one undertaking, or
— one or more undertakings

acquire, whether by purchase of securities or assets, by contract or by any other means, direct or indirect control of the whole or parts of one or more other undertakings.

2.    The creation of a joint venture performing on a lasting basis all the functions of an autonomous economic entity, shall constitute a concentration within the meaning of paragraph 1(b).

3.    For the purposes of this Regulation, control shall be constituted by rights, contracts or any other means which, either separately or in combination and having regard to the considerations of fact or law involved, confer the possibility of exercising decisive influence on an undertaking, in particular by—
(a) ownership or the right to use all or part of the assets of an undertaking;
(b) rights or contracts which confer decisive influence on the composition, voting or decisions of the organs of an undertaking.

4.    Control is acquired by persons or undertakings which—

    (a)  are holders of the rights or entitled to rights under the contracts concerned, or

    (b)  while not being holders of such rights or entitled to rights under such contracts, have the power to exercise the rights deriving therefrom.

5.      A concentration shall not be deemed to arise where—

    (a)  credit institutions or other financial institutions or insurance companies, the normal activities of which include transactions and dealing in securities for their own account or for the account of others, hold on a temporary basis securities which they have acquired in an undertaking with a view to reselling them, provided that they do not exercise voting rights in respect of those securities with a view to determining the competitive behaviour of that undertaking or provided that they exercise such voting rights only with a view to preparing the disposal of all or part of that undertaking or of its assets or the disposal of those securities and that any such disposal takes place within one year of the date of acquisition; that period may be extended by the Commission on request where such institutions or companies can show that the disposal was not reasonably possible within the period set;

    (b)  control is acquired by an office-holder according to the law of a Member State relating to liquidation, winding up, insolvency, cessation of payments, compositions or analogous proceedings;

    (c)  the operations referred to in paragraph 1(b) are carried out by the financial holding companies referred to in Article 5(3) of the Fourth Council Directive 78/660/EEC of 25 July 1978 on the annual accounts of certain types of companies, as last amended by Directive 84/569/EEC, provided however that the voting rights in respect of the holding are exercised, in particular in relation to the appointment of members of the management and supervisory bodies of the undertakings in which they have holdings, only to maintain the full value of those investments and not to determine directly or indirectly the competitive conduct of those undertakings.

NOTES

Para 2: amended by Council Regulation (EC) No 1310/97, Art 1(3).

## Article 4

### Prior notification of concentrations

1.      Concentrations with a Community dimension defined in this Regulation shall be notified to the Commission not more than one week after the conclusion of the agreement, or the announcement of the public bid, or the acquisition of a controlling interest. That week shall begin when the first of those events occurs.

2.      A concentration which consists of a merger within the meaning of Article 3(1)(a) or in the acquisition of joint control within the meaning of Article 3(1)(b) shall be notified jointly by the parties to the merger or by those acquiring joint control as the case may be. In all other cases, the notification shall be effected by the person or undertaking acquiring control of the whole or parts of one or more undertakings.

3.      Where the Commission finds that a notified concentration falls within the scope of this Regulation, it shall publish the fact of the notification, at the same time indicating the names of the parties, the nature of the concentration and the economic sectors involved. The Commission shall take account of the legitimate interest of undertakings in the protection of their business secrets.

**Article 5**

**Calculation of turnover**

1.      Aggregate turnover within the meaning of Article 1(2) shall comprise the amounts derived by the undertakings concerned in the preceding financial year from the sale of products and the provision of services falling within the undertakings' ordinary activities after deduction of sales rebates and of value added tax and other taxes directly related to turnover. The aggregate turnover of an undertaking concerned shall not include the sale of products or the provision of services between any of the undertakings referred to in paragraph 4.

Turnover, in the Community or in a Member State, shall comprise products sold and services provided to undertakings or consumers, in the Community or in that Member State as the case may be.

2.      By way of derogation from paragraph 1, where the concentration consists in the acquisition of parts, whether or not constituted as legal entities, of one or more undertakings, only the turnover relating to the parts which are the subject of the transaction shall be taken into account with regard to the seller or sellers.

However, two or more transactions within the meaning of the first subparagraph which take place within a two-year period between the same persons or undertakings shall be treated as one and the same concentration arising on the date of the last transaction.

[3.      In place of turnover the following shall be used—
(a)   for credit institutions and other financial institutions, as regards Article 1(2) and (3), the sum of the following income items as defined in Council Directive 86/635/EEC of 8 December 1986 on the annual accounts and consolidated accounts of banks and other financial institutions, after deduction of value added tax and other taxes directly related to those items, where appropriate—
(i)    interest income and similar income;
(ii)   income from securities—
— income from shares and other variable yield securities,
— income from participating interests,
— income from shares in affiliated undertakings;
(iii)  commissions receivable;
(iv)   net profit on financial operations;
(v)    other operating income.
The turnover of a credit or financial institution in the Community or in a Member State shall comprise the income items, as defined above, which are received by the branch or division of that institution established in the Community or in the Member State in question, as the case may be;
(b)   for insurance undertakings, the value of gross premiums written which shall comprise all amounts received and receivable in respect of insurance contracts issued by or on behalf of the insurance undertakings, including also outgoing reinsurance premiums, and after deduction of taxes and parafiscal contributions or levies charged by reference to the amounts of individual premiums or the total volume of premiums; as regards Article 1(2)(b) and (3)(b), (c) and (d) and the final part of Article 1(2) and (3), gross premiums received from Community residents and from residents of one Member State respectively shall be taken into account.]

[4.    Without prejudice to paragraph 2, the aggregate turnover of an undertaking concerned within the meaning of Article 1(2) and (3) shall be calculated by adding together the respective turnovers of the following—]

    (a)  the undertaking concerned;

    (b)  those undertakings in which the undertaking concerned, directly or indirectly—

        — owns more than half the capital or business assets, or

        — has the power to exercise more than half the voting rights, or

        — has the power to appoint more than half the members of the supervisory board, the administrative board or bodies legally representing the undertakings, or

        — has the right to manage the undertakings' affairs;

    (c)  those undertakings which have in the undertaking concerned the rights or powers listed in (b);

    (d)  those undertakings in which an undertaking as referred to in (c) has the rights or powers listed in (b);

    (e)  those undertakings in which two or more undertakings as referred to in (a) to (d) jointly have the rights or powers listed in (b).

[5.    Where undertakings concerned by the concentration jointly have the rights or powers listed in paragraph 4(b), in calculating the aggregate turnover of the undertakings concerned for the purposes of Article 1(2) and (3)—]

    (a)  no account shall be taken of the turnover resulting from the sale of products or the provision of services between the joint undertaking and each of the undertakings concerned or any other undertaking connected with any one of them, as set out in paragraph 4(b) to (e);

    (b)  account shall be taken of the turnover resulting from the sale of products and the provision of services between the joint undertaking and any third undertakings. This turnover shall be apportioned equally amongst the undertakings concerned.

NOTES
    Para 3: substituted by Council Regulation (EC) No 1310/97, Art 1(4).
    Paras 4, 5: introductory sentences substituted by Council Regulation (EC) No 1310/97, Art 1(4).

## Article 6

### Examination of the notification and initiation of proceedings

1.    The Commission shall examine the notification as soon as it is received.

    (a)  Where it concludes that the concentration notified does not fall within the scope of this Regulation, it shall record that finding by means of a decision.

    (b)  Where it finds that the concentration notified, although falling within the scope of this Regulation, does not raise serious doubts as to its compatibility with the common market, it shall decide not to oppose it and shall declare that it is compatible with the common market.

    [The decision declaring the concentration compatible shall also cover restrictions directly related and necessary to the implementation of the concentration.

    (c)  Without prejudice to paragraph 1a, where the Commission finds that the concentration notified falls within the scope of this Regulation and raises serious doubts as to its compatibility with the common market, it shall decide to initiate proceedings.]

[1a.    Where the Commission finds that, following modification by the undertakings concerned, a notified concentration no longer raises serious doubts within the meaning of paragraph 1(c), it may decide to declare the concentration compatible with the common market pursuant to paragraph 1(b).

The Commission may attach to its decision under paragraph 1(b) conditions and obligations intended to ensure that the undertakings concerned comply with the commitments they have entered into *vis-à-vis* the Commission with a view to rendering the concentration compatible with the common market.]

[1b.    The Commission may revoke the decision it has taken pursuant to paragraph 1(a) or (b) where—
(a)  the decision is based on incorrect information for which one of the undertakings is responsible or where it has been obtained by deceit, or
(b)  the undertakings concerned commit a breach of an obligation attached to the decision.]

[1c.    In the cases referred to in paragraph 1c, the Commission may take a decision under paragraph 1, without being bound by the deadlines referred to in Article 10(1).]

2.    The Commission shall notify its decision to the undertakings concerned and the competent authorities of the Member States without delay.

---

NOTES
    Para 1: in sub-para (b), paragraph added and sub-para (c) substituted by Council Regulation (EC) No 1310/97, Art 1(5)(a).
    Paras 1a, 1b, 1c: inserted by Council Regulation (EC) No 1310/97, Art 1(5)(b).

---

## Article 7

### Suspension of concentrations

[1.    A concentration as defined in Article 1 shall not be put into effect either before its notification or until it has been declared compatible with the common market pursuant to a decision under Article 6(1)(b) or Article 8(2) or on the basis of a presumption according to Article 10(6).]

3.    Paragraph 1 shall not prevent the implementation of a public bid which has been notified to the Commission in accordance with Article 4(1), provided that the acquirer does not exercise the voting rights attached to the securities in question or does so only to maintain the full value of those investments and on the basis of a derogation granted by the Commission under paragraph 4.

[4.    The Commission may, on request, grant a derogation from the obligations imposed in paragraphs 1 or 3. The request to grant a derogation must be reasoned. In deciding on the request, the Commission shall take into account inter alia the effects of the suspension on one or more undertakings concerned by a concentration or on a third party and the threat to competition posed by the concentration. That derogation may be made subject to conditions and obligations in order to ensure conditions of effective competition. A derogation may be applied for and granted at any time, even before notification or after the transaction.]

[5.    The validity of any transaction carried out in contravention of paragraph 1 shall be dependent on a decision pursuant to Article 6(1)(b) or Article 8(2) or (3) or on a presumption pursuant to Article 10(6).

This Article shall, however, have no effect on the validity of transactions in securities including those convertible into other securities admitted to trading on a market which is regulated and supervised by authorities recognised by public bodies, operates regularly and is accessible directly or indirectly to the public, unless the buyer and seller knew or ought to have known that the transaction was carried out in contravention of paragraph 1.]

## Article 8

### Powers of decision of the Commission

1.    Without prejudice to Article 9, all proceedings initiated pursuant to Article 6(1)(c) shall be closed by means of a decision as provided for in paragraphs 2 to 5.

[2.    Where the Commission finds that, following modification by the undertakings concerned if necessary, a notified concentration fulfils the criterion laid down in Article 2(2) and, in the cases referred to in Article 2(4), the criteria laid down in Article 85(3) of the Treaty, it shall issue a decision declaring the concentration compatible with the common market.

It may attach to its decision conditions and obligations intended to ensure that the undertakings concerned comply with the commitments they have entered into *vis-à-vis* the Commission with a view to rendering the concentration compatible with the common market. The decision declaring the concentration compatible with the common market shall also cover restrictions directly related and necessary to the implementation of the concentration.]

[3.    Where the Commission finds that a concentration fulfils the criterion defined in Article 2(3) or, in the cases referred to in Article 2(4), does not fulfil the criteria laid down in Article 85(3) of the Treaty, it shall issue a decision declaring that the concentration is incompatible with the common market.]

4.    Where a concentration has already been implemented, the Commission may, in a decision pursuant to paragraph 3 or by separate decision, require the undertakings or assets brought together to be separated or the cessation of joint control or any other action that may be appropriate in order to restore conditions of effective competition.

5.    The Commission may revoke the decision it has taken pursuant to paragraph 2 where—
    (a) the declaration of compatibility is based on incorrect information for which one of the undertakings is responsible or where it has been obtained by deceit; or
    (b) the undertakings concerned commit a breach of an obligation attached to the decision.

6.    In the cases referred to in paragraph 5, the Commission may take a decision under paragraph 3, without being bound by the deadline referred to in Article 10(3).

## Article 9

### Referral to the competent authorities of the Member States

1.    The Commission may, by means of a decision notified without delay to the undertakings concerned and the competent authorities of the other Member States, refer a notified concentration to the competent authorities of the Member State concerned in the following circumstances.

[2.    Within three weeks of the date of receipt of the copy of the notification a Member State may inform the Commission, which shall inform the undertakings concerned, that—

(a)    a concentration threatens to create or to strengthen a dominant position as a result of which effective competition will be significantly impeded on a market within that Member State, which presents all the characteristics of a distinct market, or

(b)    a concentration affects competition on a market within that Member State, which presents all the characteristics of a distinct market and which does not constitute a substantial part of the common market.]

3.    If the Commission considers that, having regard to the market for the products or services in question and the geographical reference market within the meaning of paragraph 7, there is such a distinct market and that such a threat exists, either—

(a)    it shall itself deal with the case in order to maintain or restore effective competition on the market concerned; or

[(b)    it shall refer the whole or part of the case to the competent authorities of the Member State concerned with a view to the application of that State's national competition law.

In cases where a Member State informs the Commission that a concentration affects competition in a distinct market within its territory that does not form a substantial part of the common market, the Commission shall refer the whole or part of the case relating to the distinct market concerned, if it considers that such a distinct market is affected.]

If, however, the Commission considers that such a distinct market or threat does not exist it shall adopt a decision to that effect which it shall address to the Member State concerned.

4.    A decision to refer or not to refer pursuant to paragraph 3 shall be taken—

(a)    as a general rule within the six-week period provided for in Article 10(1), second subparagraph, where the Commission, pursuant to Article 6(1)(b), has not initiated proceedings; or

(b)    within three months at most of the notification of the concentration concerned where the Commission has initiated proceedings under Article 6(1)(c), without taking the preparatory steps in order to adopt the necessary measures under Article 8(2), second subparagraph, (3) or (4) to maintain or restore effective competition on the market concerned.

5.    If within the three months referred to in paragraph 4(b) the Commission, despite a reminder from the Member State concerned, has not taken a decision on referral in accordance with paragraph 3 nor has taken the preparatory steps referred to in paragraph 4(b), it shall be deemed to have taken a decision to refer the case to the Member State concerned in accordance with paragraph 3(b).

6.     The publication of any report or the announcement of the findings of the examination of the concentration by the competent authority of the Member State concerned shall be effected not more than four months after the Commission's referral.

7.     The geographical reference market shall consist of the area in which the undertakings concerned are involved in the supply and demand of products or services, in which the conditions of competition are sufficiently homogeneous and which can be distinguished from neighbouring areas because, in particular, conditions of competition are appreciably different in those areas. This assessment should take account in particular of the nature and characteristics of the products or services concerned, of the existence of entry barriers or of consumer preferences, of appreciable differences of the undertakings' market shares between the area concerned and neighbouring areas or of substantial price differences.

8.     In applying the provisions of this Article, the Member State concerned may take only the measures strictly necessary to safeguard or restore effective competition on the market concerned.

9.     In accordance with the relevant provisions of the Treaty, any Member State may appeal to the Court of Justice, and in particular request the application of Article 186, for the purpose of applying its national competition law.

[10.     This Article may be re-examined at the same time as the thresholds referred to in Article 1.]

---

NOTES

Para 2: substituted by Council Regulation (EC) No 1310/97, Art 1(8)(a).

Para 3: sub-para (b) substituted and sub-paragraph added by Council Regulation (EC) No 1310/97, Art 1(8)(b).

Para 10: substituted by Council Regulation (EC) No 1310/97, Art 1(8)(c).

---

## Article 10

### Time limits for initiating proceedings and for decisions

1.     The decisions referred to in Article 6(1) must be taken within one month at most. That period shall begin on the day following that of the receipt of a notification or, if the information to be supplied with the notification is incomplete, on the day following that of the receipt of the complete information.

That period shall be increased to six weeks if the Commission receives a request from a Member State in accordance with Article 9(2) [or where, after notification of a concentration, the undertakings concerned submit commitments pursuant to Article 6(1)(a), which are intended by the parties to form the basis for a decision pursuant to Article 6(1)(b).]

2.     Decisions taken pursuant to Article 8(2) concerning notified concentrations must be taken as soon as it appears that the serious doubts referred to in Article 6(1)(c) have been removed, particularly as a result of modifications made by the undertakings concerned, and at the latest by the deadline laid down in paragraph

3.     Without prejudice to Article 8(6), decisions taken pursuant to Article 8(3) concerning notified concentrations must be taken within not more than four months of the date on which proceedings are initiated.

4.    [The periods set by paragraphs 1 and 3] shall exceptionally be suspended where, owing to circumstances for which one of the undertakings involved in the concentration is responsible, the Commission has had to request information by decision pursuant to Article 11 or to order an investigation by decision pursuant to Article 13.

5.    Where the Court of Justice gives a Judgment which annuls the whole or part of a Commission decision taken under this Regulation, the periods laid down in this Regulation shall start again from the date of the Judgment.

6.    Where the Commission has not taken a decision in accordance with Article 6(1)(b) or (c) or Article 8(2) or (3) within the deadlines set in paragraphs 1 and 3 respectively, the concentration shall be deemed to have been declared compatible with the common market, without prejudice to Article 9.

NOTES

Para 1: words in square brackets added by Council Regulation (EC) No 1310/97, Art 1(9)(a),
Para 4: words in square brackets substituted by Council Regulation (EC) No 1310/97, Art 1(9)(b).

## Article 11

### Requests for information

1.    In carrying out the duties assigned to it by this Regulation, the Commission may obtain all necessary information from the Governments and competent authorities of the Member States, from the persons referred to in Article 3(1)(b), and from undertakings and associations of undertakings.

2.    When sending a request for information to a person, an undertaking or an association of undertakings, the Commission shall at the same time send a copy of the request to the competent authority of the Member State within the territory of which the residence of the person or the seat of the undertaking or association of undertakings is situated.

3.    In its request the Commission shall state the legal basis and the purpose of the request and also the penalties provided for in Article 14(1)(c) for supplying incorrect information.

4.    The information requested shall be provided, in the case of undertakings, by their owners or their representatives and, in the case of legal persons, companies or firms, or of associations having no legal personality, by the persons authorised to represent them by law or by their statutes.

5.    Where a person, an undertaking or an association of undertakings does not provide the information requested within the period fixed by the Commission or provides incomplete information, the Commission shall by decision require the information to be provided. The decision shall specify what information is required, fix an appropriate period within which it is to be supplied and state the penalties provided for in Articles 14(1)(c) and 15(1)(a) and the right to have the decision reviewed by the Court of Justice.

6.    The Commission shall at the same time send a copy of its decision to the competent authority of the Member State within the territory of which the residence of the person or the seat of the undertaking or association of undertakings is situated.

## Article 12

### Investigations by the authorities of the Member States

1.    At the request of the Commission, the competent authorities of the Member States shall undertake the investigations which the Commission considers to be necessary under Article 13(1), or which it has ordered by decision pursuant to Article 13(3). The officials of the competent authorities of the Member States responsible for conducting those investigations shall exercise their powers upon production of an authorisation in writing issued by the competent authority of the Member State within the territory of which the investigation is to be carried out. Such authorisation shall specify the subject matter and purpose of the investigation.

2.    If so requested by the Commission or by the competent authority of the Member State within the territory of which the investigation is to be carried out, officials of the Commission may assist the officials of that authority in carrying out their duties.

## Article 13

### Investigative powers of the Commission

1.    In carrying out the duties assigned to it by this Regulation, the Commission may undertake all necessary investigations into undertakings and associations of undertakings.

  To that end the officials authorised by the Commission shall be empowered—
      (a)  to examine the books and other business records;
      (b)  to take or demand copies of or extracts from the books and business records;
      (c)  to ask for oral explanations on the spot;
      (d)  to enter any premises, land and means of transport of undertakings.

2.    The officials of the Commission authorised to carry out the investigations shall exercise their powers on production of an authorisation in writing specifying the subject matter and purpose of the investigation and the penalties provided for in Article 14(1)(d) in cases where production of the required books or other business records is incomplete. In good time before the investigation, the Commission shall inform, in writing, the competent authority of the Member State within the territory of which the investigation is to be carried out of the investigation and of the identities of the authorised officials.

3.    Undertakings and associations of undertakings shall submit to investigations ordered by decision of the Commission. The decision shall specify the subject matter and purpose of the investigation, appoint the date on which it shall begin and state the penalties provided for in Articles 14(1)(d) and 15(1)(b) and the right to have the decision reviewed by the Court of Justice.

4.    The Commission shall in good time and in writing inform the competent authority of the Member State within the territory of which the investigation is to be carried out of its intention of taking a decision pursuant to paragraph 3. It shall hear the competent authority before taking its decision.

5.    Officials of the competent authority of the Member State within the territory of which the investigation is to be carried out may, at the request of that authority or of the Commission, assist the officials of the Commission in carrying out their duties.

6.      Where an undertaking or association of undertakings opposes an investigation ordered pursuant to this Article, the Member State concerned shall afford the necessary assistance to the officials authorised by the Commission to enable them to carry out their investigation. To this end the Member States shall, after consulting the Commission, take the necessary measures within one year of the entry into force of this Regulation.

## Article 14

### Fines

1.      The Commission may by decision impose on the persons referred to in Article 3(1)(b), undertakings or associations of undertakings fines of from ECU 1 000 to 50 000 where intentionally or negligently—
   (a) they fail to notify a concentration in accordance with Article 4;
   (b) they supply incorrect or misleading information in a notification pursuant to Article 4;
   (c) they supply incorrect information in response to a request made pursuant to Article 11 or fail to supply information within the period fixed by a decision taken pursuant to Article 11;
   (d) they produce the required books or other business records in incomplete form during investigations under Article 12 or 13, or refuse to submit to an investigation ordered by decision taken pursuant to Article 13.

2.      The Commission may by decision impose fines not exceeding 10% of the aggregate turnover of the undertakings concerned within the meaning of Article 5 on the persons or undertakings concerned where, either intentionally or negligently, they—
   (a) fail to comply with an obligation imposed by decision pursuant to Article 7(4) or 8(2), second subparagraph;
   (b) put into effect a concentration in breach of Article 7(1) or disregard a decision taken pursuant to Article 7(2);
   (c) put into effect a concentration declared incompatible with the common market by decision pursuant to Article 8(3) or do not take the measures ordered by decision pursuant to Article 8(4).

3.      In setting the amount of a fine, regard shall be had to the nature and gravity of the infringement.

4.      Decisions taken pursuant to paragraphs 1 and 2 shall not be of criminal law nature.

## Article 15

### Periodic penalty payments

1.      The Commission may by decision impose on the persons referred to in Article 3(1)(b), undertakings or associations of undertakings concerned periodic penalty payments of up to ECU 25 000 for each day of delay calculated from the date set in the decision, in order to compel them—
   (a) to supply complete and correct information which it has requested by decision pursuant to Article 11;
   (b) to submit to an investigation which it has ordered by decision pursuant to Article 13.

2.      The Commission may by decision impose on the persons referred to in Article 3(1)(b) or on undertakings periodic penalty payments of up to ECU 100 000 for each day of delay calculated from the date set in the decision, in order to compel them—

      (a)  to comply with an obligation imposed by decision pursuant to Article 7(4) or 8(2), second subparagraph, or

      (b)  to apply the measures ordered by decision pursuant to Article 8(4).

3.      Where the persons referred to in Article 3(1)(b), undertakings or associations of undertakings have satisfied the obligation which it was the purpose of the periodic penalty payment to enforce, the Commission may set the total amount of the periodic penalty payments at a lower figure than that which would arise under the original decision.

## Article 16

### Review by the Court of Justice

The Court of Justice shall have unlimited jurisdiction within the meaning of Article 172 of the Treaty to review decisions whereby the Commission has fixed a fine or periodic penalty payments; it may cancel, reduce or increase the fine or periodic penalty payments imposed.

## Article 17

### Professional secrecy

1.      Information acquired as a result of the application of Articles 11, 12, 13 and 18 shall be used only for the purposes of the relevant request, investigation or hearing.

2.      Without prejudice to Articles 4(3), 18 and 20, the Commission and the competent authorities of the Member States, their officials and other servants shall not disclose information they have acquired through the application of this Regulation of the kind covered by the obligation of professional secrecy.

3.      Paragraphs 1 and 2 shall not prevent publication of general information or of surveys which do not contain information relating to particular undertakings or associations of undertakings.

## Article 18

### Hearing of the parties and of third persons

1.      Before taking any decision provided for in [Article 7(4)], Article 8(2), second subparagraph, and (3) to (5), and Articles 14 and 15, the Commission shall give the persons, undertakings and associations of undertakings concerned the opportunity, at every stage of the procedure up to the consultation of the Advisory Committee, of making known their views on the objections against them.

[2.      By way of derogation from paragraph 1, a decision to grant a derogation from suspension as referred to in Article 7(4) may be taken provisionally, without the persons, undertakings or associations of undertakings concerned being given the opportunity to make known their view beforehand, provided that the Commission gives them that opportunity as soon as possible after having taken its decision.]

3.      The Commission shall base its decision only on objections on which the parties have been able to submit their observations. The rights of the defence shall be fully

respected in the proceedings. Access to the file shall be open at least to the parties directly involved, subject to the legitimate interest of undertakings in the protection of their business secrets.

4.      In so far as the Commission or the competent authorities of the Member States deem it necessary, they may also hear other natural or legal persons. Natural or legal persons showing a sufficient interest and especially members of the administrative or management bodies of the undertakings concerned or the recognised representatives of their employees shall be entitled, upon application, to be heard.

NOTES
> Para 1: words in square brackets substituted by Council Regulation (EC) No 1310/97, Art 1(10)(a).
> Para 2: substituted by Council Regulation (EC) No 1310/97, Art 1(10)(b).

## Article 19

### Liaison with the authorities of the Member States

1.      The Commission shall transmit to the competent authorities of the Member States copies of notifications within three working days and, as soon as possible, copies of the most important documents lodged with or issued by the Commission pursuant to this Regulation. [Such documents shall include commitments which are intended by the parties to form the basis for a decision pursuant to Articles 6(1)(b) or 8(2).]

2.      The Commission shall carry out the procedures set out in this Regulation in close and constant liaison with the competent authorities of the Member States, which may express their views upon those procedures. For the purposes of Article 9 it shall obtain information from the competent authority of the Member State as referred to in paragraph 2 of that Article and give it the opportunity to make known its views at every stage of the procedure up to the adoption of a decision pursuant to paragraph 3 of that Article; to that end it shall give it access to the file.

3.      An Advisory Committee on concentrations shall be consulted before any decision is taken pursuant to Article 8(2) to (5), 14 or 15, or any provisions are adopted pursuant to Article 23.

4.      The Advisory Committee shall consist of representatives of the authorities of the Member States. Each Member State shall appoint one or two representatives; if unable to attend, they may be replaced by other representatives. At least one of the representatives of a Member State shall be competent in matters of restrictive practices and dominant positions.

5.      Consultation shall take place at a joint meeting convened at the invitation of and chaired by the Commission. A summary of the case, together with an indication of the most important documents and a preliminary draft of the decision to be taken for each case considered, shall be sent with the invitation. The meeting shall take place not less than 14 days after the invitation has been sent. The Commission may in exceptional cases shorten that period as appropriate in order to avoid serious harm to one or more of the undertakings concerned by a concentration.

6.      The Advisory Committee shall deliver an opinion on the Commission's draft decision, if necessary by taking a vote. The Advisory Committee may deliver an opinion even if some members are absent and unrepresented. The opinion shall be delivered in writing and appended to the draft decision. The Commission shall take the utmost account of the opinion delivered by the Committee. It shall inform the Committee of the manner in which its opinion has been taken into account.

7. The Advisory Committee may recommend publication of the opinion. The Commission may carry out such publication. The decision to publish shall take due account of the legitimate interest of undertakings in the protection of their business secrets and of the interest of the undertakings concerned in such publication's taking place.

NOTES
Para 1: words in square brackets added by Council Regulation.(EC) No 1310/97, Art 1(11),

## Article 20

### Publication of decisions

1. The Commission shall publish the decisions which it takes pursuant to Article 8(2) to (5) in the *Official Journal of the European Communities.*

2. The publication shall state the names of the parties and the main content of the decision; it shall have regard to the legitimate interest of undertakings in the protection of their business secrets.

## Article 21

### Jurisdiction

1. Subject to review by the Court of Justice, the Commission shall have sole jurisdiction to take the decisions provided for in this Regulation.

2. No Member State shall apply its national legislation on competition to any concentration that has a Community dimension.

The first subparagraph shall be without prejudice to any Member State's power to carry out any enquiries necessary for the application of Article 9(2) or after referral, pursuant to Article 9(3), first subparagraph, indent (b), or (5), to take the measures strictly necessary for the application of Article 9(8).

3. Notwithstanding paragraphs 1 and 2, Member States may take appropriate measures to protect legitimate interests other than those taken into consideration by this Regulation and compatible with the general principles and other provisions of Community law.

Public security, plurality of the media and prudential rules shall be regarded as legitimate interests within the meaning of the first subparagraph.

Any other public interest must be communicated to the Commission by the Member State concerned and shall be recognised by the Commission after an assessment of its compatibility with the general principles and other provisions of Community law before the measures referred to above may be taken. The Commission shall inform the Member State concerned of its decision within one month of that communication.

## Article 22

### Application of the Regulation

[1. This Regulation alone shall apply to concentrations as defined in Article 3, and Regulations No 17, (EEC) No 1017/68, (EEC) No 4056/86 and (EEC) No 3975/87 shall not apply, except in relation to joint ventures that do not have a Community dimension and which have their object or effect the coordination of the competitive behaviour of undertakings that remain independent.]

[3.    If the Commission finds, at the request of a Member State or at the joint request of two or more Member States, that a concentration as defined in Article 3 that has no Community dimension within the meaning of Article 1 creates or strengthens a dominant position as a result of which effective competition would be significantly impeded within the territory of the Member State or States making the joint request, it may, in so far as that concentration affects trade between Member States, adopt the decisions provided for in Article 8(2), second subparagraph, (3) and (4).]

[4.    Articles 2(1)(a) and (b), 5, 6, 8 and 10 to 20 shall apply to a request made pursuant to paragraph 3. Article 7 shall apply to the extent that the concentration has not been put into effect on the date on which the Commission informs the parties that a request has been made.

The period within which proceedings may be initiated pursuant to Article 10(1) shall begin on the day following that of the receipt of the request from the Member State or States concerned. The request must be made within one month at most of the date on which the concentration was made known to the Member State or to all the Member States making a joint request or effected. This period shall begin on the date of the first of those events.]

5.    Pursuant to paragraph 3 the Commission shall take only the measures strictly necessary to maintain or restore effective competition within the territory of the Member State [or States] at the request of which it intervenes.

NOTES

    Paras 1, 2: substituted by para 1 by Council Regulation (EC) No 1310/97, Art 1(12)(a),
    Para 3: substituted by Council Regulation (EC) No 1310/97, Art 1(12)(b),
    Para 4: substituted by Council Regulation (EC) No 1310/97, Art 1(12)(c).
    Para 5: words in square brackets inserted by Council Regulation (EC) No 1310/97, Art 1(12)(d).

## Article 23

### Implementing provisions

The Commission shall have the power to adopt implementing provisions concerning the form, content and other details of notifications pursuant to Article 4, [time limits pursuant to Articles 7, 9, 10 and 22] and hearings pursuant to Article 18.

[The Commission shall have the power to lay down the procedure and time limits for the submission of commitments pursuant to Articles 6(1a) and 8(2).]

NOTES

    Words in square brackets substituted and sub-paragraph added by Council Regulation (EC) No 1310/97, Art 1(13)(a), (b).

## Article 24

### Relations with non-member countries

1.    The Member States shall inform the Commission of any general difficulties encountered by their undertakings with concentrations as defined in Article 3 in a non-member country.

2.    Initially not more than one year after the entry into force of this Regulation and thereafter periodically the Commission shall draw up a report examining the treatment accorded to Community undertakings, in the terms referred to in paragraphs 3 and 4,

as regards concentrations in non-member countries. The Commission shall submit those reports to the Council, together with any recommendations.

3.　　Whenever it appears to the Commission, either on the basis of the reports referred to in paragraph 2 or on the basis of other information, that a non-member country does not grant Community undertakings treatment comparable to that granted by the Community to undertakings from that non-member country, the Commission may submit proposals to the Council for an appropriate mandate for negotiation with a view to obtaining comparable treatment for Community undertakings.

4.　　Measures taken under this Article shall comply with the obligations of the Community or of the Member States, without prejudice to Article 234 of the Treaty, under international agreements, whether bilateral or multilateral.

### Article 25

### Entry into force

1.　　This Regulation shall enter into force on 21 September 1990.

2.　　This Regulation shall not apply to any concentration which was the subject of an agreement or announcement or where control was acquired within the meaning of Article 4(1) before the date of this Regulation's entry into force and it shall not in any circumstances apply to any concentration in respect of which proceedings were initiated before that date by a Member State's authority with responsibility for competition.

[3.　　As regards concentrations to which this Regulation applies by virtue of accession, the date of accession shall be substituted for the date of entry into force of this Regulation. The provision of paragraph 2, second alternative, applies in the same way to proceedings initiated by a competition authority of the new Member States or by the EFTA Surveillance Authority.]

NOTES

　　Para 3: added by the 1994 Act of Accession of the Kingdom of Norway, the Republic of Austria, the Republic of Finland and the Kingdom of Sweden, Annex I(III)(B)(4), as adjusted by Council Decision 95/1/EC, Annex I(III)(B)(4).

　　This Regulation shall be binding in its entirety and directly applicable in all Member States.

# COMMISSION NOTICE

### regarding restrictions ancillary to concentrations

### (90/C 203/05)

NOTES

　　Date of publication in OJ: OJ C203, 14.8.90, p 5.

### I Introduction

1.　　Council Regulation (EEC) No 4064/89 of 21 December 1989 on the control of concentrations between undertakings ("the Regulation") states in its 25th recital that its application is not excluded where the undertakings concerned accept restrictions which are directly related and necessary to the implementation of the concentration, hereinafter referred to as "ancillary restrictions". In the scheme of the Regulation, such restrictions are to be assessed together with the concentration itself. It follows, as confirmed by Article 8(2), second subparagraph, last sentence of the Regulation, that a decision declaring the concentration compatible also covers these restrictions. In this situation, under the provisions of Article 22, paragraphs 1 and 2, the Regulation is solely applicable, to the exclusion of Regulation No 17 as well as Regulations (EEC) No 1017/68, (EEC) No 4056/86 and (EEC) No 3975/87. This avoids parallel Commission proceedings, one concerned with the assessment of the concentration under the Regulation, and the other aimed at the application of Articles 85 and 86 to the restrictions which are ancillary to the concentration.

2.      In this notice, the Commission sets out to indicate the interpretation it gives to the notion of "restrictions directly related and necessary to the implementation of the concentration". Under the Regulation such restrictions must be assessed in relation to the concentration, whatever their treatment might be under Articles 85 and 86 if they were to be considered in isolation or in a different economic context. The Commission endeavours, within the limits set by the Regulation, to take the greatest account of business practice and of the conditions necessary for the implementation of concentrations.

This notice is without prejudice to the interpretation which may be given by the Court of Justice of the European Communities.

## II  Principles of evaluation

3.      The "restrictions" meant are those agreed on between the parties to the concentration which limit their own freedom of action in the market. They do not include restrictions to the detriment of third parties. If such restrictions are the inevitable consequence of the concentration itself, they must be assessed together with it under the provisions of Article 2 of the Regulation. If, on the contrary, such restrictive effects on third parties are separable from the concentration they may, if appropriate, be the subject of an assessment of compatibility with Articles 85 and 86 of the EEC Treaty.

4.      For restrictions to be considered "directly related" they must be ancillary to the implementation of the concentration, that is to say subordinate in importance to the main object of the concentration. They cannot be substantial restrictions wholly different in nature from those which result from the concentration itself. Neither are they contractual arrangements which are among the elements constituting the concentration, such as those establishing economic unity between previously independent parties, or organising joint control by two undertakings of another undertaking. As integral parts of the concentration, the latter arrangements constitute the very subject matter of the evaluation to be carried out under the Regulation.

Also excluded, for concentrations which are carried out in stages, are the contractual arrangements relating to the stages before the establishment of control within the meaning of Article 3, paragraphs 1 and 3 of the Regulation. For these, Articles 85 and 86 remain applicable as long as the conditions set out in Article 3 are not fulfilled.

The notion of directly related restrictions likewise excludes from the application of the Regulation additional restrictions agreed at the same time which have no direct link with the concentration. It is not enough that the additional restrictions exist in the same context as the concentration.

5.     The restrictions must likewise be "necessary to the implementation of the concentration", which means that in their absence the concentration could not be implemented or could only be implemented under more uncertain conditions, at substantially higher cost, over an appreciably longer period or with considerably less probability of success. This must be judged on an objective basis.

6.     The question of whether a restriction meets these conditions cannot be answered in general terms. In particular as concerns the necessity of the restriction, it is proper not only to take account of its nature, but equally to ensure, in applying the rule of proportionality, that its duration and subject matter, and geographic field of application, do not exceed what the implementation of the concentration reasonably requires. If alternatives are available for the attainment of the legitimate aim pursued, the undertakings must choose the one which is objectively the least restrictive of competition.

These principles will be followed and further developed by the Commission's practice in individual cases. However, it is already possible, on the basis of past experience, to indicate the attitude the Commission will take to those restrictions most commonly encountered in relation to the transfer of undertakings or parts of undertakings, the division of undertakings or of their assets following a joint acquisition of control, or the creation of concentrative joint ventures.

## III   Evaluation of common ancillary restrictions in cases of the transfer of an undertaking

*A   Non-competition clauses*

1.     Among the ancillary restrictions which meet the criteria set out in the Regulation are contractual prohibitions on competition which are imposed on the vendor in the context of a concentration achieved by the transfer of an undertaking or part of an undertaking. Such prohibitions guarantee the transfer to the acquirer of the full value of the assets transferred, which in general include both physical assets and intangible assets such as the goodwill which the vendor has accumulated or the know-how he has developed. These are not only directly related to the concentration, but are also necessary for its implementation because, in their absence, there would be reasonable grounds to expect that the sale of the undertaking or part of an undertaking could not be accomplished satisfactorily. In order to take over fully the value of the assets transferred, the acquirer must be able to benefit from some protection against competitive acts of the vendor in order to gain the loyalty of customers and to assimilate and exploit the know-how. Such protection cannot generally be considered necessary when *de facto* the transfer is limited to physical assets (such as land, buildings or machinery) or to exclusive industrial and commercial property rights (the holders of which could immediately take action against infringements by the transferor of such rights).

However, such a prohibition on competition is justified by the legitimate objective sought of implementing the concentration only when its duration, its geographical field of application, its subject matter and the persons subject to it do not exceed what is reasonably necessary to that end.

2.     With regard to the acceptable duration of a prohibition on competition, a period of five years has been recognised as appropriate when the transfer of the undertaking includes the goodwill and know-how, and a period of two years when it includes only the goodwill. However, these are not absolute rules; they do not preclude a prohibition of longer duration in particular circumstances, where for

example the parties can demonstrate that customer loyalty will persist for a period longer than two years or that the economic life cycle of the products concerned is longer than five years and should be taken into account.

3.    The geographic scope of the non-competition clause must be limited to the area where the vendor had established the products or services before the transfer. It does not appear objectively necessary that the acquirer be protected from competition by the vendor in territories which the vendor had not previously penetrated.

4.    In the same manner, the non-competition clause must be limited to products and services which form the economic activity of the undertaking transferred. In particular, in the case of a partial transfer of assets, it does not appear that the acquirer needs to be protected from the competition of the vendor in the products or services which constitute the activities which the vendor retains after the transfer.

5.    The vendor may bind himself, his subsidiaries and commercial agents. However, an obligation to impose similar restrictions on others would not qualify as an ancillary restriction. This applies in particular to clauses which would restrict the scope for resellers or users to import or export.

6.    Any protection of the vendor is not normally an ancillary restriction and is therefore to be examined under Articles 85 and 86 of the EEC Treaty.

*B  Licences of industrial and commercial property rights and of know-how*

1.    The implementation of a transfer of an undertaking or part of an undertaking generally includes the transfer to the acquirer, with a view to the full exploitation of the assets transferred, of rights to industrial or commercial property or know-how. However, the vendor may remain the owner of the rights in order to exploit them for activities other than those transferred. In these cases, the usual means for ensuring that the acquirer will have the full use of the assets transferred is to conclude licensing agreements in his favour.

2.    Simple or exclusive licences of patents, similar rights or existing know-how can be accepted as necessary for the completion of the transaction, and likewise agreements to grant such licences. They may be limited to certain fields of use, to the extent that they correspond to the activities of the undertaking transferred. Normally it will not be necessary for such licences to include territorial limitations on manufacture which reflect the territory of the activity transferred. Licences may be granted for the whole duration of the patent or similar rights or the duration of the normal economic life of the know-how. As such licences are economically equivalent to a partial transfer of rights, they need not be limited in time.

3.    Restrictions in licence agreements, going beyond what is provided above, fall outside the scope of the Regulation. They must be assessed on their merits according to Article 85(1) and (3). Accordingly, where they fulfil the conditions required, they may benefit from the block exemptions provided for by Regulation (EEC) No 2349/84 on patent licences or Regulation (EEC) No 559/89 on know-how licences.

4    The same principles are to be applied by analogy in the case of licences of trademarks, business names or similar rights. There may be situations where the vendor wishes to remain the owner of such rights in relation to activities retained, but the acquirer needs the rights to use them to market the products constituting the object of activity of the undertaking or part of an undertaking transferred.

   In such circumstances, the conclusion of agreements for the purpose of avoiding confusion between trademarks may be necessary.

C      *Purchase and supply agreements*

1.      In many cases, the transfer of an undertaking or part of an undertaking can entail the disruption of traditional lines of internal procurement and supply resulting from the previous integration of activities within the economic entity of the vendor. To make possible the break up of the economic unity of the vendor and the partial transfer of the assets to the acquirer under reasonable conditions, it is often necessary to maintain, at least for a transitional period, similar links between the vendor and the acquirer. This objective is normally attained by the conclusion of purchase and supply agreements between the vendor and the acquirer of the undertaking or part of an undertaking. Taking account of the particular situation resulting from the break up of the economic unity of the vendor such obligations, which may lead to restrictions of competition, can be recognised as ancillary. They may be in favour of the vendor as well as the acquirer.

2.      The legitimate aim of such obligations may be to ensure the continuity of supply to one or other of the parties of products necessary to the activities retained (for the vendor) or taken over (for the acquirer). Thus, there are grounds for recognising, for a transitional period, the need for supply obligations aimed at guaranteeing the quantities previously supplied within the vendor's integrated business or enabling their adjustment in accordance with the development of the market.

Their aim may also be to provide continuity of outlets for one or the other of the parties, as they were previously assured within the single economic entity. For the same reason, obligations providing for fixed quantities, possibly with a variation clause, may be recognised as necessary.

3.      However, there does not appear to be a general justification for exclusive purchase or supply obligations. Save in exceptional circumstances, for example resulting from the absence of a market or the specificity of products, such exclusivity is not objectively necessary to permit the implementation of a concentration in the form of a transfer of an undertaking or part of an undertaking.

In any event, in accordance with the principle of proportionality, the undertakings concerned are bound to consider whether there are no alternative means to the ends pursued, such as agreements for fixed quantities, which are less restrictive than exclusivity.

4.      As for the duration of procurement and supply obligations, this must be limited to a period necessary for the replacement of the relationship of dependency by autonomy in market. The duration of such a period must be objectively justified.

## IV  Evaluation of ancillary restrictions in the case of a joint acquisition

1.      As set out in the 24th recital, the Regulation is applicable when two or more undertakings agree to acquire jointly the control of one or more other undertakings, in particular by means of a public tender offer, where the object or effect is the division among themselves of the undertakings or their assets. This is a concentration implemented in two successive stages; the common strategy is limited to the acquisition of control. For the transaction to be concentrative, the joint acquisition must be followed by a clear separation of the undertakings or assets concerned.

2.      For this purpose, an agreement by the joint acquirers of an undertaking to abstain from making separate competing offers for the same undertaking, or otherwise acquiring control, may be considered an ancillary restriction.

3.     Restrictions limited to putting the division into effect are to be considered directly related and necessary to the implementation of the concentration. This will apply to arrangements made between the parties for the joint acquisition of control in order to divide among themselves the production facilities or the distribution networks together with the existing trademarks of the undertaking acquired in common. The implementation of this division may not in any circumstances lead to the coordination of the future behaviour of the acquiring undertakings.

4.     To the extent that such a division involves the break up of a pre-existing economic entity, arrangements that make the break up possible under reasonable conditions must be considered ancillary. In this regard, the principles explained above in relation to purchase and supply arrangements over a transitional period in cases of transfer of undertakings should be applied by analogy.

## V  Evaluation of ancillary restrictions in cases of concentrative joint ventures within the meaning of Article 3(2) subparagraph 2 of the Regulation

This evaluation must take account of the characteristics peculiar to concentrative joint ventures, the constituent elements of which are the creation of an autonomous economic entity exercising on a long-term basis all the functions of an undertaking, and the absence of coordination of competitive behaviour between the parent undertakings and between them and the joint venture. This condition implies in principle the withdrawal of the parent undertakings from the market assigned to the joint venture and, therefore, their disappearance as actual or potential competitors of the new entity.

### A  Non-competition obligations

To the extent that a prohibition on the parent undertakings competing with the joint venture aims at expressing the reality of the lasting withdrawal of the parents from the market assigned to the joint venture, it will be recognised as an integral part of the concentration.

### B  Licences for industrial and commercial property rights and know-how

The creation of a new autonomous economic entity usually involves the transfer of the technology necessary for carrying on the activities assigned to it, in the form of a transfer of rights and related know-how. Where the parent undertakings intend nonetheless to retain the property rights, particularly with the aim of exploitation in other fields of use, the transfer of technology to the joint venture may be accomplished by means of licences. Such licences may be exclusive, without having to be limited in duration or territory, for they serve only as a substitute for the transfer of property rights. They must therefore be considered necessary to the implementation of the concentration.

### C  Purchase and supply obligations

If the parent undertakings remain present in a market upstream or downstream of that of the joint venture, any purchase and supply agreements are to be examined in accordance with the principles applicable in the case of the transfer of an undertaking.

# COMMISSION NOTICE

of 23 December 1992

## on co-operation between national courts and the Commission in applying Articles 85 and 86 of the EEC Treaty

### (93/C 39/05)

NOTES

Date of publication in OJ: OJ C39, 13.2.93, p 6.

## I   Introduction

1.     The abolition of internal frontiers enables firms in the Community to embark on new activities and Community consumers to benefit from increased competition. The Commission considers that these advantages must not be jeopardised by restrictive or abusive practices of undertakings and that the completion of the internal market thus reaffirms the importance of the Community's competition policy and competition law.

2.     A number of national and Community institutions have contributed to the formulation of Community competition law and are responsible for its day-to-day application. For this purpose, the national competition authorities, national and Community courts and the Commission each assume their own tasks and responsibilities, in line with the principles developed by the case-law of the Court of Justice of the European Communities.

3.     If the competition process is to work well in the internal market, effective co-operation between these institutions must be ensured. The purpose of this Notice is to achieve this in relations between national courts and the Commission. It spells out how the Commission intends to assist national courts by closer co-operation in the application of Articles 85 and 86 of the EEC Treaty in individual cases.

## II   Powers

4.     The Commission is the administrative authority responsible for the implementation and for the thrust of competition policy in the Community and for this purpose has to act in the public interest. National courts, on the other hand, have the task of safeguarding the subjective rights of private individuals in their relations with one another.1

5.     In performing these different tasks, national courts and the Commission possess concurrent powers for the application of Article 85(1) and Article 86 of the Treaty. in the case of the Commission, the power is conferred by Article 89 and by the provisions adopted pursuant to Article 87 In the case of the national courts, the power derives from the direct effect of the relevant Community rules. In *BRT v Sabam*, the Court of Justice considered that "as the prohibitions of Articles 85(1) and 86 tend by their very nature to produce direct effects in relations between individuals, these Articles create direct rights in respect of the individuals concerned which the national courts must safeguard".[2]

6.     In this way, national courts are able to ensure, at the request of the litigants or on their own initiative, that the competition rules will be respected for the benefit of private individuals. In addition, Article 85(2) enables them to private individuals. In addition,

Article 85(2) enables them to determine, in accordance with the national procedural law applicable, the civil law effects of the prohibition set out in Article 85(3).3

7.    However, the Commission, pursuant to Article 9 of Regulation No 17(4),4 has sole power to exempt certain types of agreements, decisions and concerted practices from this prohibition. The Commission may exercise this power in two ways. It may take a decision exempting a specific agreement in an individual case. It may also adopt regulations granting block exemptions for certain categories of agreements, decisions or concerted practices, where it is authorised to do so by the Council, in accordance with Article 87.

8.    Although national courts are not competent to apply Article 85(3), they may nevertheless apply the decisions and regulations adopted by the Commission pursuant to that provision. The Court has on several occasions confirmed that the provisions of a regulation are directly applicable.5 The Commission considers that the same is true for the substantive provisions of an individual exemption decision.

9.    The powers of the Commission and those of national courts differ not only in their objective and content, but also in the ways in which they are exercised. The Commission exercises its powers according to the procedural rules laid down by Regulation No 17, whereas national courts exercise theirs in the context of national procedural law.

10.    In this connection, the Court of Justice has laid down the principles which govern procedures and remedies for invoking directly applicable Community law.

"Although the Treaty has made it possible in a number of instances for private persons to bring a direct action, where appropriate, before the Court of Justice, it was not intended to create new remedies in the national courts to ensure the observance of Community law other than those already laid down by national law. On the other hand. . . it must be possible for every type of action provided for by national law to be available for the purpose of ensuring observance of Community provisions having direct effect, on the same conditions concerning the admissibility and procedure as would apply were it a question of ensuring observance of national law".[6]

11.    The Commission considers that these principles apply in the event of breach of the Community competition rules; individuals and companies have access to all procedural remedies provided for by national law on the same conditions as would apply if a comparable breach of national law were involved. This equality of treatment concerns not only the definitive finding of a breach of competition rules, but embraces all the legal means capable of contributing to effective legal protection. Consequently, it is the right of parties subject to Community law that national courts should take provisional measures, that an effective end should be brought, by injunction, to the infringement of Community competition rules of which they are victims, and that compensation should be awarded for the damage suffered as a result of infringements, where such remedies are available in proceedings relating to similar national law.

12.    Here the Commission would like to make it clear that the simultaneous application of national competition law is compatible with the application of Community law, provided that it does not impair the effectiveness and uniformity of Community competition rules and the measures taken to enforce them. Any conflicts which may arise when national and Community competition law are applied simultaneously must be resolved in accordance with the principle of the

precedence of Community law.[7] The purpose of this principle is to rule out any national measure which could jeopardise the full effectiveness of the provisions of Community law.

NOTES

1   Case C-234/89 *Delimitis v Henninger Bräu* [1991] ECR I-935, paragraph 44; Case T-24/90 *Automec v Commission*, judgment of 17 September 1992, paragraphs 73 and 85 (not yet reported).
2   Case 127/73 *BRT v Sabam* [1974] ECR 51, paragraph 16.
3   Case 56/65 *LTM v MBU* [1966] ECR 337; Case 48/72 *Brasserie De Haecht v Wilkin-Janssen* [1973] ECR 77; Case 319/82 *Ciments et Bétons v Kerpen & Kerpen* [1983] ECR 4173.
4   Council Regulation No 17 of 6 February 1962: First Regulation implementing Articles 85 and 86 of the Treaty (OJ No 13, 21.2.1962, p 204/62; Special Edition 1959-62, p 87).
5   Case 63/75 *Fonderies Roubaix v Fonderies Roux* [1976] ECR 111; Case C-234/89 *Delimitis v Henniger Bräu* [1991] ECR I-935.
6   Case 158/80 *Rewe v Hauptzollamt Kiel* [1981] ECR 1805, paragraph 44; see also Case 33/76 *Rewe v Landwirtschaftskammer Saarland* [1976] ECR 1989; Case 79/83 *Harz v Deutsche Tradax* [1984] ECR 1921; Case 199/82 *Amministrazione delle Finanze dello Stato v San Giorgio* [1983] ECR 3595.
7   Case 14/68 *Walt Wilhelm and Others v Bundeskartellamt* [1969] ECR 1; Joined Cases 253/78 and 1 to 3/79 *Procureur de la République v Giry and Guerlain* [1980] ECR 2327.

## III   The exercise of powers by the Commission

13.   As the administrative authority responsible for the Community's competition policy, the Commission must serve the Community's general interest. The administrative resources at the Commission's disposal to perform its task are necessarily limited and cannot be used to deal with all the cases brought to its attention. The Commission is therefore obliged, in general, to take all organisational measures necessary for the performance of its task and, in particular, to establish priorities.[1]

14.   The Commission intends, in implementing its decision-making powers, to concentrate on notifications, complaints and own-initiative proceedings having particular political, economic or legal significance for the Community. Where these features are absent in a particular case, notifications will normally be dealt with by means of comfort letter and complaints should, as a rule, be handled by national courts or authorities.

15.   The Commission considers that there is not normally a sufficient Community interest in examining a case when the plaintiff is able to secure adequate protection of his rights before the national courts.[2] In these circumstances the complaint will normally be filed.

16.   In this respect the Commission would like to make it clear that the application of Community competition law by the national courts has considerable advantages for individuals and companies—

— the Commission cannot award compensation for loss suffered as a result of an infringement of Article 85 or Article 86. Such claims may be brought only before the national courts. Companies are more likely to avoid infringements of the Community competition rules if they risk having to pay damages or interest in such an event,

— national courts can usually adopt interim measures and order the ending of infringements more quickly than the Commission is able to do,

— before national courts, it is possible to combine a claim under Community law with a claim under national law. This is not possible in a procedure before the Commission,

— in some Member States, the courts have the power to award legal costs to the successful applicant. This is never possible in the administrative procedure before the Commission.

NOTES
1   Case T-24/90 *Automec v Commission*, judgment of 17 September 1992, paragraph 77 (not yet reported).
2   Case T-24/90, cited above, paragraphs 91 to 94.

## IV   Application of Articles 85 and 86 by national courts

17.     The national court may have to reach a decision on the application of Articles 85 and 86 in several procedural situations. In the case of civil law proceedings, two types of action are particularly frequent: actions relating to contracts and actions for damages. Under the former, the defendant usually relies on Article 85(2) to dispute the contractual obligations invoked by the plaintiff. Under the latter, the prohibitions contained in Articles 85 and 86 are generally relevant in determining whether the conduct which has given rise to the alleged injury is illegal.

18.     In such situations, the direct effect of Article 85(1) and Article 86 gives national courts sufficient powers to comply with their obligation to hand down judgment. Nevertheless, when exercising these powers, they must take account of the Commission's powers in order to avoid decisions which could conflict with those taken or envisaged by the Commission in applying Article 85(1) and Article 86, and also Article 85(3).[1]

19.     In its case-law the Court of Justice has developed a number of principles which make it possible for such contradictory decisions to be avoided.[2] The Commission feels that national courts could take account of these principles in the following manner.

*1.  Application of Article 85(1) and (2) and Article 86.*

20.     The first question which national courts have to answer is whether the agreement, decision or concerted practice at issue infringes the prohibitions laid down in Article 85(1) or Article 86 Before answering this question, national courts should ascertain whether the agreement, decision or concerted practice has already been the subject of a decision, opinion or other official statement issued by an administrative authority and in particular by the Commission. Such statements provide national courts with significant information for reaching a judgment, even if they are not formally bound by them. It should be noted in this respect that not all procedures before the Commission lead to an official decision, but that cases can also be closed by comfort letters. Whilst it is true that the Court of Justice has ruled that this type of letter does not bind national courts, it has nevertheless stated that the opinion expressed by the Commission constitutes a factor which the national courts may take into account in examining whether the agreements or conduct in question are in accordance with the provisions of Article 85(3).[3]

21.     If the Commission has not ruled on the same agreement, decision or concerted practice, the national courts can always be guided, in interpreting the Community law in question, by the case-law of the Court of Justice and the existing decisions of the Commission. It is with this in view that the Commission has, in a number of general notices,[4] specified categories of agreements that are not caught by the ban laid down in Article 85(1).

22.     On these bases, national courts should generally be able to decide whether the conduct at issue is compatible with Article 85(1) and Article 86. Nevertheless, if the Commission has initiated a procedure in a case relating to the same conduct, they may, if they consider it necessary for reasons of legal certainty, stay the proceedings while awaiting the outcome of the Commission's action.[5] A stay of proceedings may also be envisaged where national courts wish to seek the Commission's views in

accordance with the arrangements referred to in this Notice.[6] Finally, where national courts have persistent doubts on questions of compatibility, they may stay proceedings in order to bring the matter before the Court of Justice, in accordance with Article 177 of the Treaty.

23.　　However, where national courts decide to give judgment and find that the conditions for applying Article 85(1) or Article 86 are not met, they should pursue their proceedings on the basis of such a finding, even if the agreement, decision or concerted practice at issue has been notified to the Commission. Where the assessment of the facts shows that the conditions for applying the said Articles are met, national courts must rule that the conduct at issue infringes Community competition law and take the appropriate measures, including those relating to the consequences that attach to infringement of a statutory prohibition under the civil law applicable.

*2.  Application of Article 85(3).*

24.　　If the national court concludes that an agreement, decision or concerted practice is prohibited by Article 85(1), it must check whether it is or will be the subject of an exemption by the Commission under Article 85(3). Here several situations may arise.

25.—(a)  The national court is required to respect the exemption decisions taken by the Commission. Consequently, it must treat the agreement, decision or concerted practice at issue as compatible with Community law and fully recognise its civil law effects. In this respect mention should be made of comfort letters in which the Commission services state that the conditions for applying Article 85(3) have been met. The Commission considers that national courts may take account of these letters as factual elements.

26.—(b)  Agreements, decisions and concerted practices which fall within the scope of application of a block exemption regulation are automatically exempted from the prohibition laid down in Article 85(1) without the need for a Commission decision or comfort letter.[7]

27.—(c)  Agreements, decisions and concerted practices which are not covered by a block exemption regulation and which have not been the subject of an individual exemption decision or a comfort letter must, in the Commission's view, be examined in the following manner.

28.　　The national court must first examine whether the procedural conditions necessary for securing exemption are fulfilled, notably whether the agreement, decision or concerted practice has been duly notified in accordance with Article 4(1) of Regulation No 17. Where no such notification has been made, and subject to Article 4(2) of Regulation No 17, exemption under Article 85(3) is ruled out, so that the national court may decide, pursuant to Article 85(2), that the agreement, decision or concerted practice is void.

29.　　Where the agreement, decision or concerted practice has been duly notified to the Commission, the national court will assess the likelihood of an exemption being granted in the case in question in the light of the relevant criteria developed by the case law of the Court of Justice and the Court of First Instance and by previous regulations and decisions of the Commission.

30.　　Where the national court has in this way ascertained that the agreement, decision or concerted practice at issue cannot be the subject of an individual exemption, it will take the measures necessary to comply with the requirements of Article 85(1) and (2). On the other hand, if it takes the view that individual exemption is possible, the national court should suspend the proceedings while awaiting the Commission's decision. If the national court does suspend the proceedings, it nevertheless remains free, according to the rules of the applicable national law, to adopt any interim measures it deems necessary.

31. In this connection, it should be made clear that these principles do not apply to agreements, decisions and concerted practices which existed before Regulation No 17 entered into force or before that Regulation became applicable as a result of the accession of a new Member State and which were duly notified to the Commission. The national courts must consider such agreements, decisions and concerted practices to be valid so long as the Commission or the authorities of the Member States have not taken a prohibition decision or sent a comfort letter to the parties informing them that the file has been closed.[8]

32. The Commission realises that the principles set out above for the application of Articles 85 and 86 by national courts are complex and sometimes insufficient to enable those courts to perform their judicial function properly. This is particularly so where the practical application of Article 85(1) and Article 86 gives rise to legal or economic difficulties, where the Commission has initiated a procedure in the same case or where the agreement, decision or concerted practice concerned may become the subject of an individual exemption within the meaning of Article 85(3). National courts may bring such cases before the Court of Justice for a preliminary ruling, in accordance with Article 177. They may also avail themselves of the Commission's assistance according to the procedures set out below.

---

NOTES

1   Case C-234/89 *Delimitis v Henninger Bräu* [1991] ECR I-935, paragraph 47.
2   Case 48/72 *Brasserie De Haecht v Wilkin-Janssen* [1973] ECR 77; Case 127/73 *BRT v Sabam* [1974] ECR 51; Case C-234/89 *Delimitis v Henninger Bräu* [1991] ECR I-935.
3   Case 99/79 *Lancôme v Etos* (1980) ECR 2511, paragraph 11.
4   See the notices on—
      — exclusive dealing contracts with commercial agents (OJ No 139, 24.12.1962, p 2921/62),
      — agreements, decisions and concerted practices in the field of co-operation between enterprises (OJ No C75, 29.7.1968, p 3, as corrected in OJ No C84, 28.8.1968, p 14),
      — assessment of certain subcontracting agreements (OJ No C1, 3.1.1979, p 2),
      — agreements of minor importance (OJ No C231, 12.9.1986, p 2).
5   Case 127/73 *BRT v Sabam* [1974] ECR 51, paragraph 21. The procedure before the Commission is initiated by an authoritative act. A simple acknowledgment of receipt cannot be considered an authoritative act as such; Case 48/72 *Brasserie De Haecht v Wilkin-Janssen* [1973] ECR 77, paragraphs 16 and 17.
6   Case C-234/89 *Delimitis v Henninger Bräu* [1991] ECR I-935, paragraph 53, Part V of this Notice.
7   A list of the relevant regulations and the official explanatory comments relating to them is given in the Annex to this Notice.
8   Case 48/72 *Brasserie De Haecht v Wilkin-Janssen* [1973] ECR 77; Case 59/77 *De Bloss v Bouyer* [1977] ECR 2359, Case 99/79 *Lancôme v Etos* (1980) ECR 2511.

---

## V   Co-operation between national courts and the Commission

33. Article 5 of the EEC Treaty establishes the principle of constant and sincere co-operation between the Community and the Member States with a view to attaining the objectives of the Treaty, including implementation of Article 3(f), which refers to the establishment of a system ensuring that competition in the common market is not distorted. This principle involves obligations and duties of mutual assistance, both for the Member States and for the Community institutions. The Court has thus

ruled that, under Article 5 of the EEC Treaty, the Commission has a duty of sincere co-operation *vis-à-vis* judicial authorities of the Member States, who are responsible for ensuring that Community law is applied and respected in the national legal system.[1]

34.    The Commission considers that such co-operation is essential in order to guarantee the strict, effective and consistent application of Community competition law. In addition, more effective participation by the national courts in the day-to-day application of competition law gives the Commission more time to perform its administrative task, namely to steer competition policy in the Community.

35.    In the light of these considerations, the Commission intends to work towards closer co-operation with national courts in the following manner.

36.    The Commission conducts its policy so as to give the parties concerned useful pointers to the application of competition rules. To this end, it will continue its policy in relation to block exemption regulations and general notices. These general texts, the case-law of the Court of Justice and the Court of First Instance, the decisions previously taken by the Commission and the annual reports on competition policy are all elements of secondary legislation or explanations which may assist national courts in examining individual cases.

37.    If these general pointers are insufficient, national courts may, within the limits of their national procedural law, ask the Commission and in particular its Directorate-General for Competition for the following information.

First, they may ask for information of a procedural nature to enable them to discover whether a certain case is pending before the Commission, whether a case has been the subject of a notification, whether the Commission has officially initiated a procedure or whether it has already taken a position through an official decision or through a comfort letter sent by its services. If necessary, national courts may also ask the Commission to give an opinion as to how much time is likely to be required for granting or refusing individual exemption for notified agreements or practices, so as to be able to determine the conditions for any decision to suspend proceedings or whether interim measures need to be adopted.[2] The Commission, for its part, will endeavour to give priority to cases which are the subject of national proceedings suspended in this way, in particular when the outcome of a civil dispute depends on them.

38.    Next, national courts may consult the Commission on points of law. Where the application of Article 85(1) and Article 86 causes them particular difficulties, national courts may consult the Commission on its customary practice in relation to the Community law at issue. As far as Articles 85 and 86 are concerned, these difficulties relate in particular to the conditions for applying these Articles as regards the effect on trade between Member States and as regards the extent to which the restriction of competition resulting from the practices specified in these provisions is appreciable. In its replies, the Commission does not consider the merits of the case. In addition, where they have doubts as to whether a contested agreement, decision or concerted practice is eligible for an individual exemption, they may ask the Commission to provide them with an interim opinion. If the Commission says that the case in question is unlikely to qualify for an exemption, national courts will be able to waive a stay of proceedings and rule on the validity of the agreement, decision or concerted practice.

39.    The answers given by the Commission are not binding on the courts which have requested them. In its replies the Commission makes it clear that its view is not definitive and that the right for the national court to refer to the Court of Justice,

pursuant to Article 177, is not affected. Nevertheless, the Commission considers that it gives them useful guidance for resolving disputes.

40.     Lastly, national courts can obtain information from the Commission regarding factual data: statistics, market studies and economic analyses. The Commission will endeavour to communicate these data, within the limits laid down in the following paragraph, or will indicate the source from which they can be obtained.

41.     It is in the interests of the proper administration of justice that the Commission should answer requests for legal and factual information in the shortest possible time. Nevertheless, the Commission cannot accede to such requests unless several conditions are met. First, the requisite data must actually be at its disposal. Secondly, the Commission may communicate this data only in so far as permitted by the general principle of sound administrative practice.

42.     For example, Article 214 of the Treaty, as spelt out in Article 20 of Regulation No 17 for the purposes of the competition rules, requires the Commission not to disclose information of a confidential nature. In addition, the duty of sincere co-operation deriving from Article 5 is one applying to the relationship between national courts and the Commission and cannot concern the position of the parties to the dispute pending before those courts. As *amicus curiae*, the Commission is obliged to respect legal neutrality and objectivity. Consequently, it will not accede to requests for information unless they come from a national court, either directly, or indirectly through parties which have been ordered by the court concerned to provide certain information. In the latter case, the Commission will ensure that its answer reaches all the parties to the proceedings.

43.     Over and above such exchange of information, required in specific cases, the Commission is anxious to develop as far as possible a more general information policy. To this end, the Commission intends to publish an explanatory booklet regarding the application of the competition rules at national level.

44.     Lastly, the Commission also wishes to reinforce the effect of national competition judgments. To this end, it will study the possibility of extending the scope of the Convention on jurisdiction and the enforcement of judgments in civil and commercial matters to competition cases assigned to administrative courts.3 It should be noted that, in the Commission's view, competition judgments are already governed by this Convention where they are handed down in cases of a civil and commercial nature.

NOTES
1   Case C-2/88, Imm, *Zwartveld* [1990] ECR I-3365, paragraph 18; C-234/89 *Delimitis v Henninger Bräu* [1991] ECR I-935, paragraph 53.
2   See paragraphs 22 and 30 of this Notice.
3   Convention of 27 September 1968 (OJ No L304, 30.10.1978, p 77).

## VI     Final remarks

45.     This Notice does not relate to the competition rules governing the transport sector.1 Nor does it relate to the competition rules laid down in the Treaty establishing the European Coal and Steel Community.

46.     This Notice is issued for guidance and does not in any way restrict the rights conferred on individuals or companies by Community law.

47.     This Notice is without prejudice to any interpretation of the Community competition rules which may be given by the Court of Justice of the European Communities.

**48.** A summary of the answers given by the Commission pursuant to this Notice will be published annually in the Competition Report.

---

NOTES

1   Competition rules governing the transport sector: Regulation No 141/62 of the Council of 26 November 1962 exempting transport from the application of Council Regulation No 17 (OJ No 124, 28.11.1962, p 2751/62), as amended by Regulations Nos 165/65/EEC (OJ No 210, 11.12.1965, p 3141/65) and 1002/67/EEC (OJ No 306, 16.12.1967, p 1); Regulation (EEC) No 1017/68 of the Council of 19 July 1968 applying rules of competition to transport by rail, road and inland waterway (OJ No L175, 23.7.1968, p 1); Council Regulation (EEC) No 4056/86 of 22 December 1986 laying down detailed rules for the application of Articles 85 and 86 of the Treaty to maritime transport (OJ No L378, 31.12.1986, p 4); Council Regulation (EEC) No 3975/87 of 14 December 1987 laying down the procedure for the application of the rules on competition to undertakings in the air transport sector (OJ No L 374, 31.12.1987, p 1).

# ANNEX
# BLOCK EXEMPTIONS

A   ENABLING COUNCIL REGULATIONS

I   **Vertical agreements** (see under BI and BII)

Council Regulation No 19/65/EEC of 2 March 1965 on the application of Article 85(3) of the Treaty to certain categories of agreements and concerted practices (OJ, Special Edition 1965–66, p 35).

II   **Horizontal agreements** (see under BIII)

Council Regulation (EEC) No 2821/71 of 20 December 1971 on the application of Article 85(3) of the Treaty to categories of agreements, decisions and concerted practices (OJ, Special Edition 1971–III, p 1032), modified by Regulation (EEC) No 2743/72 of 19 December 1972 (OJ, Special Edition 1972, 28–30.12.1972, p 60).

B   COMMISSION BLOCK EXEMPTION REGULATIONS AND EXPLANATORY NOTICES

I   **Distribution agreements**
   1.   Commission Regulation (EEC) No 1983/83 of 22 June 1983 concerning exclusive distribution agreements (OJ L173, 30.6.1983, p 1).
   2.   Commission Regulation (EEC) No 1984/83 of 22 June 1983 concerning exclusive purchasing agreements (OJ L173, 30.6.1983, p 5).
   3.   Commission Notice concerning Commission Regulations (EEC) No 1983/83 and (EEC) No 1984/83 (OJ C101, 13.4.1984, p 2).
   4.   Commission Regulation (EEC) No 123/85 of 12 December 1984 concerning motor vehicle distribution and servicing agreements (OJ L15, 18.1.1985, p 16).
   5.   Commission Notice concerning Regulation (EEC) No 123/85 (OJ C17, 18.1.1985, p 4).
   6.   Commission Notice on the clarification of the activities of motor vehicle intermediaries (OJ C329, 18.12.1991, p 20).

II   **Licensing and franchising agreements**
   1.   Commission Regulation (EEC) No 2349/84 of 23 July 1984 concerning patent licensing agreements (OJ L219, 1681984, p 15; corrigendum OJ L280, 22.10.1985, p 32).
   2.   Commission Regulation (EEC) No 4087/88 of 30 November 1988 concerning franchising agreements (OJ L359, 28.12.1988, p 46).
   3.   Commission Regulation (EEC) No 556/89 of 30 November 1988 concerning know-how licensing agreements (OJ L61, 4.3.1989, p 1).

III   **Cooperative agreements**
   1.   Commission Regulation (EEC) No 417/85 of 19 December 1984 concerning specialisation agreements (OJ L53, 22.2.1985, p 1).
   2.   Commission Regulation (EEC) No 418/85 of 19 December 1984 concerning research and development agreements (OJ L53, 22.2.1985, p 5).

# PRESS RELEASE

of 23 December 1992

## Commission adopts notice aimed at decentralising application of EC anti-trust rules

The Commission has adopted a Notice clarifying the application of the EC's competition rules (Articles 85 and 86) by national courts. The aim of the Notice is to encourage national courts to apply EC competition rules more frequently and more efficiently, ensuring a more decentralised policy while seeking to establish a clearer delineation of responsibilities between the Commission and the national courts. Community law will therefore be applied nearer to the citizen, fully in line with the concept of subsidiarity. The Notice, which forms an integral part of the procedural reforms explained recently by Sir Leon Brittan, EC Commissioner for competition policy (Speech to CEPS on 8 December 1992), is addressed to national courts, competition authorities, lawyers and to other interested parties.

The Notice sets out to do the following: to codify the case-law of the Court of Justice on the relation between the Commission and national courts; to identify their respective fields of competence; to specify how the Commission takes account of national procedures when it establishes its priorities; and to explain how the Commission intends to assist national courts, for example by offering legal advice and access to information on statistics and on the state of its own inquiries. It also aims to reinforce the effect of national competition judgments.

*Encouraging complainants to use national courts*

The strengthened role of national courts brings with it several advantages. Recourse to national courts enables individuals to obtain adequate injunctions and immediate interim measures. They may also award damages that the Commission is not empowered to provide. In some member states, national courts have the power to award legal costs to the successful applicant, unlike the Commission. It is also possible to combine a claim under Community law with a claim under national law, something which cannot be done in a procedure before the Commission.

The Commission states in the Notice that it intends to concentrate on notifications, complaints and own-initiative proceedings which have a particular political, economic or legal significance for the Community. The Commission will encourage complainants to go to the national courts in cases where adequate redress exists there.

*Avoiding conflicts with the Commission*

Articles 85(1) and 86 give national courts sufficient powers to hand down judgments, most frequently on actions relating to contracts and actions for damages. When exercising these powers, they must take account of the Commission's powers in order to avoid decisions which conflict with those taken or envisaged by the Commission. The national courts should therefore find out whether the Commission, or any other administrative authority, has already issued a decision, opinion or official statement on a case before reaching their own decision. If the Commission has not ruled on the same case, the national courts can always be guided by the case law of the Court of Justice or by existing Commission decisions. If the Commission has opened a procedure in a case relating to the same conduct, the national courts may see fit to suspend their own proceedings while awaiting the outcome of the

Commission's action. They may of course also seek the opinion of the Court of Justice directly.

If the national courts do find an infringement of Articles 85 or 86, they should pursue their proceedings, even if the case has already been notified to the Commission. They must then rule whether the business conduct at issue infringes EC competition law, and take appropriate measures.

However, it is important to note that the Commission remains the sole authority with the jurisdiction to grant individual exemptions pursuant to Article 85(3) of the Treaty. Thus, in individual cases where an alleged infringement of Article 85(1) is being considered, national courts must check whether an agreement in breach of Article 85(1) could qualify for an exemption by the Commission under Article 85(3). National courts should always assess the likelihood of an exemption being granted by the Commission. If they think it is possible, they should suspend their proceedings where appropriate while awaiting the Commission's decision. They remain free to adopt any interim measures they deem necessary.

*Co-operation between Commission and national courts*

Both Commission and national courts are governed by obligations and duties of mutual assistance. More effective participation by the national courts in the day-to-day application of competition law gives the Commission more time to perform its administrative task of steering the EC's competition policy. Where possible, the Commission will give useful pointers to the national courts, and will continue its policy of publishing block exemption regulations and general notices.

National courts may ask the Commission for procedural information which would enable them to discover whether a case is pending before the Commission, whether it has been notified, whether the Commission has officially opened an investigation, whether it has taken a position officially or through a "comfort letter", and how much time the Commission expects to take to decide, thus enabling the national courts to plan the length of their own suspension or interim measures. The Commission will strive to give priority to cases which have been suspended by the national courts. National courts may also consult the Commission on points of law, particularly regarding its view on the effect on intra-Community trade whilst the Commission will not get involved in the merits of such cases. It will be able to provide a court with an opinion on its customary practice in relation to relevant Community law. They may also ask the Commission to provide them with an interim statement on whether a contested agreement is eligible for an individual exemption from the competition rules. The Commission answers are not binding on the national courts.

National courts can also obtain statistics, market studies and economic analyses from the Commission, which will reply in the shortest possible time. It will also publish an explanatory booklet on the application of EC competition rules at national level. The Notice covers neither the transport sector nor the ECSC Treaty.

# COMMISSION NOTICE

**on co-operation between national competition authorities and the Commission in handling cases falling within the scope of Articles 85 or 86 of the EC Treaty**

**(97/C 313/03)**

NOTES

Date of publication in OJ: OJ C313, 15.10.97, p 3

## I Role of the Member States and of the Community

1.     In competition policy the Community and the Member States perform different functions. Whereas the Community is responsible only for implementing the Community rules, Member States not only apply their domestic law but also have a hand in implementing Articles 85 and 86 of the EC Treaty.

2.     This involvement of the Member States in Community competition policy means that decision can be taken as closely as possible to the citizen (Article A of the Treaty on European Union). The decentralised application of Community competition rules also leads to a better allocation of tasks. If, by reason of its scale or effects, the proposed action can best be taken at Community level, it is for the Commission to act. Otherwise, it is for the competition authority of the Member State concerned to act.

3.     Community law is implemented by the Commission and national competition authorities, on the one hand, and national courts, on the other, in accordance with the principles developed by the Community legislature and by the Court of Justice and the Court of First Instance of the European Communities.

It is the task of national courts to safeguard the rights of private persons in their relations with one another[1]. Those rights derive from the fact that the prohibitions in Articles 85(1) and 86[2] and the exemptions granted by regulation[3] have been recognised by the Court of Justice as being directly applicable. Relations between national courts and the Commission in applying Articles 85 and 86 were spelt out in a Notice published by the Commission in 1993[4]. This Notice is the counterpart, for relations with national authorities, to that of 1993 on relations with national courts.

4.     As administrative authorities, both the Commission and national competition authorities act in the public interest in performing their general task of monitoring and enforcing the competition rules[5]. Relations between them are determined primarily by this common role of protecting the general interest. Although similar to the Notice on co-operation with national courts, this Notice accordingly reflects this special feature.

5.     The specific nature of the role of the Commission and of national competition authorities is characterised by the powers conferred on those bodies by the Council regulations adopted under Article 87 of the Treaty. Article 9(1) of Regulation No 17[6] thus provides: 'Subject to review of its decision by the Court of Justice[7], the Commission shall have sole power to declare Article 85(1) inapplicable pursuant to Article 85(3) of the Treaty'. And Article 9(3) of the same Regulation provides: 'As long as the Commission has not initiated any procedure under Article 2[8], 3[9] or 6[10], the authorities of the Member States shall remain competent to apply Article 85(1) and Article 86 in accordance with Article 88 of the Treaty.'

It follows that, provided their national law has conferred the necessary powers on them, national competition authorities are empowered to apply the prohibitions in Articles 85(1) and 86. On the other hand, for the purposes of applying Article 85(3), they do not have any powers to grant exemptions in individual cases; they must abide by the decisions and regulations adopted by the Commission under that provision. They may also take account of other measures adopted by the Commission in such cases, in particular comfort letters, treating them as factual evidence.

6.　　The Commission is convinced that enhancing the role of national competition authorities will boost the effectiveness of Articles 85 and 86 of the Treaty and, generally speaking, will bolster the application of Community competition rules throughout the Community. In the interests of safeguarding and developing the single market, the Commission considers that those provisions should be used as widely as possible. Being closer to the activities and businesses that require monitoring, national authorities are often in a better position than the Commission to protect competition.

7.　　Co-operation must therefore be organised between national authorities and the Commission. If this co-operation is to be fruitful, they will have to keep in close and constant touch.

8.　　The Commission proposes to set out in this Notice the principles it will apply in future when dealing with the cases described herein. The Notice also seeks to induce firms to approach national competition authorities more often.

9.　　This Notice describes the practical co-operation which is desirable between the Commission and national authorities. It does not affect the extent of the powers conferred by Community law on either the Commission or national authorities for the purpose of dealing with individual cases.

10.　　For cases falling within the scope of Community law, to avoid duplication of checks on compliance with the competition rules which are applicable to them, which is costly for the firms concerned, checks should wherever possible be carried out by a single authority (either a Member State's competition authority or the Commission). Control by a single authority offers advantages for businesses.

Parallel proceedings before the Commission, on the one hand, and a national competition authority, on the other, are costly for businesses whose activities fall within the scope both of Community law and of Member States' competition laws. They can lead to the repetition of checks on the same activity, by the Commission, on the one hand, and by the competition authorities of the Member States concerned, on the other.

Businesses in the Community may therefore in certain circumstances find it to their advantage if some cases falling within the scope of Community competition law were dealt with solely by national authorities. In order that this advantage may be enjoyed to the full, the Commission thinks it is desirable that national authorities should themselves apply Community law directly or, failing that, obtain, by applying their domestic law, a result similar to that which would have been obtained had Community law been applied.

11.　　What is more, in addition to the resulting benefits accruing to competition authorities in terms of mobilisation of their resources, co-operation between authorities reduces the risk of divergent decisions and hence the opportunities for those who might be tempted to do so to seek out whichever authority seemed to them to be the most favourable to their interests.

12.     Member States' competition authorities often have a more detailed and precise knowledge than the Commission of the relevant markets (particularly those with highly specific national features) and the businesses concerned. Above all, they may be in a better position than the Commission to detect restrictive practices that have not been notified or abuses of a dominant position whose effects are essentially confined to their territory.

13.     Many cases handled by national authorities involve arguments based on national law and arguments drawn from Community competition law. In the interests of keeping proceedings as short as possible, the Commission considers it preferable that national authorities should directly apply Community law themselves, instead of making firms refer to the Community-law aspects of their cases to the Commission.

14.     An increasing number of major issues in the field of Community competition law have been clarified over the last thirty years through the case-law of the Court of Justice and the Court of First Instance and through decisions taken on questions of principle and the exemption regulations adopted by the Commission. The application of that law by national authorities is thereby simplified.

15.     The Commission intends to encourage the competition authorities of all Member States to engage in this co-operation. However, the national legislation of several Member States does not currently provide competition authorities with the procedural means of applying Articles 85(1) and 86. In such Member States conduct caught by the Community provisions can be effectively dealt with by national authorities only under national law.

In the Commission's view, it is desirable that national authorities should apply Articles 85 or 86 of the Treaty, if appropriate in conjunction with their domestic competition rules, when handling cases that fall within the scope of those provisions.

16.     Where authorities are not in a position to do this and hence can apply only their national law to such cases, the application of that law should 'not prejudice the uniform application throughout the common market of the Community rules on cartels and of the full effect of the measures adopted in implementation of those rules'[11]. At the very least, the solution they find to a case falling within the scope of Community law must be compatible with that law, Member States being forbidden, given the primacy of Community law over national competition law[12] and the obligation to co-operate in good faith laid down in Article 5 of the Treaty[13], to take measures capable of defeating the practical effectiveness of Articles 85 and 86.

17.     Divergent decisions are more likely to be reached where a national authority applies its national law rather than Community law. Where a Member State's competition authority applies Community law, it is required to comply with any decisions taken previously by the Commission in the same proceedings. Where the case has merely been the subject of a comfort letter, then, according to the Court of Justice, although this type of letter does not bind national courts, the opinion expressed by the Commission constitutes a factor which the national courts may take into account in examining whether the agreements on conduct in question are in accordance with the provisions of Article 85[14]. In the Commission's view, the same holds true for national authorities.

18.     Where an infringement of Articles 85 or 86 is established by Commission decision, that decision precludes the application of a domestic legal provision authorising what the Commission has prohibited. The objective of the prohibitions in

Articles 85(1) and 86 is to guarantee the unity of the common market and the preservation of undistorted competition in that market. They must be strictly complied with if the functioning of the Community regime is not to be endangered[15].

19.　The legal position is less clear as to whether national authorities are allowed to apply their more stringent national competition law where the situation they are assessing has previously been the subject of an individual exemption decision of the Commission or is covered by a block exemption Regulation. In *Walt Wilhelm*, the Court stated that the Treaty 'permits the Community authorities to carry out certain positive, though indirect, actions with a view to promoting a harmonious development of economic activities within the whole Community' (paragraph 5 of the judgment). In *Bundeskartellamt v Volkswagen and VAG Leasing*[16], the Commission contended that national authorities may not prohibit exempted agreements. The uniform application of Community law would be frustrated every time an exemption granted under Community law was made to depend on the relevant national rules. Otherwise, not only would a given agreement be treated differently depending on the law of each Member State, thus detracting from the uniform application of Community law, but the full effectiveness of an act giving effect to the Treaty—which an exemption under Article 85(3) undoubtedly is—would also be disregarded. In the case in point, however, the Court did not have to settle the question.

20.　If the Commission's Directorate-General for Competition sends a comfort letter in which it expresses the opinion that an agreement or a practice is incompatible with Article 85 of the Treaty but states that, for reasons to do with its internal priorities, it will not propose to the Commission that it take a decision thereon in accordance with the formal procedures laid down in Regulation No 17, it goes without saying that the national authorities in whose territory the effects of the agreement or practice are felt may take action in respect of that agreement or practice.

21.　In the case of a comfort letter in which the Directorate-General for Competition expresses the opinion that an agreement does restrict competition within the meaning of Article 85(1) but qualifies for exemption under Article 85(3), the Commission will call upon national authorities to consult it before they decide whether to adopt a different decision under Community or national law.

22.　As regards comfort letters in which the Commission expresses the opinion that, on the basis of the information in its possession, there is no need for it to take any action under Article 85(1) or Article 86 of the Treaty, 'that fact cannot by itself have the result of preventing the national authorities from applying to those agreements' or practices 'provisions of national competition law which may be more rigorous than Community law in this respect. The fact that a practice has been held by the Commission not to fall within the ambit of the prohibition contained in Article 85(1) and (2)' or Article 86, 'the scope of which is limited to agreements' or dominant positions 'capable of affecting trade between Member States, in no way prevents that practice from being considered by the national authorities from the point of view of the restrictive effects which it may produce nationally'. (Judgment of the Court of Justice in *Procureur de la République v Giry and Guerlain*[17]).

---

NOTES
1　Case T-24/90 *Automec v EC Commission (Automec II)* [1992] ECR II-2223, para 85.
2　Case 127/733 *BRT v SABAM* [1974] ECR 51, para 16.
3　Case 63/75 *Fonderies Roubaix-Wattrelos v Fonderies A Roux* [1976] ECR 111.
4　Notice on co-operation between national courts and the Commission in applying Articles 85 and 86 of the EEC Treaty, OJ C39, 13.2.9, p 6.

5  *Automec II*, see n 1 above, para 85.

6  Council Regulation 17 of 6 February 1962: First Regulation implementing Articles 85 and 86 of the Treaty; OJ 13, 21.2.62, p 204/62 (English Special Edition 1959-62, p 87).

7  Now by the Court of First Instance and, on appeal, by the Court of Justice.

8  Negative clearance.

9  Termination of infringements—prohibition decisions.

10  Decisions pursuant to Article 85(3).

11  Case 14/68 *Walt Wilhelm v Bundeskartellamt* [1969] ECR 1, para 4.

12  *Walt Wilhelm*, see n 11 above, para 6; Case 66/86 *Ahmed Saeed Flugreisen v Zentrale Zur Bekämpfung Unlauteren Wettbewerbs* [1989] ECR 803, para 48.

13  Case C-165/91 *Van Munster v Rijksdienst voor Pensioenen* [1994] ECR I-4661, para 32.

14  Case 99/79 *Lancôme v Etos* [1980] ECR 2511, para 11, cited in the abovementioned notice on co-operation between national courts and the Commission in applying Articles 85 and 86.

15  4th Report on Competition Policy (1974), point 45.

16  Case C-266/93 [1995] ECR I-3477; see also the Opinion of Advocate-General Tesauro in the same case, para 51.

17  Joined Cases 253/78 and 1–3/79 *Procureur de la République v Giry and Guerlain* [1980] ECR 2327, para 18.

## II  Guidelines on case allocation

23.     Co-operation between the Commission and national competition authorities has to comply with the current legal framework. First, if it is to be caught by Community law and not merely by national competition law, the conduct in question must be liable to have an appreciable effect on trade between Member States. Secondly, the Commission has sole power to declare Article 85(1) of the Treaty inapplicable under Article 85(3).

24.     In practice, decisions taken by a national authority can apply effectively only to restrictions of competition whose impact is felt essentially within its territory. This is the case in particular with the restrictions referred to in Article 4(2)(1) of Regulation No 17, namely agreements, decisions or concerted practices the only parties to which are undertakings from one Member State and which, though they do not relate either to imports or to exports between Member States, may affect intra-Community trade[1]. It is extremely difficult from a legal standpoint for such an authority to conduct investigations outside its home country, such as when on-the-spot inspections need to be carried out on businesses, and to ensure that its decisions are enforced beyond its national borders. The upshot is that the Commission usually has to handle cases involving businesses whose relevant activities are carried on in more than one Member State.

25.     A national authority having sufficient resources in terms of manpower and equipment and having had the requisite powers conferred on it, also needs to be able to deal effectively with any cases covered by the Community rules which it proposes to take on. The effectiveness of a national authority's action is dependent on its powers of investigation, the legal means it has at its disposal for settling a case—including the power to order interim measures in an emergency—and the penalties it is empowered to impose on businesses found guilty of infringing the competition rules. Differences between the rules of procedure applicable in the various Member States should not, in the Commission's view, lead to outcomes which differ in their effectiveness when similar cases are being dealt with.

26.     In deciding which cases to handle itself, the Commission will take into account the effects of the restrictive practice or abuse of a dominant position and the nature of the infringement.

In principle, national authorities will handle cases the effects of which are felt mainly in their territory and which appear upon preliminary examination unlikely to qualify for exemption under Article 85(3). However, the Commission reserves the right to take on certain cases displaying a particular Community interest.

*Mainly national effects*

27.    First of all, it should be pointed out that the only cases at issue here are those which fall within the scope of Articles 85 and 86.

That being so, the existing and foreseeable effects of a restrictive practice or abuse of a dominant position may be deemed to be closely linked to the territory in which the agreement or practice is applied and to the geographic market for the goods or services in question.

28.    Where the relevant geographic market is limited to the territory of a single Member State and the agreement or practice is applied only in that State, the effects of the agreement or practice must be deemed to occur mainly within that State even if, theoretically, the agreement or practice is capable of affecting trade between Member States.

*Nature of the infringement: cases that cannot be exempted*

29.    The following considerations apply to cases brought before the Commission, to cases brought before a national competition authority and to cases which both may have to deal with.

A distinction should be drawn between infringements of Article 85 of the Treaty and infringements of Article 86.

30.    The Commission has exclusive powers under Articles 85(3) of the Treaty to declare the provisions of Article 85(1) inapplicable. Any notified restrictive practice that prima facie qualifies for exemption must therefore be examined by the Commission, which will take account of the criteria developed in this area by the Court of Justice and the Court of First Instance and also by the relevant regulations and its own previous decisions.

31.    The Commission also has exclusive responsibility for investigation complaints against decisions it has taken under its exclusive powers, such as a decision to withdraw an exemption previously granted by it under Article 85(3)[2].

32.    No such limitation exists, however, on implementation of Article 86 of the Treaty. The Commission and the Member States have concurrent competence to investigate complaints and to prohibit abuses of dominant positions.

*Cases of particular significance to the Community*

33.    Some cases considered by the Commission to be of particular Community interest will more often be dealt with by the Commission even if, inasmuch as they satisfy the requirements set out above (points 27–28 and 29–32), they can be dealt with by a national authority.

34.    This category includes cases which raise a new point of law, that is to say, those which have not yet been the subject of a Commission decision or a judgment of the Court of Justice or Court of First Instance.

35.    The economic magnitude of a case is not in itself sufficient reason for its being dealt with by the Commission. The position might be different where access to the relevant market by firms from other Member States is significantly impeded.

36.    Cases involving alleged anti-competitive behaviour by a public undertaking, an undertaking to which a Member State has granted special or exclusive rights within the meaning of Article 90(1) of the Treaty, or an undertaking entrusted with the operation of services of general economic interest or having the character of a revenue-producing monopoly within the meaning of Article 90(2) of the Treaty may also be of particular Community interest.

NOTES

    1    It is possible that an agreement, 'although it does not relate either to imports or to exports between Member States' within the meaning of art 4 of Regulation No 17, 'may affect trade between Member States' within the meaning of Article 85(1) of the Treaty (judgment of the Court of Justice in Case 43/69 *Bilger v Jehle* [1970] ECR 127, para 5).
    2    Case T-24/90 *Automec v EC Commission (Automec II)* [1992] ECR II-2223, para 75.

## III  Co-operation in cases which the Commission deals with first

37.    Cases dealt with by the Commission have three possible origins: own-initiative proceedings, notifications and complaints. By their very nature, own-initiative proceedings do not lend themselves to decentralised processing by national competition authorities.

38.    The exclusivity of the Commission's powers to apply Article 85(3) of the Treaty in individual cases means that cases notified to the Commission under Article 4(1) of Regulation No 17 by parties seeking exemption under Article 85(3) cannot be dealt with by a national competition authority on the Commission's initiative. According to the case-law of the Court of First Instance, these exclusive powers confer on the applicant the right to obtain from the Commission a decision on the substance of his request for exemption[1].

39.    National competition authorities may deal, at the Commission's request, with complaints that do not involve the application of Article 85(3), namely those relating to restrictive practices which must be notified under Articles 4(1), 5(1) and 25 of Regulation No 17 but have not been notified to the Commission and those based on alleged infringement of Article 86 of the Treaty. On the other hand, complaints concerning matters falling within the scope of the Commission's exclusive powers, such as withdrawal of exemption, cannot be usefully handled by a national competition authority[2].

40.    The criteria set out at points 23 to 36 above in relation to the handling of a case by the Commission or a national authority, in particular as regards the territorial extent of the effects of a restrictive practice or dominant position (points 27–28), should be taken into account.

*Commission's right to reject a complaint*

41.    It follows from the case-law of the Court of First Instance that the Commission is entitled under certain conditions to reject a complaint which does not display sufficient Community interest to justify further investigation[3].

42.    The Commission's resultant right to reject a complaint stems from the concurrent competence of the Commission, national courts and—where they have the power—national competition authorities to apply Articles 85(1) and 86 and from the consequent protection available to complainants before the courts and administrative authorities. With regard to that concurrent competence, it has been consistently held by the Court of Justice and the Court of First Instance that Article 3 of Regulation No

17 (the legal basis for the right to lodge a complaint with the Commission for alleged infringement of Article 85 or Article 86) does not entitle an applicant under that Article to obtain from the Commission a decision within the meaning of Article 189 of the Treaty as to whether or not the alleged infringement has occurred[4].

*Conditions for rejecting a complaint*

43.     The investigation of a complaint by a national authority presupposes that the following specific conditions, derived from the case-law of the Court of First Instance, are met.

44.     The first of these conditions is that, in order to assess whether or not there is a Community interest in having a case investigated further, the Commission must first undertake a careful examination of the questions of fact and law set out in the complaint[5]. In accordance with the obligation imposed on it by Article 190 of the Treaty to state the reasons for its decisions, the Commission has to inform the complainant of the legal and factual considerations which have induced it to conclude that the complaint does not display a sufficient Community interest to justify further investigation. The Commission cannot therefore confine itself to an abstract reference to the Community interest[6].

45.     In assessing whether it is entitled to reject a complaint for lack of any Community interest, the Commission must balance the significance of the alleged infringement as regards the functioning of the common market, the probability of its being able to establish the existence of the infringement, and the extent of the investigative measures required for it to perform, under the best possible conditions, its task of making sure that Articles 85 and 86 are complied with[7]. In particular, as the Court of First Instance held in *BEMIM*[8], where the effects of the infringements alleged in a complaint are essentially confined to the territory of one Member State and where proceedings have been brought before the courts and competent administrative authorities of that Member State by the complainant against the body against which the complaint was made, the Commission is entitled to reject the complaint for lack of any sufficient Community interest in further investigation of the case, provided however that the rights of the complainant can be adequately safeguarded. As to whether the effects of the restrictive practice are localised, such is the case in particular with practices to which the only parties are undertakings from one Member State and which, although they do not relate either to imports or to exports between Member States, within the meaning of point 1 of Article 4(2) of Regulation No 17[9], are capable of affecting intra-Community trade. As regards the safeguarding of the complainant's rights, the Commission considers that the referral of the matter to the national authority concerned needs must protect them quite adequately. On this latter point, the Commission takes the view that the effectiveness of the national authority's action depends notably on whether that authority is able to take interim measures if it deems it necessary, without prejudice to the possibility, found in the law of certain Member States, that such measures may be taken with the requisite degree of effectiveness by a court.

*Procedure*

46.     Where the Commission considers these conditions to have been met, it will ask the competition authority of the Member State in which most of the effects of the contested agreement or practice are felt if it would agree to investigate and decide on the complaint. Where the competition authority agrees to do so, the Commission will reject the complaint pending before it on the ground that it does not display sufficient

Community interest and will refer the matter to the national competition authority, either automatically or at the complainant's request. The Commission will place the relevant documents in its possession at the national authority's disposal[10].

47. With regard to investigation of the complaint, it should be stressed that, in accordance with the ruling given by the Court of Justice in Case C-67/91[11] (the *Spanish banks* case), national competition authorities are not entitled to use as evidence, for the purposes of applying either national rules or the Community competition rules, unpublished information contained in replies to requests for information sent to firms under Article 11 of Regulation No 17 or information obtained as a result of any inspections carried out under Article 14 of that Regulation. This information can nevertheless be taken into account, where appropriate, to justify instituting national proceedings[12].

NOTES

1 Case T-23/90 *Peugeot v EC Commission* [1991] ECR II-653, para 47.

2 Case T-24/90 *Automec v EC Commission (Automec II)* [1992] ECR II-2223, para 75.

3 *Automec II*, see n 2 above, para 85; cited in Case T-114/92 *BEMIM v EC Commission* [1995] ECR II-147, para 80, and in Case T-77/95 *SFEI v EC Commission* [1997] ECR II-1, paras 29 and 55.

4 See in particular Case 125/78 *GEMA v EC Commission* [1979] ECR 3173, para 17, and Case T-16/91 *Rendo v EC Commission* [1992] ECR II-2417, para 98.

5 *Automec II*, see n 2 above, para 82.

6 *Automec II*, see n 2 above, para 85.

7 *Automec II*, see n 2 above, paragraph 86, cited in *BEMIM*, see n 3 above, para 80.

8 See n 3 above, para 86.

9 See footnote 1, at page 237.

10 However, in the case of information accompanied by a request for confidentiality with a view to protecting the informant's anonymity, an institution which accepts such information is bound, under Article 214 of the Treaty, to comply with such a condition (Case 145/83 *Adams v EC Commission* [1985] ECR 3539). The Commission will thus not divulge to national authorities the name of an informant who wishes to remain anonymous unless the person concerned withdraws, at the Commission's request, his request for anonymity vis-à-vis the national authority which may be dealing with his complaint.

11 Case C-67/91 *Dirección General de Defensa de la Competencia v Asociación Española de Banca Privada (AEB)* [1992] ECR I-4785, operative part.

12 See n 11 above, paras 39 and 43.

## IV Co-operation in case which a national authority deals with first

### Introduction

48. At issue here are cases falling within the scope of Community competition law which a national competition authority handles on its own initiative, applying Articles 85(1) or 86, either alone or in conjunction with its national competition rules, or, where it cannot do so, its national rules alone. This covers all cases within this field which a national authority investigates before the Commission—where appropriate—does so, irrespective of their procedural origin (own-initiative proceedings, notification, complaint, etc). These cases are therefore those which fulfil the conditions set out in Part II (Guidelines on case allocation) of this Notice.

49. As regards cases which they deal with under Community law, it is desirable that national authorities should systematically inform the Commission of any proceedings they initiate. The Commission will pass on this information to the authorities in the other Member States.

50. This co-operation is especially necessary in regard to cases of particular significance to the Community within the meaning of points 33–36. This category includes (*a*) all cases raising a new point of law, the aim being to avoid decisions,

whether based on national law or on Community law, which are incompatible with the latter; (*b*) among cases of the utmost importance from an economic point of view, only those in which access by firms from other Member States to the relevant national market is significantly impeded; and (*c*) certain cases in which a public undertaking or an undertaking treated as equivalent to a public undertaking (within the meaning of Article 90(1) and (2) of the Treaty) is suspected of having engaged in an anti-competitive practice. Each national authority must determine, if necessary after consulting the Commission, whether a given case fits into one of these sub-categories.

51.    Such cases will be investigated by national competition authorities in accordance with the procedures laid down by their national law, whether they are acting with a view to applying the Community competition rules or applying their national competition rules[1].

52.    The Commission also takes the view that, like national courts to which competition cases involving Articles 85 or 86 have been referred, national competition authorities applying those provisions are always at liberty, within the limits of their national procedural rules and subject to Article 214 of the Treaty, to seek information from the Commission on the state of any proceedings which the Commission may have set in motion and as to the likelihood of its giving an official ruling, pursuant to Regulation No 17, on cases which they are investigating on their own initiative. Under the same circumstances, national competition authorities may contact the Commission where the concrete application of Article 85(1) or of Article 86 raises particular difficulties, in order to obtain the economic and legal information which the Commission is in a position to supply to them[2].

53.    The Commission is convinced that close co-operation with national authorities will forestall any contradictory decisions. But if, 'during national proceedings, it appears possible that the decision to be taken by the Commission at the culmination of a procedure still in progress concerning the same agreement may conflict with the effects of the decision of the national authorities, it is for the latter to take the appropriate measures' (*Walt Wilhelm*) to ensure that measures implementing Community competition law are fully effective. The Commission takes the view that these measures should generally consist in national authorities staying their proceedings pending the outcome of the proceedings being conducted by the Commission. Where a national authority applies its national law, such a stay of proceedings would be based on the principles of the primacy of Community law (*Walt Wilhelm*)[3] and legal certainty, and where it applies Community law, on the principle of legal certainty alone. For its part, the Commission will endeavour to deal as a matter of priority with cases subject to national proceedings thus stayed. A second possibility may, however, be envisaged, whereby the Commission is consulted before adopting the national decision. The consultations would consist, due regard being had to the judgment in the Spanish banks case, in exchanging any documents preparatory to the decisions envisaged, so that Member States' authorities might be able to take account of the Commission's position in their own decision without the latter having to be deferred until such time as the Commission's decision has been taken.

---

NOTES

1    Case C-67/91 *Dirección General de Defensa de la Competencia v Asociación Española de Banca Privada (AEB)* [1992] ECR I-4785, para 32.

2    Case C-234/89 *Delimitis v Henninger Bräu* [1991] ECR I-935, para 53.

3    Case 14/68 *Walt Wilhelm v Bundeskartellamt* [1969] ECR I, paras 8, 9, 5 respectively.

## Procedure

### *In respect of complaints*

54.     Since complainants cannot force the Commission to take a decision as to whether the infringement they allege has actually occurred, and since the Commission is entitled to reject a complaint which lacks a sufficient Community interest, national competition authorities should not have any special difficulty in handling complaints submitted initially to them involving matters that fall within the scope of the Community competition rules.

### *In respect of notifications*

55.     Although they form a very small percentage of all notifications to the Commission, special consideration needs to be given to notifications to the Commission of restrictive practices undergoing investigation by a national authority made for dilatory purposes. A dilatory notification is one where a firm, threatened with a decision banning a restrictive practice which a national authority is poised to take following an investigation under Article 85(1) or under national law, notifies the disputed agreement to the Commission and asks for it to be exempted under Article 85(3) of the Treaty. Such a notification is made in order to induce the Commission to initiate a proceeding under Articles 2, 3 or 6 of Regulation No 17 and hence, by virtue of Article 9(3) of that Regulation, to remove from Member States' authorities the power to apply the provisions of Article 85(1). The Commission will not consider a notification to be dilatory until after it has contacted the national authority concerned and checked that the latter agrees with its assessment. The Commission calls upon national authorities, moreover, to inform it of their own accord of any notifications they receive which, in their view, are dilatory in nature.

56.     A similar situation arises where an agreement is notified to the Commission with a view to preventing the imminent initiation of national proceedings which might result in the prohibition of that agreement[1].

57.     The Commission recognises, of course, that a firm requesting exemption is entitled to obtain from it a decision on the substance of its request (see point 38). However, if the Commission takes the view that such notification is chiefly aimed at suspending the national proceedings, given its exclusive powers to grant exemptions it considers itself justified in not examining it as a matter of priority.

58.     The national authority which is investigating the matter and has therefore initiated proceedings should normally ask the Commission for its provisional opinion on the likelihood of its exempting the agreement now notified to it. Such a request will be superfluous where, 'in the light of the relevant criteria developed by the case-law of the Court of Justice and the Court of First Instance and by previous regulations and decisions of the Commission, the national authority has ascertained that the agreement, decision or concerted practice at issue cannot be the subject of an individual exemption'[2].

59.     The Commission will deliver its provisional opinion on the likelihood of an exemption being granted, in the light of a preliminary examination of the questions of fact and law involved, as quickly as possible once the complete notification is received. Examination of the notification having revealed that the agreement in question is unlikely to qualify for exemption under Article 85(3) and that its effects are mainly confined to one Member State, the opinion will state that further investigation of the matter is not a Commission priority.

60.     The Commission will transmit this opinion in writing to the national authority investigating the case and to the notifying parties. It will state in its letter that it will be highly unlikely to take a decision on the matter before the national authority to which it was referred has taken its final decision and that the notifying parties retain their immunity from any fines the Commission might impose.

61.     In its reply, the national authority, after taking note of the Commission's opinion, should undertake to contact the Commission forthwith if its investigation leads it to a conclusion which differs from that opinion. This will be the case if, following its investigation, the national authority concludes that the agreement in question should not be banned under Article 85(1) of the Treaty or, if that provision cannot be applied, under the relevant national law. The national authority should also undertake to forward a copy of its final decision on the matter to the Commission. Copies of the correspondence will be sent to the competition authorities of the other Member States for information.

62.     The Commission will not itself initiate proceedings in the same case before the proceedings pending before the national authority have been completed; in accordance with Article 9(3) of Regulation No 17, such action would have the effect of taking the matter out of the hands of the national authority. The Commission will do this only in quite exceptional circumstances—in a situation where, against all expectations, the national authority is liable to find that there has been no infringement of Articles 85 or 86 or of its national competition law, or where the national proceedings are unduly long drawn-out.

63.     Before initiating proceedings the Commission will consult the national authority to discover the factual or legal grounds for that authority's proposed favourable decision or the reasons for the delay in the proceedings.

NOTES
   1    With respect to agreements not subject to notification pursuant to point 1 of art 4(2) of Regulation No 17, points 56 and 57 of this Notice also apply mutatis mutandis to express requests for exemption.
   2    Points 29 and 30 of the Notice on co-operation between national courts and the Commission.

## V  Concluding remarks

64.     This Notice is without prejudice to any interpretation by the Court of First Instance and the Court of Justice.

65.     In the interests of effective, consistent application of Community law throughout the Union, and legal simplicity and certainty for the benefit of undertakings, the Commission calls upon those Member States which have not already done so to adopt legislation enabling their competition authority to implement Articles 85(1) and 86 of the Treaty effectively.

66.     In applying this Notice, the Commission and the competent authorities of the Member States and their officials and other staff will observe the principle of professional secrecy in accordance with Article 20 of Regulation No 17.

67.     This Notice does not apply to competition rules in the transport sector, owing to the highly specific way in which cases arising in that sector are handled from a procedural point of view[1].

68.     The actual application of this Notice, especially in terms of the measures considered desirable to facilitate its implementation, will be the subject of an annual review carried out jointly by the authorities of the Member States and the Commission.

69.    This Notice will be reviewed no later than at the end of the fourth year after its adoption.

NOTES
    1    Council Regulation No 141/62 of 26 November 1962 exempting transport from the application of Council Regulation No 17 (OJ 124, 28.11.62, p 2753; English Special Edition 1959-62, p 291), as amended by Regulations Nos 165/65/EEC (OJ 210, 11.12.65, p 314) and 1002/67/EEC (OJ 306, 16.12.67, p 1); Council Regulation (EEC) No 1017/68 of 19 July 1968 applying rules of competition to transport by rail, road and inland waterway (OJ L 175, 23.7.68. p 1; English Special Edition 1968 I, p 302); Council Regulation (EEC) No 4056/86 of 22 December 1986 laying down detailed rules for the application of Articles 85 and 86 of the Treaty to maritime transport (OJ L 378, 31.12.86, p 4); Council Regulation (EEC) 3975/87 of 14 December 1987 laying down the procedure for the application of the rules on competition to undertakings in the air transport sector (OJ L 374, 31.12.87, p 1); and Commission Regulation (EC) No 870/95 of 20 April 1995 on the application of Article 85(3) of the Treaty to certain categories of agreements, decisions and concerted practices between liner shipping companies (consortia) pursuant to Council Regulation (EEC) No 479/92 (OJ L 89, 21.4.95, p 7).

# COMMISSION NOTICE

## on the definition of the relevant market for the purposes of Community competition law

NOTES
    Date of publiation in OJ: OJ C372, 9.12.97, p 5.

## I  Introduction

1.    The purpose of this notice is to provide guidance as to how the Commission applies the concept of relevant product and geographic market in its ongoing enforcement of Community competition law, in particular the application of Council Regulation 17/62 and (EEC) 4064/89, their equivalents in other sectoral applications such as transport, coal and steel, and agriculture, and the relevant provisions of the EEA Agreement[1]. Throughout this notice, references to Articles 85 and 86 of the Treaty and to merger control are to be understood as referring to the equivalent provisions in the EEA Agreement and the ECSC Treaty.

2.    Market definition is a tool to identify and define the boundaries of competition between firms. It serves to establish the framework within which competition policy is applied by the Commission. The main purpose of market definition is to identify in a systematic way the competitive constraints that the undertakings involved[2] face. The objective of defining a market in both its product and geographic dimension is to identify those actual competitors of the undertakings involved that are capable of constraining those undertakings' behaviour and of preventing them from behaving independently of effective competitive pressure. It is from this perspective that the market definition makes it possible inter alia to calculate market shares that would convey meaningful information regarding market power for the purposes of assessing dominance or for the purposes of applying Article 85.

3.    It follows from point 2 that the concept of 'relevant' market is different from other definitions of market often used in other contexts. For instance, companies often

use the term 'market' to refer to the area where it sells its products or to refer broadly to the industry or sector where it belongs.

4.      The definition of the relevant market in both its product and its geographic dimensions often has a decisive influence on the assessment of a competition case. By rendering public the procedures which the Commission follows when considering market definition and by indicating the criteria and evidence on which it relies to reach a decision, the Commission expects to increase the transparency of its policy and decision-making in the area of competition policy.

5.      Increased transparency will also result in companies and their advisers being able to better anticipate the possibility that the Commission may raise competition concerns in an individual case. Companies could, therefore, take such a possibility into account in their own internal decision-making when contemplating, for instance, acquisitions, the creation of joint ventures, or the establishment of certain agreements. It is also intended that companies should be in a better position to understand what sort of information the Commission considers relevant for the purposes of market definition.

6.      The Commission's interpretation 'relevant' market is without prejudice to the interpretation which may be given by the Court of Justice or the Court of First Instance of the European Communities.

## II  Definition of relevant market

### Definition of relevant product market and relevant geographic market

7.      The Regulations based on Articles 85 and 86 of the Treaty, in particular in section 6 of Form A/B with respect to Regulation No 17, as well as in section 6 of Form CO with respect to Regulation (EEC) 4064/89 on the control of concentrations having a Community dimension have laid down the following definitions. 'Relevant product markets' are defined as follows:
> 'A relevant product market comprises all those products and/or services which are regarded as interchangeable or substitutable by the consumer, by reason of the products' characteristics, their prices and their intended use.'

8.      'Relevant geographic markets' are defined as follows:
> 'The relevant geographic market comprises the area in which the undertakings concerned are involved in the supply and demand of products or services, in which the conditions of competition are sufficiently homogeneous and which can be distinguished from neighbouring areas because the conditions of competition are appreciably different in those areas'.

9.      The relevant market within which to assess a given competition issue is therefore established by the combination of the product and geographic markets. The Commission interprets the definitions in paragraphs 7 and 8 (which reflect the case law of the Court of Justice and the Court of First Instance as well as its own decision-making practice) according to the orientations defined in this notice.

### Concept of relevant market and objectives of Community competition policy

10.      The concept of relevant market is closely related to the objectives pursued under Community competition policy. For example, under the Community's merger control, the objective in controlling structural changes in the supply of a product/service is to prevent the creation or reinforcement of a dominant position as a result

of which effective competition would be significantly impeded in a substantial part of the common market. Under the Community's competition rules, a dominant position is such that a firm or group of firms would be in a position to behave to an appreciable extent independently of its competitors, customers and ultimately of its consumers[3]. Such a position would usually arise when a firm or group of firms accounted for a large share of the supply in any given market, provided that other factors analysed in the assessment (such as entry barriers, customers' capacity, etc) point in the same direction.

11. The same approach is followed by the Commission in its application of Article 86 of the Treaty to firms that enjoy a single or collective dominant position. Within the meaning of Regulation No 17, the Commission has the power to investigate and bring to an end abuses of such a dominant position, which must also be defined by reference to the relevant market. Markets may also need to be defined in the application of Article 85 of the Treaty, in particular, in determining whether an appreciable restriction of competition exists or in establishing if the condition pursuant to Article 85(3)(b) for an exemption from the application of Article 85(1) is met.

12. The criteria for defining the relevant market are applied generally for the analysis of certain types of behaviour in the market and for the analysis of structural changes in the supply of products. This methodology, though, might lead to different results depending on the nature of the competition issue being examined. For instance, the scope of the geographic market might be different when analysing a concentration, where the analysis is essentially prospective, from an analysis of past behaviour. The different time horizon considered in each case might lead to the result that different geographic markets are defined for the same products depending on whether the Commission is examining a change in the structure of supply, such as a concentration or a cooperative joint venture, or examining issues relating to certain past behaviour.

## Basic principles for market definition

*Competitive constraints*

13. Firms are subject to three main sources of competitive constraints: demand substitutability, supply substitutability and potential competition. From an economic point of view, for the definition of the relevant market, demand substitution constitutes the most immediate and effective disciplinary force on the suppliers of a given product, in particular in relation to their pricing decisions. A firm or a group of firms cannot have a significant impact on the prevailing conditions of sale, such as prices, if its customers are in a position to switch easily to available substitute products or to suppliers located elsewhere. Basically, the exercise of market definition consists in identifying the effective alternative sources of supply for the customers of the undertakings involved, in terms both of products/services and of geographic location of suppliers.

14. The competitive constraints arising from supply side substitutability other than those described in paras 20–23 and from potential competition are in general less immediate and in any case require an analysis of additional factors. As a result such constraints are taken into account at the assessment stage of competition analysis.

*Demand substitution*

15. The assessment of demand substitution entails a determination of the range of products which are viewed as substitutes by the consumer. One way of making this determination can be viewed as a speculative experiment, postulating a hypothetical

small, lasting change in relative prices and evaluating the likely reactions of customers to that increase. The exercise of market definition focuses on prices for operational and practical purposes, and more precisely on demand substitution arising from small, permanent changes in relative prices. This concept can provide clear indications as to the evidence that is relevant to define markets.

16.    Conceptually, this approach means that, starting from the type of products that the undertakings involved sell and the area in which they sell them, additional products and areas will be included in, or excluded from, the market definition depending on whether competition from these other products and areas affect or restrain sufficiently the pricing of the parties' products in the short term.

17.    The question to be answered is whether the parties' customers would switch to readily available substitutes or to suppliers located elsewhere in response to a hypothetical small (in the range 5%–10%) but permanent relative price increase in the products and areas being considered. If substitution were enough to make the price increase unprofitable because of the resulting loss of sales, additional substitutes and areas are included in the relevant market. This would be done until the set of products and geographical areas is such that small, permanent increases in relative prices would be profitable. The equivalent analysis is applicable in cases concerning the concentration of buying power, where the starting point would then be the supplier and the price test serves to identify the alternative distribution channels or outlets for the supplier's products. In the application of these principles, careful account should be taken of certain particular situations as described within paragraphs 56 and 58.

18.    A practical example of this test can be provided by its application to a merger of, for instance, soft-drink bottlers. An issue to examine in such a case would be to decide whether different flavours of soft drinks belong to the same market. In practice, the question to address would be whether consumers of flavour A would switch to other flavours when confronted with a permanent price increase of 5% to 10% for flavour A. If a sufficient number of consumers would switch to, say, flavour B, to such an extent that the price increase for flavour A would not be profitable owing to the resulting loss of sales, then the market would comprise at least flavours A and B. The process would have to be extended in addition to other available flavours until a set of products is identified for which a price rise would not induce a sufficient substitution in demand.

19.    Generally, and in particular for the analysis of merger cases, the price to take into account will be the prevailing market price. This might not be the case where the prevailing price has been determined in the absence of sufficient competition. In particular for the investigation of abuses of dominant positions, the fact that the prevailing price might already have been substantially increased will be taken into account.

*Supply substitution*

20.    Supply-side substitutability may also be taken into account when defining markets in those situations in which its effects are equivalent to those of demand substitution in terms of effectiveness and immediacy. This requires that suppliers be able to switch production to the relevant products and market them in the short term[4] without incurring significant additional costs or risks in response to small and permanent changes in relative prices. When these conditions are met, the additional production that is put on the market will have a disciplinary effect on the competitive behaviour of the companies involved. Such an impact in terms of effectiveness and immediacy is equivalent to the demand substitution effect.

21.     These situations typically arise when companies market a wide range of qualities or grades of one product; even if, for a given final customer or group of consumers, the different qualities are not substitutable, the different qualities will be grouped into one product market, provided that most of the suppliers are able to offer and sell the various qualities immediately and without the significant increases in costs described above. In such cases, the relevant product market will encompass all products that are substitutable in demand and supply, and the current sales of those products will be aggregated so as to give the total value or volume of the market. The same reasoning may lead to group different geographic areas.

22.     A practical example of the approach to supply-side substitutability when defining product markets is to be found in the case of paper. Paper is usually supplied in a range of different qualities, from standard writing paper to high quality papers to be used, for instance, to publish art books. From a demand point of view, different qualities of paper cannot be used for any given use, ie an art book or a high quality publication cannot be based on lower quality papers. However, paper plants are prepared to manufacture the different qualities, and production can be adjusted with negligible costs and in a short time-frame. In the absence of particular difficulties in distribution, paper manufacturers are able therefore, to compete for orders of the various qualities, in particular if orders are passed with sufficient lead time to allow for modification of production plans. Under such circumstances, the Commission would not define a separate market for each quality of paper and its respective use. The various qualities of paper are included in the relevant market, and their sales added up to estimate total market value and volume.

23.     When supply-side substitutability would entail the need to adjust significantly existing tangible and intangible assets, additional investments, strategic decisions or time delays, it will not be considered at the stage of market definition. Examples where supply-side substitution did not induce the Commission to enlarge the market are offered in the area of consumer products, in particular for branded beverages. Although bottling plants may in principle bottle different beverages, there are costs and lead times involved (in terms of advertising, product testing and distribution) before the products can actually be sold. In these cases, the effects of supply-side substitutability and other forms of potential competition would then be examined at a later stage.

*Potential competition*

24.     The third source of competitive constraint, potential competition, is not taken into account when defining markets, since the conditions under which potential competition will actually represent an effective competitive constraint depend on the analysis of specific factors and circumstances related to the conditions of entry. If required, this analysis is only carried out at a subsequent stage, in general once the position of the companies involved in the relevant market has already been ascertained, and when such position gives rise to concerns from a competition point of view.

## III  Evidence relied on to define relevant markets

## The process of defining the relevant market in practice

*Product dimension*

25.     There is a range of evidence permitting an assessment of the extent to which substitution would take place. In individual cases, certain types of evidence will be determinant, depending very much on the characteristics and specificity of the industry

and products or services that are being examined. The same type of evidence may be of no importance in other cases. In most cases, a decision will have to be based on the consideration of a number of criteria and different items of evidence. The Commission follows an open approach to empirical evidence, aimed at making an effective use of all available information which may be relevant in individual cases. The Commission does not follow a rigid hierarchy of different sources of information or types of evidence.

26.     The process of defining relevant markets may be summarised as follows: on the basis of the preliminary information available or information submitted by the undertakings involved, the Commission will usually be in a position to broadly establish the possible relevant markets within which, for instance, a concentration or a restriction of competition has to be assessed. In general, and for all practical purposes when handling individual cases, the question will usually be to decide on a few alternative possible relevant markets. For instance, with respect to the product market, the issue will often be to establish whether product A and product B belong or do not belong to the same product market. It is often the case that the inclusion of product B would be enough to remove any competition concerns.

27.     In such situations it is not necessary to consider whether the market includes additional products, or to reach a definitive conclusion on the precise product market. If under the conceivable alternative market definitions the operation in question does not raise competition concerns, the question of market definition will be left open, reducing thereby the burden on companies to supply information.

*Geographic dimension*

28.     The Commission's approach to geographic market definition might be summarised as follows: it will take a preliminary view of the scope of the geographic market on the basis of broad indications as to the distribution of market shares between the parties and their competitors, as well as a preliminary analysis of pricing and price differences at national and Community or EEA level. This initial view is used basically as a working hypothesis to focus the Commission's enquiries for the purposes of arriving at a precise geographic market definition.

29.     The reasons behind any particular configuration of prices and market shares need to be explored. Companies might enjoy high market shares in their domestic markets just because of the weight of the past, and conversely, a homogeneous presence of companies throughout the EEA might be consistent with national or regional geographic markets. The initial working hypothesis will therefore be checked against an analysis of demand characteristics (importance of national or local preferences, current patterns of purchases of customers, product differentiation/brands, other) in order to establish whether companies in different areas do indeed constitute a real alternative source of supply for consumers. The theoretical experiment is again based on substitution arising from changes in relative prices, and the question to answer is again whether the customers of the parties would switch their orders to companies located elsewhere in the short term and at a negligible cost.

30.     If necessary, a further check on supply factors will be carried out to ensure that those companies located in differing areas do not face impediments in developing their sales on competitive terms throughout the whole geographic market. This analysis will include an examination of requirements for a local presence in order to sell in that area the conditions of access to distribution channels, costs associated with setting up a

distribution network, and the presence or absence of regulatory barriers arising from public procurement, price regulations, quotas and tariffs limiting trade or production, technical standards, monopolies, freedom of establishment, requirements for administrative authorisations, packaging regulations, etc. In short, the Commission will identify possible obstacles and barriers isolating companies located in a given area from the competitive pressure of companies located outside that area, so as to determine the precise degree of market interpenetration at national, European or global level.

31.    The actual pattern and evolution of trade flows offers useful supplementary indications as to the economic importance of each demand or supply factor mentioned above, and the extent to which they may or may not constitute actual barriers creating different geographic markets. The analysis of trade flows will generally address the question of transport costs and the extent to which these may hinder trade between different areas, having regard to plant location, costs of production and relative price levels.

*Market integration in the Community*

32.    Finally, the Commission also takes into account the continuing process of market integration, in particular in the Community when defining geographic markets, especially in the area of concentrations and structural joint ventures. The measures adopted and implemented in the internal market programme to remove barriers to trade and further integrate the Community markets cannot be ignored when assessing the effects on competition of a concentration or a structural joint venture. A situation where national markets have been artificially isolated from each other because of the existence of legislative barriers that have now been removed will generally lead to a cautious assessment of past evidence regarding prices, market shares or trade patterns. A process of market integration that would, in the short term, lead to wider geographic markets may therefore be taken into consideration when defining the geographic market for the purposes of assessing concentrations and joint ventures.

*The process of gathering evidence*

33.    When a precise market definition is deemed necessary, the Commission will often contact the main customers and the main companies in the industry to enquire into their views about the boundaries of product and geographic markets and to obtain the necessary factual evidence to reach a conclusion. The Commission might also contact the relevant professional associations, and companies active in upstream markets, so as to be able to define, in so far as necessary, separate product and geographic markets, for different levels of production or distribution of the products/services in question. It might also request additional information to the undertakings involved.

34.    Where appropriate, the Commission will address written requests for information to the market players mentioned above. These requests will usually include questions relating to the perceptions of companies about reactions to hypothetical price increases and their views of the boundaries of the relevant market. They will also ask for provision of the factual information the Commission deems necessary to reach a conclusion on the extent of the relevant market. The Commission might also discuss with marketing directors or other officers of those companies to gain a better understanding on how negotiations between suppliers and customers take place and better understand issues relating to the definition of the relevant market. Where

appropriate, they might also carry out visits or inspections to the premises of the parties, their customers and/or their competitors, in order to better understand how products are manufactured and sold.

35.     The type of evidence relevant to reach a conclusion as to the product market can be categorised as follows:

### Evidence to define markets—product dimension

36.     An analysis of the product characteristics and its intended use allows the Commission, as a first step, to limit the field of investigation of possible substitutes. However, product characteristics and intended use are insufficient to show whether two products are demand substitutes. Functional interchangeability or similarity in characteristics may not, in themselves, provide sufficient criteria, because the responsiveness of customers to relative price changes may be determined by other considerations as well. For example, there may be different competitive constraints in the original equipment market for car components and in spare parts, thereby leading to a separate delineation of two relevant markets. Conversely, differences in product characteristics are not in themselves sufficient to exclude demand substitutability, since this will depend to a large extent on how customers value different characteristics.

37.     The type of evidence the Commission considers relevant to assess whether two products are demand substitutes can be categorised as follows:

38.     *Evidence of substitution in the recent past* In certain cases, it is possible to analyse evidence relating to recent past events or shocks in the market that offer actual examples of substitution between two products. When available, this sort of information will normally be fundamental for market definition. If there have been changes in relative prices in the past (all else being equal), the reactions in terms of quantities demanded will be determinant in establishing substitutability. Launches of new products in the past can also offer useful information, when it is possible to precisely analyse which products have lost sales to the new product.

39.     There are a number of *quantitative tests* that have specifically been designed for the purpose of delineating markets. These tests consist of various econometric and statistical approaches estimates of elasticities and cross-price elasticities[5] for the demand of a product, tests based on similarity of price movements over time, the analysis of causality between price series and similarity of price levels and/or their convergence. The Commission takes into account the available quantitative evidence capable of withstanding rigorous scrutiny for the purposes of establishing patterns of substitution in the past.

40.     *Views of customers and competitors* The Commission often contacts the main customers and competitors of the companies involved in its enquiries, to gather their views on the boundaries of the product market as well as most of the factual information it requires to reach a conclusion on the scope of the market. Reasoned answers of customers and competitors as to what would happen if relative prices for the candidate products were to increase in the candidate geographic area by a small amount (for instance of 5%–10%) are taken into account when they are sufficiently backed by factual evidence.

41.     *Consumer preferences* In the case of consumer goods, it may be difficult for the Commission to gather the direct views of end consumers about substitute products. *Marketing studies* that companies have commissioned in the past and that are used by

companies in their own decision-making as to pricing of their products and/or marketing actions may provide useful information for the Commission's delineation of the relevant market. Consumer surveys on usage patterns and attitudes, data from consumers' purchasing patterns, the views expressed by retailers and more generally, market research studies submitted by the parties and their competitors are taken into account to establish whether an economically significant proportion of consumers consider two products as substitutable, also taking into account the importance of brands for the products in question. The methodology followed in consumer surveys carried out ad-hoc by the undertakings involved or their competitors for the purposes of a merger procedure or a procedure pursuant to Regulation No 17 will usually be scrutinised with utmost care. Unlike pre-existing studies, they have not been prepared in the normal course of business for the adoption of business decisions.

42.   *Barriers and costs associated with switching demand to potential substitutes*  There are a number of barriers and costs that might prevent the Commission from considering two prima facie demand substitutes as belonging to one single product market. It is not possible to provide an exhaustive list of all the possible barriers to substitution and of switching costs. These barriers or obstacles might have a wide range of origins, and in its decisions, the Commission has been confronted with regulatory barriers or other forms of State intervention, constraints arising in downstream markets, need to incur specific capital investment or loss in current output in order to switch to alternative inputs, the location of customers, specific investment in production process, learning and human capital investment, retooling costs or other investments, uncertainty about quality and reputation of unknown suppliers, and others.

43.   *Different categories of customers and price discrimination*  The extent of the product market might be narrowed in the presence of distinct groups of customers. A distinct group of customers for the relevant product may constitute a narrower, distinct market when such a group could be subject to price discrimination. This will usually be the case when two conditions are met: (*a*) it is possible to identify clearly which group an individual customer belongs to at the moment of selling the relevant products to him, and (*b*) trade among customers or arbitrage by third parties should not be feasible.

## Evidence for defining markets—geographic dimension

44.   The type of evidence the Commission considers relevant to reach a conclusion as to the geographic market can be categorised as follows:

45.   *Past evidence of diversion of orders to other areas*  In certain cases, evidence on changes in prices between different areas and consequent reactions by customers might be available. Generally, the same quantitative tests used for product market definition might as well be used in geographic market definition, bearing in mind that international comparisons of prices might be more complex due to a number of factors such as exchange rate movements, taxation and product differentiation.

46.   *Basic demand characteristics*  The nature of demand for the relevant product may in itself determine the scope of the geographical market. Factors such as national preferences or preferences for national brands, language, culture and life style, and the need for a local presence have a strong potential to limit the geographic scope of competition.

47.   *Views of customers and competitors*  Where appropriate, the Commission will contact the main customers and competitors of the parties in its enquiries, to gather their views on the boundaries of the geographic market as well as most of the factual

information it requires to reach a conclusion on the scope of the market when they are sufficiently backed by factual evidence.

48.　　*Current geographic pattern of purchases* An examination of the customers' current geographic pattern of purchases provides useful evidence as to the possible scope of the geographic market. When customers purchase from companies located anywhere in the Community or the EEA on similar terms, or they procure their supplies through effective tendering procedures in which companies from anywhere in the Community or the EEA submit bids, usually the geographic market will be considered to be Community-wide.

49.　　*Trade flows/pattern of shipments* When the number of customers is so large that it is not possible to obtain through them a clear picture of geographic purchasing patterns, information on trade flows might be used alternatively, provided that the trade statistics are available with a sufficient degree of detail for the relevant products. Trade flows, and above all, the rationale behind trade flows provide useful insights and information for the purpose of establishing the scope of the geographic market but are not in themselves conclusive.

50.　　*Barriers and switching costs associated to divert orders to companies located in other areas* The absence of trans-border purchases or trade flows, for instance, does not necessarily mean that the market is at most national in scope. Still, barriers isolating the national market have to be identified before it is concluded that the relevant geographic market in such a case is national. Perhaps the clearest obstacle for a customer to divert its orders to other areas is the impact of transport costs and transport restrictions arising from legislation or from the nature of the relevant products. The impact of transport costs will usually limit the scope of the geographic market for bulky, low-value products, bearing in mind that a transport disadvantage might also be compensated by a comparative advantage in other costs (labour costs or raw materials). Access to distribution in a given area, regulatory barriers still existing in certain sectors, quotas and custom tariffs might also constitute barriers isolating a geographic area from the competitive pressure of companies located outside that area. Significant switching costs in procuring supplies from companies located in other countries constitute additional sources of such barriers.

51.　　On the basis of the evidence gathered, the Commission will then define a geographic market that could range from a local dimension to a global one, and there are examples of both local and global markets in past decisions of the Commission.

52.　　The paragraphs above describe the different factors which might be relevant to define markets. This does not imply that in each individual case it will be necessary to obtain evidence and assess each of these factors. Often in practice the evidence provided by a subset of these factors will be sufficient to reach a conclusion, as shown in the past decisional practice of the Commission.

## IV Calculation of market share

53.　　The definition of the relevant market in both its product and geographic dimensions allows the identification of the suppliers and the customers/consumers active on that market. On that basis, a total market size and market shares for each supplier can be calculated on the basis of their sales of the relevant products in the relevant area. In practice, the total market size and market shares are often available from market sources, ie companies' estimates, studies commissioned from industry consultants and/or trade associations. When this is not the case, or when available estimates are not reliable, the Commission will usually ask each supplier in the relevant market to provide its own sales in order to calculate total market size and market shares.

54.     If sales are usually the reference to calculate market shares, there are nevertheless other indications that, depending on the specific products or industry in question, can offer useful information such as, in particular, capacity, the number of players in bidding markets, units of fleet as in aerospace, or the reserves held in the case of sectors such as mining.

55.     As a rule of thumb, both volume sales and value sales provide useful information. In cases of differentiated products, sales in value and their associated market share will usually be considered to better reflect the relative position and strength of each supplier.

## V  Additional considerations

56.     There are certain areas where the application of the principles above has to be undertaken with care. This is the case when considering primary and secondary markets, in particular, when the behaviour of undertakings at a point in time has to be analysed pursuant to Article 86. The method of defining markets in these cases is the same, ie assessing the responses of customers based on their purchasing decisions to relative price changes, but taking into account as well, constraints on substitution imposed by conditions in the connected markets. A narrow definition of market for secondary products, for instance, spare parts, may result when compatibility with the primary product is important. Problems of finding compatible secondary products together with the existence of high prices and a long lifetime of the primary products may render relative price increases of secondary products profitable. A different market definition may result if significant substitution between secondary products is possible or if the characteristics of the primary products make quick and direct consumer responses to relative price increases of the secondary products feasible.

57.     In certain cases, the existence of chains of substitution might lead to the definition of a relevant market where products or areas at the extreme of the market are not directly substitutable. An example might be provided by the geographic dimension of a product with significant transport costs. In such cases, deliveries from a given plant are limited to a certain area around each plant by the impact of transport costs. In principle, such an area could constitute the relevant geographic market. However, if the distribution of plants is such that there are considerable overlaps between the areas around different plants, it is possible that the pricing of those products will be constrained by a chain substitution effect, and lead to the definition of a broader geographic market. The same reasoning may apply if product B is a demand substitute for products A and C. Even if products A and C are not direct demand substitutes, they might be found to be in the same relevant product market since their respective pricing might be constrained by substitution to B.

58.     From a practical perspective, the concept of chains of substitution has to be corroborated by actual evidence, for instance related to price interdependence at the extremes of the chains of substitution, in order to lead to an extension of the relevant market in an individual case. Price levels at the extremes of the chains would have to be of the same magnitude as well.

---

NOTES

    1   The focus of assessment in State aid cases is the aid recipient and the industry/sector concerned rather than identification of competitive constraints faced by the aid recipient. When consideration of

market power and therefore of the relevant market are raised in any particular case, elements of the approach outlined here might serve as a basis for the assessment of State aid cases.

2    For the purposes of this notice, the undertakings involved will be, in the case of a concentration, the parties to the concentration, in investigations within the meaning of Article 86 of the Treaty, the undertaking being investigated or the complainants; for investigations within the meaning of Article 85, the parties to the Agreement.

3    Definition given by the Court of Justice in its judgment of 13 February 1979 in Case 85/76 [1979] ECR 461 *Hoffmann La Roche*, and confirmed in subsequent judgments.

4    That is such a period that does not entail a significant adjustment of existing tangible and intangible assets (see para 23).

5    Own-price elasticity of demand for product X is a measure of the responsiveness of demand for X to percentage change in its own price. Cross-price elasticity between products X and Y is the responsiveness of demand for product X to percentage change in the price of product Y.

# COMMISSION NOTICE

### on agreements of minor importance which do not fall under Article 85(1) of the Treaty establishing the European Community

### (97/C 372/04)

NOTES

Date of publication in OJ:  OJ C 372, 9.12.97, p 13.

## I

1.    The Commission considers it important to facilitate co-operation between undertakings where such co-operation is economically desirable without presenting difficulties from the point of view of competition policy. To this end, it published the notice concerning agreements, decisions and concerted practices in the field of co-operation between enterprises[1] listing a number of agreements that by their nature cannot be regarded as being in restraint of competition. Furthermore, in the notice concerning its assessment of certain subcontracting agreements[2] the Commission considered that that type of contract, which offers all undertakings opportunities for development, does not automatically fall within the scope of Article 85(1). The notice concerning the assessment of co-operative joint ventures pursuant to Article 85 of the EC Treaty[3] describes in detail the conditions under which the agreements in question do not fall under the prohibition of restrictive agreements. By issuing this notice which replaces the Commission notice of 3 September 1986[4], the Commission is taking a further step towards defining the scope of Article 85(1), in order to facilitate co-operation between undertakings.

2.    Article 85(1) prohibits agreements which may affect trade between Member States and which have as their object or effect the prevention, restriction or distortion of competition within the common market. The Court of Justice of the European Communities has clarified that this provision is not applicable where the impact of the agreement on intra-Community trade or on competition is not appreciable. Agreements which are not capable of significantly affecting trade between Member States are not caught by Article 85. They should therefore be examined on the basis, and within the framework, of national legislation alone. This is also the case for agreements whose actual or potential effect remains limited to the territory of only one Member State or of one or more third countries. Likewise, agreements which do not have as their object

or their effect an appreciable restriction of competition are not caught by the prohibition contained in Article 85(1).

3.      In this notice the Commission, by setting quantitative criteria and by explaining their application, has given a sufficiently concrete meaning to the term 'appreciable' for undertakings to be able to judge for themselves whether their agreements do not fall within the prohibition pursuant to Article 85(1) by virtue of their minor importance. The quantitative definition of appreciability, however, serves only as a guideline: in individual cases even agreements between undertakings which exceed the threshold set out below may still have only a negligible effect on trade between Member States or on competition within the common market and are therefore not caught by Article 85(1). This notice does not contain an exhaustive description of restrictions which fall outside Article 85(1). It is generally recognised that even agreements which are not of minor importance can escape the prohibition on agreements on account of their exclusively favourable impact on competition.

4.      The benchmarks provided by the Commission in this notice should eliminate the need to have the legal status of agreements covered by it established through individual Commission decisions; notification for this purpose will no longer be necessary for such agreements. However, if it is doubtful whether, in an individual case, an agreement is likely to affect trade between Member States or to restrict competition to any significant extent, undertakings are free to apply for negative clearance or to notify the agreement pursuant to Council Regulations No 17[5], (EEC) 1017/69[6], (EEC) 4056/86[7] and (EEC) 3975/87[8].

5.      In cases covered by this notice, and subject to points 11 and 20, the Commission will not institute any proceedings either on application or on its own initiative. Where undertakings have failed to notify an agreement falling within the scope of Article 85(1) because they assumed in good faith that the agreement was covered by this notice, the Commission will not consider imposing fines.

6.      This notice is likewise applicable to decisions by associations of undertakings and to concerted practices.

7.      This notice is without prejudice to the competence of national courts to apply Article 85. However, it constitutes a factor which those courts may take into account when deciding a pending case. It is also without prejudice to any interpretation of Article 85 which may be given by the Court of Justice or the Court of First Instance of the European Communities.

8.      This notice is without prejudice to the application of national competition laws.

## II

9.      The Commission holds the view that agreements between undertakings engaged in the production or distribution of goods or in the provision of services do not fall under the prohibition in Article 85(1) if the aggregate market shares held by all of the participating undertakings do not exceed, on any of the relevant markets:

   (*a*)   the 5% threshold, where the agreement is made between undertakings operating at the same level of production or of marketing ('horizontal' agreement);

   (*b*)   the 10% threshold, where the agreement is made between undertakings operating at different economic levels ('vertical' agreement).

In the case of a mixed horizontal/vertical agreement or where it is difficult to classify the agreement as either horizontal or vertical, the 5% threshold is applicable.

10.    The Commission also holds the view that the said agreements do not fall under the prohibition of Article 85(1) if the market shares given at point 9 are exceeded by no more than one-tenth during two successive financial years.

11.    With regard to:
   (a)  horizontal agreements which have as their object
      —  to fix prices or to limit production or sales, or
      —  to share markets or sources of supply,
   (b)  vertical agreements which have as their object
      —  to fix resale prices, or
      —  to confer territorial protection on the participating undertakings or third undertakings,

the applicability of Article 85(1) cannot be ruled out even where the aggregate market shares held by all of the participating undertakings remain below the thresholds mentioned in points 9 and 10.

The Commission considers, however, that in the first instance it is for the authorities and courts of the Member States to take action on any agreements envisaged above in (a) and (b). Accordingly it will only intervene in such cases when it considers that the interest of the Community so demands, and in particular if the agreements impair the proper functioning of the internal market.

12.    For the purposes of this notice, 'participating undertakings' are:
   (a)  undertakings being parties to the agreement;
   (b)  undertakings in which a party to the agreement, directly or indirectly,
      —  owns more than half of the capital or business assets, or
      —  has the power to exercise more than half of the voting rights, or
      —  has the power to appoint more than half of the members of the supervisory board, board of management or bodies legally representing the undertakings, or
      —  has the right to manage the undertaking's business;
   (c)  undertakings which directly or indirectly have over a party to the agreement the rights or powers listed in (b);
   (d)  undertakings over which an undertaking referred to in (c) has, directly or indirectly, the rights or powers listed in (b).

Undertakings over which several undertakings as referred to in (a) to (d) jointly have, directly or indirectly, the rights or powers set out in (b) shall also be considered to be participating undertakings.

13.    In order to calculate the market share, it is necessary to determine the relevant market; for this, the relevant product market and the relevant geographic market must be defined.

14.    The relevant product market comprises any products or services which are regarded as interchangeable or substitutable by the consumer, by reason of their characteristics, prices and intended use.

15.    The relevant geographic market comprises the area in which the participating undertakings are involved in the supply of relevant products or services, in which the conditions of competition are sufficiently homogeneous, and which can be distinguished

from neighbouring geographic areas because, in particular, conditions of competition are appreciably different in those areas.

16.    When applying points 14 and 15, reference should be had to the notice on the definition of the relevant market under Community competition law[9].

17.    In the case of doubt about the delimitation of the relevant geographic market, undertakings may take the view that their agreement has no appreciable effect on intra-Community trade or on competition when the market share thresholds indicated in points 9 and 10 are not exceeded in any Member State. This view, however, does not preclude the application of national competition law to the agreements in question.

18.    Chapter II of this notice shall not apply where in a relevant market competition is restricted by the cumulative effects of parallel networks of similar agreements established by several manufacturers or dealers.

## III

19.    Agreements between small and medium-sized undertakings, as defined in the Annex to Commission recommendation 96/280/EC[10] are rarely capable of significantly affecting trade between Member States and competition within the common market. Consequently, as a general rule, they are not caught by the prohibition in Article 85(1). In cases where such agreements exceptionally meet the conditions for the application of that provision, they will not be of sufficient Community interest to justify any intervention. This is why the Commission will not institute any proceedings, either on request or on its own initiative, to apply the provisions of Article 85(1) to such agreements, even if the thresholds set out in points 9 and 10 above are exceeded.

20.    The Commission nevertheless reserves the right to intervene in such agreements:
   (*a*)  where they significantly impede competition in a substantial part of the relevant market,
   (*b*)  where, in the relevant market, competition is restricted by the cumulative effect of parallel networks of similar agreements made between several producers or dealers.

NOTES
   1 OJ C75, 29.7.68, p 3, as corrected in OJ C84, 28.8.68, p 14.
   2 OJ C1, 3.1.79, p 2.
   3 OJ C43, 16.2.93, p 2.
   4 OJ C231, 12.9.86, p 2.
   5 OJ 13, 21.2.62, p 204/62.
   6 OJ L175, 23.7.68, p 1.
   7 OJ L378, 31.12.86, p 4.
   8 OJ L374, 31.12.87, p 1.
   9 OJ C372, 9.12.97, p 5.
   10 OJ L107, 30.4.96, p 4.

# GUIDELINES

## on the method of setting fines imposed pursuant to Article 15 (2) of Regulation No 17 and Article 65 (5) of the ECSC Treaty

### (98/C 9/03)

NOTE

Date of publication in OJ: OJ C9, 14.1.98, p 3.

The principles outlined here should ensure the transparency and impartiality of the Commission's decisions, in the eyes of the undertakings and of the Court of Justice alike, while upholding the discretion which the Commission is granted under the relevant legislation to set fines within the limit of 10 % of overall turnover. This discretion must, however, follow a coherent and non-discriminatory policy which is consistent with the objectives pursued in penalising infringements of the competition rules.

The new method of determining the amount of a fine will adhere to the following rules, which start from a basic amount that will be increased to take account of aggravating circumstances or reduced to take account of attenuating circumstances.

## 1. Basic amount

The basic amount will be determined according to the gravity and duration of the infringement, which are the only criteria referred to in Article 15 (2) of Regulation No 17.

### A. *Gravity*

In assessing the gravity of the infringement, account must be taken of its nature, its actual impact on the market, where this can be measured, and the size of the relevant geographic market.

Infringements will thus be put into one of three categories: minor infringements, serious infringements and very serious infringements

— *minor infringements*:
These might be trade restrictions, usually of a vertical nature, but with a limited market impact and affecting only a substantial but relatively limited part of the Community market.
Likely fines: ECU 1 000 to ECU 1 million.

— *serious infringements*:
These will more often than not be horizontal or vertical restrictions of the same type as above, but more rigorously applied, with a wider market impact, and with effects in extensive areas of the common market. There might also be abuse of a dominant position (refusals to supply, discrimination, exclusion, loyalty discounts made by dominant firms in order to shut competitors out of the market, etc.).
Likely fines: ECU 1 million to ECU 20 million.

— *very serious infringements*:
These will generally be horizontal restrictions such as price cartels and market-sharing quotas, or other practices which jeopardise the proper functioning of the single market, such as the partitioning of national

markets and clear-cut abuse of a dominant position by undertakings holding a virtual monopoly (see Decisions 91/297/EEC, 91/298/EEC, 91/299/EEC, 91/300/EEC and 91/301/EEC[1] - Soda Ash, 94/815/EC[2] – Cement, 94/601/EC[3] – Cartonboard, 92/163/EC[4] – Tetra Pak, and 94/215/ ECSC[5] - Steel beams).
Likely fines: above ECU 20 million

Within each of these categories, and in particular as far as serious and very serious infringements are concerned, the proposed scale of fines will make it possible to apply differential treatment to undertakings according to the nature of the infringement committed.

It will also be necessary to take account of the effective economic capacity of offenders to cause significant damage to other operators, in particular consumers, and to set the fine at a level which ensures that it has a sufficiently deterrent effect.

Generally speaking, account may also be taken of the fact that large undertakings usually have legal and economic knowledge and infrastructures which enable them more easily to recognise that their conduct constitutes an infringement and be aware of the consequences stemming from it under competition law.

Where an infringement involves several undertakings (e.g. cartels), it might be necessary in some cases to apply weightings to the amounts determined within each of the three categories in order to take account of the specific weight and, therefore, the real impact of the offending conduct of each undertaking on competition, particularly where there is considerable disparity between the sizes of the undertakings committing infringements of the same type.

Thus, the principle of equal punishment for the same conduct may, if the circumstances so warrant, lead to different fines being imposed on the undertakings concerned without this differentiation being governed by arithmetic calculation.

B. *Duration*
   — infringements of short duration (in general, less than one year): no increase in amount,
   — infringements of medium duration (in general, one to five years): increase of up to 50 % in the amount determined for gravity,
   — infringements of long duration (in general, more than five years): increase of up to 10 % per year in the amount determined for gravity.

This approach will therefore point to a possible increase in the amount of the fine.

Generally speaking, the increase in the fine for long-term infringements represents a considerable strengthening of the previous practice with a view to imposing effective sanctions on restrictions which have had a harmful impact on consumers over a long period. Moreover, this new approach is consistent with the expected effect of the notice of 18 July 1996 on the non-imposition or reduction of fines in cartel cases[6]. The risk of having to pay a much larger fine, proportionate to the duration of the infringement, will necessarily increase the incentive to denounce it or to cooperate with the Commission.

The basic amount will result from the addition of the two amounts established in accordance with the above:

x      gravity + y duration = basic amount

## 2.    Aggravating circumstances

The basic amount will be increased where there are aggravating circumstances such as:
— repeated infringement of the same type by the same undertaking(s),
— refusal to cooperate with or attempts to obstruct the Commission in carrying out its investigations,
— role of leader in, or instigator of the infringement,
— retaliatory measures against other undertakings with a view to enforcing practices which constitute an infringement,
— need to increase the penalty in order to exceed the amount of gains improperly made as a result of the infringement when it is objectively possible to estimate that amount,
— other.

## 3.  Attenuating circumstances

The basic amount will be reduced where there are attenuating circumstances such as:
— an exclusively passive or 'follow-my-leader' role in the infringement,
— non-implementation in practice of the offending agreements or practices,
— termination of the infringement as soon as the Commission intervenes (in particular when it carries out checks),
— existence of reasonable doubt on the part of the undertaking as to whether the restrictive conduct does indeed constitute an infringement,
— infringements committed as a result of negligence or unintentionally,
— effective cooperation by the undertaking in the proceedings, outside the scope of the Notice of 18 July 1996 on the non-imposition or reduction of fines in cartel cases,
— other.

## 4.  Application of the Notice of 18 July 1996 on the non-imposition or reduction of fines [7]

## 5.  General comments

(a)    It goes without saying that the final amount calculated according to this method (basic amount increased or reduced on a percentage basis) may not in any case exceed 10 % of the worldwide turnover of the undertakings, as laid down by Article 15 (2) of Regulation No 17. In the case of agreements which are illegal under the ECSC Treaty, the limit laid down by Article 65 (5) is twice the turnover on the products in question, increased in certain cases to a maximum of 10 % of the undertaking's turnover on ECSC products.

The accounting year on the basis of which the worldwide turnover is determined must, as far as possible, be the one preceding the year in which the decision is taken or, if figures are not available for that accounting year, the one immediately preceding it.

(b)    Depending on the circumstances, account should be taken, once the above calculations have been made, of certain objective factors such as a specific economic context, any economic or financial benefit derived by the offenders (see Twenty-first report on competition policy, point 139), the specific characteristics of the undertakings in question and their real ability to pay in a specific social context, and the fines should be adjusted accordingly.

(c)     In cases involving associations of undertakings, decisions should as far as possible be addressed to and fines imposed on the individual undertakings belonging to the association. If this is not possible (e.g. where there are several thousands of affiliated undertakings), and except for cases falling within the ECSC Treaty, an overall fine should be imposed on the association, calculated according to the principles outlined above but equivalent to the total of individual fines which might have been imposed on each of the members of the association.

(d)     The Commission will also reserve the right, in certain cases, to impose a 'symbolic' fine of ECU 1 000, which would not involve any calculation based on the duration of the infringement or any aggravating or attenuating circumstances. The justification for imposing such a fine should be given in the text of the decision.

NOTES
1   OJ L152, 15.6.91, p 54.
2   OJ L343, 30.12.94, p 1.
3   OJ L243, 19.9.94, p 1.
4   OJ L72, 18.3.92, p 1.
5   OJ L116, 6.5.94, p 1.
6   OJ C207, 18.7.96 p 4.
7   See footnote 6.

## CONSUMER PROTECTION

# COUNCIL DIRECTIVE

of 10 September 1984

**[concerning misleading and comparative advertising]**

**(84/450/EEC)**

NOTES
  Date of publication in OJ: OJ L 250, 19.9.84, p 17.
  Title amended by Council Directive 97/55/EC, Art 1(1).

THE COUNCIL OF THE EUROPEAN COMMUNITIES,

Having regard to the Treaty establishing the European Economic Community, and in particular Article 100 thereof,

Having regard to the proposal from the Commission,

Having regard to the opinion of the European Parliament,

Having regard to the opinion of the Economic and Social Committee,

Whereas the laws against misleading advertising now in force in the Member States differ widely; whereas, since advertising reaches beyond the frontiers of individual Member States, it has a direct effect on the establishment and the functioning of the common market;

Whereas misleading advertising can lead to distortion of competition within the common market;

Whereas advertising, whether or not it induces a contract, affects the economic welfare of consumers;

Whereas misleading advertising may cause a consumer to take decisions prejudicial to him when acquiring goods or other property, or using services, and the differences between the laws of the Member States not only lead, in many cases, to inadequate levels of consumer protection, but also hinder the execution of advertising campaigns beyond national boundaries and thus affect the free circulation of goods and provision of services;

Whereas the second programme of the European Economic Community for a consumer protection and information policy provides for appropriate action for the protection of consumers against misleading and unfair advertising;

Whereas it is in the interest of the public in general, as well as that of consumers and all those who, in competition with one another, carry on a trade, business, craft or profession, in the common market, to harmonise in the first instance national provisions against misleading advertising and that, at a second stage, unfair advertising and, as far as necessary, comparative advertising should be dealt with, on the basis of appropriate Commission proposals;

Whereas minimum and objective criteria for determining whether advertising is misleading should be established for this purpose;

Whereas the laws to be adopted by Member States against misleading advertising must be adequate and effective;

Whereas persons or organisations regarded under national law as having a legitimate interest in the matter must have facilities for initiating proceedings against misleading advertising, either before a court or before an administrative authority which is competent to decide upon complaints or to initiate appropriate legal proceedings;

Whereas it should be for each Member State to decide whether to enable the courts or administrative authorities to require prior recourse to other established means of dealing with the complaint;

Whereas the courts or administrative authorities must have powers enabling them to order or obtain the cessation of misleading advertising;

Whereas in certain cases it may be desirable to prohibit misleading advertising even before it is published; whereas, however, this in no way implies that Member States are under an obligation to introduce rules requiring the systematic prior vetting of advertising;

Whereas provision should be made for accelerated procedures under which measures with interim or definitive effect can be taken;

Whereas it may be desirable to order the publication of decisions made by courts or administrative authorities or of corrective statements in order to eliminate any continuing effects of misleading advertising;

Whereas administrative authorities must be impartial and the exercise of their powers must be subject to judicial review;

Whereas the voluntary control exercised by self-regulatory bodies to eliminate misleading advertising may avoid recourse to administrative or judicial action and ought therefore to be encouraged;

Whereas the advertiser should be able to prove, by appropriate means, the material accuracy of the factual claims he makes in his advertising, and may in appropriate cases be required to do so by the court or administrative authority;

Whereas this Directive must not preclude Member States from retaining or adopting provisions with a view to ensuring more extensive protection of consumers, persons carrying on a trade, business, craft or profession, and the general public,

## HAS ADOPTED THIS DIRECTIVE—

### Article 1

[The purpose of this Directive is to protect consumers, persons carrying on a trade or business or practising a craft or profession and the interests of the public in general against misleading advertising and the unfair consequences thereof and to lay down the conditions under which comparative advertising is permitted].

---

NOTES
Substituted by Council Directive 97/55/EC, Art 1(2).

---

### Article 2

For the purposes of this Directive—
1. "advertising" means the making of a representation in any form in connection with a trade, business, craft or profession in order to promote the supply of goods or services, including immovable property, rights and obligations;
2. "misleading advertising" means any advertising which in any way, including its presentation, deceives or is likely to deceive the persons to whom it is addressed or whom it reaches and which, by reason of its deceptive nature, is likely to affect their economic behaviour or which, for those reasons, injures or is likely to injure a competitor;
   [2a "comparative advertising" means any advertising which explicitly or by implication identifies a competitor or goods or services offered by a competitor.]
3. "person" means any natural or legal person.

---

NOTES
Para 2a: inserted by Council Directive 97/55/EC, Art 1(3).

---

### Article 3

In determining whether advertising is misleading, account shall be taken of all its features, and in particular of any information it contains concerning—
(a) the characteristics of goods or services, such as their availability, nature, execution, composition, method and date of manufacture or provision,

fitness for purpose, uses, quantity, specification, geographical or commercial origin or the results to be expected from their use, or the results and material features of tests or checks carried out on the goods or services;
  (b) the price or the manner in which the price is calculated, and the conditions on which the goods are supplied or the services provided;
  (c) the nature, attributes and rights of the advertiser such as his identity and assets, his qualifications and ownership of industrial, commercial or intellectual property rights or his awards and distinctions.

## [Article 3a

1.    Comparative advertising shall, as far as the comparison is concerned, be permitted when the following conditions are met:
  (a) it is not misleading according to Articles 2 (2), 3 and 7 (1);
  (b) it compares goods or services meeting the same needs or intended for the same purpose;
  (c) it objectively compares one or more material, relevant, verifiable and representative features of those goods and services, which may include price;
  (d) it does not create confusion in the market place between the advertiser and a competitor or between the advertiser's trade marks, trade names, other distinguishing marks, goods or services and those of a competitor;
  (e) it does not discredit or denigrate the trade marks, trade names, other distinguishing marks, goods, services, activities, or circumstances of a competitor;
  (f) for products with designation of origin, it relates in each case to products with the same designation;
  (g) it does not take unfair advantage of the reputation of a trade mark, trade name or other distinguishing marks of a competitor or of the designation of origin of competing products;
  (h) it does not present goods or services as imitations or replicas of goods or services bearing a protected trade mark or trade name.

2.    Any comparison referring to a special offer shall indicate in a clear and unequivocal way the date on which the offer ends or, where appropriate, that the special offer is subject to the availability of the goods and services, and, where the special offer has not yet begun, the date of the start of the period during which the special price or other specific conditions shall apply.]

---

NOTES

Inserted by Council Directive 97/55/EC, Art 1(4).

## Article 4

[1.    Member States shall ensure that adequate and effective means exist to combat misleading advertising and for the compliance with the provisions on comparative advertising in the interests of consumers as well as competitors and the general public.

Such means shall include legal provisions under which persons or organisations regarded under national law as having a legitimate interest in prohibiting misleading advertising or regulating comparative advertising may:
  (a) take legal action against such advertising; and/or

(b) bring such advertising before an administrative authority competent either to decide on complaints or to initiate appropriate legal proceedings.]

It shall be for each Member State to decide which of these facilities shall be available and whether to enable the courts or administrative authorities to require prior recourse to other established means of dealing with complaints, including those referred to in Article 5.

2.     Under the legal provisions referred to in paragraph 1, Member States shall confer upon the courts or administrative authorities powers enabling them, in cases where they deem such measures to be necessary taking into account all the interests involved and in particular the public interest—

[— to order the cessation of, or to institute appropriate legal proceedings for an order for the cessation of, misleading advertising or unpermitted comparative advertising, or

— if the misleading advertising or unpermitted comparative advertising has not yet been published but publication is imminent, to order the prohibition of, or to institute appropriate legal proceedings for an order for the prohibition of, such publication,]

even without proof of actual loss or damage or of intention or negligence on the part of the advertiser.

Member States shall also make provision for the measures referred to in the first subparagraph to be taken under an accelerated procedure—

— either with interim effect, or
— with definitive effect,

on the understanding that it is for each Member State to decide which of the two options to select.

[Furthermore, Member States may confer upon the courts or administrative authorities powers enabling them, with a view to eliminating the continuing effects of misleading advertising or unpermitted comparative advertising, the cessation of which has been ordered by a final decision—]

— to require publication of that decision in full or in part and in such form as they deem adequate,
— to require in addition the publication of a corrective statement.

3.     The administrative authorities referred to in paragraph 1 must—

(a) be composed so as not to cast doubt on their impartiality;
(b) have adequate powers, where they decide on complaints, to monitor and enforce the observance of their decisions effectively;
(c) normally give reasons for their decisions.

Where the powers referred to in paragraph 2 are exercised exclusively by an administrative authority, reasons for its decisions shall always be given. Furthermore in this case, provision must be made for procedures whereby improper or unreasonable exercise of its powers by the administrative authority or improper or unreasonable failure to exercise the said powers can be the subject of judicial review.

NOTES

Para 1: substituted by Council Directive 97/55/EC, Art 1(5).
Para 2: words in square brackets substituted by Council Directive 97/55/EC, Art 1(6).

**[Article 5**

This Directive does not exclude the voluntary control, which Member States may encourage, of misleading or comparative advertising by self-regulatory bodies and recourse to such bodies by the persons or organisations referred to in article 4 if proceedings before such bodies are in addition to the court or administrative proceedings referred to in that Article.]

NOTES

Substituted by Council Directive 97/55/EC, Art 1(7).

**Article 6**

Member States shall confer upon the courts or administrative authorities powers enabling them in the civil or administrative proceedings provided for in Article 4—

[(a) to require the advertiser to furnish evidence as to the accuracy of factual claims in advertising if, taking into account the legitimate interest of the advertiser and any other party to the proceedings, such a requirement appears appropriate on the basis of the circumstances of the particular case and in the case of comparative advertising to require the advertiser to furnish such evidence in a short period of time; and]

(b) to consider factual claims as inaccurate if the evidence demanded in accordance with (a) is not furnished or is deemed insufficient by the court or administrative authority.

NOTES

Words in square brackets substituted by Council Directive 97/55/EC, Art 1(8).

**[Article 7**

1.     This Directive shall not preclude Member States from retaining or adopting provisions with a view to ensuring more extensive protection, with regard to misleading advertising, for consumers, persons carrying on a trade, business, craft or profession, and the general public.

2.     Paragraph 1 shall not apply to comparative advertising as far as the comparison is concerned.

3.     The provisions of this Directive shall apply without prejudice to Community provisions on advertising for specific products and/or services or to restrictions or prohibitions on advertising in particular media.

4.     The provisions of this Directive concerning comparative advertising shall not oblige Member States which, in compliance with the provisions of the Treaty, maintain or introduce advertising bans regarding certain goods or services, whether imposed directly or by a body or organisation responsible, under the law of the Member States, for regulating the exercise of a commercial, industrial, craft or professional activity, to permit comparative advertising regarding those goods or services. Where these bans are limited to particular media, the Directive shall apply to the media not covered by these bans.

5.     Nothing in this Directive shall prevent Member States from, in compliance with the provisions of the Treaty, maintaining or introducing bans or limitations on the use of comparisons in the advertising of professional services, whether imposed directly or by a body or organisation responsible, under the law of the Member States, for regulating the exercise of a professional activity.]

NOTES
Substituted by Council Directive 97/55/EC, Art 1(9).

### Article 8

Member States shall bring into force the measures necessary to comply with this Directive by 1 October 1986 at the latest. They shall forthwith inform the Commission thereof.

Member States shall communicate to the Commission the text of all provisions of national law which they adopt in the field covered by this Directive.

### Article 9

This Directive is addressed to the Member States.

# COUNCIL DIRECTIVE

of 25 July 1985

**on the approximation of the laws, regulations and administrative provisions of the Member States concerning liability for defective products**

**(85/374/EEC)**

NOTES
Date of publication in OJ: OJ L210, 7.8.85, p 29.

THE COUNCIL OF THE EUROPEAN COMMUNITIES,

Having regard to the Treaty establishing the European Economic Community, and in particular Article 100 thereof,

Having regard to the proposal from the Commission,

Having regard to the opinion of the European Parliament,

Having regard to the opinion of the Economic and Social Committee,

Whereas approximation of the laws of the Member States concerning the liability of the producer for damage caused by the defectiveness of his products is necessary because the existing divergences may distort competition and affect the movement of goods within the common market and entail a differing degree of protection of the consumer against damage caused by a defective product to his health or property;

Whereas liability without fault on the part of the producer is the sole means of adequately solving the problem, peculiar to our age of increasing technicality, of a fair apportionment of the risks inherent in modern technological production;

Whereas liability without fault should apply only to movables which have been industrially produced; whereas, as a result, it is appropriate to exclude liability for agricultural products and game, except where they have undergone a processing of an industrial nature which could cause a defect in these products; whereas the liability provided for in this Directive should also apply to movables which are used in the construction of immovables or are installed in immovables;

Whereas protection of the consumer requires that all producers involved in the production process should be made liable, in so far as their finished product, component part or any raw material supplied by them was defective; whereas, for the same reason, liability should extend to importers of products into the Community and to persons who present themselves as producers by affixing their name, trade mark or other distinguishing feature or who supply a product the producer of which cannot be identified;

Whereas, in situations where several persons are liable for the same damage, the protection of the consumer requires that the injured person should be able to claim full compensation for the damage from any one of them;

Whereas, to protect the physical well-being and property of the consumer, the defectiveness of the product should be determined by reference not to its fitness for use but to the lack of the safety which the public at large is entitled to expect; whereas the safety is assessed by excluding any misuse of the product not reasonable under the circumstances;

Whereas a fair apportionment of risk between the injured person and the producer implies that the producer should be able to free himself from liability if he furnishes proof as to the existence of certain exonerating circumstances;

Whereas the protection of the consumer requires that the liability of the producer remains unaffected by acts or omissions of other persons having contributed to cause the damage; whereas, however, the contributory negligence of the injured person may be taken into account to reduce or disallow such liability;

Whereas the protection of the consumer requires compensation for death and personal injury as well as compensation for damage to property; whereas the latter should nevertheless be limited to goods for private use or consumption and be subject to a deduction of a lower threshold of a fixed amount in order to avoid litigation in an excessive number of cases; whereas this Directive should not prejudice compensation for pain and suffering and other non-material damages payable, where appropriate, under the law applicable to the case;

Whereas a uniform period of limitation for the bringing of action for compensation is in the interests both of the injured person and of the producer;

Whereas products age in the course of time, higher safety standards are developed and the state of science and technology progresses; whereas, therefore, it would not be reasonable to make the producer liable for an unlimited period for the defectiveness of his product; whereas, therefore, liability should expire after a reasonable length of time, without prejudice to claims pending at law;

Whereas, to achieve effective protection of consumers, no contractual derogation should be permitted as regards the liability of the producer in relation to the injured person;

Whereas under the legal systems of the Member States an injured party may have a claim for damages based on grounds of contractual liability or on grounds of non-contractual liability other than that provided for in this Directive; in so far as these provisions also serve to attain the objective of effective protection of consumers, they should remain unaffected by this Directive; whereas, in so far as effective protection of consumers in the sector of pharmaceutical products is already also attained in a Member State under a special liability system, claims based on this system should similarly remain possible;

Whereas, to the extent that liability for nuclear injury or damage is already covered in all Member States by adequate special rules, it has been possible to exclude damage of this type from the scope of this Directive;

Whereas, since the exclusion of primary agricultural products and game from the scope of this Directive may be felt, in certain Member States, in view of what is expected for the protection of consumers, to restrict unduly such protection, it should be possible for a Member State to extend liability to such products;

Whereas, for similar reasons, the possibility offered to a producer to free himself from liability if he proves that the state of scientific and technical knowledge at the time when he put the product into circulation was not such as to enable the existence of a defect to be discovered may be felt in certain Member States to restrict unduly the protection of the consumer; whereas it should therefore be possible for a Member State to maintain in its legislation or to provide by new legislation that this exonerating circumstance is not admitted; whereas, in the case of new legislation, making use of this derogation should, however, be subject to a Community stand-still procedure, in order to raise, if possible, the level of protection in a uniform manner throughout the Community;

Whereas, taking into account the legal traditions in most of the Member States, it is inappropriate to set any financial ceiling on the producer's liability without fault; whereas, in so far as there are, however, differing traditions, it seems possible to admit that a Member State may derogate from the principle of unlimited liability by providing a limit for the total liability of the producer for damage resulting from a death or personal injury and caused by identical items with the same defect, provided that this limit is established at a level sufficiently high to guarantee adequate protection of the consumer and the correct functioning of the common market;

Whereas the harmonisation resulting from this cannot be total at the present stage, but opens the way towards greater harmonisation; whereas it is therefore necessary that the Council receive at regular intervals, reports from the Commission on the application of this Directive, accompanied, as the case may be, by appropriate proposals;

Whereas it is particularly important in this respect that a re-examination be carried out of those parts of the Directive relating to the derogations open to the Member States, at the expiry of a period of sufficient length to gather practical experience on the effects of these derogations on the protection of consumers and on the functioning of the common market,

HAS ADOPTED THIS DIRECTIVE—

## Article 1

The producer shall be liable for damage caused by a defect in his product.

## Article 2

For the purpose of this Directive "product" means all movables, with the exception of primary agricultural products and game, even though incorporated into another movable or into an immovable. "Primary agricultural products" means the products of the soil, of stock-farming and of fisheries, excluding products which have undergone initial processing. "Product" includes electricity.

## Article 3

1.    "Producer" means the manufacturer of a finished product, the producer of any raw material or the manufacturer of a component part and any person who, by putting his name, trade mark or other distinguishing feature on the product presents himself as its producer.

2.    Without prejudice to the liability of the producer, any person who imports into the Community a product for sale, hire, leasing or any form of distribution in the course of his business shall be deemed to be a producer within the meaning of this Directive and shall be responsible as a producer.

3.    Where the producer of the product cannot be identified, each supplier of the product shall be treated as its producer unless he informs the injured person, within a reasonable time, of the identity of the producer or of the person who supplied him with the product. The same shall apply, in the case of an imported product, if this product does not indicate the identity of the importer referred to in paragraph 2, even if the name of the producer is indicated.

## Article 4

The injured person shall be required to prove the damage, the defect and the causal relationship between defect and damage.

## Article 5

Where, as a result of the provisions of this Directive, two or more persons are liable for the same damage, they shall be liable jointly and severally, without prejudice to the provisions of national law concerning the rights of contribution or recourse.

## Article 6

1.    A product is defective when it does not provide the safety which a person is entitled to expect, taking all circumstances into account, including—
  (a)  the presentation of the product;
  (b)  the use to which it could reasonably be expected that the product would be put;
  (c)  the time when the product was put into circulation.

2.    A product shall not be considered defective for the sole reason that a better product is subsequently put into circulation;

## Article 7

The producer shall not be liable as a result of this Directive if he proves—
  (a)  that he did not put the product into circulation; or
  (b)  that, having regard to the circumstances, it is probable that the defect which caused the damage did not exist at the time when the product was put into circulation by him or that this defect came into being afterwards; or
  (c)  that the product was neither manufactured by him for sale or any form of distribution for economic purpose nor manufactured or distributed by him in the course of his business; or
  (d)  that the defect is due to compliance of the product with mandatory regulations issued by the public authorities; or
  (e)  that the state of scientific and technical knowledge at the time when he put the product into circulation was not such as to enable the existence of the defect to be discovered; or
  (f)   in the case of a manufacturer of a component, that the defect is attributable to the design of the product in which the component has been fitted or to the instructions given by the manufacturer of the product.

## Article 8

1.    Without prejudice to the provisions of national law concerning the right of contribution or recourse, the liability of the producer shall not be reduced when the damage is caused both by a defect in product and by the act or omission of a third party.

2.    The liability of the producer may be reduced or disallowed when, having regard to all the circumstances, the damage is caused both by a defect in the product and by the fault of the injured person or any person for whom the injured person is responsible.

## Article 9

For the purpose of Article 1, "damage" means—
  (a)  damage caused by death or by personal injuries;
  (b)  damage to, or destruction of, any item of property other than the defective product itself, with a lower threshold of 500 ECU, provided that the item of property—

    (i)  is of a type ordinarily intended for private use or consumption, and

    (ii)  was used by the injured person mainly for his own private use or consumption.

This Article shall be without prejudice to national provisions relating to non-material damage.

## Article 10

1.    Member States shall provide in their legislation that a limitation period of three years shall apply to proceedings for the recovery of damages as provided for in this Directive. The limitation period shall begin to run from the day on which the plaintiff became aware, or should reasonably have become aware, of the damage, the defect and the identity of the producer.

2.    The laws of Member States regulating suspension or interruption of the limitation period shall not be affected by this Directive.

## Article 11

Member States shall provide in their legislation that the rights conferred upon the injured person pursuant to this Directive shall be extinguished upon the expiry of a period of 10 years from the date on which the producer put into circulation the actual product which caused the damage, unless the injured person has in the meantime instituted proceedings against the producer.

## Article 12

The liability of the producer arising from this Directive may not, in relation to the injured person, be limited or excluded by a provision limiting his liability or exempting him from liability.

## Article 13

This Directive shall not affect any rights which an injured person may have according to the rules of the law of contractual or non-contractual liability or a special liability system existing at the moment when this Directive is notified.

## Article 14

This Directive shall not apply to injury or damage arising from nuclear accidents and covered by international conventions ratified by the Member States.

## Article 15

1.    Each Member State may—
    (a)  by way of derogation from Article 2, provide in its legislation that within the meaning of Article 1 of this Directive "product" also means primary agricultural products and game;
    (b)  by way of derogation from Article 7(e), maintain or, subject to the procedure set out in paragraph 2 of this Article, provide in this legislation that the producer shall be liable even if he proves that the state of scientific and technical knowledge at the time when he put the product into circulation was not such as to enable the existence of a defect to be discovered.

2.      A Member State wishing to introduce the measure specified in paragraph 1(b) shall communicate the text of the proposed measure to the Commission. The Commission shall inform the other Member States thereof.

The Member State concerned shall hold the proposed measure in abeyance for nine months after the Commission is informed and provided that in the meantime the Commission has not submitted to the Council a proposal amending this Directive on the relevant matter. However, if within three months of receiving the said information, the Commission does not advise the Member State concerned that it intends submitting such a proposal to the Council, the Member State may take the proposed measure immediately.

If the Commission does submit to the Council such a proposal amending this Directive within the aforementioned nine months, the Member State concerned shall hold the proposed measure in abeyance for a further period of 18 months from the date on which the proposal is submitted.

3.      Ten years after the date of notification of this Directive, the Commission shall submit to the Council a report on the effect that rulings by the courts as to the application of Article 7(e) and of paragraph 1(b) of this Article have on consumer protection and the functioning of the common market. In the light of this report the Council, acting on a proposal from the Commission and pursuant to the terms of Article 100 of the Treaty, shall decide whether to repeal Article 7(e).

### Article 16

1.      Any Member State may provide that a producer's total liability for damage resulting from a death or personal injury and caused by identical items with the same defect shall be limited to an amount which may not be less than 70 million ECU.

2.      Ten years after the date of notification of this Directive, the Commission shall submit to the Council a report on the effect on consumer protection and the functioning of the common market of the implementation of the financial limit on liability by those Member States which have used the option provided for in paragraph 1. In the light of this report the Council, acting on a proposal from the Commission and pursuant to the terms of Article 100 of the Treaty, shall decide whether to repeal paragraph 1.

### Article 17

This Directive shall not apply to products put into circulation before the date on which the provisions referred to in Article 19 enter into force.

### Article 18

1.      For the purposes of this Directive, the ECU shall be that defined by Regulation (EEC) No 3180/781, as amended by Regulation (EEC) No 2626/842. The equivalent in national currency shall initially be calculated at the rate obtaining on the date of adoption of this Directive.

2.      Every five years the Council, acting on a proposal from the Commission, shall examine and, if need be, revise the amounts in this Directive, in the light of economic and monetary trends in the Community.

### Article 19

1.      Member States shall bring into force, not later than three years from the date of notification of this Directive, the laws, regulations and administrative provisions

necessary to comply with this Directive. They shall forthwith inform the Commission thereof.

2.     The procedure set out in Article 15(2) shall apply from the date of notification of this Directive.

NOTES
This Directive was notified to the Member States on 30 July 1985.

## Article 20

Member States shall communicate to the Commission the texts of the main provisions of national law which they subsequently adopt in the field governed by this Directive.

## Article 21

Every five years the Commission shall present a report to the Council on the application of this Directive and, if necessary, shall submit appropriate proposals to it.

## Article 22

This Directive is addressed to the Member States.

# COUNCIL DIRECTIVE

of 29 June 1992

## on general product safety

## (92/59/EEC)

NOTES
The Directive has been implemented in the UK by the General Product Safety Regulations 1994, SI 1994/2328.
Date of publication in OJ: OJ L228, 11.8.92, p 24.

THE COUNCIL OF THE EUROPEAN COMMUNITIES,
Having regard to the Treaty establishing the European Economic Community, and in particular Article 100a thereof,
Having regard to the proposal from the Commission,
In co-operation with the European Parliament,
Having regard to the opinion of the Economic and Social Committee,
Whereas it is important to adopt measures with the aim of progressively establishing the internal market over a period expiring on 31 December 1992; whereas the internal market is to comprise an area without internal frontiers in which the free movement of goods, persons, services and capital is ensured;
Whereas some Member States have adopted horizontal legislation on product safety, imposing, in particular, a general obligation on economic operators to market only safe products; whereas those legislations differ in the level of protection afforded to persons; whereas such disparities and the absence of horizontal legislation in other Member States are liable to create barriers to trade and distortions of competition within the internal market;
Whereas it is very difficult to adopt Community legislation for every product which exists or may be developed; whereas there is a need for a broadly-based, legislative framework of a

horizontal nature to deal with those products, and also to cover lacunae in existing or forthcoming specific legislation, in particular with a view to ensuring a high level of protection of safety and health of persons, as required by Article 100a(3) of the Treaty;

Whereas it is therefore necessary to establish on a Community level a general safety requirement for any product placed on the market that is intended for consumers or likely to be used by consumers; whereas certain second-hand goods should nevertheless be excluded by their nature;

Whereas production equipment, capital goods and other products used exclusively in the context of a trade or business are not covered by this Directive;

Whereas, in the absence of more specific safety provisions, within the framework of Community regulations, covering the products concerned, the provisions of this Directive are to apply;

Whereas when there are specific rules of Community law, of the total harmonisation type, and in particular rules adopted on the basis of the new approach, which lay down obligations regarding product safety, further obligations should not be imposed on economic operators as regards the placing on the market of products covered by such rules;

Whereas, when the provisions of specific Community regulations cover only certain aspects of safety or categories of risks in respect of the product concerned, the obligations of economic operators in respect of such aspects are determined solely by those provisions;

Whereas it is appropriate to supplement the duty to observe the general safety requirement by an obligation on economic operators to supply consumers with relevant information and adopt measures commensurate with the characteristics of the products, enabling them to be informed of the risks that these products might present;

Whereas in the absence of specific regulations, criteria should be defined whereby product safety can be assessed;

Whereas Member States must establish authorities responsible for monitoring product safety and with powers to take the appropriate measures;

Whereas it is necessary in particular for the appropriate measures to include the power for Member States to organise, immediately and efficiently, the withdrawal of dangerous products already placed on the market;

Whereas it is necessary for the preservation of the unity of the market to inform the Commission of any measure restricting the placing on the market of a product or requiring its withdrawal from the market except for those relating to an event which is local in effect and in any case limited to the territory of the Member State concerned; whereas such measures can be taken only in compliance with the provisions of the Treaty, and in particular Articles 30 to 36;

Whereas this Directive applies without prejudice to the notification procedures in Council Directive 83/189/EEC of 28 March 1983 laying down a procedure for the provision of information in the field of technical standards and regulations and in Commission Decision 88/383/EEC of 24 February 1988 providing for the improvement of information on safety, hygiene and health at work;

Whereas effective supervision of product safety requires the setting-up at national and Community levels of a system of rapid exchange of information in emergency situations in respect of the safety of a product and whereas the procedure laid down by Council Decision 89/45/EEC of 21 December 1988 on a Community system for the rapid exchange of information on dangers arising from the use of consumer products should therefore be incorporated into this Directive and the above Decision should be repealed; whereas it is also advisable for this Directive to take over the detailed procedures adopted under the above Decision and to give the Commission, assisted by a committee, power to adapt them;

Whereas, moreover, equivalent notification procedures already exist for pharmaceuticals, which come under Directives 75/319/EEC and 81/851/EEC, concerning animal diseases referred to in Directive 82/894/EEC, for products of animal origin covered by Directive 89/662/EEC, and in the form of the system for the rapid exchange of information in radiological emergencies under Decision 87/600/Euratom;

Whereas it is primarily for Member States, in compliance with the Treaty and in particular with Articles 30 to 36 thereof, to take appropriate measures with regard to dangerous products located within their territory;

Whereas in such a situation the decision taken on a particular product could differ from one Member State to another; whereas such a difference may entail unacceptable disparities in consumer protection and constitute a barrier to intra-Community trade;

Whereas it may be necessary to cope with serious product-safety problems which affect or could affect, in the immediate future, all or a large part of the Community and which, in view of the nature of the safety problem posed by the product cannot be dealt with effectively in a manner commensurate with the urgency of the problem under the procedures laid down in the specific rules of Community law applicable to the products or category of products in question;

Whereas it is therefore necessary to provide for an adequate mechanism allowing, in the last resort, for the adoption of measures applicable throughout the Community, in the form of a decision addressed to the Member States, in order to cope with emergency situations as mentioned above; whereas such a decision is not of direct application to economic operators and must be incorporated into a national instrument; whereas measures adopted under such a procedure can be no more than interim measures that have to be taken by the Commission assisted by a committee of representatives of the Member States; whereas, for reasons of co-operation with the Member States, it is appropriate to provide for a regulatory committee according to procedure III(b) of Decision 87/373/EEC;

Whereas this Directive does not affect victims' rights within the meaning of Council Directive 85/374/EEC of 25 July 1985 on the approximation of the laws, regulations and administrative provisions of the Member States concerning liability for defective products;

Whereas it is necessary that Member States provide for appropriate means of redress before the competent courts in respect of measures taken by the competent authorities which restrict the placing on the market of a product or require its withdrawal;

Whereas it is appropriate to consider, in the light of experience, possible adaptation of this Directive, particularly as regards extension of its scope and provisions on emergency situations and intervention at Community level;

Whereas, in addition, the adoption of measures concerning imported products with a view to preventing risks to the safety and health of persons must comply with the Community's international obligations,

HAS ADOPTED THIS DIRECTIVE—

# TITLE I
## Objective—Scope—Definitions

**Article 1**

1.    The purpose of the provisions of this Directive is to ensure that products placed on the market are safe.

2.    The provisions of this Directive shall apply in so far as there are no specific provisions in rules of Community law governing the safety of the products concerned.

In particular, where specific rules of Community law contain provisions imposing safety requirements on the products which they govern, the provisions of Articles 2 to 4 of this Directive shall not, in any event, apply to those products.

Where specific rules of Community law contain provisions governing only certain aspects of product safety or categories of risks for the products concerned, those are the provisions which shall apply to the products concerned with regard to the relevant safety aspects or risks.

**Article 2**

For the purposes of this Directive—
(a) *product* shall mean any product intended for consumers or likely to be used by consumers, supplied whether for consideration or not in the course of a commercial activity and whether new, used or reconditioned.

However, this Directive shall not apply to second-hand products supplied as antiques or as products to be repaired or reconditioned prior to being used, provided that the supplier clearly informs the person to whom he supplies the product to that effect;

(b) *safe product* shall mean any product which, under normal or reasonably foreseeable conditions of use, including duration, does not present any risk or only the minimum risks compatible with the product's use, considered as acceptable and consistent with a high level of protection for the safety and health of persons, taking into account the following points in particular—
— the characteristics of the product, including its composition, packaging, instructions for assembly and maintenance,
— the effect on other products, where it is reasonably foreseeable that it will be used with other products,
— the presentation of the product, the labelling, any instructions for its use and disposal and any other indication or information provided by the producer,
— the categories of consumers at serious risk when using the product, in particular children.

The feasibility of obtaining higher levels of safety or the availability of other products presenting a lesser degree of risk shall not constitute grounds for considering a product to be "unsafe" or "dangerous";

(c) *dangerous product* shall mean any product which does not meet the definition of "safe product" according to point (b) hereof;

(d) *producer* shall mean—
— the manufacturer of the product, when he is established in the Community, and any other person presenting himself as the manufacturer by affixing to the product his name, trade mark or other distinctive mark, or the person who reconditions the product,
— the manufacturer's representative, when the manufacturer is not established in the Community or, if there is no representative established in the Community, the importer of the product,
— other professionals in the supply chain, insofar as their activities may affect the safety properties of a product placed on the market.

(e) *distributor* shall mean any professional in the supply chain whose activity does not affect the safety properties of a product.

## TITLE II
## General safety requirement

**Article 3**

1. Producers shall be obliged to place only safe products on the market.

2. Within the limits of their respective activities, producers shall—
— provide consumers with the relevant information to enable them to assess the risks inherent in a product throughout the normal or reasonably foreseeable period of its use, where such risks are not immediately obvious without adequate warnings, and to take precautions against those risks.

Provision of such warnings does not, however, exempt any person from compliance with the other requirements laid down in this Directive,
— adopt measures commensurate with the characteristics of the products which they supply, to enable them to be informed of risks which these products might present and to take appropriate action including, if necessary, withdrawing the product in question from the market to avoid these risks.

The above measures shall for example include, whenever appropriate, marking of the products or product batches in such a way that they can be identified, sample testing of marketed products, investigating complaints made and keeping distributors informed of such monitoring.

3.    Distributors shall be required to act with due care in order to help to ensure compliance with the general safety requirement, in particular by not supplying products which they know or should have presumed, on the basis of the information in their possession and as professionals, do not comply with this requirement. In particular, within the limits of their respective activities, they shall participate in monitoring the safety of products placed on the market, especially by passing on information on product risks and co-operating in the action taken to avoid these risks.

### Article 4

1.    Where there are no specific Community provisions governing the safety of the products in question, a product shall be deemed safe when it conforms to the specific rules of national law of the Member State in whose territory the product is in circulation, such rules being drawn up in conformity with the Treaty, and in particular Articles 30 and 36 thereof, and laying down the health and safety requirements which the product must satisfy in order to be marketed.

2.    In the absence of specific rules as referred to in paragraph 1, the conformity of a product to the general safety requirement shall be assessed having regard to voluntary national standards giving effect to a European standard or, where they exist, to Community technical specifications or, failing these, to standards drawn up in the Member State in which the product is in circulation, or to the codes of good practice in respect of health and safety in the sector concerned or to the state of the art and technology and to the safety which consumers may reasonably expect.

3.    Conformity of a product with the provisions mentioned in paragraphs 1 or 2 shall not bar the competent authorities of the Member States from taking appropriate measures to impose restrictions on its being placed on the market or to require its withdrawal from the market where there is evidence that, despite such conformity, it is dangerous to the health and safety of consumers.

# TITLE III
## Obligations and powers of the Member States

### Article 5

Member States shall adopt the necessary laws, regulations and administrative provisions to make producers and distributors comply with their obligations under this Directive in such a way that products placed on the market are safe.

In particular, Member States shall establish or nominate authorities to monitor the compliance of products with the obligation to place only safe products on the market and arrange for such authorities to have the necessary powers to take the appropriate measures incumbent upon them under this Directive, including the possibility of imposing suitable penalties in the event of failure to comply with the obligations deriving from this Directive. They shall notify the Commission of the said authorities; the Commission shall pass on the information to the other Member States.

### Article 6

1.    For the purposes of Article 5, Member States shall have the necessary powers, acting in accordance with the degree or risk and in conformity with the Treaty, and

in particular Articles 30 and 36 thereof, to adopt appropriate measures with a view, inter alia, to—

    (a)  organising appropriate checks on the safety properties of products, even after their being placed on the market as being safe, on an adequate scale, up to the final stage of use or consumption;

    (b)  requiring all necessary information from the parties concerned;

    (c)  taking samples of a product or a product line and subjecting them to safety checks;

    (d)  subjecting product marketing to prior conditions designed to ensure product safety and requiring that suitable warnings be affixed regarding the risks which the product may present;

    (e)  making arrangements to ensure that persons who might be exposed to a risk from a product are informed in good time and in a suitable manner of the said risk by, inter alia, the publication of special warnings;

    (f)  temporarily prohibiting, for the period required to carry out the various checks, anyone from supplying, offering to supply or exhibiting a product or product batch, whenever there are precise and consistent indications that they are dangerous;

    (g)  prohibiting the placing on the market of a product or product batch which has proved dangerous and establishing the accompanying measures needed to ensure that the ban is complied with;

    (h)  organising the effective and immediate withdrawal of a dangerous product or product batch already on the market and, if necessary, its destruction under appropriate conditions.

2.    The measures to be taken by the competent authorities of the Member States under this Article shall be addressed, as appropriate, to—

    (a)  the producer;

    (b)  within the limits of their respective activities, distributors and in particular the party responsible for the first stage of distribution on the national market;

    (c)  any other person, where necessary, with regard to co-operation in action taken to avoid risks arising from a product.

## TITLE IV
### Notification and Exchanges of Information

### Article 7

1.    Where a Member State takes measures which restrict the placing of a product or a product batch on the market or require its withdrawal from the market, such as provided for in Article 6(1)(d) to (h), the Member State shall, to the extent that such notification is not required under any specific Community legislation, inform the Commission of the said measures, specifying its reasons for adopting them. This obligation shall not apply where the measures relate to an event which is local in effect and in any case limited to the territory of the Member State concerned.

2.    The Commission shall enter into consultations with the parties concerned as quickly as possible. Where the Commission concludes, after such consultations, that the measure is justified, it shall immediately inform the Member State which initiated the action and the other Member States. Where the Commission concludes, after such consultations, that the measure is not justified, it shall immediately inform the Member State which initiated the action.

# TITLE V
## Emergency situations and action at Community level

**Article 8**

1.     Where a Member State adopts or decides to adopt emergency measures to prevent, restrict or impose specific conditions on the possible marketing or use, within its own territory, of a product or product batch by reason of a serious and immediate risk presented by the said product or product batch to the health and safety of consumers, it shall forthwith inform the Commission thereof, unless provision is made for this obligation in procedures of a similar nature in the context of other Community instruments.

This obligation shall not apply if the effects of the risk do not, or cannot, go beyond the territory of the Member State concerned.

Without prejudice to the provisions of the first subparagraph, Member States may pass on to the Commission any information in their possession regarding the existence of a serious and immediate risk before deciding to adopt the measures in question.

2.     On receiving this information, the Commission shall check to see whether it complies with the provisions of this Directive and shall forward it to the other Member States, which, in turn, shall immediately inform the Commission of any measures adopted.

3.     Detailed procedures for the Community information system described in this Article are set out in the Annex. They shall be adapted by the Commission in accordance with the procedure laid down in Article 11.

**Article 9**

If the Commission becomes aware, through notification given by the Member States or through information provided by them, in particular under Article 7 or Article 8, of the existence of a serious and immediate risk from a product to the health and safety of consumers in various Member States and if—

(a)   one or more Member States have adopted measures entailing restrictions on the marketing of the product or requiring its withdrawal from the market, such as those provided for in Article 6(1)(d) to (h);

(b)   Member States differ on the adoption of measures to deal with the risk in question;

(c)   the risk cannot be dealt with, in view of the nature of the safety issue posed by the product and in a manner compatible with the urgency of the case, under the other procedures laid down by the specific Community legislation applicable to the product or category of products concerned; and

(d)   the risk can be eliminated effectively only by adopting appropriate measures applicable at Community level, in order to ensure the protection of the health and safety of consumers and the proper functioning of the common market,

the Commission, after consulting the Member States and at the request of at least one of them, may adopt a decision, in accordance with the procedure laid down in Article 11, requiring Member States to take temporary measures from among those listed in Article 6(1)(d) to (h).

## Article 10

1.     The Commission shall be assisted by a Committee on Product Safety Emergencies, hereinafter referred to as "the Committee", composed of the representatives of the Member States and chaired by a representative of the Commission.

2.     Without prejudice to Article 9(c), there shall be close co-operation between the Committee referred to in paragraph 1 and the other Committees established by specific rules of Community law to assist the Commission as regards the health and safety aspects of the product concerned.

## Article 11

1.     The Commission representative shall submit to the Committee a draft of the measures to be taken. The Committee, having verified that the conditions listed in Article 9 are fulfilled, shall deliver its opinion on the draft within a time limit which the Chairman may lay down according to the urgency of the matter but which may not exceed one month. The opinion shall be delivered by the majority laid down in Article 148(2) of the Treaty for adoption of decisions by the Council on a proposal from the Commission. The votes of the representatives of the Member States within the Committee shall be weighted in the manner set out in that Article. The Chairman shall not vote.

   The Commission shall adopt the measures in question, if they are in accordance with the opinion of the Committee. If the measures proposed are not in accordance with the Committee's opinion, or in the absence of an opinion, the Commission shall forthwith submit to the Council a proposal regarding the measures to be taken. The Council shall act by a qualified majority.

   If the Council has not acted within 15 days of the date on which the proposal was submitted to it, the measures proposed shall be adopted by the Commission unless the Council has decided against them by a simple majority.

2.     Any measure adopted under this procedure shall be valid for no longer than three months. That period may be prolonged under the same procedure.

3.     Member States shall take all necessary measures to implement the decisions adopted under this procedures within less than 10 days.

4.     The competent authorities of the Member States responsible for carrying out measures adopted under this procedures shall, within one month, give the parties concerned an opportunity to submit their views and shall inform the Commission accordingly.

## Article 12

The Member States and the Commission shall take the steps necessary to ensure that their officials and agents are required not to disclose information obtained for the purposes of this Directive which, by its nature, is covered by professional secrecy, except for information relating to the safety properties of a given product which must be made public if circumstances so require, in order to protect the health and safety of persons.

## TITLE VI
## Miscellaneous and final provisions

## Article 13

This Directive shall be without prejudice to Directive 85/374/EEC.

## Article 14

1.    Any decision adopted under this Directive and involving restrictions on the placing of a product on the market, or requiring its withdrawal from the market, must state the appropriate reasons on which it is based. It shall be notified as soon as possible to the party concerned and shall indicate the remedies available under the provisions in force in the Member State in question and the time limits applying to such remedies.

The parties concerned shall, whenever feasible, be given an opportunity to submit their views before the adoption of the measure. If this has not been done in advance because of the urgency of the measures to be taken, such opportunity shall be given in due course after the measure has been implemented.

Measures requiring the withdrawal of a product from the market shall take into consideration the need to encourage distributors, users and consumers to contribute to the implementation of such measures.

2.    Member States shall ensure that any measure taken by the competent authorities involving restrictions on the placing of a product on the market or requiring its withdrawal from the market can be challenged before the competent courts.

3.    Any decision taken by virtue of this Directive and involving restrictions on the placing of a product on the market or requiring its withdrawal from the market shall be entirely without prejudice to assessment of the liability of the party concerned, in the light of the national criminal law applying in the case in question.

## Article 15

Every two years following the date of adoption, the Commission shall submit a report on the implementation of this Directive to the European Parliament and the Council.

## Article 16

Four years from the date referred to in Article 17(1), on the basis of a Commission report on the experience acquired, together with appropriate proposals, the Council shall decide whether to adjust this Directive, in particular with a view to extending its scope as laid down in Article 1(1) and Article 2(a), and whether the provisions of Title V should be amended.

## Article 17

1.    Member States shall adopt the laws, regulations and administrative provisions necessary to comply with this Directive by 29 June 1994 at the latest. They shall forthwith inform the Commission thereof. The provisions adopted shall apply with effect from 29 June 1994.

2.    When these measures are adopted by the Member States, they shall contain a reference to this Directive or be accompanied by such a reference on the occasion of their official publication. The methods of making such a reference shall be laid down by the Member States.

3.    Member States shall communicate to the Commission the text of the provisions of national law which they adopt in the area covered by this Directive.

## Article 18

Decision 89/45/EEC is hereby repealed on the date referred to in Article 17(1).

**Article 19**

This Directive is addressed to the Member States.

Done at Luxembourg, 29 June 1992.

# COUNCIL DIRECTIVE

of 5 April 1993

### on unfair terms in consumer contracts

### (93/13/EEC)

NOTES

The Directive has been implemented in the UK by the Unfair Terms in Consumer Contracts Regulations 1994, SI 1994/3159.

Date of publication in OJ: OJ L95, 21.4.93, p 29.

## THE COUNCIL OF THE EUROPEAN COMMUNITIES,

Having regard to the Treaty establishing the European Economic Community, and in particular Article 100A thereof,

Having regard to the proposal from the Commission,

In co-operation with the European Parliament,

Having regard to the opinion of the Economic and Social Committee,

Whereas it is necessary to adopt measures with the aim of progressively establishing the internal market before 31 December 1992; whereas the internal market comprises an area without internal frontiers in which goods, persons, services and capital move freely;

Whereas the laws of Member States relating to the terms of contract between the seller of goods or supplier of services, on the one hand, and the consumer of them, on the other hand, show many disparities, with the result that the national markets for the sale of goods and services to consumers differ from each other and that distortions of competition may arise amongst the sellers and suppliers, notably when they sell and supply in other Member States;

Whereas, in particular, the laws of Member States relating to unfair terms in consumer contracts show marked divergences;

Whereas it is the responsibility of the Member States to ensure that contracts concluded with consumers do not contain unfair terms;

Whereas, generally speaking, consumers do not know the rules of law which, in Member States other than their own, govern contracts for the sale of goods or services; whereas this lack of awareness may deter them from direct transactions for the purchase of goods or services in another Member State;

Whereas, in order to facilitate the establishment of the internal market and to safeguard the citizen in his role as consumer when acquiring goods and services under contracts which are governed by the laws of Member States other than his own, it is essential to remove unfair terms from those contracts;

Whereas sellers of goods and suppliers of services will thereby be helped in their task of selling goods and supplying services, both at home and throughout the internal market; whereas competition will thus be stimulated, so contributing to increased choice for Community citizens as consumers;

Whereas the two Community programmes for a consumer protection and information policy underlined the importance of safeguarding consumers in the matter of unfair terms of contract; whereas this protection ought to be provided by laws and regulations which are either harmonised at Community level or adopted directly at that level;

Whereas in accordance with the principle laid down under the heading "Protection of the economic interests of the consumers", as stated in those programmes: "acquirers of goods and services should be protected against the abuse of power by the seller or supplier, in particular against one-sided standard contracts and the unfair exclusion of essential rights in contracts";

Whereas more effective protection of the consumer can be achieved by adopting uniform rules of law in the matter of unfair terms; whereas those rules should apply to all contracts concluded between sellers or suppliers and consumers; whereas as a result inter alia contracts relating to employment, contracts relating to succession rights, contracts relating to rights under family law and contracts relating to the incorporation and organisation of companies or partnership agreements must be excluded from this Directive;

Whereas the consumer must receive equal protection under contracts concluded by word of mouth and written contracts regardless, in the latter case, of whether the terms of the contract are contained in one or more documents;

Whereas, however, as they now stand, national laws allow only partial harmonisation to be envisaged; whereas, in particular, only contractual terms which have not been individually negotiated are covered by this Directive; whereas Member States should have the option, with due regard for the Treaty, to afford consumers a higher level of protection through national provisions that are more stringent than those of this Directive;

Whereas the statutory or regulatory provisions of the Member States which directly or indirectly determine the terms of consumer contracts are presumed not to contain unfair terms; whereas, therefore, it does not appear to be necessary to subject the terms which reflect mandatory statutory or regulatory provisions and the principles or provisions of international conventions to which the Member States or the Community are party; whereas in that respect the wording "mandatory statutory or regulatory provisions" in Article 1 (2) also covers rules which, according to the law, shall apply between the contracting parties provided that no other arrangements have been established;

Whereas Member States must however ensure that unfair terms are not included, particularly because this Directive also applies to trades, business or professions of a public nature;

Whereas it is necessary to fix in a general way the criteria for assessing the unfair character of contract terms;

Whereas the assessment, according to the general criteria chosen, of the unfair character of terms, in particular in sale or supply activities of a public nature providing collective services which take account of solidarity among users, must be supplemented by a means of making an overall evaluation of the different interests involved; whereas this constitutes the requirement of good faith; whereas, in making an assessment of good faith, particular regard shall be had to the strength of the bargaining positions of the parties, whether the consumer had an inducement to agree to the term and whether the goods or services were sold or supplied to the special order of the consumer; whereas the requirement of good faith may be satisfied by the seller or supplier where he deals fairly and equitably with the other party whose legitimate interests he has to take into account;

Whereas, for the purposes of this Directive, the annexed list of terms can be of indicative value only and, because of the cause of the minimal character of the Directive, the scope of these terms may be the subject of amplification or more restrictive editing by the Member States in their national laws;

Whereas the nature of goods or services should have an influence on assessing the unfairness of contractual terms;

Whereas, for the purposes of this Directive, assessment of unfair character shall not be made of terms which describe the main subject matter of the contract nor the quality/price ratio of the goods or services supplied; whereas the main subject matter of the contract and the price/quality ratio may nevertheless be taken into account in assessing the fairness of other terms; whereas it follows, inter alia, that in insurance contracts, the terms which clearly define or circumscribe the insured risk and the insurer's liability shall not be subject to such assessment since these restrictions are taken into account in calculating the premium paid by the consumer;

Whereas contracts should be drafted in plain, intelligible language, the consumer should actually be given an opportunity to examine all the terms and, if in doubt, the interpretation most favourable to the consumer should prevail;

Whereas Member States should ensure that unfair terms are not used in contracts concluded with consumers by a seller or supplier and that if, nevertheless, such terms are so used, they will not bind the consumer, and the contract will continue to bind the parties upon those terms if it is capable of continuing in existence without the unfair provisions;

Whereas there is a risk that, in certain cases, the consumer may be deprived of protection under this Directive by designating the law of a non-Member country as the law applicable to the contract; whereas provisions should therefore be included in this Directive designed to avert this risk;

Whereas persons or organisations, if regarded under the law of a Member State as having a legitimate interest in the matter, must have facilities for initiating proceedings concerning terms of contract drawn up for general use in contracts concluded with consumers, and in particular unfair terms, either before a court or before an administrative authority competent to decide upon complaints or to initiate appropriate legal proceedings; whereas this possibility does not, however, entail prior verification of the general conditions obtaining in individual economic sectors;

Whereas the courts or administrative authorities of the Member States must have at their disposal adequate and effective means of preventing the continued application of unfair terms in consumer contracts,

HAS ADOPTED THIS DIRECTIVE—

### Article 1

1.  The purpose of this Directive is to approximate the laws, regulations and administrative provisions of the Member States relating to unfair terms in contracts concluded between a seller or supplier and a consumer.

2.  The contractual terms which reflect mandatory statutory or regulatory provisions and the provisions or principles of international conventions to which the Member States or the Community are party, particularly in the transport area, shall not be subject to the provisions of this Directive.

### Article 2

For the purposes of this Directive—
  - (a) "unfair terms" means the contractual terms defined in Article 3;
  - (b) "consumer" means any natural person who, in contracts covered by this Directive, is acting for purposes which are outside his trade, business or profession;
  - (c) "seller or supplier" means any natural or legal person who, in contracts covered by this Directive, is acting for purposes relating to his trade, business or profession, whether publicly owned or privately owned.

### Article 3

1.  A contractual term which has not been individually negotiated shall be regarded as unfair if, contrary to the requirement of good faith, it causes a significant imbalance in the parties' rights and obligations arising under the contract, to the detriment of the consumer.

2.  A term shall always be regarded as not individually negotiated where it has been drafted in advance and the consumer has therefore not been able to influence the substance of the term, particularly in the context of a pre-formulated standard contract.

The fact that certain aspects of a term or one specific term have been individually negotiated shall not exclude the application of this Article to the rest of a contract if an overall assessment of the contract indicates that it is nevertheless a pre-formulated standard contract.

Where any seller or supplier claims that a standard term has been individually negotiated, the burden of proof in this respect shall be incumbent on him.

3.  The Annex shall contain an indicative and non-exhaustive list of the terms which may be regarded as unfair.

### Article 4

1.  Without prejudice to Article 7, the unfairness of a contractual term shall be assessed, taking into account the nature of the goods or services for which the contract was concluded and by referring, at the time of conclusion of the contract, to all the circumstances attending

the conclusion of the contract and to all the other terms of the contract or of another contract on which it is dependent.

2.      Assessment of the unfair nature of the terms shall relate neither to the definition of the main subject matter of the contract nor to the adequacy of the price and remuneration, on the one hand, as against the services or goods supplies in exchange, on the other, in so far as these terms are in plain intelligible language.

## Article 5

In the case of contracts where all or certain terms offered to the consumer are in writing, these terms must always be drafted in plain, intelligible language. Where there is doubt about the meaning of a term, the interpretation most favourable to the consumer shall prevail. This rule on interpretation shall not apply in the context of the procedures laid down in Article 7(2).

## Article 6

1.      Member States shall lay down that unfair terms used in a contract concluded with a consumer by a seller or supplier shall, as provided for under their national law, not be binding on the consumer and that the contract shall continue to bind the parties upon those terms if it is capable of continuing in existence without the unfair terms.

2.      Member States shall take the necessary measures to ensure that the consumer does not lose the protection granted by this Directive by virtue of the choice of the law of a non-Member country as the law applicable to the contract if the latter has a close connection with the territory of the Member States.

## Article 7

1.      Member States shall ensure that, in the interests of consumers and of competitors, adequate and effective means exist to prevent the continued use of unfair terms in contracts concluded with consumers by sellers or suppliers.

2.      The means referred to in paragraph 1 shall include provisions whereby persons or organisations, having a legitimate interest under national law in protecting consumers, may take action according to the national law concerned before the courts or before competent administrative bodies for a decision as to whether contractual terms drawn up for general use are unfair, so that they can apply appropriate and effective means to prevent the continued use of such terms.

3.      With due regard for national laws, the legal remedies referred to in paragraph 2 may be directed separately or jointly against a number of sellers or suppliers from the same economic sector or their associations which use or recommend the use of the same general contractual terms or similar terms.

## Article 8

Member States may adopt or retain the most stringent provisions compatible with the Treaty in the area covered by this Directive, to ensure a maximum degree of protection for the consumer.

## Article 9

The Commission shall present a report to the European Parliament and to the Council concerning the application of this Directive five years at the latest after the date in Article 10(1).

**Article 10**

1.    Member States shall bring into force the laws, regulations and administrative provisions necessary to comply with this Directive no later than 31 December 1994. They shall forthwith inform the Commission thereof.

These provisions shall be applicable to all contracts concluded after 31 December 1994.

2.    When Member States adopt these measures, they shall contain a reference to this Directive or shall be accompanied by such reference on the occasion of their official publication. The methods of making such a reference shall be laid down by the Member States.

3.    Member States shall communicate the main provisions of national law which they adopt in the field covered by this Directive to the Commission.

**Article 11**

This Directive is addressed to the Member States.

Done at Luxembourg, 5 April 1993.

## ANNEX
## TERMS REFERRED TO IN ARTICLE 3(3)

1.    Terms which have the object or effect of—
    (a)    excluding or limiting the legal liability of a seller or supplier in the event of the death of a consumer or personal injury to the latter resulting from an act or omission of that seller or supplier;
    (b)    inappropriately excluding or limiting the legal rights of the consumer *vis-à-vis* the seller or supplier or another party in the event of total or partial non-performance or inadequate performance by the seller or supplier of any of the contractual obligations, including the option of offsetting a debt owed to the seller or supplier against any claim which the consumer may have against him;
    (c)    making an agreement binding on the consumer whereas provision of services by the seller or supplier is subject to a condition whose realisation depends on his own will alone;
    (d)    permitting the seller or supplier to retain sums paid by the consumer where the latter decides not to conclude or perform the contract, without providing for the consumer to receive compensation of an equivalent amount from the seller or supplier where the latter is the party cancelling the contract;
    (e)    requiring any consumer who fails to fulfil his obligation to pay a disproportionately high sum in compensation;
    (f)    authorising the seller or supplier to dissolve the contract on a discretionary basis where the same facility is not granted to the consumer, or permitting the seller or supplier to retain the sums paid for services not yet supplied by him where it is the seller or supplier himself who dissolves the contract;
    (g)    enabling the seller or supplier to terminate a contract of indeterminate duration without reasonable notice except where there are serious grounds for doing so;
    (h)    automatically extending a contract of fixed duration where the consumer does not indicate otherwise, when the deadline fixed for the consumer to express this desire not to extend the contract is unreasonably early;
    (i)    irrevocably binding the consumer to terms with which he had no real opportunity of becoming acquainted before the conclusion of the contract;
    (j)    enabling the seller or supplier to alter the terms of the contract unilaterally without a valid reason which is specified in the contract;
    (k)    enabling the seller or supplier to alter unilaterally without a valid reason any characteristics of the product or service to be provided;

(l) providing for the price of goods to be determined at the time of delivery or allowing a seller of goods or supplier of services to increase their price without in both cases giving the consumer the corresponding right to cancel the contract if the final price is too high in relation to the price agreed when the contract was concluded;

(m) giving the seller or supplier the right to determine whether the goods or services supplied are in conformity with the contract, or giving him the exclusive right to interpret any term of the contract;

(n) limiting the seller's or supplier's obligation to respect commitments undertaken by his agents or making his commitments subject to compliance with a particular formality;

(o) obliging the consumer to fulfil all his obligations where the seller or supplier does not perform his;

(p) giving the seller or supplier the possibility of transferring his rights and obligations under the contract, where this may serve to reduce the guarantees for the consumer, without the latter's agreement;

(q) excluding or hindering the consumer's right to take legal action or exercise any other legal remedy, particularly by requiring the consumer to take disputes exclusively to arbitration not covered by legal provisions, unduly restricting the evidence available to him or imposing on him a burden of proof which, according to the applicable law, should lie with another party to the contract.

2. Scope of subparagraphs (g), (j) and (l)—

(a) Subparagraph (g) is without hindrance to terms by which a supplier of financial services reserves the right to terminate unilaterally a contract of indeterminate duration without notice where there is a valid reason, provided that the supplier is required to inform the other contracting party or parties thereof immediately.

(b) Subparagraph (j) is without hindrance to terms under which a supplier of financial services reserves the right to alter the rate of interest payable by the consumer or due to the latter, or the amount of other charges for financial services without notice where there is a valid reason, provided that the supplier is required to inform the other contracting party or parties thereof at the earliest opportunity and that the latter are free to dissolve the contract immediately.

Subparagraph (j) is also without hindrance to terms under which a seller or supplier reserves the right to alter unilaterally the conditions of a contract of indeterminate duration, provided that he is required to inform the consumer with reasonable notice and that the consumer is free to dissolve the contract.

(c) Subparagraphs (g), (j) and (l) do not apply to—

— transactions in transferable securities, financial instruments and other products or services where the price is linked to fluctuations in a stock exchange quotation or index or a financial market rate that the seller or supplier does not control;

— contracts for the purchase or sale of foreign currency, traveller's cheques or international money orders denominated in foreign currency;

(d) Subparagraph (l) is without hindrance to price-indexation clauses, where lawful, provided that the method by which prices vary is explicitly described.

**FREE MOVEMENT OF GOODS**

# COMMISSION DIRECTIVE

of 22 December 1969

**based on the provisions of Article 33(7), on the abolition of measures which have an effect equivalent to quantitative restrictions on imports and are not covered by other provisions adopted in pursuance of the EEC Treaty**

**(70/50/EEC)**

NOTES

   Date of publication in OJ: OJ L13, 19.1.70, p 29.
   This Directive is spent and is included within the scope of this work for the purpose of historical analysis only.

THE COMMISSION OF THE EUROPEAN COMMUNITIES,

   Having regard to the provisions of the Treaty establishing the European Economic Community, and in particular Article 33(7) thereof;

   Whereas for the purpose of Article 30 *et seq* "measures" means laws, regulations, administrative provisions, administrative practices, and all instruments issuing from a public authority, including recommendations;

   Whereas for the purposes of this Directive "administrative practices" means any standard and regularly followed procedure of a public authority; whereas "recommendations" means any instruments issuing from a public authority which, while not legally binding on the addressees thereof, cause them to pursue a certain conduct;

   Whereas the formalities to which imports are subject do not as a general rule have an effect equivalent to that of quantitative restrictions and, consequently, are not covered by this Directive;

   Whereas certain measures adopted by Member States, other than those applicable equally to domestic and imported products, which were operative at the date of entry into force of the Treaty and are not covered by other provisions adopted in pursuance of the Treaty, either preclude importation or make it more difficult or costly than the disposal of domestic production;

   Whereas such measures must be considered to include those which make access of imported products to the domestic market, at any marketing stage, subject to a condition which is not laid down for domestic products or to a condition differing from that laid down for domestic products, and more difficult to satisfy, so that a burden is thus placed on imported products only;

   Whereas such measures must also be considered to include those which, at any marketing stage, grant to domestic products a preference, other than an aid, to which conditions may or may not be attached, and where such measures totally or partially preclude the disposal of imported products;

   Whereas such measures hinder imports which could otherwise take place, and thus have an effect equivalent to quantitative restrictions on imports;

   Whereas effects on the free movement of goods of measures which relate to the marketing of products and which apply equally to domestic and imported products are not as a general rule equivalent to those of quantitative restrictions, since such effects are normally inherent in the disparities between rules applied by Member States in this respect;

   Whereas, however, such measures may have a restrictive effect on the free movement of goods over and above that which is intrinsic to such rules;

   Whereas such is the case where imports are either precluded or made more difficult or costly than the disposal of domestic production and where such effect is not necessary for the attainment of an objective within the scope of the powers for the regulation of trade left to

Member States by the Treaty; whereas such is in particular the case where the said objective can be attained just as effectively by other means which are less of a hindrance to trade; whereas such is also the case where the restrictive effect of these provisions on the free movement of goods is out of proportion to their purpose;

Whereas these measures accordingly have an effect equivalent to that of quantitative restrictions on imports;

Whereas the customs union cannot be achieved without the abolition of such measures having an equivalent effect to quantitative restrictions on imports;

Whereas Member States must abolish all measures having equivalent effect by the end of the transitional period at the latest, even if no Commission Directive expressly requires them to do so;

Whereas the provisions concerning the abolition of quantitative restrictions and measures having equivalent effect between Member States apply both to products originating in and exported by Member States and to products originating in third countries and put into free circulation in the other Member States;

Whereas Article 33(7) does not apply to measures of the kind referred to which fall under other provisions of the Treaty, and in particular those which fall under Articles 37(1) and 44 of the Treaty or form an integral part of a national organisation of an agricultural market;

Whereas Article 33(7) does not apply to the charges and taxation referred to in Article 12 *et seq* and Article 95 *et seq* or to the aids mentioned in Article 92;

Whereas the provisions of Article 33(7) do not prevent the application, in particular, of Articles 36 and 223;

## HAS ADOPTED THIS DIRECTIVE—

### Article 1

The purpose of this Directive is to abolish the measures referred to in Articles 2 and 3, which were operative at the date of entry into force of the EEC Treaty.

### Article 2

1.　This Directive covers measures, other than those applicable equally to domestic or imported products, which hinder imports which could otherwise take place, including measures which make importation more difficult or costly than the disposal of domestic production.

2.　In particular, it covers measures which make imports or the disposal, at any marketing stage, of imported products subject to a condition rather than a formality—which is required in respect of imported products only, or a condition differing from that required for domestic products and more difficult to satisfy. Equally, it covers, in particular, measures which favour domestic products or grant them a preference, other than an aid, to which conditions may or may not be attached.

3.　The measures referred to must be taken to include those measures which—
- (a) lay down, for imported products only, minimum or maximum prices below or above which imports are prohibited, reduced or made subject to conditions liable to hinder importation;
- (b) lay down less favourable prices for imported products than for domestic products;
- (c) fix profit margins or any other price components for imported products only or fix these differently for domestic products and for imported products, to the detriment of the latter;
- (d) preclude any increase in the price of the imported product corresponding to the supplementary costs and charges inherent in importation;

(e) fix the prices of products solely on the basis of the cost price or the quality of domestic products at such a level as to create a hindrance to importation;

(f) lower the value of an imported product, in particular by causing a reduction in its intrinsic value, or increase its costs;

(g) make access of imported products to the domestic market conditional upon having an agent or representative in the territory of the importing Member State;

(h) lay down conditions of payment in respect of imported products only, or subject imported products to conditions which are different from those laid down for domestic products and more difficult to satisfy;

(i) require, for imports only, the giving of guarantees or making of payments on account;

(j) subject imported products only to conditions, in respect, in particular of shape, size, weight, composition, presentation, identification or putting up, or subject imported products to conditions which are different from those for domestic products and more difficult to satisfy;

(k) hinder the purchase by private individuals of imported products only, or encourage, require or give preference to the purchase of domestic products only;

(1) totally or partially preclude the use of national facilities or equipment in respect of imported products only, or totally or partially confine the use of such facilities or equipment to domestic products only;

(m) prohibit or limit publicity in respect of imported products only, or totally or partially confine publicity to domestic products only;

(n) prohibit, limit or require stocking in respect of imported products only; totally or partially confine the use of stocking facilities to domestic products only, or make the stocking of imported products subject to conditions which are different from those required for domestic products and more difficult to satisfy;

(o) make importation subject to the granting of reciprocity by one or more Member States;

(p) prescribe that imported products are to conform, totally or partially, to rules other than those of the importing country;

(q) specify time limits for imported products which are insufficient or excessive in relation to the normal course of the various transactions to which these time limits apply;

(r) subject imported products to controls or, other than those inherent in the customs clearance procedure, to which domestic products are not subject or which are stricter in respect of imported products than they are in respect of domestic products, without this being necessary in order to ensure equivalent protection;

(s) confine names which are not indicative of origin or source to domestic products only.

## Article 3

This Directive also covers measures governing the marketing of products which deal, in particular, with shape, size, weight, composition, presentation, identification or putting up and which are equally applicable to domestic and imported products, where the restrictive effect of such measures on the free movement of goods exceeds the effects intrinsic to trade rules.

This is the case, in particular, where—
— the restrictive effects on the free movement of goods are out of proportion to their purpose;
— the same objective can be attained by other means which are less of a hindrance to trade.

Communication from the Commission concerning the consequences of the judgment given by the Court of Justice on 20 February 1979 in Case 120/78 ("Cassis de Dijon")

NOTES
Date of publication in OJ: OJ L19, 24.1.78, p 7.

# COMMUNICATION FROM THE COMMISSION CONCERNING THE CONSEQUENCES OF THE JUDGMENT GIVEN BY THE COURT OF JUSTICE ON 20 FEBRUARY 1979 IN CASE 120/78 ("CASSIS DE DIJON")

**The following is the text of a letter which has been sent to the Member States; the European Parliament and the Council which have also been notified of it.**

NOTES
Date of publication in OJ: OJ C256, 3.10.80, p 2.

In the Commission's Communication of 6 November 1978 on "Safeguarding free trade within the Community", it was emphasised that the free movement of goods is being affected by a growing number of restrictive measures.

The judgment delivered by the Court of Justice on 20 February 1979 in Case 120/78 (the "Cassis de Dijon" case), and recently reaffirmed in the judgment of 26 June 1980 in Case 788/79, has given the Commission some interpretative guidance enabling it to monitor more strictly the application of the Treaty rules on the free movement of goods, particularly Articles 30 to 36 of the EEC Treaty.

The Court gives a very general definition of the barriers to free trade which are prohibited by the provisions of Article 30 *et seq* of the EEC Treaty. These are taken to include "any national measure capable of hindering, directly or indirectly, actually or potentially, intra-Community trade".

In its judgment of 20 February 1979 the Court indicates the scope of this definition as it applies to technical and commercial rules.

Any product lawfully produced and marketed in one Member State must, in principle, be admitted to the market of any other Member State.

Technical and commercial rules, even those equally applicable to national and imported products, may create barriers to trade only where those rules are necessary to satisfy mandatory requirements and to serve a purpose which is in the general interest and for which they are an essential guarantee. This purpose must be such as to take precedence over the requirements of the free movement of goods, which constitutes one of the fundamental rules of the Community.

The conclusions in terms of policy which the Commission draws from this new guidance are set out below.

— Whereas Member States may, with respect to domestic products and in the absence of relevant Community provisions, regulate the terms on which such products are marketed, the case is different for products imported from other Member States.

Any product imported from another Member State must in principle be admitted to the territory of the importing Member State if it has been lawfully produced, that is, conforms to the rules and processes of manufacture that are customarily and traditionally accepted in the exporting country, and is marketed in the territory of the latter.

This principle implies that Member States, when drawing up commercial or technical rules liable to affect the free movement of goods, may not take an exclusively national viewpoint and take account only of requirements confined to domestic products. The proper functioning of the common market demands that each Member State also give consideration to the legitimate requirements of other Member States.

— Only under very strict conditions does the Court accept exceptions to this principle; barriers to trade resulting from differences between commercial and technical rules are only admissible—
   — if the rules are necessary, that is appropriate and not excessive, in order to satisfy mandatory requirements (public health, protection of consumers or the environment, the fairness of commercial transactions, etc);
   — if the rules serve a purpose in the general interest which is compelling enough to justify an exception to a fundamental rule of the Treaty such as the free movement of goods;
   — if the rules are essential for such a purpose to be attained, ie are the means which are the most appropriate and at the same time least hinder trade.

The Court's interpretation has induced the Commission to set out a number of guidelines.

— The principles deduced by the Court imply that a Member State may not in principle prohibit the sale in its territory of a product lawfully produced and marketed in another Member State even if the product is produced according to technical or quality requirements which differ from those imposed on its domestic products. Where a product "suitably and satisfactorily" fulfils the legitimate objective of a Member State's own rules (public safety, protection of the consumer or the environment, etc), the importing country cannot justify prohibiting its sale in its territory by claiming that the way it fulfils the objective is different from that imposed on domestic products.

In such a case, an absolute prohibition of sale could not be considered "necessary" to satisfy a "mandatory requirement" because it would not be an "essential guarantee" in the sense defined in the Court's judgment.

The Commission will therefore have to tackle a whole body of commercial rules which lay down that products manufactured and marketed in one Member State must fulfil technical or qualitative conditions in order to be admitted to the market of another and specifically in all cases where the trade barriers occasioned by such rules are inadmissible according to the very strict criteria set out by the Court.

The Commission is referring in particular to rules covering the composition, designation, presentation and packaging of products as well as rules requiring compliance with certain technical standards.

— The Commission's work of harmonisation will henceforth have to be directed mainly at national laws having an impact on the functioning of the common market where barriers to trade to be removed arise from national provisions which are admissible under the criteria set by the Court.

The Commission will be concentrating on sectors deserving priority because of their economic relevance to the creation of a single internal market.

To forestall later difficulties, the Commission will be informing Member States of potential objections, under the terms of Community law, to provisions they may be considering introducing which come to the attention of the Commission.

It will be producing suggestions soon on the procedures to be followed in such cases.

The Commission is confident that this approach will secure greater freedom of trade for the Community's manufacturers, so strengthening the industrial base of the Community, while meeting the expectations of consumers.

**FREE MOVEMENT OF PERSONS**

# COUNCIL DIRECTIVE

of 25 February 1964

**on the co-ordination of special measures concerning the movement and residence of foreign nationals which are justified on grounds of public policy, public security or public health**

**(64/221/EEC)**

NOTES
   Date of publication in OJ: OJ L56, 3.4.64, p 850.

## Article 1

1.    The provisions of this Directive shall apply to any national of a Member State who resides in or travels to another Member State of the Community, either in order to pursue an activity as an employed or self-employed person, or as a recipient of services.

2.    These provisions shall apply also to the spouse and to members of the family who come within the provisions of the regulations and directives adopted in this field in pursuance of the Treaty.

## Article 2

1.    This Directive relates to all measures concerning entry into their territory, issue or renewal of residence permits, or expulsion from their territory, taken by Member States on grounds of public policy, public security or public health.

2.    Such grounds shall not be invoked to service economic ends.

## Article 3

1.    Measures taken on grounds of public policy or of public security shall be based exclusively on the personal conduct of the individual concerned.

2.    Previous criminal convictions shall not in themselves constitute grounds for the taking of such measures.

3.    Expiry of the identity card or passport used by the person concerned to enter the host country and to obtain a residence permit shall not justify expulsion from the territory.

4.    The State which issued the identity card or passport shall allow the holder of such document to re-enter its territory without any formality even if the document is no longer valid or the nationality of the holder is in dispute.

## Article 4

1.    The only diseases or disabilities justifying refusal of entry into a territory or refusal to issue a first residence permit shall be those listed in the Annex to this Directive.

2.     Diseases or disabilities occurring after a first residence permit has been issued shall not justify refusal to renew the residence permit or expulsion from the territory.

3.     Member States shall not introduce new provisions or practices which are more restrictive than those in force at the date of notification of this Directive.

## Article 5

1.     A decision to grant or to refuse a first residence permit shall be taken as soon as possible and in any event not later than six months from the date of application for the permit.

The person concerned shall be allowed to remain temporarily in the territory pending a decision either to grant or to refuse a residence permit.

2.     The host country may, in cases where this is considered essential, request the Member State of origin of the applicant, and if need be other Member States, to provide information concerning any previous police record. Such enquiries shall not be made as a matter of routine. The Member State consulted shall give its reply within two months.

## Article 6

The person concerned shall be informed of the grounds of public policy, public security, or public health upon which the decision taken in his case is based, unless this is contrary to the interests of the security of the State involved.

## Article 7

The person concerned shall be officially notified of any decision to refuse the issue or renewal of a residence permit or to expel him from the territory. The period allowed for leaving the territory shall be stated in this notification. Save in cases of urgency, this period shall be not less than fifteen days if the person concerned has not yet been granted a residence permit and not less than one month in all other cases.

## Article 8

The person concerned shall have the same legal remedies in respect of any decision concerning entry, or refusing the issue or renewal of a residence permit, or ordering expulsion from the territory, as are available to nationals of the State concerned in respect of acts of the administration.

## Article 9

1.     Where there is no right of appeal to a court of law, or where such appeal may be only in respect of the legal validity of the decision, or where the appeal cannot have suspensory effect, a decision refusing renewal of a residence permit or ordering the expulsion of the holder of a residence permit from the territory shall not be taken by the administrative authority, save in cases of urgency, until an opinion has been obtained from a competent authority of the host country before which the person concerned enjoys such rights of defence and of assistance or representation as the domestic law of that country provides for.

This authority shall not be the same as that empowered to take the decision refusing renewal of the residence permit or ordering expulsion.

2.     Any decision refusing the issue of a first residence permit or ordering expulsion of the person concerned before the issue of the permit shall, where that person so requests, be referred for consideration to the authority whose prior opinion is required under paragraph 1. The person concerned shall then be entitled to submit his defence in person, except where this would be contrary to the interests of national security.

**Article 10**

1.     Member States shall within six months of notification of this Directive put into force the measures necessary to comply with its provisions and shall forthwith inform the Commission thereof.

2.     Member States shall ensure that the texts of the main provisions of national law which they adopt in the field governed by this Directive are communicated to the Commission.

**Article 11**

This Directive is addressed to the Member States.

# COUNCIL REGULATION

of 15 October 1968

**on freedom of movement for workers within the Community**

**(1612/68/EEC)**

NOTES
Date of publication in OJ: OJ L257, 19.10.68, p 2.

## PART 1
## EMPLOYMENT AND WORKERS' FAMILIES

### Title I
### Eligibility for Employment

**Article 1**

1.     Any national of a Member State, shall, irrespective of his place of residence, have the right to take up an activity as an employed person, and to pursue such activity, within the territory of another Member State in accordance with the provisions laid down by law, regulation or administrative action governing the employment of nationals of that State.

2.     He shall, in particular, have the right to take up available employment in the territory of another Member State with the same priority as nationals of that State.

**Article 2**

Any national of a Member State and any employer pursuing an activity in the territory of a Member State may exchange their applications for and offers of employment, and may conclude and perform contracts of employment in accordance with the provisions in force laid down by law, regulation or administrative action, without any discrimination resulting therefrom.

### Article 3

1.      Under this Regulation, provisions laid down by law, regulation or administrative action or administrative practices of a Member State shall not apply—
> — where they limit application for and offers of employment, or the right of foreign nationals to take up and pursue employment or subject these to conditions not applicable in respect of their own nationals; or
> — where, though applicable irrespective of nationality their exclusive or principal aim or effect is to keep nationals of other Member States away from the employment offered.

This provision shall not apply to conditions relating to linguistic knowledge required by reason of the nature of the post to be filled.

2.      There shall be included in particular among the provisions or practices of a Member State referred to in the first subparagraph of paragraph 1 those which—
> (a) prescribe a special recruitment procedure for foreign nationals;
> (b) limit or restrict the advertising of vacancies in the press or through any other medium or subject it to conditions other than those applicable in respect of employers pursuing their activities in the territory of that Member State;
> (c) subject eligibility for employment to conditions of registration with employment offices or impede recruitment of individual workers, where persons who do not reside in the territory of that State are concerned.

### Article 4

1.      Provisions laid down by law, regulation or administrative action of the Member States which restrict by number or percentage the employment of foreign nationals in any undertaking, branch of activity or region, or at a national level, shall not apply to nationals of the other Member States.

2.      When in a Member State the granting of any benefit to undertakings is subject to a minimum percentage of national workers being employed, nationals of the other Member States shall be counted as national workers, subject to the provisions of the Council Directive of 15 October 1963.

### Article 5

A national of a Member State who seeks employment in the territory of another Member State shall receive the same assistance there as that afforded by the employment offices in that State to their own nationals seeking employment.

### Article 6

1.      The engagement and recruitment of a national of one Member State for a post in another Member State shall not depend on medical, vocational or other criteria which are discriminatory on grounds of nationality by comparison with those applied to nationals of the other Member State who wish to pursue the same activity.

2.      Nevertheless, a national who holds an offer in his name from an employer in a Member State other than that of which he is a national may have to undergo a vocational test, if the employer expressly requests this when making his offer of employment.

# TITLE II
# EMPLOYMENT AND EQUALITY OF TREATMENT

## Article 7

1.    A worker who is a national of a Member State may not, in the territory of another Member State, be treated differently from national workers by reason of his nationality in respect of any conditions of employment and work, in particular as regards remuneration, dismissal, and should he become unemployed, reinstatement or re-employment;

2.    He shall enjoy the same social and tax advantages as national workers.

3.    He shall also, by virtue of the same right and under the same conditions as national workers, have access to training in vocational schools and retraining centres.

4.    Any clause of a collective or individual agreement or of any other collective regulation concerning eligibility for employment, employment, remuneration and other conditions of work or dismissal shall be null and void in so far as it lays down or authorises discriminatory conditions in respect of workers who are nationals of the other Member States.

## Article 8

1.    A worker who is a national of a Member State and who is employed in the territory of another Member State shall enjoy equality of treatment as regards membership of trade unions and the exercise of rights attaching thereto, including the right to vote [and to be eligible for the administration or management posts of a trade union]; he may be excluded from taking part in the management of bodies governed by public law and from holding an office governed by public law. Furthermore, he shall have the right of eligibility for workers' representative bodies in the undertaking. The provisions of this Article shall not affect laws or regulations in certain Member States which grant more extensive rights to workers coming from the other Member States.

2.    . . .

---

NOTES

   Para 1: words in square brackets inserted by Council Regulation 312/76, Art 1(1).
   Para 2: repealed by Council Regulation 312/76, Art 1(2).

---

## Article 9

1.    A worker who is a national of a Member State and who is employed in the territory of another Member State shall enjoy all the rights and benefits accorded to national workers in matters of housing, including ownership of the housing he needs.

2.    Such worker may, with the same right as nationals, put his name down on the housing lists in the region in which he is employed, where such lists exist; he shall enjoy the resultant benefits and priorities.

   If his family has remained in the country whence he came, they shall be considered for this purpose as residing in the said region, where national workers benefit from a similar presumption.

## TITLE III
## WORKERS' FAMILIES

**Article 10**

1.     The following shall, irrespective of their nationality, have the right to install themselves with a worker who is a national of one Member State and who is employed in the territory of another Member State—

(a)  his spouse and their descendants who are under the age of 21 years or are dependants;

(b)  dependent relatives in the ascending line of the worker and his spouse.

2.     Member States shall facilitate the admission of any member of the family not coming within the provisions of paragraph 1 if dependent on the worker referred to above or living under his roof in the country whence he comes.

3.     For the purposes of paragraphs 1 and 2, the worker must have available for his family housing considered as normal for national workers in the region where he is employed; this provision, however must not give rise to discrimination between national workers and workers from the other Member States.

**Article 11**

Where a national of a Member State is pursuing an activity as an employed or self-employed person in the territory of another Member State, his spouse and those of the children who are under the age of 21 years or dependent on him shall have the right to take up any activity as an employed person throughout the territory of that same State, even if they are not nationals of any Member State.

**Article 12**

The children of a national of a Member State who is or has been employed in the territory of another Member State shall be admitted to that State's general educational, apprenticeship and vocational training courses under the same conditions as the nationals of that State, if such children are residing in its territory.

Member States shall encourage all efforts to enable such children to attend these courses under the best possible conditions.

# COUNCIL DIRECTIVE

of 15 October 1968

**on the abolition of restrictions on movement and residence within the Community for workers of Member States and their families**

**(68/360/EEC)**

NOTES

Date of publication in OJ: OJ L257, 18.10.68, p 13.

**Article 1**

Member States shall, acting as provided in this Directive, abolish restrictions on the movement and residence of nationals of the said States and of members of their families to whom Regulation (EEC) No 1612/68 applies.

## Article 2

1.    Member States shall grant the nationals referred to in Article 1 the right to leave their territory in order to take up activities as employed persons and to pursue such activities in the territory of another Member State. Such right shall be exercised simply on production of a valid identity card or passport. Members of the family shall enjoy the same right as the national on whom they are dependent.

2.    Member States shall, acting in accordance with their laws, issue to such nationals, or renew, an identity card or passport, which shall state in particular the holder's nationality.

3.    The passport must be valid at least for all Member States and for countries through which the holder must pass when travelling between Member States. Where a passport is the only document on which the holder may lawfully leave the country, its period of validity shall be not less than five years.

4.    Member States may not demand from the nationals referred to in Article 1 any exit visa or any equivalent document.

## Article 3

1.    Member States shall allow the persons referred to in Article 1 to enter their territory simply on production of a valid identity card or passport.

2.    No entry visa or equivalent document may be demanded save from members of the family who are not nationals of a Member State. Member States shall accord to such persons every facility for obtaining any necessary visas.

## Article 4

1.    Member States shall grant the right of residence in their territory to the persons referred to in Article 1 who are able to produce the documents listed in paragraph 3.

2.    As proof of the right of residence, a document entitled "Residence Permit for a National of a Member State of the EEC" shall be issued. This document must include a statement that it has been issued pursuant to Regulation (EEC) No 1612/68 and to the measures taken by the Member States for the implementation of the present Directive. The text of such statement is given in the Annex to this Directive.

3.    For the issue of a Residence Permit for a national of a Member State of the EEC, Member States may require only the production of the following documents;
   — by the worker—
      (a)  the document with which he entered their territory;
      (b)  a confirmation of engagement from the employer or a certificate of employment;
   — by the members of the worker's family—
      (c)  the document with which they entered the territory;
      (d)  a document issued by the competent authority of the state of origin or the state whence they came, proving their relationship;
      (e)  in the cases referred to in Article 10(1) and (2) of Regulation (EEC) No 1612/68, a document issued by the competent authority of the State of origin or the State whence they came, testifying that they are dependent on the worker or that they live under his roof in such country.

4.      A member of the family who is not a national of a Member State shall be issued with a residence document which shall have the same validity as that issued to the worker on whom he is dependent.

## Article 5

Completion of the formalities for obtaining a residence permit shall not hinder the immediate beginning of employment under a contract concluded by the applicants.

## Article 6

1.      The residence permit—
    (a) must be valid throughout the territory of the Member State which issued it;
    (b) must be valid for at least five years from the date of issue and be automatically renewable.

2.      Breaks in residence not exceeding six consecutive months and absence on military service shall not affect the validity of a residence permit.

3.      Where a worker is employed for a period exceeding three months but not exceeding a year in the service of an employer in the host State or in the employ of a person providing services, the host Member State shall issue him a temporary residence permit, the validity of which may be limited to the expected period of the employment.

Subject to the provisions of Article 8(1)(c), a temporary residence permit shall be issued also to a seasonal worker employed for a period of more than three months. The period of employment must be shown in the documents referred to in paragraph 4(3)(b).

## Article 7

1.      A valid residence permit may not be withdrawn from a worker solely on the grounds that he is no longer in employment, either because he is temporarily incapable of work as a result of illness or accident, or because he is involuntarily unemployed, this being duly confirmed by the competent employment office.

2.      When the residence permit is renewed for the first time, the period of residence may be restricted, but not to less than twelve months, where the worker has been involuntarily unemployed in the Member State for more than twelve consecutive months.

## Article 8

1.      Member States shall, without issuing a residence permit, recognise the right of residence in their territory of—
    (a) a worker pursuing an activity as an employed person, where the activity is not expected to last for more than three months. The document with which the person concerned entered the territory and a statement by the employer on the expected duration of the employment shall be sufficient to cover his stay; a statement by the employer shall not, however, be required in the case of workers coming within the provisions of the Council Directive of 25 February 1964 on the attainment of freedom of establishment and freedom to provide services in respect of the activities of intermediaries in commerce, industry and small craft industries.
    (b) a worker who, while having his residence in the territory of a Member State to which he returns as a rule, each day or at least once a week, is employed

in the territory of another Member State. The competent authority of the State where he is employed may issue such worker with a special permit valid for five years and automatically renewable;

(c) a seasonal worker who holds a contract of employment stamped by the competent authority of the Member State on whose territory he has come to pursue his activity.

2.    In all cases referred to in paragraph 1, the competent authorities of the host Member State may require the worker to report his presence in the territory.

### Article 9

1.    The residence documents granted to nationals of a Member State of the EEC referred to in this Directive shall be issued and renewed free of charge or on payment of an amount not exceeding the dues and taxes charged for the issue of identity cards to nationals.

2.    The visa referred to in Article 3(2) and the stamp referred to in Article 8(1)(c) shall be free of charge.

3.    Member States shall take the necessary steps to simplify as much as possible the formalities and procedure for obtaining the documents mentioned in paragraph 1.

### Article 10

Member States shall not derogate from the provisions of this Directive save on grounds of public policy, public security or public health.

# COMMISSION REGULATION

of 29 June 1970

**on the right of workers to remain in the territory of a Member State after having been employed in that State**

**(1251/70/EEC)**

NOTES

Date of publication in OJ: OJ L142, 1.7.70, p 24.

### Article 1

The provisions of this Regulation shall apply to nationals of a Member State who have worked as employed persons in the territory of another Member State and to members of their families, as defined in Article 10 of Council Regulation (EEC) No 1612/68 on freedom of movement for workers within the Community.

### Article 2

1.    The following shall have the right to remain permanently in the territory of a Member State—

(a) a worker who, at the time of termination of his activity, has reached the age laid down by the law of that Member State for entitlement to an old-

age pension and who has been employed in that State for at least the last twelve months and has resided there continuously for more than three years;
(b) a worker who, having resided continuously in the territory of that State for more than two years, ceases to work there as an employed person as a result of permanent incapacity to work. If such incapacity is the result of an accident at work or an occupational disease entitling him to a pension for which an institution of that State is entirely or partially responsible, no condition shall be imposed as to length of residence;
(c) a worker who, after three years continuous employment and residence in the territory of that State, works as an employed person in the territory of another Member State, while retaining his residence in the territory of the first State, to which he returns, as a rule, each day or at least once a week.

Periods of employment completed in this way in the territory of the other Member State shall, for the purposes of entitlement to the rights referred to in subparagraphs (a) and (b), be considered as having been completed in the territory of the State of residence.

2.     The conditions as to length of residence and employment laid down in paragraph 1(a) and the condition as to length of residence laid down in paragraph 1(b) shall not apply if the worker's spouse is a national of the Member State concerned or has lost the nationality of that State by marriage to that worker.

## Article 3

1.     The members of a worker's family referred to in Article 1 of this Regulation who are residing with him in the territory of a Member State shall be entitled to remain there permanently if the worker has acquired the right to remain in the territory of that State in accordance with Article 2, and to do so even after his death.

2.     If, however, the worker dies during his working life and before having acquired the right to remain in the territory of the State concerned, members of his family shall be entitled to remain there permanently on condition that—
— the worker, on the date of his decease, had resided continuously in the territory of that Member State for at least 2 years; or
— his death resulted from an accident at work or an occupational disease; or
— the surviving spouse is a national of the State of residence or lost the nationality of that State by marriage to that worker.

## Article 4

1.     Continuity of residence as provided for in Articles 2(1) and 3(2) may be attested by any means of proof in use in the country of residence. It shall not be affected by temporary absences not exceeding a total of three months per year, nor by longer absences due to compliance with the obligations of military service.

2.     Periods of involuntary unemployment, duly recorded by the competent employment office, and absences due to illness or accident shall be considered as periods of employment within the meaning of Article 2(1).

## Article 5

1.     The person entitled to the right to remain shall be allowed to exercise it within two years from the time of becoming entitled to such right pursuant to Article 2(1)(a)

and (b) and Article 3. During such period he may leave the territory of the Member State without adversely affecting such right.

2.     No formality shall be required on the part of the person concerned in respect of the exercise of the right to remain.

## Article 6

1.     Persons coming under the provisions of this Regulation shall be entitled to a residence permit which—

    (a)  shall be issued and renewed free of charge or on payment of a sum not exceeding the dues and taxes payable by nationals for the issue or renewal identity documents;

    (b)  must be valid throughout the territory of the Member State issuing it;

    (c)  must be valid for at least five years and be renewable automatically.

2.     Periods of non-residence not exceeding six consecutive months shall not affect the validity of the residence permit.

## Article 7

The right to equality of treatment, established by Council Regulation (EEC) No 1612/68, shall apply also to persons coming under the provisions of this Regulation.

## Article 8

1.     This Regulation shall not affect any provisions laid down by law, regulation or administrative action of one Member State which would be more favourable to nationals of other Member States.

2.     Member States shall facilitate re-admission to their territories of workers who have left those territories after having resided there permanently for a long period and having been employed there and who wish to return there when they have reached retirement age or are permanently incapacitated for work.

# COUNCIL DIRECTIVE

of 21 May 1973

**on the abolition of restrictions on movement and residence within the Community for nationals of Member States with regard to establishment and the provision of services**

**(73/148/EEC)**

NOTES

    Date of publication in OJ: OJ L172, 28.6.73, p 14.

## Article 1

1.     The Member States shall, acting as provided in this Directive, abolish restrictions on the movements and residence of—

    (a)  nationals of a Member State who are established or who wish to establish themselves in another Member State in order to pursue activities as self-employed persons, or who wish to provide services in that state;

(b) nationals of Member States wishing to go to another Member State as recipients of services;

(c) the spouse and the children under twenty-one years of age of such nationals, irrespective of their nationality;

(d) the relatives in the ascending and descending lines of such nationals and of the spouse of such nationals, which relatives are dependent on them, irrespective of their nationality.

2. Member States shall favour the admission of any other member of the family of a national referred to in paragraph 1(a) or (b) or of the spouse of that national, which member is dependent on that national or spouse of that national or who in the country of origin was living under the same roof.

## Article 2

1. Member States shall grant the persons referred to in Article 1 the right to leave their territory. such right shall be exercised simply on production of a valid identity card or passport. members of the family shall enjoy the same right as the national on whom they are dependent.

2. Member States shall, acting in accordance with their laws, issue to their nationals, or renew, an identity card or passport, which shall state in particular the holder's nationality.

3. The passport must be valid at least for all member states and for countries through which the holder must pass when travelling between Member States. Where a passport is the only document on which the holder may lawfully leave the country, its period of validity shall be not less than five years.

4. Member States may not demand from the persons referred to in Article 1 any exit visa or any equivalent requirement.

## Article 3

1. Member States shall grant to the persons referred to in Article 1 right to enter their territory merely on production of a valid identity card or passport.

2. No entry visa or equivalent requirement may be demanded save in respect of members of the family who do have the nationality of a Member State. Member States shall afford to such persons every facility for obtaining any necessary visas.

## Article 4

1. Each Member State shall grant the right of permanent residence to nationals of other Member States who establish themselves within its territory in order to pursue activities as self-employed persons, when the restrictions on these activities have been abolished pursuant to the Treaty.

As proof of the right of residence, a document entitled "Residence Permit for a National of a Member State of the European Communities" shall be issued. This document shall be valid for not less than five years from the date of issue and shall be automatically renewable.

Breaks in residence not exceeding six consecutive months and absence on military service shall not affect the validity of a residence permit.

A valid residence permit may not be withdrawn from a national referred to in Article 1(1)(a) solely on the grounds that he is no longer in employment because he is temporarily incapable of work as a result of illness or accident.

Any national of a Member State who is not specified in the first subparagraph but who is authorised under the laws of another Member State to pursue an activity within its territory shall be granted a right of abode for a period not less than that of the authorisation granted for the pursuit of the activity in question.

However, any national referred to in subparagraph 1 and to whom the provisions of the preceding subparagraph apply as a result of a change of employment shall retain his residence permit until the date on which it expires.

2.      The right of residence for persons providing and receiving services shall be of equal duration with the period during which the services are provided.

Where such period exceeds three months, the Member State in the territory of which the services are performed shall issue a right of abode as proof of the right of residence.

Where the period does not exceed three months, the identity card or passport with which the person concerned entered the territory shall be sufficient to cover his stay. The Member State may, however, require the person concerned to report his presence in the territory.

3.      A member of the family who is not a national of a Member State shall be issued with a residence document which shall have the same validity as that issued to the national on whom he is dependent.

## Article 5

The right of residence shall be effective throughout the territory of the Member State concerned.

## Article 6

An applicant for a residence permit or right of abode shall not be required by a Member State to produce anything other than the following, namely—
    (a)  the identity card or passport with which he or she entered its territory;
    (b)  proof that he or she comes within one of the classes of person referred to in Articles 1 and 4.

## Article 7

1.      The residence documents granted to nationals of a Member State shall be issued and renewed free of charge or on payment of an amount not exceeding the dues and taxes charged for the issue of identity cards to nationals. These provisions shall also apply to documents and certificates required for the issue and renewal of such residence documents.

2.      The visas referred to in Article 3(2) shall be free of charge.

3.      Member States shall take the necessary steps to simplify as much as possible the formalities and the procedure for obtaining the documents mentioned in paragraph 1.

## Article 8

Member States shall not derogate from the provisions of this Directive save on grounds of public policy, public security or public health.

# COUNCIL DIRECTIVE

of 17 December 1974

## concerning the right of nationals of a Member State to remain in the territory of another Member State after having pursued therein an activity in a self-employed capacity

## (75/34/EEC)

NOTES

Date of publication in OJ: OJ L14, 20.1.75, p 10.

### Article 1

Member States shall, under the conditions laid down in this Directive, abolish restrictions on the right to remain in their territory in favour of nationals of another Member State who have pursued activities as self-employed persons in their territory, and members of their families, as defined in Article 1 of Directive No 73/148/EEC.

### Article 2

1.     Each Member State shall recognise the right to remain permanently in its territory of—

(a) any person who, at the time of termination of his activity, has reached the age laid down by the law of that State for entitlement to an old-age pension and who has pursued his activity in that State for at least the previous twelve months and has resided there continuously for more than three years.

Where the law of that Member State does not grant the right to an old-age pension to certain categories of self-employed workers, the age requirement shall be considered as satisfied when the beneficiary reaches 65 years of age;

(b) any person who, having resided continuously in the territory of that State for more than two years, ceases to pursue his activity there as a result of permanent incapacity to work.

If such incapacity is the result of an accident at work or an occupational illness entitling him to a pension which is payable in whole or in part by an institution of that State no condition shall be imposed as to length of residence;

(c) any person who, after three years continuous activity and residence in the territory of that State, pursues his activity in the territory of another Member State, while retaining his residence in the territory of the first State, to which he returns, as a rule, each day or at least once a week.

Periods of activity so completed in the territory of the other Member State shall, for the purposes of entitlement to the rights referred to in (a) and (b), be considered as having been completed in the territory of the State of residence.

2.     The conditions as to length of residence and activity laid down in paragraph 1(a) and the condition as to length of residence laid down in paragraph 1(b) shall not apply if the spouse of the self-employed person is a national of the Member State concerned or has lost the nationality of that State by marriage to that person.

## Article 3

1.     Each Member State shall recognise the right of the members of the self-employed person's family referred to in Article 1 who are residing with him in the territory of that State to remain there permanently, if the person concerned has acquired the right to remain in the territory of that State in accordance with Article 2. This provision shall continue to apply even after the death of the person concerned.

2.     If, however, the self-employed person dies during his working life and before having acquired the right to remain in the territory of the State concerned, that State shall recognise the right of the members of his family to remain there permanently on condition that—

— the person concerned, on the date of his decease, had resided continuously in its territory for at least two years; or
— his death resulted from an accident at work or an occupational illness; or
— the surviving spouse is a national of that State or lost such nationality by marriage to the person concerned.

## Article 4

1.     Continuity of residence as provided for in Articles 2(1) and 3(2) may be attested by any means of proof in use in the country of residence. It may not be affected by temporary absences not exceeding a total of three months per year, nor by longer absences due to compliance with the obligations of military service.

2.     Periods of inactivity due to circumstances outside the control of the person concerned or of inactivity owing to illness or accident must be considered as periods of activity within the meaning of Article 2(1).

## Article 5

1.     Member States shall allow the person entitled to the right to remain to exercise such right within two years from the time of becoming entitled thereto pursuant to Article 2(1)(a) and (b) and Article 3. During this period the beneficiary must be able to leave the territory of the Member State without adversely affecting such right.

2.     Member States shall not require the person concerned to comply with any particular formality in order to exercise the right to remain.

## Article 6

1.     Member States shall recognise the right of persons having the right to remain in their territory to a residence permit, which must—

(a) be issued and renewed free of charge or on payment of a sum not exceeding the dues and taxes payable by nationals for the issue or renewal of identity cards;
(b) by valid throughout the territory of the Member State issuing it;
(c) be valid for five years and renewable automatically.

2.     Periods of non-residence not exceeding six consecutive months and longer absences due to compliance with the obligations of military service may not affect the validity of a residence permit.

## Article 7

Member States shall apply to persons having the right to remain in their territory the right of equality of treatment recognised by the Council Directives on the abolition of restrictions on freedom of establishment pursuant to Title III of the General Programme which provides for such abolition.

### Article 8

1.　This Directive shall not affect any provisions laid down by law, regulation or administrative action of any Member State which would be more favourable to nationals of other Member States.

2.　Member States shall facilitate re-admission to their territories of self-employed persons who left those territories after having resided there permanently for a long period while pursuing an activity there and who wish to return when they have reached retirement age as defined in Article 2(1) (a) or are permanently incapacitated for work.

### Article 9

Member States may not derogate from the provisions of this Directive save on grounds of public policy, public security or public health.

# COUNCIL DIRECTIVE

### of 18 June 1992

### on a second general system for the recognition of professional education and training to supplement Directive 89/48/EEC

### (92/51/EEC)

NOTES
　Date of publication in OJ: OJ L209, 24.7.92, p 25.

## CHAPTER I

### Article 1

### Definitions

For the purposes of this Directive, the following definitions shall apply—
　(a) *diploma*—　any evidence of education and training or any set of such evidence—
　　　— which has been awarded by a competent authority in a Member State, designated in accordance with the laws, regulations or administrative provisions of that State,
　　　— which shows that the holder has successfully completed—
　　　　(i) either a post-secondary course other than that referred to in the second indent of Article 1(a) of Directive 89/48/EEC, of at least one year's duration or of equivalent duration on a part-time basis, one of the conditions of entry of which is, as a general rule, the successful completion of the secondary course required to obtain entry to university or higher education, as well as the professional training which may be required in addition to that post-secondary course;
　　　　(ii) or one of the education and training courses in Annex C, and

— which shows that the holder has the professional qualifications required for the taking up or pursuit of a regulated profession in that Member State,

provided that the education and training attested by this evidence was received mainly in the Community, or outside the Community at teaching establishments which provide education and training in accordance with the laws, regulations or administrative provisions of a Member State, or that the holder thereof has three years professional experience certified by the Member State which recognised third-country evidence of education and training.

The following shall be treated in the same way as a diploma within the meaning of the first subparagraph: any evidence of education and training or any set of such evidence awarded by a competent authority in a Member State if it is awarded on the successful completion of education and training received in the Community and recognised by a competent authority in that member State as being of an equivalent level and if it confers the same rights in respect of the taking up and pursuit of a regulated profession in that Member State;

(b) *certificate*— any evidence of education and training or any set of such evidence—

— which has been awarded by a competent authority in a Member State, designated in accordance with the laws, regulations or administrative provisions of that State,

— which shows that the holder, after having followed a secondary course, has completed—

either a course of education or training other than courses referred to in point (a), provided at an educational or training establishment or on the job, or in combination at an educational or training establishment and on the job, and complemented, where appropriate, by the probationary or professional practice required in addition to this course,

or the probationary or professional practice required in addition to this secondary course, or

— which shows that the holder, after having followed a secondary course of a technical or vocational nature has completed, where necessary,

either a course of education or training as referred to in the previous indent, or the probationary or professional practice required in addition to this secondary course of a technical or vocational nature and

— which shows that the holder has the professional qualifications required for the taking up or pursuit of a regulated profession in that Member State,

provided that the education and training attested by this evidence was received mainly in the Community, or outside the Community at teaching establishments which provide education and training in accordance with the laws, regulations or administrative provisions of a Member State, or that the holder thereof has two years professional experience certified by the Member State which recognised third-country evidence of education and training.

The following shall be treated in the same way as a certificate, within the meaning of the first subparagraph—any evidence of education and training or any set of such evidence awarded by a competent authority in a Member

State if it is awarded on the successful completion of education and training received in the Community and recognised by a competent authority in a Member State as being of an equivalent level and if it confers the same rights in respect of the taking up and pursuit of a regulated profession in that Member State;

(c) *attestation of competence*— any evidence of qualifications—

— attesting to education and training not forming part of a set constituting a diploma within the meaning of Directive 89/48/EEC or a diploma or certificate within the meaning of this Directive, or

— awarded following an assessment of the personal qualities, aptitudes or knowledge which it is considered essential that the applicant have for the pursuit of a profession by an authority designated in accordance with the laws, regulations or administrative provisions of a Member State, without proof of prior education and training being required;

(d) *host Member State*— any Member State in which a national of a Member State applies to pursue a profession subject to regulation in that Member State, other than the State in which he obtained his evidence of education and training or attestation of competence or first pursued the profession in question;

(e) *regulated profession*— the regulated professional activity or range of activities which constitute this profession in a Member State;

(f) *regulated professional activity*— a professional activity the taking up or pursuit of which, or one of its modes of pursuit in a Member State, is subject, directly or indirectly, by virtue of laws, regulations or administrative provisions, to the possession of evidence of education and training or an attestation of competence. The following in particular shall constitute a mode of pursuit of a regulated professional activity—

— pursuit of an activity under a professional title, in so far as the use of such a title is reserved to the holders of evidence of education and training or an attestation of competence governed by laws, regulations or administrative provisions,

— pursuit of a professional activity relating to health, in so far as remuneration and/or reimbursement for such an activity is subject by virtue of national social security arrangements to the possession of evidence of education and training or an attestation of competence.

Where the first subparagraph does not apply, a professional activity shall be deemed to be a regulated professional activity if it is pursued by the members of an association or organisation the purpose of which is, in particular, to promote and maintain a high standard in the professional field concerned and which, to achieve that purpose, is recognised in a special form by a Member State and—

— awards evidence of education and training to its members,

— ensures that its members respect the rules of professional conduct which it prescribes, and

— confers on them the right to use a professional title or designatory letters, or to benefit from a status corresponding to that education and training.

Whenever a Member State grants the recognition referred to in the second subparagraph to an association or organisation which satisfies the conditions of that subparagraph, it shall inform the Commission thereof;

(g) *regulated education and training*— any education and training which—

— is specifically geared to the pursuit of a given profession, and

—  comprises a course or courses complemented, where appropriate, by professional training or probationary or professional practice, the structure and level of which are determined by the laws, regulations or administrative provisions of that Member State or which are monitored or approved by the authority designated for that purpose;

(h) *professional experience*— the actual and lawful pursuit of the profession concerned in a Member State;

(i) *adaptation period*— the pursuit of a regulated profession in the host Member State under the responsibility of a qualified member of that profession, such period of supervised practice possibly being accompanied by further education and training. This period of supervised practice shall be the subject of an assessment. The detailed rules governing the adaptation period and its assessment shall be laid down by the competent authorities in the host Member State.

The status enjoyed in the host Member State by the person undergoing the period of supervised practice, in particular in the matter of right of residence as well as of obligations, social rights and benefits, allowances and remuneration, shall be established by the competent authorities in that Member State in accordance with applicable Community law;

(j) *aptitude test*  a test limited to the professional knowledge of the applicant, made by the competent authorities of the host Member State with the aim of assessing the ability of the applicant to pursue a regulated profession in that Member State.

In order to permit this test to be carried out, the competent authorities shall draw up a list of subjects which, on the basis of a comparison of the education and training required in the Member State and that received by the applicant, are not covered by the evidence of education and training possessed by the applicant. These subjects may cover both theoretical knowledge and practical skills required for the pursuit of the profession.

This aptitude test must take account of the fact that the applicant is a qualified professional in the Member State of origin or the Member State from which he comes. It shall cover subjects to be selected from those on the list referred to in the second subparagraph, knowledge of which is essential to the pursuit of the profession in the host Member State. The test may also include knowledge of the professional rules applicable to the activities in question in the host Member State. The detailed application of the aptitude test shall be determined by the competent authorities of that State.

The status in the host Member State of the applicant who wishes to prepare himself for the aptitude test in that State shall be determined by the competent authorities in that State, in accordance with applicable Community law.

## CHAPTER II

**Article 2**

**Scope**

This Directive shall apply to any national of a Member State wishing to pursue a regulated profession in a host Member State in a self-employed capacity or as an employed person.

This Directive shall apply to neither professions which are the subject of a specific Directive establishing arrangements for the mutual recognition of diplomas by Member States, nor activities covered by a Directive listed in Annex A.

The Directives listed in Annex B shall be made applicable to the pursuit as an employed person of the activities covered by those Directives.

# CHAPTER III

*System for recognition where a host Member State requires possession of a diploma within the meaning of this Directive or Directive 89/48/EEC*

## Article 3

Without prejudice to Directive 89/48/EEC, where, in a host Member State, the taking up or pursuit of a regulated profession is subject to possession of a diploma, as defined in this Directive or in Directive 89/48/EEC, the competent authority may not, on the grounds of inadequate qualifications, refuse to authorise a national of a Member State to take up or pursue that profession on the same conditions as those which apply to its own nationals—

(a) if the applicant holds the diploma, as defined in this Directive or in Directive 89/48/EEC, required in another Member State for the taking up or pursuit of the profession in question in its territory, such diploma having been awarded in a Member State; or

(b) if the applicant has pursued the profession in question full-time for two years, or for an equivalent period on a part-time basis, during the previous 10 years in another Member State which does not regulate that profession within the meaning of either Article 1(e) and the first subparagraph of Article 1(f) of this Directive or Article 1(c) and the first subparagraph of Article 1(d) of Directive 89/48/EEC, and possesses evidence of education and training which—

— has been awarded by a competent authority in a Member State, designated in accordance with the laws, regulations or administrative provisions of that State, and

— either shows that the holder has successfully completed a post-secondary course, other than that referred to in the second indent of Article 1(a) of Directive 89/48/EEC, of at least one year's duration, or of equivalent duration on a part-time basis, one of the conditions of entry of which is, as a general rule, the successful completion of the secondary course required to obtain entry to university or higher education, as well as any professional training which is an integral part of that post-secondary course,

— or attests to regulated education and training referred to in Annex D, and

— has prepared the holder for the pursuit of his profession.

However, the two years professional experience referred to above may not be required where the evidence of education and training held by the applicant and referred to in this point is awarded on completion of regulated education and training.

The following shall be treated in the same way as the evidence of education and training referred to in the first subparagraph of this point: any evidence of education and training or any set of such evidence awarded by a competent authority in a Member

State if it is awarded on the completion of education and training received in the Community and is recognised by that Member State as being of an equivalent level, provided that the other Member States and the Commission have been notified of this recognition. By way of derogation from the first subparagraph of this Article, the host Member State is not required to apply this Article where the taking up or pursuit of a regulated profession is subject in its country to possession of a diploma as defined in Directive 89/48/EEC, one of the conditions for the issue of which shall be the completion of a post-secondary course of more than four years duration.

## Article 4

1.      Notwithstanding Article 3, the host Member State may also require the applicant—

(a)  to provide evidence of professional experience, where the duration of the education and training adduced in support of his application, as laid down in points (a) and (b) of the first subparagraph of Article 3, is at least one year less than that required in the host Member State. In this event, the period of professional experience required may not exceed—

— twice the shortfall in duration of education and training where the shortfall relates to a post-secondary course and/or to a period of probationary practice carried out under the control of a supervising professional person and ending with an examination,

— the shortfall where the shortfall relates to professional practice acquired with the assistance of a qualified member of the profession concerned.

In the case of diplomas within the meaning of the second subparagraph of Article 1(a), the duration of education and training recognised as being of an equivalent level shall be determined as for the education and training defined in the first subparagraph of Article 1(a).

When these provisions are applied, account must be taken of the professional experience referred to in point (b) of the first subparagraph of Article 3.

In any event, the professional experience required may not exceed four years.

Professional experience may not, however, be required of an applicant holding a diploma attesting to a post-secondary course as referred to in the second indent of Article 1(a) or a diploma as defined in Article 1(a) of Directive 89/48/EEC who wishes to pursue his profession in a host Member State which requires the possession of a diploma or evidence of education and training attesting to one of the courses of education and training as referred to in Annexes C and D;

(b)  to complete an adaptation period not exceeding three years or take an aptitude test where—

— the theoretical and/or practical matters covered by the education and training which he has received as laid down in points (a) or (b) of the first subparagraph of Article 3 differ substantially from those covered by the diploma, as defined in this Directive or in Directive 89/48/EEC, required in the host Member State, or

— in the case referred to in point (a) of the first subparagraph of Article 3, the profession regulated in the host Member State comprises one or more regulated professional activities which do not form part of the profession regulated in the Member State from which the applicant originates or comes and that difference corresponds to specific education and training required in the host Member State and covers theoretical and/or practical matters which differ substantially from those covered by the diploma, as defined in this Directive or in Directive 89/48/EEC, adduced by the applicant, or

— in the case referred to in point (b) of the first subparagraph of Article 3, the profession regulated in the host Member State comprises one or more regulated professional activities which do not form part of the profession pursued by the applicant in the Member State from which he originates or comes, and that difference corresponds to specific education and training required in the host Member State and covers theoretical and/or practical matters which differ substantially from those covered by the evidence of education and training adduced by the applicant.

Should the host Member State make use of this possibility, it must give the applicant the right to choose between an adaptation period and an aptitude test. Where the host Member State, which requires a diploma as defined in Directive 89/48/EEC or in this Directive, intends to introduce derogations from an applicant's right to choose, the procedure laid down in Article 14 shall apply.

By way of derogation from the second subparagraph of this point, the host Member State may reserve the right to choose between the adaptation period and the aptitude test if—

— a profession is involved the pursuit of which requires a precise knowledge of national law and in respect of which the provision of advice and/or assistance concerning national law is an essential and constant feature of the professional activity, or

— where the host Member State makes access to the profession or its pursuit subject to the possession of a diploma as defined in Directive 89/48/EEC, one of the conditions for the award of which is the completion of a post-secondary course of at least three years duration or an equivalent period on a part-time basis and the applicant holds either a diploma as defined in this Directive or evidence of education and training within the meaning of point (b) of the first subparagraph of Article 3 and not covered by Article 3 (b) of Directive 89/48/EEC.

2.      However, the host Member State may not apply the provisions of paragraph 1(a) and (b) cumulatively.

## CHAPTER IV

*System for recognition where a host Member State requires possession of a diploma and the applicant is the holder of a certificate or has received corresponding education and training*

### Article 5

Where, in a host Member State, the taking up or pursuit of a regulated profession is subject to possession of a diploma, the competent authority may not, on the grounds of inadequate qualifications, refuse to authorise a national of a Member State to take up or pursue that profession on the same conditions as those which apply to its own nationals—

(a)  if the applicant holds the certificate required in another Member State for the taking up or pursuit of the same profession in its territory, such certificate having been awarded in a Member State; or

    (b)  if the applicant has pursued the same profession full-time for two years during the previous 10 years in another Member State which does not regulate that profession, within the meaning of Article 1(e) and the first subparagraph of Article 1(f), and possesses evidence of education and training—

    — which was been awarded by a competent authority in a Member State, designated in accordance with the laws, regulations or administrative provisions of that State, and

    — which shows that the holder, after having followed a secondary course, has completed: either a course of professional education or training other than courses referred to in point (a), provided at an educational or training establishment or on the job, or in combination at an educational or training establishment and on the job and complemented, where appropriate, by the probationary or professional practice which is an integral part of that training course, or the probationary or professional practice which is an integral part of that secondary course, or

    — which shows that the holder, after having followed a secondary course of a technical or vocational nature has completed, where necessary, either a course of professional education or training as referred to in the previous indent, or the period of probationary or professional practice which is an integral part of that secondary course of a technical or vocational nature and

    — which has prepared the holder for the pursuit of this profession.

However, the two years professional experience referred to above may not be required where the evidence of education and training held by the applicant and referred to in this point is awarded on completion of regulated education and training. Nevertheless, the host Member State may require the applicant to undergo an adaptation period not exceeding three years or take an aptitude test. The host Member State must give the applicant the right to choose between an adaptation period and an aptitude test.

Where the host Member State intends to introduce derogations from an applicant's right to choose, the procedure laid down in Article 14 shall apply.

# CHAPTER V

*System for recognition where a host Member State requires possession of a certificate*

## Article 6

Where, in the host Member State, the taking up or pursuit of a regulated profession is subject to possession of a certificate, the competent authority may not, on the grounds of inadequate qualifications, refuse to authorise a national of a Member State to take up or pursue that profession on the same conditions as those which apply to its own nationals—

    (a)  if the applicant holds the diploma, as defined in this Directive or in Directive 89/48/EEC, or the certificate required in another Member State for the taking up or pursuit of the profession in question in its territory, such diploma having been awarded in a Member State; or

    (b)  if the applicant has pursued the profession in question full-time for two years or for an equivalent period on a part-time basis during the previous

10 years in another Member State which does not regulate that profession, within the meaning of Article 1(e) and the first subparagraph of Article 1(f), and possesses evidence of education and training—

— which has been awarded by a competent authority in a Member State, designated in accordance with the laws, regulations or administrative provisions of that State, and

— which shows that the holder has successfully completed a post-secondary course other than that referred to in the second indent of Article 1(a) of Directive 89/48/EEC, of at least one year's duration or of equivalent duration on a part-time basis, one of the conditions of entry of which is, as a general rule, the completion of the secondary course required to obtain entry to university or higher education, as well as any professional training which is an integral part of that post-secondary course, or

— which shows that the holder, after having followed a secondary course, has completed: either a course of education or training for a profession other than courses referred to in point (a), provided at an educational establishment or on the job, or in combination at an educational establishment and on the job and complemented, where appropriate, by the probationary or professional practice which is an integral part of that training course, or the probationary or professional practice which is an integral part of that secondary course, or

— which shows that the holder, after having followed a secondary course of a technical or vocational nature has completed, where necessary, either a course of education or training for a profession as referred to in the previous indent, or the period of probationary or professional practice which is an integral part of that secondary course of a technical or vocational nature and

— which has prepared the holder for the pursuit of this profession.

However, the two years professional experience referred to above may not be required where the evidence of education and training held by the applicant and referred to in this point is awarded on completion of regulated education and training.

(c) If the applicant who does not hold any diploma, certificate or other evidence of education and training within the meaning of Article 3 (b) or of point (b) of this Article has pursued the profession in question full-time for three consecutive years, or for an equivalent period on a part-time basis, during the previous 10 years in another Member State which does not regulate that profession within the meaning of Article 1(e) and the first subparagraph of Article 1(f).

The following shall be treated in the same way as the evidence of education and training referred to under (b) in the first subparagraph: any evidence of education and training or any set of such evidence awarded by a competent authority in a Member State if it is awarded on the completion of education and training received in the Community and is recognised by that Member State as being of an equivalent level, provided that the other Member States and the Commission have been notified of this recognition.

## Article 7

Without prejudice to Article 6, a host Member State may also require the applicant to—

(a)   complete an adaptation period not exceeding two years or to take an aptitude test when the education and training which he received in accordance with points (a) or (b) of the first subparagraph of Article 5 relates to theoretical or practical matters differing substantially from those covered by the certificate required in the host Member State, or where there are differences in the fields of activity characterised in the host Member State by specific education and training relating to theoretical or practical matters differing substantially from those covered by the applicant's evidence of formal qualifications.

Should the host Member State make use of this possibility, it must give the applicant the right to choose between an adaptation period and an aptitude test. Where the host Member State which requires a certificate intends to introduce derogations as regards an applicant's right to choose, the procedure laid down in Article 14 shall apply;

(b)   undergo an adaptation period not exceeding two years or take an aptitude test where, in the instance referred to in point (c) of the first subparagraph of Article 6, he does not hold a diploma, certificate or other evidence of education and training. The host Member State may reserve the right to choose between an adaptation period and an aptitude test.

## CHAPTER VI

*Special systems for recognition of other qualifications*

### Article 8

Where, in the host Member State, the taking up or pursuit of a regulated profession is subject to possession of an attestation of competence, the competent authority may not, on the grounds of inadequate qualifications, refuse to authorise a national of a Member State to take up or pursue that profession on the same conditions as those which apply to its own nationals—

(a)   if the applicant holds the attestation of competence required in another Member State for the taking up or pursuit of the same profession in its territory, such attestation having been awarded in a Member State; or

(b)   if the applicant provides proof of qualifications obtained in other Member States, and giving guarantees, in particular in the matter of health, safety, environmental protection and consumer protection, equivalent to those required by the laws, regulations or administrative provisions of the host Member State.

If the applicant does not provide proof of such an attestation or of such qualifications the laws, regulations or administrative provisions of the host Member State shall apply.

### Article 9

Where, in the host Member State, the taking up or pursuit of a regulated profession is subject only to possession of evidence of education attesting to general education at primary or secondary school level, the competent authority may not, on the grounds of inadequate qualifications, refuse to authorise a national of a Member State to take up or pursue that profession on the same conditions as those which apply to its own nationals if the applicant possesses formal qualifications of the corresponding level, awarded in another Member State.

This evidence of formal qualifications must have been awarded by a competent authority in that Member State, designated in accordance with its own laws, regulations or administrative provisions.

# CHAPTER VII

*Other measures to facilitate the effective exercise of the right of establishment, freedom to provide services and freedom of movement of employed persons*

## Article 10

1.      Where the competent authority of the host Member State requires of persons wishing to take up a regulated profession proof that they are of good character or repute or that they have not been declared bankrupt, or suspends or prohibits the pursuit of that profession in the event of serious professional misconduct or a criminal offence, that State shall accept as sufficient evidence, in respect of nationals of Member States wishing to pursue that profession in its territory, the production of documents issued by competent authorities in the Member State of origin or the Member State from which the foreign national comes showing that those requirements are met.

Where the competent authorities of the Member State of origin or of the Member State from which the foreign national comes do not issue the documents referred to in the first subparagraph, such documents shall be replaced by a declaration on oath—or, in Member States where there is no provision for declaration on oath, by a solemn declaration—made by the person concerned before a competent judicial or administrative authority or, where appropriate, a notary or qualified professional body of the Member State of origin or the Member State from which the person comes; such authority or notary shall issue written confirmation attesting the authenticity of the declaration on oath or solemn declaration.

2.      Where the competent authority of the host Member State requires of nationals of that Member State wishing to take up or pursue a regulated profession a statement of physical of mental health, that authority shall accept as sufficient evidence in this respect the production of the document required in the Member State of origin or the Member State from which the foreign national comes.

Where the Member State of origin or the Member State from which the foreign national comes does not impose any requirements of this nature on those wishing to take up or pursue the profession in question, the host Member State shall accept from such nationals a statement issued by a competent authority in that State corresponding to the statement issued in the host Member State.

3.      The competent authority of the host Member State may require that the documents and statements referred to in paragraphs 1 and 2 are presented no more than three months after their date of issue.

4.      Where the competent authority of the host Member State requires nationals of that Member State wishing to take up or pursue a regulated profession to take an oath or make solemn declaration and where the form of such oath or declaration cannot be used by nationals of other Member States, that authority shall ensure that an appropriate and equivalent form of oath or declaration is offered to the person concerned.

## Article 11

1.      The competent authorities of host Member States shall recognise the right of nationals of Member States who fulfil the conditions for the taking up and pursuit of

a regulated profession in their territory to use the professional title of the host Member State corresponding to that profession.

2.    The competent authority of the host Member State shall recognise the right of nationals of Member States who fulfil the conditions for the taking up and pursuit of a regulated profession in the territory to use their lawful academic title and, where appropriate, the abbreviation thereof deriving from their Member State of origin or the Member State from which they come, in the language of that State. The host Member State may require this title to be followed by the name and location of the establishment or examining board which awarded it.

3.    Where a profession is regulated in the host Member State by an association or organisation referred to in Article 1(f), nationals of Member States shall be entitled to use the professional title or designatory letters conferred by that organisation or association only on proof of membership.

Where the association or organisation makes membership subject to certain qualification requirements, it may apply these to nationals of other Member States who are in possession of a diploma within the meaning of Article 1(a), a certificate within the meaning of Article 1(b) or evidence of education and training or qualification within the meaning of point (b) of the first subparagraph of Article 3, point (b) of the first subparagraph of Article 5 or Article 9 in accordance only with this Directive, in particular Articles 3, 4 and 5.

**Article 12**

1.    The host Member State shall accept as means of proof that the conditions laid down in Articles 3 to 9 are satisfied the documents issued by the competent authorities in the Member States, which the person concerned shall submit in support of his application to pursue the profession concerned.

2.    The procedure for examining an application to pursue a regulated profession shall be completed as soon as possible and the outcome communicated in a reasoned decision of the competent authority in the host Member State not later than four months after presentation of all the documents relating to the person concerned. A remedy shall be available against this decision or the absence thereof, before a court or tribunal in accordance with the provisions of national law.

# CHAPTER VIII

*Procedure for coordination*

**Article 13**

1.    Member States shall designate, within the period provided for in Article 17, the competent authorities empowered to receive the applications and take the decisions referred to in this Directive. They shall communicate this information to the other Member States and to the Commission.

2.    Each Member State shall designate a person responsible for coordinating the activities of the authorities referred to in paragraph 1 and shall inform the other Member States and the Commission to that effect. His role shall be to promote uniform application of this Directive to all the professions concerned. This coordinator shall be a member of the coordinating group set up under the aegis of the Commission by Article 9(2) of Directive 89/48/EEC.

The coordinating group set up under the aforementioned provision of Directive 89/48/EEC shall also be required to—

— facilitate the implementation of this Directive,
— collect all useful information for its application in the Member States, particularly information relating to the establishment of an indicative list of regulated professions and to the disparities between the qualifications awarded in the Member States with a view to assisting the competent authorities of the Member States in their task of assessing whether substantial differences exist.

The group may be consulted by the Commission on any changes to the existing system which may be contemplated.

3.     The Member States shall take measures to provide the necessary information on the recognition of diplomas and certificates and on other conditions governing the taking up of the regulated professions within the framework of this Directive. To carry out this task they may call upon the existing information networks and, where appropriate, the relevant professional associations or organisations. The Commission shall take the necessary initiatives to ensure the development and coordination of the communication of the necessary information.

## CHAPTER IX

*Procedure for derogating from the right to choose between adaptation period and aptitude test*

### Article 14

1.     If, pursuant to the second sentence of the second subparagraph of Article 4(1)(b), the third subparagraph of Article 5, or the second sentence of the second subparagraph of Article 7(a), a Member State proposes not to grant applicants the right to choose between an adaptation period and an aptitude test, it shall immediately communicate to the Commission the corresponding draft provision. It shall at the same time notify the Commission of the grounds which make the enactment of such a provision necessary.

The Commission shall immediately notify the other Member States of any draft which it has received; it may also consult the coordinating group referred to in Article 13(2) on the draft.

2.     Without prejudice to the possibility for the Commission and the other Member States to make comments on the draft, the Member State may adopt the provision only if the Commission has not taken a decision to the contrary within three months.

3.     At the request of a Member State or the Commission, Member States shall communicate to them, without delay, the definitive text of any provision arising from the application of this Article.

## CHAPTER XI

*Other provisions*

### Article 16

Following the expiry of the period provided for in Article 17, Member States shall communicate to the Commission, every two years, a report on the application of the system introduced. In addition to general remarks, this report shall contain a statistical summary of the decisions taken and a description of the main problems arising from the application of this Directive.

## Article 17

1. Member States shall adopt the laws, regulations and administrative provisions necessary for them to comply with this Directive before 18 June 1994. They shall forthwith inform the Commission thereof.

When Member States adopt these measures, the latter shall include a reference to this Directive or be accompanied by such reference at the time of their official publication. The methods of making such a reference shall be laid down by the Member States.

2. Member States shall communicate to the Commission the texts of the main provisions of national law which they adopt in the field governed by this Directive.

## Article 18

Five years at the latest following the date specified in Article 17, the Commission shall report to the European Parliament, the Council and the Economic and Social Committee on the progress of the application of this Directive.

After conducting all necessary consultations, the Commission shall present its conclusions as to any changes which need to be made to this Directive. At the same time the Commission shall, where appropriate, submit proposals for improving the existing rules in the interest of facilitating freedom of movement, right of establishment and freedom to provide services.

## Article 19

This Directive is addressed to the Member States.

INDUSTRIAL/INTELLECTUAL PROPERTY

# COUNCIL DIRECTIVE

of 14 May 1991

## on the legal protection of computer programs

## (91/250/EEC)

NOTES

Date of publication in OJ: OJ L122, 17.5.91, p 42.

## THE COUNCIL OF THE EUROPEAN COMMUNITIES,

Having regard to the Treaty establishing the European Economic Community and in particular Article 100a thereof,

Having regard to the proposal from the Commission,

In co-operation with the European Parliament,

Having regard to the opinion of the Economic and Social Committee,

Whereas computer programs are at present not clearly protected in all Member States by existing legislation and such protection, where it exists, has different attributes;

Whereas the development of computer programs requires the investment of considerable human, technical and financial resources while computer programs can be copied at a fraction of the cost needed to develop them independently;

Whereas computer programs are playing an increasingly important role in a broad range of industries and computer program technology can accordingly be considered as being of fundamental importance for the Community's industrial development;

Whereas certain differences in the legal protection of computer programs offered by the laws of the Member States have direct and negative effects on the functioning of the common market as regards computer programs and such differences could well become greater as Member States introduce new legislation on this subject;

Whereas existing differences having such effects need to be removed and new ones prevented from arising, while differences not adversely affecting the functioning of the common market to a substantial degree need not be removed or prevented from arising;

Whereas the Community's legal framework on the protection of computer programs can accordingly in the first instance be limited to establishing that Member States should accord protection to computer programs under copyright law as literary works and, further, to establishing who and what should be protected, the exclusive rights on which protected persons should be able to rely in order to authorise or prohibit certain acts and for how long the protection should apply;

Whereas, for the purpose of this Directive, the term 'computer program' shall include programs in any form, including those which are incorporated into hardware; whereas this term also includes preparatory design work leading to the development of a computer program provided that the nature of the preparatory work is such that a computer program can result from it at a later stage;

Whereas, in respect of the criteria to be applied in determining whether or not a computer program is an original work, no tests as to the qualitative or aesthetic merits of the program should be applied;

Whereas the Community is fully committed to the promotion of international standardisation;

Whereas the function of a computer program is to communicate and work together with other components of a computer system and with users and, for this purpose, a logical and, where appropriate, physical interconnection and interaction is required to permit all elements of software and hardware to work with other software and hardware and with users in all the ways in which they are intended to function;

Whereas the parts of the program which provide for such interconnection and interaction between elements of software and hardware are generally known as 'interfaces';

Whereas this functional interconnection and interaction is generally known as 'interoperability'; whereas such interoperability can be defined as the ability to exchange information and mutually to use the information which has been exchanged;

Whereas, for the avoidance of doubt, it has to be made clear that only the expression of a computer program is protected and that ideas and principles which underlie any element of a program, including those which underlie its interfaces, are not protected by copyright under this Directive;

Whereas, in accordance with this principle of copyright, to the extent that logic, algorithms and programming languages comprise ideas and principles, those ideas and principles are not protected under this Directive;

Whereas, in accordance with the legislation and jurisprudence of the Member States and the international copyright conventions, the expression of those ideas and principles is to be protected by copyright;

Whereas, for the purposes of this Directive, the term 'rental' means the making available for use, for a limited period of time and for profit-making purposes, of a computer program or a copy thereof; whereas this term does not include public lending, which, accordingly, remains outside the scope of this Directive;

Whereas the exclusive rights of the author to prevent the unauthorised reproduction of his work have to be subject to a limited exception in the case of a computer program to allow the reproduction technically necessary for the use of that program by the lawful acquirer;

Whereas this means that the acts of loading and running necessary for the use of a copy of a program which has been lawfully acquired, and the act of correction of its errors, may not be prohibited by contract; whereas, in the absence of specific contractual provisions, including when a copy of the program has been sold, any other act necessary for the use of the copy of a program may be performed in accordance with its intended purpose by a lawful acquirer of that copy;

Whereas a person having a right to use a computer program should not be prevented from performing acts necessary to observe, study or test the functioning of the program, provided that these acts do not infringe the copyright in the program;

Whereas the unauthorised reproduction, translation, adaptation or transformation of the form of the code in which a copy of a computer program has been made available constitutes an infringement of the exclusive rights of the author;

Whereas, nevertheless, circumstances may exist when such a reproduction of the code and translation of its form within the meaning of Article 4(a) and (b) are indispensable to obtain the necessary information to achieve the interoperability of an independently created program with other programs;

Whereas it has therefore to be considered that in these limited circumstances only, performance of the acts of reproduction and translation by or on behalf of a person having a right to use a copy of the program is legitimate and compatible with fair practice and must therefore be deemed not to require the authorisation of the rightholder;

Whereas an objective of this exception is to make it possible to connect all components of a computer system, including those of different manufacturers, so that they can work together;

Whereas such an exception to the author's exclusive rights may not be used in a way which prejudices the legitimate interests of the rightholder or which conflicts with a normal exploitation of the program;

Whereas, in order to remain in accordance with the provisions of the Berne Convention for the Protection of Literary and Artistic Works, the term of protection should be the life of the author and fifty years from the first of January of the year following the year of his death or, in the case of an anonymous or pseudonymous work, 50 years from the first of January of the year following the year in which the work is first published;

Whereas protection of computer programs under copyright laws should be without prejudice to the application, in appropriate cases, of other forms of protection; whereas, however, any contractual provisions contrary to Article 6 or to the exceptions provided for in Article 5(2) and (3) should be null and void;

Whereas the provisions of this Directive are without prejudice to the application of the competition rules under Articles 85 and 86 of the Treaty if a dominant supplier refuses to make information available which is necessary for interoperability as defined in this Directive;

Whereas the provisions of this Directive should be without prejudice to specific requirements of Community law already enacted in respect of the publication of interfaces in the telecommunications sector or Council Decisions relating to standardisation in the field of information technology and telecommunication;

Whereas this Directive does not affect derogations provided for under national legislation in accordance with the Berne Convention on points not covered by this Directive,

HAS ADOPTED THIS DIRECTIVE—

## Article 1

1.    In accordance with the provisions of this Directive, Member States shall protect computer programs, by copyright, as literary works within the meaning of the Berne Convention for the Protection of Literary and Artistic Works. For the purposes of this Directive, the term 'computer programs' shall include their preparatory design material.

2.    Protection in accordance with this Directive shall apply to the expression in any form of a computer program. Ideas and principles which underlie any element of a computer program, including those which underlie its interfaces, are not protected by copyright under this Directive.

3.    A computer program shall be protected if it is original in the sense that it is the author's own intellectual creation. No other criteria shall be applied to determine its eligibility for protection.

## Article 2

### Authorship of computer programs

1.    The author of a computer program shall be the natural person or group of natural persons who has created the program or, where the legislation of the Member State permits, the legal person designated as the rightholder by that legislation. Where collective works are recognised by the legislation of a Member State, the person considered by the legislation of the Member State to have created the work shall be deemed to be its author.

2.    In respect of a computer program created by a group of natural persons jointly, the exclusive rights shall be owned jointly.

3.    Where a computer program is created by an employee in the execution of his duties or following the instructions given by his employer, the employer exclusively shall be entitled to exercise all economic rights in the program so created, unless otherwise provided by contract.

## Article 3

### Beneficiaries of protection

Protection shall be granted to all natural or legal persons eligible under national copyright legislation as applied to literary works.

## Article 4

### Restricted Acts

Subject to the provisions of Articles 5 and 6, the exclusive rights of the rightholder within the meaning of Article 2, shall include the right to do or to authorise—

(a) the permanent or temporary reproduction of a computer program by any means and in any form, in part or in whole. Insofar as loading, displaying, running, transmission or storage of the computer program necessitate such reproduction, such acts shall be subject to authorisation by the rightholder;

(b) the translation, adaptation, arrangement and any other alteration of a computer program and the reproduction of the results thereof, without prejudice to the rights of the person who alters the program;

(c) any form of distribution to the public, including the rental, of the original computer program or of copies thereof. The first sale in the Community of a copy of a program by the rightholder or with his consent shall exhaust the distribution right within the Community of that copy, with the exception of the right to control further rental of the program or a copy thereof.

## Article 5

### Exceptions to the restricted acts

1.    In the absence of specific contractual provisions, the acts referred to in Article 4(a) and (b) shall not require authorisation by the rightholder where they are necessary for the use of the computer program by the lawful acquirer in accordance with its intended purpose, including for error correction.

2.    The making of a back-up copy by a person having a right to use the computer program may not be prevented by contract insofar as it is necessary for that use.

3.    The person having a right to use a copy of a computer program shall be entitled, without the authorisation of the rightholder, to observe, study or test the functioning of the program in order to determine the ideas and principles which underlie any element of the program if he does so while performing any of the acts of loading, displaying, running, transmitting or storing the program which he is entitled to do.

## Article 6

### Decompilation

1.    The authorisation of the rightholder shall not be required where reproduction of the code and translation of its form within the meaning of Article 4(a) and (b) are indispensable to obtain the information necessary to achieve the interoperability of an independently created computer program with other programs, provided that the following conditions are met—

(a) these acts are performed by the licensee or by another person having a right to use a copy of a program, or on their behalf by a person authorised to do so;

(b) the information necessary to achieve interoperability has not previously been readily available to the persons referred to in subparagraph (a); and

(c) these acts are confined to the parts of the original program which are necessary to achieve interoperability.

2.    The provisions of paragraph 1 shall not permit the information obtained through its application—

(a) to be used for goals other than to achieve the interoperability of the independently created computer program;

(b) to be given to others, except when necessary for the interoperability of the independently created computer program; or

(c) to be used for the development, production or marketing of a computer program substantially similar in its expression, or for any other act which infringes copyright.

3.    In accordance with the provisions of the Berne Convention for the protection of Literary and Artistic Works, the provisions of this Article may not be interpreted in such a way as to allow its application to be used in a manner which unreasonably prejudices the right holder's legitimate interests or conflicts with a normal exploitation of the computer program.

## Article 7

### Special measures of protection

1.    Without prejudice to the provisions of Articles 4, 5 and 6, Member States shall provide, in accordance with their national legislation, appropriate remedies against a person committing any of the acts listed in subparagraphs (a), (b) and (c) below—
   (a) any act of putting into circulation a copy of a computer program knowing, or having reason to believe, that it is an infringing copy;
   (b) the possession, for commercial purposes, of a copy of a computer program knowing, or having reason to believe, that it is an infringing copy;
   (c) any act of putting into circulation, or the possession for commercial purposes of, any means the sole intended purpose of which is to facilitate the unauthorised removal or circumvention of any technical device which may have been applied to protect a computer program.

2.    Any infringing copy of a computer program shall be liable to seizure in accordance with the legislation of the Member State concerned.

3.    Member States may provide for the seizure of any means referred to in paragraph 1(c).

## Article 9

### Continued application of other legal provisions

1.    The provisions of this Directive shall be without prejudice to any other legal provisions such as those concerning patent rights, trade-marks, unfair competition, trade secrets, protection of semi-conductor products or the law of contract. Any contractual provisions contrary to Article 6 or to the exceptions provided for in Article 5(2) and (3) shall be null and void.

2.    The provisions of this Directive shall apply also to programs created before 1 January 1993 without prejudice to any acts concluded and rights acquired before that date.

## Article 10

### Final provisions

1.    Member States shall bring into force the laws, regulations and administrative provisions necessary to comply with this Directive before 1 January 1993.

   When Member States adopt these measures, the latter shall contain a reference to this Directive or shall be accompanied by such reference on the occasion of their official publication. The methods of making such a reference shall be laid down by the Member States.

2.    Member States shall communicate to the Commission the provisions of national law which they adopt in the field governed by this Directive.

## Article 11

This Directive is addressed to the Member States.

# COUNCIL REGULATION

of 20 December 1993

## on the Community trade mark

## (40/94/EC)

NOTES
   Date of publication in OJ: OJ L11, 14.1.94, p 1.

THE COUNCIL OF THE EUROPEAN UNION,

   Having regard to the Treaty establishing the European Community, and in particular Article 235 thereof,

   Having regard to the proposal from the Commission,

   Having regard to the opinion of the European Parliament,

   Having regard to the opinion of the Economic and Social Committee,

   Whereas it is desirable to promote throughout the Community a harmonious development of economic activities and a continuous and balanced expansion by completing an internal market which functions properly and offers conditions which are similar to those obtaining in a national market; whereas in order to create a market of this kind and make it increasingly a single market, not only must be barriers to free movement of goods and services be removed and arrangements be instituted which ensure that competition is not distorted, but, in addition, legal conditions must be created which enable undertakings to adapt their activities to the scale of the Community, whether in manufacturing and distributing goods or in providing services; whereas for those purposes, trade marks enabling the products and services of undertakings to be distinguished by identical means throughout the entire Community, regardless of frontiers, should feature amongst the legal instruments which undertakings have at their disposal;

   Whereas action by the Community would appear to be necessary for the purpose of attaining the Community's said objectives; whereas such action involves the creation of Community arrangements for trade marks whereby undertakings can by means of one procedural system obtain Community trade marks to which uniform protection is given and which produce their effects throughout the entire area of the Community; whereas the principle of the unitary character of the Community trade mark thus stated will apply unless otherwise provided for in this Regulation;

   Whereas the barrier of territoriality of the rights conferred on proprietors of trade marks by the laws of the Member States cannot be removed by approximation of laws; whereas in order to open up unrestricted economic activity in the whole of the common market for the benefit of undertakings, trade marks need to be created which are governed by a uniform Community law directly applicable in all Member States;

   Whereas since the Treaty has not provided the specific powers to establish such a legal instrument, Article 235 of the Treaty should be applied;

   Whereas the Community law relating to trade marks nevertheless does not replace the laws of the Member States on trade marks; whereas it would not in fact appear to be justified to require undertakings to apply for registration of their trade marks as Community trade marks; whereas national trade marks continue to be necessary for those undertakings which do not want protection of their trade marks at Community level;

   Whereas the rights in a Community trade mark may not be obtained otherwise than by registration, and registration is to be refused in particular if the trade mark is not distinctive, if it is unlawful or if it conflicts with earlier rights;

   Whereas the protection afforded by a Community trade mark, the function of which is in particular to guarantee the trade mark as an indication of origin, is absolute in the case of identity between the mark and the sign and the goods or services; whereas the protection applies also in cases of similarity between the mark and the sign and the goods or services; whereas an interpretation should be given of the concept of similarity in relation to the likelihood of confusion; whereas the likelihood of confusion, the appreciation of which depends on numerous elements and, in particular, on the recognition of the trade mark on the market, the association which can be made with the used or registered sign, the degree of similarity between the trade mark and the sign and between the goods or services identified, constitutes the specific condition for such protection;

Whereas it follows from the principle of free flow of goods that the proprietor of a Community trade mark must not be entitled to prohibit its use by a third party in relation to goods which have been put into circulation in the Community, under the trade mark, by him or with his consent, save where there exist legitimate reasons for the proprietor to oppose further commercialisation of the goods;

Whereas there is no justification for protecting Community trade marks or, as against them, any trade mark which has been registered before them, except where the trade marks are actually used;

Whereas a Community trade mark is to be regarded as an object of property which exists separately from the undertakings whose goods or services are designated by it; whereas accordingly, it must be capable of being transferred, subject to the overriding need to prevent the public being misled as a result of the transfer. It must also be capable of being charged as security in favour of a third party and of being the subject matter of licences;

Whereas administrative measures are necessary at Community level for implementing in relation to every trade mark the trade mark law created by this Regulation; whereas it is therefore essential, while retaining the Community's existing institutional structure and balance of powers, to establish an Office for Harmonisation in the Internal Market (trade marks and designs) which is independent in relation to technical matters and has legal, administrative and financial autonomy; whereas to this end it is necessary and appropriate that it should be a body of the Community having legal personality and exercising the implementing powers which are conferred on it by this Regulation, and that it should operate within the framework of Community law without detracting from the competencies exercised by the Community Institutions;

Whereas it is necessary to ensure that parties who are affected by decisions made by the Office are protected by the law in a manner which is suited to the special character of trade mark law; whereas to that end provision is made for an appeal to lie from decisions of the examiners and of the various divisions of the Office; whereas if the department whose decision is contested does not rectify its decision it is to remit the appeal to a Board of Appeal of the Office, which is to decide on it; whereas decisions of the Boards of Appeal are, in turn, amenable to actions before the Court of Justice of the European Communities, which has jurisdiction to annul or to alter the contested decision;

Whereas under Council Decision 88/591/ECSC, EEC, Euratom of 24 October 1988 establishing a Court of First Instance of the European Communities, as amended by Decision 93/350/Euratom, ECSC, EEC of 8 June 1993, that Court shall exercise at the first instance the jurisdiction conferred on the Court of Justice by the Treaties establishing the Communities— with particular regard to appeals lodged under the second subparagraph of Article 173 of the EC Treaty—and by the acts adopted in implementation thereof, save as otherwise provided in an act setting up a body governed by Community law; whereas the jurisdiction which this Regulation confers on the Court of Justice to cancel and reform decisions of the appeal courts shall accordingly be exercised at the first instance by the Court in accordance with the above Decision;

Whereas in order to strengthen the protection of Community trade marks the Member States should designate, having regard to their own national system, as limited a number as possible of national courts of first and second instance having jurisdiction in matters of infringement and validity of Community trade marks;

Whereas decisions regarding the validity and infringement of Community trade marks must have effect and cover the entire area of the Community, as this is the only way of preventing inconsistent decisions on the part of the courts and the Office and of ensuring that the unitary character of Community trade marks is not undermined; whereas the rules contained in the Brussels Convention of Jurisdiction and the Enforcement of Judgments in Civil and Commercial Matters will apply to all actions at law relating to Community trade marks, save where this Regulation derogates from those rules;

Whereas contradictory judgments should be avoided in actions which involve the same acts and the same parties and which are brought on the basis of a Community trade mark and parallel national trade marks; whereas for this purpose, when the actions are brought in the same Member State, the way in which this is to be achieved is a matter for national procedural rules, which are not prejudiced by this Regulation, whilst when the actions are brought in different Member States, provisions modelled on the rules on lis pendens and related actions of the abovementioned Brussels Convention appear appropriate;

Whereas in order to guarantee the full autonomy and independence of the Office, it is considered necessary to grant it an autonomous budget whose revenue comes principally from fees paid by the users of the system; whereas however, the Community budgetary procedure remains applicable as far as any subsidies chargeable to general budget of the European Communities are concerned; whereas moreover, the auditing of accounts should be undertaken by the Court of Auditors;

Whereas implementing measures are required for the Regulation's application, particularly as regards the adoption and amendment of fees regulations and an Implementing Regulation; whereas such measures should be adopted by the Commission, assisted by a Committee composed of representatives of the Member States, in accordance with the procedural rules laid down in Article 2, procedure III(b), of Council Decision 87/373/EEC of 13 July 1987 laying down the procedures for the exercise of implementing powers conferred on the Commission,

HAS ADOPTED THIS REGULATION—

# TITLE I
# GENERAL PROVISIONS

## Article 1

### Community trade mark

1.    A trade mark for goods or services which is registered in accordance with the conditions contained in this Regulation and in the manner herein provided is hereinafter referred to as a 'Community trade mark'.

2.    A Community trade mark shall have a unitary character. It shall have equal effect throughout the Community: it shall not be registered, transferred or surrendered or be the subject of a decision revoking the rights of the proprietor or declaring it invalid, nor shall its use be prohibited, save in respect of the whole Community. This principle shall apply unless otherwise provided in this Regulation.

## Article 2

### Office

An Office for Harmonisation in the Internal Market (trade marks and designs), hereinafter referred to as 'the Office', is hereby established.

## Article 3

### Capacity to act

For the purpose of implementing this Regulation, companies or firms and other legal bodies shall be regarded as legal persons if, under the terms of the law governing them, they have the capacity in their own name to have rights and obligations of all kinds, to make contracts or accomplish other legal acts and to sue and be sued.

## TITLE II
## THE LAW RELATING TO TRADE MARKS

## SECTION 1
## DEFINITION OF A COMMUNITY TRADE MARK
## OBTAINING A COMMUNITY TRADE MARK

### Article 4

### Signs of which a Community trade mark may consist

A Community trade mark may consist of any signs capable of being represented graphically, particularly words, including personal names, designs, letters, numerals, the shape of goods or of their packaging, provided that such signs are capable of distinguishing the goods or services of one undertaking from those of other undertakings.

### Article 5

### Persons who can be proprietors of Community trade marks

1.     The following natural or legal persons, including authorities established under public law, may be proprietors of Community trade marks—
   (a)   nationals of the Member States; or
   [(b)  nationals of other States which are parties to the Paris Convention for the protection of industrial property, hereinafter referred to as 'the Paris Convention', or to the Agreement establishing the World Trade Organisations;]
   (c)   nationals of States which are not parties to the Paris Convention who are domiciled or have their seat or who have real and effective industrial or commercial establishments within the territory of the Community or of a State which is party to the Paris Convention; or
   [(d)  nationals, other than those referred to under subparagraph (c), of any State which is not party to the Paris Convention or to the Agreement establishing the World Trade Organisation and which, according to published findings, accords to nationals of all the Member States the same protection for trade marks as it accords to its own nationals and, if nationals of the Member States are required to prove registration in the country of origin, recognises the registration of Community trade marks as such proof.]

2.     With respect to the application of paragraph 1, stateless persons as defined by Article 1 of the Convention relating to the Status of Stateless Persons signed at New York on 28 September 1954, and refugees as defined by Article 1 of the Convention relating to the Status of Refugees signed at Geneva on 28 July 1951 and modified by the Protocol relating to the Status of Refugees signed at New York on 31 January 1967, shall be regarded as nationals of the country in which they have their habitual residence.

3.     Persons who are nationals of a State covered by paragraph 1(d) must prove that the trade mark for which an application for a Community trade mark has been submitted is registered in the State of origin, unless, according to published findings, the trade marks of nationals of the Member States are registered in the State of origin in question without proof of prior registration as a Community trade mark or as a national trade mark in a Member State.

---

NOTES

Para 1: sub-paras (b), (d) substituted by Council Regulation 3288/94/EC, Art 1(1), (2).

---

## Article 6

### Means whereby a Community trade mark is obtained

A Community trade mark shall be obtained by registration.

## Article 7

### Absolute grounds for refusal

1.　The following shall not be registered—
   (a) signs which do not conform to the requirements of Article 4;
   (b) trade marks which are devoid of any distinctive character;
   (c) trade marks which consist exclusively of signs or indications which may serve, in trade, to designate the kind, quality, quantity, intended purpose, value, geographical origin or the time of production of the goods or of rendering of the service, or other characteristics of the goods or service;
   (d) trade marks which consist exclusively of signs or indications which have become customary in the current language or in the bona fide and established practices of the trade;
   (e) signs which consist exclusively of—
      (i) the shape which results from the nature of the goods themselves; or
      (ii) the shape of goods which is necessary to obtain a technical result; or
      (iii) the shape which gives substantial value to the goods;
   (f) trade marks which are contrary to public policy or to accepted principles of morality;
   (g) trade marks which are of such a nature as to deceive the public, for instance as to the nature, quality or geographical origin of the goods or service;
   (h) trade marks which have not been authorised by the competent authorities and are to be refused pursuant to Article 6*ter* of the Paris Convention;
   (i) trade marks which include badges, emblems or escutcheons other than those covered by Article 6*ter* of the Paris Convention and which are of particular public interest, unless the consent of the appropriate authorities to their registration has been given.
   [(j) trade marks for wines which contain or consist of a geographical indication identifying wines or for spirits which contain or consist of a geographical indication identifying spirits with respect to such wines or spirits not having that origin.]

2.　Paragraph 1 shall apply notwithstanding that the grounds of non-registrability obtain in only part of the Community.

3.　Paragraph 1(b), (c) and (d) shall not apply if the trade mark has become distinctive in relation to the goods or services for which registration is requested in consequence of the use which has been made of it.

---

NOTES
　　Para 1: sub-para (j) added by Council Regulation 3288/94/EC, Art 1(3).

---

## Article 8

### Relative grounds for refusal

1.　Upon opposition by the proprietor of an earlier trade mark, the trade mark applied for shall not be registered—

(a) if it is identical with the earlier trade mark and the goods or services for which registration is applied for are identical with the goods or services for which the earlier trade mark is protected;

(b) if because of its identity with or similarity to the earlier trade mark and the identity or similarity of the goods or services covered by the trade marks there exists a likelihood of confusion on the part of the public in the territory in which the earlier trade mark is protected; the likelihood of confusion includes the likelihood of association with the earlier trade mark.

2.    For the purposes of paragraph 1, 'Earlier trade marks' means—

(a) trade marks of the following kinds with a date of application for registration which is earlier than the date of application for registration of the Community trade mark, taking account, where appropriate, of the priorities claimed in respect of those trade marks—

(i) Community trade marks;

(ii) trade marks registered in a Member State, or, in the case of Belgium, the Netherlands or Luxembourg, at the Benelux Trade Mark Office;

(iii) trade marks registered under international arrangements which have effect in a Member State;

(b) applications for the trade marks referred to in subparagraph (a), subject to their registration;

(c) trade marks which, on the date of application for registration of the Community trade mark, or, where appropriate, of the priority claimed in respect of the application for registration of the Community trade mark, are well known in a Member State, in the sense in which the words 'well known' are used in Article 6*bis* of the Paris Convention.

3.    Upon opposition by the proprietor of the trade mark, a trade mark shall not be registered where an agent or representative of the proprietor of the trade mark applies for registration thereof in his own name without the proprietor's consent, unless the agent or representative justifies his action.

4.    Upon opposition by the proprietor of a non-registered trade mark or of another sign used in the course of trade of more than mere local significance, the trade mark applied for shall not be registered where and to the extent that, pursuant to the law of the Member State governing that sign,

(a) rights to that sign were acquired prior to the date of application for registration of the Community trade mark, or the date of the priority claimed for the application for registration of the Community trade mark;

(b) that sign confers on its proprietor the right to prohibit the use of a subsequent trade mark.

5.    Furthermore, upon opposition by the proprietor of an earlier trade mark within the meaning of paragraph 2, the trade mark applied for shall not be registered where it is identical with or similar to the earlier trade mark and is to be registered for goods or services which are not similar to those for which the earlier trade mark is registered, where in the case of an earlier Community trade mark the trade mark has a reputation in the Community and, in the case of an earlier national trade mark, the trade mark has a reputation in the Member State concerned and where the use without due cause of the trade mark applied for would take unfair advantage of, or be detrimental to, the distinctive character or the repute of the earlier trade mark.

## SECTION 2
## EFFECTS OF COMMUNITY TRADE MARKS

### Article 9

### Rights conferred by a Community trade mark

1.    A Community trade mark shall confer on the proprietor exclusive rights therein. The proprietor shall be entitled to prevent all third parties not having his consent from using in the course of trade—

   (a) any sign which is identical with the Community trade mark in relation to goods or services which are identical with those for which the Community trade mark is registered;

   (b) any sign where, because of its identity with or similarity to the Community trade mark and the identity or similarity of the goods or services covered by the Community trade mark and the sign, there exists a likelihood of confusion on the part of the public; the likelihood of confusion includes the likelihood of association between the sign and the trade mark;

   (c) any sign which is identical with or similar to the Community trade mark in relation to goods or services which are not similar to those for which the Community trade mark is registered, where the latter has a reputation in the Community and where use of that sign without due cause takes unfair advantage of, or is detrimental to, the distinctive character or the repute of the Community trade mark.

2.    The following, inter alia, may be prohibited under paragraph 1—

   (a) affixing the sign to the goods or to the packaging thereof;

   (b) offering the goods, putting them on the market or stocking them for these purposes under that sign, or offering or supplying services thereunder;

   (c) importing or exporting the goods under that sign;

   (d) using the sign on business papers and in advertising.

3.    The rights conferred by a Community trade mark shall prevail against third parties from the date of publication of registration of the trade mark. Reasonable compensation may, however, be claimed in respect of matters arising after the date of publication of a Community trade mark application, which matters would, after publication of the registration of the trade mark, be prohibited by virtue of that publication. The court seized of the case may not decide upon the merits of the case until the registration has been published.

### Article 10

### Reproduction of Community trade marks in dictionaries

If the reproduction of a Community trade mark in a dictionary, encyclopaedia or similar reference work gives the impression that it constitutes the generic name of the goods or services for which the trade mark is registered, the publisher of the work shall, at the request of the proprietor of the Community trade mark, ensure that the reproduction of the trade mark at the latest in the next edition of the publication is accompanied by an indication that it is a registered trade mark.

## Article 11

### Prohibition on the use of a Community trade mark registered in the name of an agent or representative

Where a Community trade mark is registered in the name of the agent or representative of a person who is the proprietor of that trade mark, without the proprietor's authorisation, the latter shall be entitled to oppose the use of his mark by his agent or representative if he has not authorised such use, unless the agent or representative justifies his action.

## Article 12

### Limitation of the effects of a Community trade mark

A Community trade mark shall not entitle the proprietor to prohibit a third party from using in the course of trade—
  (a)  his own name or address;
  (b)  indications concerning the kind, quality, quantity, intended purpose, value, geographical origin, the time of production of the goods or of rendering of the service, or other characteristics of the goods or service;
  (c)  the trade mark where it is necessary to indicate the intended purpose of a product or service, in particular as accessories or spare parts,

provided he uses them in accordance with honest practices in industrial or commercial matters.

## Article 13

### Exhaustion of the rights conferred by a Community trade mark

1.    A Community trade mark shall not entitle the proprietor to prohibit its use in relation to goods which have been put on the market in the Community under that trade mark by the proprietor or with his consent.

2.    Paragraph 1 shall not apply where there exist legitimate reasons for the proprietor to oppose further commercialisation of the goods, especially where the condition of the goods is changed or impaired after they have been put on the market.

## Article 14

### Complementary application of national law relating to infringement

1.    The effects of Community trade marks shall be governed solely by the provisions of this Regulation. In other respects, infringement of a Community trade mark shall be governed by the national law relating to infringement of a national trade mark in accordance with the provisions of Title X.

2.    This Regulation shall not prevent actions concerning a Community trade mark being brought under the law of Member States relating in particular to civil liability and unfair competition.

3.    The rules of procedure to be applied shall be determined in accordance with the provisions of Title X.

## SECTION 3
## USE OF COMMUNITY TRADE MARKS

### Article 15

**Use of Community trade marks**

1.    If, within a period of five years following registration, the proprietor has not put the Community trade mark to genuine use in the Community in connection with the goods or services in respect of which it is registered, or if such use has been suspended during an uninterrupted period of five years, the Community trade mark shall be subject to the sanctions provided for in this Regulation, unless there are proper reasons for non-use.

2.    The following shall also constitute use within the meaning of paragraph 1—
   (a) use of the Community trade mark in a form differing in elements which do not alter the distinctive character of the mark in the form in which it was registered;
   (b) affixing of the Community trade mark to goods or to the packaging thereof in the Community solely for export purposes.

3.    Use of the Community trade mark with the consent of the proprietor shall be deemed to constitute use by the proprietor.

## SECTION 4
## COMMUNITY TRADE MARKS AS OBJECTS OF PROPERTY

### Article 16

**Dealing with Community trade marks as national trade marks**

1.    Unless Articles 17 to 24 provide otherwise, a Community trade mark as an object of property shall be dealt with in its entirety, and for the whole area of the Community, as a national trade mark registered in the Member State in which, according to the Register of Community trade marks,
   (a) the proprietor has his seat or his domicile on the relevant date; or
   (b) where subparagraph (a) does not apply, the proprietor has an establishment on the relevant date.

2.    In cases which are not provided for by paragraph 1, the Member State referred to in that paragraph shall be the Member State in which the seat of the Office is situated.

3.    If two or more persons are mentioned in the Register of Community trade marks as joint proprietors, paragraph 1 shall apply to the joint proprietor first mentioned; failing this, it shall apply to the subsequent joint proprietors in the order in which they are mentioned. Where paragraph 1 does not apply to any of the joint proprietors, paragraph 2 shall apply.

### Article 17

**Transfer**

1.    A Community trade mark may be transferred, separately from any transfer of the undertaking in respect of some or all of the goods or services for which it is registered.

2.     A transfer of the whole of the undertaking shall include the transfer of the Community trade mark except where, in accordance with the law governing the transfer, there is agreement to the contrary or circumstances clearly dictate otherwise. This provision shall apply to the contractual obligation to transfer the undertaking.

3.     Without prejudice to paragraph 2, an assignment of the Community trade mark shall be made in writing and shall require the signature of the parties to the contract, except when it is a result of a judgment; otherwise it shall be void.

4.     Where it is clear from the transfer documents that because of the transfer the Community trade mark is likely to mislead the public concerning the nature, quality or geographical origin of the goods or services in respect of which it is registered, the Office shall not register the transfer unless the successor agrees to limit registration of the Community trade mark to goods or services in respect of which it is not likely to mislead.

5.     On request of one of the parties a transfer shall be entered in the Register and published.

6.     As long as the transfer has not been entered in the Register, the successor in title may not invoke the rights arising from the registration of the Community trade mark.

7.     Where there are time limits to be observed *vis-à-vis* the Office, the successor in title may make the corresponding statements to the Office once the request for registration of the transfer has been received by the Office.

8.     All documents which require notification to the proprietor of the Community trade mark in accordance with Article 77 shall be addressed to the person registered as proprietor.

## Article 18

### Transfer of a trade mark registered in the name of an agent

Where a Community trade mark is registered in the name of the agent or representative of a person who is the proprietor of that trade mark, without the proprietor's authorisation, the latter shall be entitled to demand the assignment in his favour of the said registration, unless such agent or representative justifies his action.

## Article 22

### Licensing

1.     A Community trade mark may be licensed for some or all of the goods or services for which it is registered and for the whole or part of the Community. A licence may be exclusive or non-exclusive.

2.     The proprietor of a Community trade mark may invoke the rights conferred by that trade mark against a licensee who contravenes any provision in his licensing contract with regard to its duration, the form covered by the registration in which the trade mark may be used, the scope of the goods or services for which the licence is granted, the territory in which the trade mark may be affixed, or the quality of the goods manufactured or of the services provided by the licensee.

3.     Without prejudice to the provisions of the licensing contract, the licensee may bring proceedings for infringement of a Community trade mark only if its proprietor consents thereto. However, the holder of an exclusive licence may bring such proceedings if the proprietor of the trade mark, after formal notice, does not himself bring infringement proceedings within an appropriate period.

4.      A licensee shall, for the purpose of obtaining compensation for damage suffered by him, be entitled to intervene in infringement proceedings brought by the proprietor of the Community trade mark.

5.      On request of one of the parties the grant or transfer of a licence in respect of a Community trade mark shall be entered in the Register and published.

## Article 23

### Effects *vis-à-vis* third parties

1.      Legal acts referred to in Article 17, 19 and 22 concerning a Community trade mark shall only have effects *vis-à-vis* third parties in all the Member States after entry in the Register. Nevertheless, such an act, before it is so entered, shall have effect *vis-à-vis* third parties who have acquired rights in the trade mark after the date of that act but who knew of the act at the date on which the rights were acquired.

2.      Paragraph 1 shall not apply in the case of a person who acquires the Community trade mark or a right concerning the Community trade mark by way of transfer of the whole of the undertaking or by any other universal succession.

3.      The effects *vis-à-vis* third parties of the legal acts referred to in Article 20 shall be governed by the law of the Member State determined in accordance with Article 16.

4.      Until such time as common rules for the Member States in the field of bankruptcy enter into force, the effects *vis-à-vis* third parties of bankruptcy or like proceedings shall be governed by the law of the Member State in which such proceedings are first brought within the meaning of national law or of conventions applicable in this field.

## Article 24

### The application for a Community trade mark as an object of property

Articles 16 to 23 shall apply to applications for Community trade marks.

# TITLE III
# APPLICATION FOR COMMUNITY TRADE MARKS
## SECTION 1
## FILING OF APPLICATIONS AND THE CONDITIONS WHICH GOVERN THEM

## Article 25

### Filing of applications

1.      An application for a Community trade mark shall be filed, at the choice of the applicant,
   (a) at the Office; or
   (b) at the central industrial property office of a Member State or at the Benelux Trade Mark Office. An application filed in this way shall have the same effect as if it had been filed on the same date at the Office.

2.      Where the application is filed at the central industrial property office of a Member State or at the Benelux Trade Mark Office, that office shall take all steps to

forward the application to the Office within two weeks after filing. It may charge the applicant a fee which shall not exceed the administrative costs of receiving and forwarding the application.

3.      Applications referred to in paragraph 2 which reach the Office more than one month after filing shall be deemed withdrawn.

4.      Ten years after the entry into force of this Regulation, the Commission shall draw up a report on the operation of the system of filing applications for Community trade marks, together with any proposals for modifying this system.

**Article 143**

**Entry into force**

1.      This Regulation shall enter into force on the 60th day following that of its publication in the Official Journal of the European Communities.

2.      The Member States shall within three years following entry into force of this Regulation take the necessary measures for the purpose of implementing Articles 91 and 110 hereof and shall forthwith inform the Commission of those measures.

3.      Applications for Community trade marks may be filed at the Office from the date fixed by the Administrative Board on the recommendation of the President of the Office.

4.      Applications for Community trade marks filed within three months before the date referred to in paragraph 3 shall be deemed to have been filed on that date.

This Regulation shall be binding in its entirety and directly applicable in all Member States.

Statement by the Council and the Commission on the seat of the Office for Harmonisation in the Internal Market (trade marks and designs)[1]

'In adopting the Regulation on the Community Trade Mark, the Council and the Commission note—
— that the representatives of the Governments of the Member States, meeting at Head of State and Government level on 29 October 1993, decided that the Office for Harmonisation in the Internal Market (trade marks and designs) should have its seat in Spain, in a town to be determined by the Spanish Government;
— that the Spanish Government has designated Alicante as the seat of the Office.'

NOTES
1      Date of publication in OJ: OJ L11, 14.1.94, p 36.

# COMMISSION REGULATION

of 31 January 1996

## on the application of Article 85(3) of the Treaty to certain categories of technology transfer agreements

### (240/96/EC)

NOTES
Date of publication in OJ: OJ L31, 9.2.96, p 2.

## THE COMMISSION OF THE EUROPEAN COMMUNITIES,

Having regard to the Treaty establishing the European Community,

Having regard to Council Regulation No 19/65/EEC of 2 March 1965 on the application of Article 85(3) of the Treaty to certain categories of agreements and concerted practices, as last amended by the Act of Accession of Austria, Finland and Sweden, and in particular Article 1 thereof,

Having published a draft of this Regulation,

After consulting the Advisory Committee on Restrictive Practices and Dominant Positions,

Whereas—

(1) Regulation No 19/65/EEC empowers the Commission to apply Article 85(3) of the Treaty by regulation to certain categories of agreements and concerted practices falling within the scope of Aricle 85(1) which include restrictions imposed in relation to the acquisition or use of industrial property rights—in particular of patents, utility models, designs or trademarks—or to the rights arising out of contracts for assignment of, or the right to use, a method of manufacture of knowledge relating to use or to the application of industrial processes.

(2) The Commission has made use of this power by adopting Regulation (EEC) No 2349/84 of 23 July 1984 on the application of Article 85(3) of the Treaty to certain categories of patent licensing agreements, as last amended by Regulation (EC) No 2131/95, and Regulation (EEC) No 556/89 of 30 November 1988 on the application of Article 85(3) of the Treaty to certain categories of know-how licensing agreements, as last amended by the Act of Accession of Austria, Finland and Sweden.

(3) These two block exemptions ought to be combined into a single regulation covering technology transfer agreements, and the rules governing patent licensing agreements and agreements for the licensing of know-how ought to be harmonised and simplified as far as possible, in order to encourage the dissemination of technical knowledge in the Community and to promote the manufacture of technically more sophisticated products. In those circumstances Regulation (EEC) No 556/89 should be repealed.

(4) This Regulation should apply to the licensing of Member States' own patents, Community patents and European patents ('pure' patent licensing agreements). It should also apply to agreements for the licensing of non-patented technical information such as descriptions of manufacturing processes, recipes, formulae, designs or drawings, commonly termed 'know-how' ('pure' know-how licensing agreements), and to combined patent and know-how licensing agreements ('mixed' agreements), which are playing an increasingly important role in the transfer of technology. For the purposes of this Regulation, a number of terms are defined in Article 10.

(5) Patent or know-how licensing agreements are agreements whereby one undertaking which holds a patent or know-how ('the licensor') permits another undertaking ('the licensee') to exploit the patent thereby licensed, or communicates the know-how to it, in particular for purposes of manufacture, use or putting on the market. In the light of experience acquired so far, it is possible to define a category of licensing agreements covering all or part of the common market which are capable of falling within the scope of Article 85(1) but which can normally be regarded as satisfying the conditions laid down in Article 85(3), where patents are necessary for the achievement of the objects of the licensed technology by a mixed agreement or where know-how—whether it is ancillary to patents or independent of them—is secret, substantial and identified in any appropriate form. These criteria are intended only to ensure that the licensing of the know-how or the grant of the patent licence justifies a block exemption of obligations restricting competition. This is without prejudice to the right of the parties to include in the contract provisions regarding other obligations, such as the obligation to pay royalties, even if the block exemption no longer applies.

(6) It is appropriate to extend the scope of this Regulation to pure or mixed agreements containing the licensing of intellectual property rights other than patents (in particular, trademarks, design rights and copyright, especially software protection), when such additional licensing contributes to the achievement of the objects of the licensed technology and contains only ancillary provisions.

(7) Where such pure or mixed licensing agreements contain not only obligations relating to territories within the common market but also obligations relating to non-member countries, the presence of the latter does not prevent this Regulation from applying to the obligations

relating to territories within the common market. Where licensing agreements for non-member countries or for territories which extend beyond the frontiers of the Community have effects within the common market which may fall within the scope of Article 85(1), such agreements should be covered by this Regulation to the same extent as would agreements for territories within the common market.

(8) The objective being to facilitate the dissemination of technology and the improvement of manufacturing processes, this Regulation should apply only where the licensee himself manufactures the licensed products or has them manufactured for his account, or where the licensed product is a service, provides the service himself or has the service provided for his account, irrespective of whether or not the licensee is also entitled to use confidential information provided by the licensor for the promotion and sale of the licensed product. The scope of this Regulation should therefore exclude agreements solely for the purpose of sale. Also to be excluded from the scope of this Regulation are agreements relating to marketing know-how communicated in the context of franchising arrangements and certain licensing agreements entered into in connection with arrangements such as joint ventures or patent pools and other arrangements in which a licence is granted in exchange for other licences not related to improvements to or new applications of the licensed technology. Such agreements pose different problems which cannotat present be dealt with in a single regulation (Article 5).

(9) Given the similarity between sale and exclusive licensing, and the danger that the requirements of this Regulation might be evaded by presenting as assignments what are in fact exclusive licenses restrictive of competition, this Regulation should apply to agreements concerning the assignment and acquisition of patents or know-how where the risk associated with exploitation remains with the assignor. It should also apply to licensing agreements in which the licensor is not the holder of the patent or know-how but is authorised by the holder to grant the licence (as in the case of sub-licences) and to licensing agreements in which the parties' rights or obligations are assumed by connected undertakings (Article 6).

(10) Exclusive licensing agreements, ie agreements in which the licensor undertakes not to exploit the licensed technology in the licensed territory himself or to grant further licences there, may not be in themselves incompatible with Article 85(1) where they are concerned with the introduction and protection of a new technology in the licensed territory, by reason of the scale of the research which has been undertaken, of the increase in the level of competition, in particular inter-brand competition, and of the competitiveness of the undertakings concerned resulting from the dissemination of innovation within the Community. In so far as agreements of this kind fall, in other circumstances, within the scope of Article 85(1), it is appropriate to include them in Article 1 in order that they may also benefit from the exemption.

(11) The exemption of export bans on the licensor and on the licensees does not prejudice any developments in the case law of the Court of Justice in relation to such agreements, notably with respect to Articles 30 to 36 and Article 85(1). This is also the case, in particular, regarding the prohibition on the licensee from selling the licensed product in territories granted to other licensees (passive competition).

(12) The obligations listed in Article 1 generally contribute to improving the production of goods and to promoting technical progress. They make the holders of patents or know-how more willing to grant licences and licensees more inclined to undertake the investment required to manufacture, use and put on the market a new product or to use a new process. Such obligations may be permitted under this Regulation in respect of territories where the licensed product is protected by patents as long as these remain in force.

(13) Since the point at which the know-how ceases to be secret can be difficult to determine, it is appropriate, in respect of territories where the licensed technology comprises know-how only, to limit such obligations to a fixed number of years. Moreover, in order to provide sufficient periods of protection, it is appropriate to take as the starting-point for such periods the date on which the product is first put on the market in the Community by a licensee.

(14) Exemption under Article 85(3) of longer periods of territorial protection for know-how agreements, in particular in order to protect expensive and risky investment or where the parties were not competitors at the date of the grant of the licence, can be granted only by individual decision. On the other hand, parties are free to extend the term of their agreements in order to exploit any subsequent improvement and to provide for the payment of additional royalties. However, in such cases, further periods of territorial protection may be allowed only

starting from the date of licensing of the secret improvements in the Community, and by individual decision. Where the research for improvements results in innovations which are distinct from the licensed technology the parties may conclude a new agreement benefitting from an exemption under this Regulation.

(15) Provision should also be made for exemption of an obligation on the licensee not to put the product on the market in the territories of other licensees, the permitted period for such an obligation (this obligation would ban not just active competition but passive competition too) should, however, be limited to a few years from the date on which the licensed product is first put on the market in the Community by a licensee, irrespective of whether the licensed technology comprises know-how, patents or both in the territories concerned.

(16) The exemption of territorial protection should apply for the whole duration of the periods thus permitted, as long as the patents remain in force or the know-how remains secret and substantial. The parties to a mixed patent and know-how licensing agreement must be able to take advantage in a particular territory of the period of protection conferred by a patent or by the know-how, whichever is the longer.

(17) The obligations listed in Article 1 also generally fulfil the other conditions for the application of Article 85(3). Consumers will, as a rule, be allowed a fair share of the benefit resulting from the improvement in the supply of goods on the market. To safeguard this effect, however, it is right to exclude from the application of Article 1 cases where the parties agree to refuse to meet demand from users or resellers within their respective territories who would resell for export, or to take other steps to impede parallel imports. The obligations referred to above thus only impose restrictions which are indispensable to the attainment of their objectives.

(18) It is desirable to list in this Regulation a number of obligations that are commonly found in licensing agreements but are normally not restrictive of competition, and to provide that in the event that because of the particular economic or legal circumstances they should fall within Article 85(1), they too will be covered by the exemption. This list, in Article 2, is not exhaustive.

(19) This Regulation must also specify what restrictions or provisions may not be included in licensing agreements if these are to benefit from the block exemption. The restrictions listed in Article 3 may fall under the prohibition of Article 85(1), but in their case there can be no general presumption that, although they relate to the transfer of technology, they will lead to the positive effects required by Article 85(3), as would be necessary for the granting of a block exemption. Such restrictions can be declared exempt only by an individual decision, taking account of the market position of the undertakings concerned and the degree of concentration on the relevant market.

(20) The obligations on the licensee to cease using the licensed technology after the termination of the agreement (Article 2(1)(3)) and to make improvements available to the licensor (Article 2(1)(4)) do not generally restrict competition. The post-term use ban may be regarded as a normal feature of licensing, as otherwise the licensor would be forced to transfer his know-how or patents in perpetuity. Undertakings by the licensee to grant back to the licensor a licence for improvements to the licensed know-how and/or patents are generally not restrictive of competition if the licensee is entitled by the contract to share in future experience and inventions made by the licensor. On the other hand, a restrictive effect on competition arises where the agreement obliges the licensee to assign to the licensor rights to improvements of the originally licensed technology that he himself has brought about (Article 3(6)).

(21) The list of clauses which do not prevent exemption also includes an obligation on the licensee to keep paying royalties until the end of the agreement independently of whether or not the licensed know-how has entered into the public domain through the action of third parties or of the licensee himself (Article 2(1)(7)). Moreover, the parties must be free, in order to facilitate payment, to spread the royalty payments for the use of the licensed technology over a period extending beyond the duration of the licensed patents, in particular by setting lower royalty rates. As a rule, parties do not need to be protected against the foreseeable financial consequences of an agreement freely entered into, and they should therefore be free to choose the appropriate means of financing the technology transfer and sharing between them the risks of such use. However, the setting of rates of royalty so as to achieve one of the restrictions listed in Article 3 renders the agreement ineligible for the block exemption.

(22) An obligation on the licensee to restrict his exploitation of the licensed technology to one or more technical fields of application ('fields of use') or to one or more product markets

is not caught by Article 85(1) either, since the licensor is entitled to transfer the technology only for a limited purpose (Article 2(1)(8)).

(23) Clauses whereby the parties allocate customers within the same technological field of use or the same product market, either by an actual prohibition on supplying certain classes of customer or through an obligation with an equivalent effect, would also render the agreement ineligible for the block exemption where the parties are competitors for the contract products (Article 3(4)). Such restrictions between undertakings which are not competitors remain subject to the opposition procedure. Article 3 does not apply to cases where the patent or know-how licence is granted in order to provide a single customer with a second source of supply. In such a case, a prohibition on the second licensee from supplying persons other than the customer concerned is an essential condition for the grant of a second licence, since the purpose of the transaction is not to create an independent supplier in the market. The same applies to limitations on the quantities the licensee may supply to the customer concerned (Article 2(1)(13)).

(24) Besides the clauses already mentioned, the list of restrictions which render the block exemption inapplicable also includes restrictions regarding the selling prices of the licensed product or the quantities to be manufactured or sold, since they seriously limit the extent to which the licensee can exploit the licensed technology and since quantity restrictions particularly may have the same effect as export bans (Article 3(1) and (5)). This does not apply where a licence is granted for use of the technology in specific production facilities and where both a specific technology is communicated for the setting-up, operation and maintenance of these facilities and the licensee is allowed to increase the capacity of the facilities or to set up further facilities for its own use on normal commercial terms. On the other hand, the licensee may lawfully be prevented from using the transferred technology to set up facilities for third parties, since the purpose of the agreement is not to permit the licensee to give other producers access to the licensor's technology while it remains secret or protected by patent (Article 2(1)(12)).

(25) Agreements which are not automatically covered by the exemption because they contain provisions that are not expressly exempted by this Regulation and not expressly excluded from exemption, including those listed in Article 4(2), may, in certain circumstances, nonetheless be presumed to be eligible for application of the block exemption. It will be possible for the Commission rapidly to establish whether this is the case on the basis of the information undertakings are obliged to provide under Commission Regulation (EC) No 3385/94. The Commission may waive the requirement to supply specific information required in form A/B but which it does not deem necessary. The Commission will generally be content with communication of the text of the agreement and with an estimate, based on directly available data, of the market structure and of the licensee's market share. Such agreements should therefore be deemed to be covered by the exemption provided for in this Regulation where they are notified to the Commission and the Commission does not oppose the application of the exemption within a specified period of time.

(26) Where agreements exempted under this Regulation nevertheless have effects incompatible with Article 85(3), the Commission may withdraw the block exemption, in particular where the licensed products are not faced with real competition in the licensed territory (Article 7). This could also be the case where the licensee has a strong position on the market. In assessing the competition the Commission will pay special attention to cases where the licensee has more than 40% of the whole market for the licensed products and of all the products or services which customers consider interchangeable or substitutable on account of their characteristics, prices and intended use.

(27) Agreements which come within the terms of Articles 1 and 2 and which have neither the object nor the effect of restricting competition in any other way need no longer be notified. Nevertheless, undertakings will still have the right to apply in individual cases for negative clearance or for exemption under Article 85(3) in accordance with Council Regulation No 17, as last amended by the Act of Accession of Austria, Finland and Sweden. They can in particular notify agreements obliging the licensor not to grant other licences in the territory, where the licensee's market share exceeds or is likely to exceed 40%,

HAS ADOPTED THIS REGULATION—

## Article 1

1.    Pursuant to Article 85(3) of the Treaty and subject to the conditions set out below, it is hereby declared that Article 85(1) of the Treaty shall not apply to pure patent licensing or know-how licensing agreements and to mixed patent and know-how licensing agreements, including those agreements containing ancillary provisions relating to intellectual property rights other than patents, to which only two undertakings are party and which include one or more of the following obligations—

  (1)  an obligation on the licensor not to license other undertakings to exploit the licensed technology in the licensed territory;
  (2)  an obligation on the licensor not to exploit the licensed technology in the licensed territory himself;
  (3)  an obligation on the licensee not to exploit the licensed technology in the territory of the licensor within the common market;
  (4)  an obligation on the licensee not to manufacture or use the licensed product, or use the licensed process, in territories within the common market which are licensed to other licensees;
  (5)  an obligation on the licensee not to pursue an active policy of putting the licensed product on the market in the territories within the common market which are licensed to other licensees, and in particular not to engage in advertising specifically aimed at those territories or to establish any branch or maintain an distribution depot there;
  (6)  an obligation on the licensee not to put the licensed product on the market in the territories licensed to other licensees within the common market in response to unsolicited orders;
  (7)  an obligation on the licensee to use only the licensor's trademark or get up to distinguish the licensed product during the term of the agreement, provided that the licensee is not prevented from identifying himself as the manufacturer of the licensed products;
  (8)  an obligation on the licensee to limit his production of the licensed product to the quantities he requires in manufacturing his own products and to sell the licensed product only as an integral part of or a replacement part for his own products or otherwise in connection with the sale of his own products, provided that such quantities are freely determined by the licensee.

2.    Where the agreement is a pure patent licensing agreement, the exemption of the obligations referred to in paragraph 1 is granted only to the extent that and for as long as the licensed product is protected by parallel patents, in the territories respectively of the licensee (points (1), (2), (7) and (8)), the licensor (point (3)) and other licensees (points (4) and (5)). The exemption of the obligation referred to in point (6) of paragraph 1 is granted for a period not exceeding five years from the date when the licensed product is first put on the market within the common market by one of the licensees, to the extent that and for as long as, in these territories, this product is protected by parallel patents.

3.    Where the agreement is a pure know-how licensing agreement, the period for which the exemption of the obligations referred to in points (1) to (5) of paragraph 1 is granted may not exceed ten years from the date when the licensed product is first put on the market within the common market by one of the licensees.

The exemption of the obligation referred to in point (6) of paragraph 1 is granted for a period not exceeding five years from the date when the licensed product is first put on the market within the common market by one of the licensees.

The obligations referred to in points (7) and (8) of paragraph 1 are exempted during the lifetime of the agreement for as long as the know-how remains secret and substantial.

However, the exemption in paragraph 1 shall apply only where the parties have identified in any appropriate form the initial know-how and any subsequent improvements to it which become available to one party and are communicated to the other party pursuant to the terms of the agreement and to the purpose thereof, and only for as long as the know-how remains secret and substantial.

4.      Where the agreement is a mixed patent and know-how licensing agreement, the exemption of the obligations referred to in points (1) to (5) of paragraph 1 shall apply in Member States in which the licensed technology is protected by necessary patents for as long as the licensed product is protected in those Member States by such patents if the duration of such protection exceeds the periods specified in paragraph 3.

The duration of the exemption provided in point (6) of paragraph 1 may not exceed the five-year period provided for in paragraphs 2 and 3.

However, such agreements qualify for the exemption referred to in paragraph 1 only for as long as the patents remain in force or to the extent that the know-how is identified and for as long as it remains secret and substantial whichever period is the longer.

5.      The exemption provided for in paragraph 1 shall also apply where in a particular agreement the parties undertake obligations of the types referred to in that paragraph but with a more limited scope than is permitted by that paragraph.

## Article 2

1.      Article 1 shall apply notwithstanding the presence in particular of any. of the following clauses, which are generally not restrictive of competition—

(1) an obligation on the licensee not to divulge the know-how communicated by the licensor; the licensee may be held to this obligation after the agreement has expired;

(2) an obligation on the licensee not to grant sublicences or assign the licence;

(3) an obligation on the licensee not to exploit the licensed know-how or patents after termination of the agreement in so far and as long as the know-how is still secret or the patents are still in force;

(4) an obligation on the licensee to grant to the licensor a licence in respect of his own improvements to or his new applications of the licensed technology, provided—

— that, in the case of severable improvements, such a licence is not exclusive, so that the licensee is free to use his own improvements or to license them to third parties, in so far as that does not involve disclosure of the know-how communicated by the licensor that is still secret,

— and that the licensor undertakes to grant an exclusive or non-exclusive licence of his own improvements to the licensee;

(5) an obligation on the licensee to observe minimum quality specifications, including technical specifications, for the licensed product or to procure goods or services from the licensor or from an undertaking designated by the licensor, in so far as these quality specifications, products or services are necessary for—

(a) a technically proper exploitation of the licensed technology; or

(b) ensuring that the product of the licensee conforms to the minimum quality specifications that are applicable to the licensor and other licensees;

and to allow the licensor to carry out related checks;

(6) obligations—
  (a) to inform the licensor of misappropriation of the know-how or of infringements of the licensed patents; or
  (b) to take or to assist the licensor in taking legal action against such misappropriation or infringements;
(7) an obligation on the licensee to continue paying the royalties—
  (a) until the end of the agreement in the amounts, for the periods and according to the methods freely determined by the parties, in the event of the know-how becoming publicly known other than by action of the licensor, without prejudice to the payment of any additional damages in the event of the know-how becoming publicly known by the action of the licensee in breach of the agreement;
  (b) over a period going beyond the duration of the licensed patents, in order to facilitate payment;
(8) an obligation on the licensee to restrict his exploitation of the licensed technology to one or more technical fields of application covered by the licensed technology or to one or more product markets;
(9) an obligation on the licensee to pay a minimum royalty or to produce a minimum quantity of the licensed product or to carry out a minimum number of operations exploiting the licensed technology;
(10) an obligation on the licensor to grant the licensee any more favourable terms that the licensor may grant to another undertaking after the agreement is entered into;
(11) an obligation on the licensee to mark the licensed product with an indication of the licensor's name or of the licensed patent;
(12) an obligation on the licensee not to use the licensor's technology to construct facilities for third parties; this is without prejudice to the right of the licensee to increase the capacity of his facilities or to set up additional facilities for his own use on normal commercial terms, including the payment of additional royalties;
(13) an obligation on the licensee to supply only a limited quantity of the licensed product to a particular customer, where the licence was granted so that the customer might have a second source of supply inside the licensed territory; this provision shall also apply where the customer is the licensee, and the licence which was granted in order to provide a second source of supply provides that the customer is himself to manufacture the licensed products or to have them manufactured by a subcontractor;
(14) a reservation by the licensor of the right to exercise the rights conferred by a patent to oppose the exploitation of the technology by the licensee outside the licensed territory;
(15) a reservation by the licensor of the right to terminate the agreement if the licensee contests the secret or substantial nature of the licensed know-how or challenges the validity of licensed patents within the common market belonging to the licensor or undertakings connected with him;
(16) a reservation by the licensor of the right to terminate the licence agreement of a patent if the licensee raises the claim that such a patent is not necessary;
(17) an obligation on the licensee to use his best endeavours to manufacture and market the licensed product;
(18) a reservation by the licensor of the right to terminate the exclusivity granted to the licensee and to stop licensing improvements to him when the licensee enters into competition within the common market with the

licensor, with undertakings connected with the licensor or with other undertakings in respect of research and development, production, use or distribution of competing products, and to require the licensee to prove that the licensed know-how is not being used for the production of products and the provision of services other than those licensed.

2.  In the event that, because of particular circumstances, the clauses referred to in paragraph 1 fall within the scope of Article 85(1), they shall also be exempted even if they are not accompanied by any of the obligations exempted by Article 1.

3.  The exemption in paragraph 2 shall also apply where an agreement contains clauses of the types referred to in paragraph 1 but with a more limited scope than is permitted by that paragraph.

## Article 3

Article 1 and Article 2(2) shall not apply where—
  (1) one party is restricted in the determination of prices, components of prices or discounts for the licensed products;
  (2) one party is restricted from competing within the common market with the other party, with undertakings connected with the other party or with other undertakings in respect of research and development, production, use or distribution of competing products without prejudice to the provisions of Article 2(1)(17) and (18);
  (3) one or both of the parties are required without any objectively justified reason—
      (a) to refuse to meet orders from users or resellers in their respective territories who would market products in other territories within the common market;
      (b) to make it difficult for users or resellers to obtain the products from other resellers within the common market, and in particular to exercise intellectual property rights or take measures so as to prevent users or resellers from obtaining outside, or from putting on the market in the licensed territory products which have been lawfully put on the market within the common market by the licensor or with his consent;
      or do so as a result of a concerted practice between them;
  (4) the parties were already competing manufacturers before the grant of the licence and one of them is restricted, within the same technical field of use or within the same product market, as to the customers he may serve, in particular by being prohibited from supplying certain classes of user, employing certain forms of distribution or, with the aim of sharing customers, using certain types of packaging for the products, save as provided in Article 1(1)(7) and Article 2(1)(13);
  (5) the quantity of the licensed products one party may manufacture or sell or the number of operations exploiting the licensed technology he may carry out are subject to limitations, save as provided in Article (1)(8) and Article 2(1)(13);
  (6) the licensee is obliged to assign in whole or in part to the licensor rights to improvements to or new applications of the licensed technology;
  (7) the licensor is required, albeit in separate agreements or through automatic prolongation of the initial duration of the agreement by the inclusion of any new improvements, for a period exceeding that referred to in Article 1(2) and (3) not to license other undertakings to exploit the licensed technology

in the licensed territory, or a party is required for a period exceeding that
referred to in Article 1(2) and (3) or Article 1(4) not to exploit the licensed
technology in the territory of the other party or of other licensees.

## Article 4

1.    The exemption provided for in Articles 1 and 2 shall also apply to agreements
containing obligations restrictive of competition which are not covered by those
Articles and do not fall within the scope of Article 3, on condition that the agreements
in question are notified to the Commission in accordance with the provisions of
Articles 1, 2 and 3 of Regulation (EC) No 3385/94 and that the Commission does not
oppose such exemption within a period of four months.

2.    Paragraph 1 shall apply, in particular, where—
(a) the licensee is obliged at the time the agreement is entered into to accept
quality specifications or further licences or to procure goods or services
which are not necessary for a technically satisfactory exploitation of the
licensed technology or for ensuring that the production of the licensee
conforms to the quality standards that are respected by the licensor and
other licensees;
(b) the licensee is prohibited from contesting the secrecy or the substantiality
of the licensed know-how or from challenging the validity of patents
licensed within the common market belonging to the licensor or
undertakings connected with him.

3.    The period of four months referred to in paragraph 1 shall run from the date
on which the notification takes effect in accordance with Article 4 of Regulation (EC)
No 3385/94.

4.    The benefit of paragraphs 1 and 2 may be claimed for agreements notified
before the entry into force of this Regulation by submitting a communication to the
Commission referring expressly to this Article and to the notification. Paragraph 3 shall
apply *mutatis mutandis*.

5.    The Commission may oppose the exemption within a period of four months.
It shall oppose exemption if it receives a request to do so from a Member State within
two months of the transmission to the Member State of the notification referred to in
paragraph 1 or of the communication referred to in paragraph 4. This request must be
justified on the basis of considerations relating to the competition rules of the Treaty.

6.    The Commission may withdraw the opposition to the exemption at any time.
However, where the opposition was raised at the request of a Member State and this
request is maintained, it may be withdrawn only after consultation of the Advisory
Committee on Restrictive Practices and Dominant Positions.

7.    If the opposition is withdrawn because the undertakings concerned have shown
that the conditions of Article 85(3) are satisfied, the exemption shall apply from the date
of notification.

8.    If the opposition is withdrawn because the undertakings concerned have
amended the agreement so that the conditions of Article 85(3) are satisfied, the
exemption shall apply from the date on which the amendments take effect.

9.    If the Commission opposes exemption and the opposition is not withdrawn,
the effects of the notification shall be governed by the provisions of Regulation No 17.

**Article 5**

1.   This Regulation shall not apply to—
   (1) agreements between members of a patent or know-how pool which relate to the pooled technologies;
   (2) licensing agreements between competing undertakings which hold interests in a joint venture, or between one of them and the joint venture, if the licensing agreements relate to the activities of the joint venture;
   (3) agreements under which one party grants the other a patent and/or know-how licence and in exchange the other party, albeit in separate agreements or through connected undertakings, grants the first party a patent, trademark or know-how licence or exclusive sales rights, where the parties are competitors in relation to the products covered by those agreements;
   (4) licensing agreements containing provisions relating to intellectual property rights other than patents which are not ancillary;
   (5) agreements entered into solely for the purpose of sale.

2.   This Regulation shall nevertheless apply—
   (1) to agreements to which paragraph 1(2) applies, under which a parent undertaking grants the joint venture a patent or know-how licence, provided that the licensed products and the other goods and services of the participating undertakings which are considered by users to be interchangeable or substitutable in view of their characteristics, price and intended use represent—
      — in case of a licence limited to production, not more than 20%, and
      — in case of a licence covering production and distribution, not more than 10%;
   of the market for the licensed products and all interchangeable or substitutable goods and services;
   (2) to agreements to which paragraph 1(1) applies and to reciprocal licences within the meaning of paragraph 1(3), provided the parties are not subject to any territorial restriction within the common market with regard to the manufacture, use or putting on the market of the licensed products or to the use of the licensed or pooled technologies.

3.   This Regulation shall continue to apply where, for two consecutive financial years, the market shares in paragraph 2(1) are not exceeded by more than one-tenth; where that limit is exceeded, this Regulation shall continue to apply for a period of six months from the end of the year in which the limit was exceeded.

**Article 6**

This Regulation shall also apply to—
   (1) agreements where the licensor is not the holder of the know-how or the patentee, but is authorised by the holder or the patentee to grant a licence;
   (2) assignments of know-how, patents or both where the risk associated with exploitation remains with the assignor, in particular where the sum payable in consideration of the assignment is dependent on the turnover obtained by the assignee in respect of products made using the know-how or the patents, the quantity of such products manufactured or the number of operations carried out employing the know-how or the patents;
   (3) licensing agreements in which the rights or obligations of the licensor or the licensee are assumed by undertakings connected with them.

**Article 7**

The Commission may withdraw the benefit of this Regulation, pursuant to Article 7 of Regulation No 19/65/EEC, where it finds in a particular case that an agreement exempted by this Regulation nevertheless has certain effects which are incompatible with the conditions laid down in Article 85(3) of the Treaty, and in particular where—

    (1)  the effect of the agreement is to prevent the licensed products from being exposed to effective competition in the licensed territory from identical goods or services or from goods or services considered by users as interchangeable or substitutable in view of their characteristics, price and intended use, which may in particular occur where the licensee's market share exceeds 40%;

    (2)  without prejudice to Article 1(1)(6), the licensee refuses, without any objectively justified reason, to meet unsolicited orders from users or resellers in the territory of other licensees;

    (3)  the parties—

        (a)  without any objectively justified reason, refuse to meet orders from users or resellers in their respective territories who would market the products in other territories within the common market; or

        (b)  make it difficult for users or resellers to obtain the products from other resellers within the common market, and in particular where they exercise intellectual property rights or take measures so as to prevent resellers or users from obtaining outside, or from putting on the market in the licensed territory products which have been lawfully put on the market within the common market by the licensor or with his consent;

    (4)  the parties were competing manufacturers at the date of the grant of the licence and obligations on the licensee to produce a minimum quantity or to use his best endeavours as referred to in Article 2(1), (9) and (17) respectively have the effect of preventing the licensee from using competing technologies.

**Article 8**

1.      For purposes of this Regulation—

    (a)  patent applications;

    (b)  utility models;

    (c)  applications for registration of utility models;

    (d)  topographies of semiconductor products;

    (e)  *certificats d'utilitè* and *certificats d'addition* under French law;

    (f)  applications for *certificats d'utilitè* and *certificats d'addition* under French law;

    (g)  supplementary protection certificates for medicinal products or other products for which such supplementary protection certificates may be obtained;

    (h)  plant breeder's certificates,

shall be deemed to be patents.

2.    This Regulation shall also apply to agreements relating to the exploitation of an invention if an application within the meaning of paragraph 1 is made in respect of the invention for a licensed territory after the date when the agreements were entered into but within the time-limits set by the national law or the international convention to be applied.

3.     This Regulation shall furthermore apply to pure patent or know-how licensing agreements or to mixed agreements whose initial duration is automatically prolonged by the inclusion of any new improvements, whether patented or not, communicated by the licensor, provided that the licensee has the right to refuse such improvements or each party has the right to terminate the agreement at the expiry of the initial term of an agreement and at least every three years thereafter.

### Article 9

1.     Information acquired pursuant to Article 4 shall be used only for the purposes of this Regulation.

2.     The Commission and the authorities of the Member States, their officials and other servants shall not disclose information acquired by them pursuant to this Regulation of the kind covered by the obligation of professional secrecy.

3.     The provisions of paragraphs 1 and 2 shall not prevent publication of general information or surveys which do not contain information relating to particular undertakings or associations of undertakings.

### Article 10

For purposes of this Regulation—

    (1)  'know-how' means a body of technical information that is secret, substantial and identified in any appropriate form;

    (2)  'secret' means that the know-how package as a body or in the precise configuration and assembly of its components is not generally known or easily accessible, so that part of its value consists in the lead which the licensee gains when it is communicated to him; it is not limited to the narrow sense that each individual component of the know-how should be totally unknown or unobtainable outside the licensor's business;

    (3)  'substantial' means that the know-how includes information which must be useful, ie can reasonably be expected at the date of conclusion of the agreement to be capable of improving the competitive position of the licensee, for example by helping him to enter a new market or giving him an advantage in competition with other manufacturers or providers of services who do not have access to the licensed secret know-how or other comparable secret know-how;

    (4)  'identified' means that the know-how is described or recorded in such a manner as to make it possible to verify that it satisfies the criteria of secrecy and substantiality and to ensure that the licensee is not unduly restricted in his exploitation of his own technology, to be identified the know-how can either be set out in the licence agreement or in a separate document or recorded in any other appropriate form at the latest when the know-how is transferred or shortly thereafter, provided that the separate document or other record can be made available if the need arises;

    (5)  'necessary patents' are patents where a licence under the patent is necessary for the putting into effect of the licensed technology in so far as, in the absence of such a licence, the realisation of the licensed technology would not be possible or would by possible only to a lesser extent or in more difficult or costly conditions. Such patents must therefore be of technical, legal or economic interest to the licensee;

    (6)  'licensing agreement' means pure patent licensing agreements and pure know-how licensing agreements as well as mixed patent and know-how licensing agreements;

(7) 'licensed technology' means the initial manufacturing know-how or the necessary product and process patents, or both, existing at the time the first licensing agreement is concluded, and improvements subsequently made to the know-how or patents, irrespective of whether and to what extent they are exploited by the parties or by other licensees;

(8) 'the licensed products' are goods or services the production or provision of which requires the use of the licensed technology;

(9) 'the licensee's market share' means the proportion which the licensed products and other goods or services provided by the licensee, which are considered by users to be interchangeable or substitutable for the licensed products in view of their characteristics, price and intended use, represent the entire market for the licensed products and all other interchangeable or substitutable goods and services in the common market or a substantial part of it;

(10) 'exploitation' refers to any use of the licensed technology in particular in the production, active or passive sales in a territory even if not coupled with manufacture in that territory, or leasing of the licensed products;

(11) 'the licensed territory' is the territory covering all or at least part of the common market where the licensee is entitled to exploit the licensed technology;

(12) 'territory of the licensor' means territories in which the licensor has not granted any licences for patents and/or know-how covered by the licensing agreement;

(13) 'parallel patents' means patents which, in spite of the divergences which remain in the absence of any unification of national rules concerning industrial property, protect the same invention in various Member States;

(14) 'connected undertakings' means—

    (a) undertakings in which a party to the agreement, directly or indirectly—
- owns more than half the capital or business assets, or
- has the power to exercise more than half the voting rights, or
- has the power to appoint more than half the members of the supervisory board, board of directors or bodies legally representing the undertaking, or
- has the right to manage the affairs of the undertaking;

    (b) undertakings which, directly or indirectly, have in or over a party to the agreement the rights or powers listed in (a);

    (c) undertakings in which an undertaking referred to in (b), directly or indirectly, has the rights or powers listed in (a);

    (d) undertakings in which the parties to the agreement or undertakings connected with them jointly have the rights or powers listed in (a): such jointly controlled undertakings are considered to be connected with each of the parties to the agreement;

(15) 'ancillary provisions' are provisions relating to the exploitation of intellectual property rights other than patents, which contain no obligations restrictive of competition other than those also attached to the licensed know-how or patents and exempted under this Regulation;

(16) 'obligation' means both contractual obligation and a concerted practice;

(17) 'competing manufacturers' or manufacturers of 'competing products' means manufacturers who sell products which, in view of their characteristics, price and intended use, are considered by users to be interchangeable or substitutable for the licensed products.

**Article 11**

1.    Regulation (EEC) No 556/89 is hereby repealed with effect from 1 April 1996.

2.    Regulation (EEC) No 2349/84 shall continue to apply until 31 March 1996.

3.    The prohibition in Article 85(1) of the Treaty shall not apply to agreements in force on 31 March 1996 which fulfil the exemption requirements laid down by Regulation (EEC) No 2349/84 or (EEC) No 556/89.

**Article 12**

1.    The Commission shall undertake regular assessments of the application of this Regulation, and in particular of the opposition procedure provided for in Article 4.

2.    The Commission shall draw up a report on the operation of this Regulation before the end of the fourth year following its entry into force and shall, on that basis, assess whether any adaptation of the Regulation is desirable.

**Article 13**

This Regulation shall enter into force on 1 April 1996.

It shall apply until 31 March 2006.

Article 11(2) of this Regulation shall, however, enter into force on 1 January 1996.

This Regulation shall be binding in its entirety and directly applicable in all Member States.

### SOCIAL POLICY: EQUAL PAY AND TREATMENT

# COUNCIL DIRECTIVE

of 10 February 1975

## on the approximation of the laws of the Member States relating to the application of the principle of equal pay for men and women

### (75/117/EEC)

NOTES

Date of publication in OJ: OJ L45, 19.2.75, p 19.

## Article 1

The principle of equal pay for men and women outlined in Article 119 of the Treaty, hereinafter called "principle of equal pay", means, for the same work or for work to which equal value is attributed, the elimination of all discrimination on grounds of sex with regard to all aspects and conditions of remuneration.

In particular, where a job classification system is used for determining pay, it must be based on the same criteria for both men and women and so drawn up as to exclude any discrimination on grounds of sex.

## Article 2

Member States shall introduce into their national legal systems such measures as are necessary to enable all employees who consider themselves wronged by failure to apply the principle of equal pay to pursue their claims by judicial process after possible recourse to other competent authorities.

## Article 3

Member States shall abolish all discrimination between men and women arising from laws, regulations or administrative provisions which is contrary to the principle of equal pay.

## Article 4

Member States shall take the necessary measures to ensure that provisions appearing in collective agreements, wage scales, wage agreements or individual contracts of employment which are contrary to the principle of equal pay shall be, or may be declared, null and void or may be amended.

## Article 5

Member States shall take the necessary measures to protect employees against dismissal by the employer as a reaction to a complaint within the undertaking or to any legal proceedings aimed at enforcing compliance with the principle of equal pay.

## Article 6

Member States shall, in accordance with their national circumstances and legal systems, take the measures necessary to ensure that the principle of equal pay is applied. They shall see that effective means are available to take care that this principle is observed.

### Article 7

Member States shall take care that the provisions adopted pursuant to this Directive together with the relevant provisions already in force, are brought to the attention of employees by all appropriate means, for example at their place of employment.

# COUNCIL DIRECTIVE

of 9 February 1976

### on the implementation of the principle of equal treatment for men and women as regards access to employment, vocational training and promotion, and working conditions

### (76/207/EEC)

NOTES

Date of publication in OJ: OJ L39, 14.2.76, p 40.

### Article 1

1.    The purpose of this Directive is to put into effect in the Member States the principle of equal treatment for men and women as regards access to employment, including promotion, and to vocational training and as regards working conditions and, on the conditions referred to in paragraph 2, social security. This principle is hereinafter referred to as "the principle of equal treatment".

2.    With a view to ensuring the progressive implementation of the principle of equal treatment in matters of social security, the Council, acting on a proposal from the Commission, will adopt provisions defining its substance, its scope and the arrangements for its application.

### Article 2

1.    For the purposes of the following provisions, the principle of equal treatment shall mean that there shall be no discrimination whatsoever on grounds of sex either directly or indirectly by reference in particular to marital or family status.

2.    This Directive shall be without prejudice to the right of Member States to exclude from its field of application those occupational activities and, where appropriate, the training leading thereto, for which, by reason of their nature of the context in which they are carried out, the sex of the worker constitutes a determining factor.

3.    This Directive shall be without prejudice to provisions concerning the protection of women, particularly as regards pregnancy and maternity.

4.    This Directive shall be without prejudice to measures to promote equal opportunity for men and women, in particular by removing existing inequalities which affect women's opportunities in the areas referred to in Article 1(1).

## Article 3

1.    Application of the principle of equal treatment means that there shall be no discrimination whatsoever on grounds of sex in the conditions, including selection criteria, for access to all jobs or posts, whatever the sector or branch of activity, and to all levels of the occupational hierarchy—

2.    To this end, Member States shall take the measures necessary to ensure that—
   (a)  any laws, regulations and administrative provisions contrary to the principle of equal treatment shall be abolished;
   (b)  any provisions contrary to the principle of equal treatment which are included in collective agreements, individual contracts of employment, internal rules of undertakings, or in rules governing the independent occupations and professions shall be, or may be declared, null and void or may be amended;
   (c)  those laws, regulations and administrative provisions contrary to the principle of equal treatment when the concern for protection which originally inspired them is no longer well founded shall be revised; and that where similar provisions are included in collective agreements labour and management shall be requested to undertake the desired revision.

## Article 4

Application of the principle of equal treatment with regard to access to all types and to all levels, of vocational guidance, vocational training, advanced vocational training and retraining, means that Member States shall take all necessary measures to ensure that—
   (a)  any laws, regulations and administrative provisions contrary to the principle of equal treatment shall be abolished;
   (b)  any provisions contrary to the principle of equal treatment which are included in collective agreements, individual contracts of employment, internal rules of undertakings or in rules governing the independent occupations and professions shall be, or may be declared, null and void or may be amended;
   (c)  without prejudice to the freedom granted in certain Member States to certain private training establishments, vocational guidance, vocational training, advanced vocational training and retraining shall be accessible on the basis of the same criteria and at the same levels without any discrimination on grounds of sex.

## Article 5

1.    Application of the principle of equal treatment with regard to working conditions, including the conditions governing dismissal, means that men and women shall be guaranteed the same conditions without discrimination on grounds of sex.

2.    To this end, Member States shall take the measures necessary to ensure that—
   (a)  any laws, regulations and administrative provisions contrary to the principle of equal treatment shall be abolished;
   (b)  any provisions contrary to the principle of equal treatment which are included in collective agreements, individual contracts of employment, internal rules of undertakings or in rules governing the independents occupations and professions shall be, or may be declared, null and void or may be amended;

(c) those laws, regulations and administrative provisions contrary to the principle of equal treatment when the concern for protection which originally inspired them is no longer well founded shall be revised; and that where similar provisions are included in collective agreements labour and management shall be requested to undertake the desired revision.

**Article 6**

Member States shall introduce into their national legal systems such measures as are necessary to enable all persons who consider themselves wronged by failure to apply to them the principle of equal treatment within the meaning of Articles 3, 4 and 5 to pursue their claims by judicial process after possible recourse to other competent authorities.

**Article 7**

Member States shall take the necessary measures to protect employees against dismissal by the employer as a reaction to a complaint within the undertaking or to any legal proceedings aimed at enforcing compliance with the principle of equal treatment.

# COUNCIL DIRECTIVE

of 19 December 1978

**on the progressive implementation of the principle of equal treatment for men and women in matters of social security**

**(79/7/EEC)**

NOTES

Date of publication in OJ: OJ L6, 10.1.79, p 24.

**Article 1**

The purpose of this Directive is the progressive implementation, in the field of social security and other elements of social protection provided for in Article 3, of the principle of equal treatment for men and women in matters of social security, hereinafter referred to as 'the principle of equal treatment'.

**Article 2**

This Directive shall apply to the working population—including self-employed persons, workers and self-employed persons whose activity is interrupted by illness, accident or involuntary unemployment and persons seeking employment—and to retired or invalided workers and self-employed persons.

**Article 3**

1.     This Directive shall apply to—
        (a) statutory schemes which provide protection against the following risks—
           — sickness,
           — invalidity,

— old age,
— accidents at work and occupational diseases,
— unemployment;
(b) social assistance, in so far as it is intended to supplement or replace the schemes referred to in (a).

2. This Directive shall not apply to the provisions concerning survivors' benefits nor to those concerning family benefits, except in the case of family benefits granted by way of increases of benefits due in respect of the risks referred to in paragraph 1(a).

3. With a view to ensuring implementation of the principle of equal treatment in occupational schemes, the Council, acting on a proposal from the Commission, will adopt provisions defining its substance, its scope and the arrangements for its application.

## Article 4

1. The principle of equal treatment means that there shall be no discrimination whatsoever on ground of sex either directly, or indirectly by reference in particular to marital or family status, in particular as concerns—
— the scope of the schemes and the conditions of access thereto,
— the obligation to contribute and the calculation of contributions,
— the calculation of benefits including increases due in respect of a spouse and for dependants and the conditions governing the duration and retention of entitlement to benefits.

2. The principle of equal treatment shall be without prejudice to the provisions relating to the protection of women on the grounds of maternity.

## Article 5

Member States shall take the measures necessary to ensure that any laws, regulations and administrative provisions contrary to the principle of equal treatment are abolished.

## Article 6

Member States shall introduce into their national legal systems such measures as are necessary to enable all persons who consider themselves wronged by failure to apply the principle of equal treatment to pursue their claims by judicial process, possibly after recourse to other competent authorities.

## Article 7

1. This Directive shall be without prejudice to the right of Member States to exclude from its scope—
(a) the determination of pensionable age for the purposes of granting old-age and retirement pensions and the possible consequences thereof for other benefits;
(b) advantages in respect of old-age pension schemes granted to persons who have brought up children; the acquisition of benefit entitlements following periods of interruption of employment due to the bringing up of children;
(c) the granting of old-age or invalidity benefit entitlements by virtue of the derived entitlements of a wife;
(d) the granting of increases of long-term invalidity, old-age, accidents at work and occupational disease benefits for a dependent wife;

(e) the consequences of the exercise, before the adoption of this Directive, of a right of option not to acquire rights to incur obligations under a statutory scheme.

2.    Member States shall periodically examine matters excluded under paragraph 1 in order to ascertain, in the light of social developments in the matter concerned, whether there is justification for maintaining the exclusions concerned.

### Article 8

1.    Member States shall bring into force the laws, regulations and administrative provisions necessary to comply with this Directive within six years of its notification. They shall immediately inform the Commission thereof.

2.    Member States shall communicate to the Commission the text of laws, regulations and administrative provisions which they adopt in the field covered by this Directive, including measures adopted pursuant to Article 7(2).

They shall inform the Commission of their reasons for maintaining any existing provisions on the matters referred to in Article 7(1) and of the possibilities for reviewing them at a later date.

### Article 9

Within seven years of notification of this Directive, Member States shall forward all information necessary to the Commission to enable it to draw up a report on the application of this Directive for submission to the Council and to propose such further measures as may be required for the implementation of the principle of equal treatment.

### Article 10

This Directive is addressed to the Member States.

# COUNCIL DIRECTIVE

of 24 July 1986

## on the implementation of the principle of equal treatment for men and women in occupational social security schemes

### (86/378/EEC)

NOTES

Date of publication in OJ: OJ L225, 12.8.86, p 40.

### Article 1

The object of this Directive is to implement, in occupational social security schemes, the principle of equal treatment for men and women, hereinafter referred to as "the principle of equal treatment".

### [Article 2

1.    "Occupational social security schemes" means schemes not governed by Directive 79/7/EEC whose purpose is to provide workers, whether employees or self-

employed, in an undertaking or group of undertakings, area of economic activity, occupational sector or group of such sectors with benefits intended to supplement the benefits provided by statutory social security schemes or to replace them, whether membership of such schemes is compulsory or optional.

2.     This Directive does not apply to—
   (a)  individual contracts for self-employed workers,
   (b)  schemes for self-employed workers having only one member,
   (c)  insurance contracts to which the employer is not a party, in the case of salaried workers;
   (d)  optional provisions of occupational schemes offered to participants individually to guarantee them—
         — either additional benefits, or
         — a choice of date on which the normal benefits for self-employed workers will start, or a choice between several benefits;
   (e)  occupational schemes in so far as benefits are financed by contributions paid by workers on a voluntary basis.

3.     This Directive does not preclude an employer granting to persons who have already reached the retirement age for the purposes of granting a pension by virtue of an occupational scheme, but who have not yet reached the retirement age for the purposes of granting a statutory retirement pension, a pension supplement, the aim of which is to make equal or more nearly equal the overall amount of benefit paid to these persons in relation to the amount paid to persons of the other sex in the same situation who have already reached the statutory retirement age, until the persons benefiting from the supplement reach the statutory retirement age.]

NOTES
Substituted by Council Directive 96/97/EC, Art 1(1).

**[Article 3**

This Directive shall apply to members of the working population, including self-employed persons, persons whose activity is interrupted by illness, maternity, accident or involuntary unemployment and persons seeking employment, to retired and disabled workers and to those claiming under them, in accordance with national law and/or practice.]

NOTES
Substituted by Council Directive 96/97/EC, Art 1(2).

**Article 4**

This Directive shall apply to—
   (a)  occupational schemes which provide protection against the following risks—
         — sickness,
         — invalidity,
         — old age, including early retirement,
         — industrial accidents and occupational diseases,
         — unemployment;
   (b)  occupational schemes which provide for other social benefits, in cash or in kind, and in particular survivors' benefits and family allowances, if such

benefits are accorded to employed persons and thus constitute a consideration paid by the employer to the worker by reason of the latter's employment.

## Article 5

1.    Under the conditions laid down in the following provisions, the principle of equal treatment implies that there shall be no discrimination on the basis of sex, either directly or indirectly, by reference in particular to marital or family status, especially as regards—
— the scope of the schemes and the conditions of access to them;
— the obligation to contribute and the calculation of contributions;
— the calculation of benefits, including supplementary benefits due in respect of a spouse or dependants, and the conditions governing the duration and retention of entitlement to benefits.

2.    The principle of equal treatment shall not prejudice the provisions relating to the protection of women by reason of maternity.

## [Article 6

1.    Provisions contrary to the principle of equal treatment shall include those based on sex, either directly or indirectly, in particular by reference to marital or family status, for—
(a) determining the persons who may participate in an occupational scheme;
(b) fixing the compulsory or optional nature of participation in an occupational scheme;
(c) laying down different rules as regards the age of entry into the scheme or the minimum period of employment or membership of the scheme required to obtain the benefits thereof;
(d) laying down different rules, except as provided for in points (h) and (i), for the reimbursement of contributions where a worker leaves a scheme without having fulfilled the conditions guaranteeing a deferred right to long-term benefits;
(e) setting different conditions for the granting of benefits or restricting such benefits to workers of one or other of the sexes;
(f) fixing different retirement ages;
(g) suspending the retention or acquisition of rights during periods of maternity leave or leave for family reasons which are granted by law or agreement and are paid by the employer;
(h) setting different levels of benefit, except in so far as may be necessary to take account of actuarial calculation factors which differ according to sex in the case of contribution-defined schemes.
In the case of funded defined-benefit schemes, certain elements (examples of which are annexed) may be unequal where the inequality of the amounts results from the effects of the use of the actuarial factors differing according to sex at the time when the scheme's funding is implemented;
(i) setting different levels for worker's contributions;
setting different levels for employer's contributions, except—
— in the case of defined-contribution schemes if the aim is to equalize the amount of the final benefits or to make them more nearly equal for both sexes,

— in the case of funded defined-benefit schemes where the employer's contributions are intended to cover the adequacy of the funds necessary to cover the cost of the benefits defined,

(j) laying down different standards or standards applicable only to workers of a specified sex, except as provided for in points (h) and (i), as regards the guarantee or retention of entitlement to deferred benefits when a worker leaves a scheme.

2.   Where the granting of benefits within the scope of this Directive is left to the discretion of the scheme's management bodies, the latter must comply with the principle of equal treatment.]

NOTES
Substituted by Council Directive 96/97/EC, Art 1(3).

## Article 7

Member States shall take all necessary steps to ensure that—

(a) provisions contrary to the principle of equal treatment in legally compulsory collective agreements, staff rules of undertakings or any other arrangements relating to occupational schemes are null and void, or may be declared null and void or amended;

(b) schemes containing such provisions may not be approved or extended by administrative measures.

## [Article 8

1.   Member States shall take the necessary steps to ensure that the provisions of occupational schemes for self-employed workers contrary to the principle of equal treatment are revised with effect from 1 January 1993 at the latest.

2.   This Directive shall not preclude rights and obligations relating to a period of membership of an occupational scheme prior to revision of that scheme from remaining subject to the provisions of the scheme in force during that period.]

NOTES
Substituted by Council Directive 96/97/EC, Art 1(4).

## [Article 9

As regards schemes for self-employed workers, Member States may defer compulsory application of the principle of equal treatment with regard to—

(a) determination of pensionable age for the granting of old-age or retirement pensions, and the possible implications for other benefits—

— either until the date on which such equality is achieved in statutory schemes,

— or, at the latest, until such equality is prescribed by a directive.

(b) survivors' pensions until Community law establishes the principle of equal treatment in statutory social security schemes in that regard;

(c) the application of the first subparagraph of point (i) of Article 6(1) to take account of the different actuarial calculation factors, at the latest until 1 January 1999.]

NOTES
Substituted by Council Directive 96/97/EC, Art 1(5).

## [Article 9a

Where men and women may claim a flexible pensionable age under the same conditions, this shall not be deemed to be incompatible with this Directive.]

NOTES
Inserted by Council Directive 96/97/EC, Art 1(6).

## Article 10

Member States shall introduce into their national legal systems such measures as are necessary to enable all persons who consider themselves injured by failure to apply the principle of equal treatment to pursue their claims before the courts, possibly after bringing the matters before other competent authorities.

## Article 11

Member States shall take all the necessary steps to protect worker against dismissal where this constitutes a response on the part of the employer to a complaint made at undertaking level or to the institution of legal proceedings aimed at enforcing compliance with the principle of equal treatment.

## Article 12

1.      Member States shall bring into force such laws, regulations and administrative provisions as are necessary in order to comply with this Directive at the latest three years after notification thereof. They shall immediately inform the Commission thereof.

2.      Member States shall communicate to the Commission at the latest five years after notification of this Directive all information necessary to enable the Commission to draw up a report on the application of this Directive for submission to the Council.

## Article 13

This Directive is addressed to the Member States.

## [ANNEX

Examples of elements which may be unequal, in respect of funded defined-benefit schemes, as referred to in Article 6(h)—
— conversion into a capital sum of part of a periodic pension,
— transfer of pension rights,
— a reversionary pension payable to a dependant in return for the surrender of part of a pension,
— a reduced pension where the worker opts to take early retirement.]

NOTES
Added by Council Directive 96/97/EC, Art 1(7).

# COUNCIL DIRECTIVE

of 11 December 1986

**on the application of the principle of equal treatment between men and women engaged in an activity, including agriculture, in a self-employed capacity, and on the protection of self-employed women during pregnancy and motherhood**

**(86/613/EEC)**

NOTES

Date of publication in OJ: OJ L 359, 19.12.86, p 56.

## SECTION I

*Aims and scope*

### Article 1

The purpose of this Directive is to ensure, in accordance with the following provisions, application in the Member States of the principle of equal treatment as between men and women engaged in an activity in a self-employed capacity, or contributing to the pursuit of such an activity, as regards those aspects not covered by Directives 76/207/EEC and 79/7/EEC.

### Article 2

This Directive covers—
    (a)  self-employed workers, ie all persons pursuing a gainful activity for their own account, under the conditions laid down by national law, including farmers and members of the liberal professions;
    (b)  their spouses, not being employees or partners, where they habitually, under the conditions laid down by national law, participate in the activities of the self-employed worker and perform the same tasks or ancillary tasks.

### Article 3

For the purposes of this Directive the principle of equal treatment implies the absence of all discrimination on grounds of sex, either directly or indirectly, by reference in particular to marital or family status.

## SECTION II

*Equal treatment between self-employed male and female workers—position of the spouses without professional status of self-employed workers—protection of self-employed workers or wives of self-employed workers during pregnancy and motherhood*

### Article 4

As regards self-employed persons, Member States shall take the measures necessary to ensure the elimination of all provisions which are contrary to the principle of equal treatment as defined in Directive 76/207/EEC, especially in respect of the establishment, equipment or extension of a business or the launching or extension of any other form of self-employed activity including financial facilities.

### Article 5

Without prejudice to the specific conditions for access to certain activities which apply equally to both sexes, Member States shall take the measures necessary to ensure that the conditions for the formation of a company between spouses are not more restrictive than the conditions for the formation of a company between unmarried persons.

### Article 6

Where a contributory social security system for self-employed workers exists in a Member State, that Member State shall take the necessary measures to enable the spouses referred to in Article 2(b) who are not protected under the self-employed worker's social security scheme to join a contributory social security scheme voluntarily.

### Article 7

Member States shall undertake to examine under what conditions recognition of the work of the spouses referred to in Article 2(b) may be encouraged and, in the light of such examination, consider any appropriate steps for encouraging such recognition.

### Article 8

Member States shall undertake to examine whether, and under what conditions, female self-employed workers and the wives of self-employed workers may, during interruptions in their occupational activity owing to pregnancy or motherhood,
- have access to services supplying temporary replacements or existing national social services, or
- be entitled to cash benefits under a social security scheme or under any other public social protection system.

## SECTION III

*General and final provisions*

### Article 9

Member States shall introduce into their national legal systems such measures as are necessary to enable all persons who consider themselves wronged by failure to apply the principle of equal treatment in self-employed activities to pursue their claims by judicial process, possibly after recourse to other competent authorities.

### Article 10

Member States shall ensure that the measures adopted pursuant to this Directive, together with the relevant provisions already in force, are brought to the attention of bodies representing self-employed workers and vocational training centres.

### Article 11

The Council shall review this Directive, on a proposal from the Commission, before 1 July 1993.

### Article 12

1.    Member States shall bring into force the laws, regulations and administrative provisions necessary to comply with this Directive not later than 30 June 1989.

However, if a Member State which, in order to comply with Article 5 of this Directive, has to amend its legislation on matrimonial rights and obligations, the date on which such Member State must comply with Article 5 shall be 30 June 1991.

2.   Member States shall immediately inform the Commission of the measures taken to comply with this Directive.

### Article 13

Member States shall forward to the Commission, not later than 30 June 1991, all the information necessary to enable it to draw up a report on the application of this Directive for submission to the Council.

### Article 14

This Directive is addressed to the Member States.

# COUNCIL DIRECTIVE

of 19 October 1992

**on the introduction of measures to encourage improvements in the safety and health of pregnant workers and workers who have recently given birth or are breastfeeding (tenth individual Directive within the meaning of Article 16(1) of Directive 89/391)**

**(92/85/EEC)**

NOTES

Date of publication in OJ: OJ L348, 28.11.92, p 1.

THE COUNCIL OF THE EUROPEAN COMMUNITIES,

Having regard to the Treaty establishing the European Economic Community, and in particular Article 118a thereof,

Having regard to the proposal from the Commission, drawn up after consultation with the Advisory Committee on Safety, Hygiene and Health Protection at work,

In co-operation with the European Parliament,

Having regard to the opinion of the Economic and Social Committee,

Whereas Article 118a of the Treaty provides that the Council shall adopt, by means of directives, minimum requirements for encouraging improvements, especially in the working environment, to protect the safety and health of workers;

Whereas this Directive does not justify any reduction in levels of protection already achieved in individual Member States, the Member States being committed, under the Treaty, to encouraging improvements in conditions in this area and to harmonising conditions while maintaining the improvements made;

Whereas, under the terms of Article 118a of the Treaty, the said directives are to avoid imposing administrative, financial and legal constraints in a way which would hold back the creation and development of small and medium-sized undertakings;

Whereas, pursuant to Decision 74/325/EEC, as last amended by the 1985 Act of Accession, the Advisory Committee on Safety, Hygiene and Health Protection at Work is consulted by the Commission on the drafting of proposals in this field;

Whereas the Community Charter of the fundamental social rights of workers, adopted at the Strasbourg European Council on 9 December 1989 by the Heads of State or Government of 11 Member States, lays down, in paragraph 19 in particular, that—

'Every worker must enjoy satisfactory health and safety conditions in his working environment. Appropriate measures must be taken in order to achieve further harmonisation of conditions in this area while maintaining the improvements made';

Whereas the Commission, in its action programme for the implementation of the Community Charter of the fundamental social rights of workers, has included among its aims the adoption by the Council of a Directive on the protection of pregnant women at work;

Whereas Article 15 of Council Directive 89/391/EEC of 12 June 1989 on the introduction of measures to encourage improvements in the safety and health of workers at work provides that particularly sensitive risk groups must be protected against the dangers which specifically affect them;

Whereas pregnant workers, workers who have been recently given birth or who are breastfeeding must be considered a specific risk group in many respects, and measures must be taken with regard to their safety and health;

Whereas the protection of the safety and health of pregnant workers, workers who have recently given birth or workers who are breastfeeding should not treat women on the labour market unfavourably nor work to the detriment of directives concerning equal treatment for men and women;

Whereas some types of activities may pose a specific risk, for pregnant workers, workers who have recently given birth or workers who are breastfeeding, of exposure to dangerous agents, processes or working conditions; whereas such risks must therefore be assessed and the result of such assessment communicated to female workers and/or their representatives;

Whereas, further, should the result of this assessment reveal the existence of a risk to the safety or health of the female worker, provision must be made for such worker to be protected;

Whereas pregnant workers and workers who are breastfeeding must not engage in activities which have been assessed as revealing a risk of exposure, jeopardising safety and health, to certain particularly dangerous agents or working conditions;

Whereas provision should be made for pregnant workers, workers who have recently given birth or workers who are breastfeeding not to be required to work at night where such provision is necessary from the point of view of their safety and health;

Whereas the vulnerability of pregnant workers, workers who have recently given birth or who are breastfeeding makes it necessary for them to be granted the right to maternity leave of at least 14 continuous weeks, allocated before and/or after confinement, and renders necessary the compulsory nature of maternity leave of at least two weeks, allocated before and/or after confinement;

Whereas the risk of dismissal for reasons associated with their condition may have harmful effects on the physical and mental state of pregnant workers, workers who have recently given birth or who are breastfeeding; whereas provision should be made for such dismissal to be prohibited;

Whereas measures for the organisation of work concerning the protection of the health of pregnant workers, workers who have recently given birth or workers who are breastfeeding would serve no purpose unless accompanied by the maintenance of rights linked to the employment contract, including maintenance of payment and/or entitlement to an adequate allowance;

Whereas, moreover, provision concerning maternity leave would also serve no purpose unless accompanied by the maintenance of rights linked to the employment contract and/or entitlement to an adequate allowance;

Whereas the concept of an adequate allowance in the case of maternity leave must be regarded as a technical point of reference with a view to fixing the minimum level of protection and should in no circumstances be interpreted as suggesting an analogy between pregnancy and illness.

HAS ADOPTED THIS DIRECTIVE—

# SECTION I
# PURPOSE AND DEFINITIONS

## Article 1

## Purpose

1.    The purpose of this Directive, which is the tenth individual Directive within the meaning of Article 16(1) of Directive 89/391/EEC, is to implement measures to

encourage improvements in the safety and health at work of pregnant workers and workers who have recently given birth or who are breastfeeding.

2.      The provisions of Directive 89/391/EEC, except for Article 2(2) thereof, shall apply in full to the whole area covered by paragraph 1, without prejudice to any more stringent and/or specific provisions contained in this Directive.

3.      This Directive may not have the effect of reducing the level of protection afforded to pregnant workers, workers who have recently given birth or who are breastfeeding as compared with the situation which exists in each Member State on the date on which this Directive is adopted.

## Article 2

### Definitions

For the purposes of this Directive—

(a) *pregnant worker* shall mean a pregnant worker who informs her employer of her condition, in accordance with national legislation and/or national practice;

(b) *worker who has recently given birth* shall mean a worker who has recently given birth within the meaning of national legislation and/or national practice and who informs her employer of her condition, in accordance with that legislation and/or practice;

(c) *worker who is breastfeeding* shall mean a worker who is breastfeeding within the meaning of national legislation and/or national practice and who informs her employer of her condition, in accordance with that legislation and/or practice.

# SECTION II
# GENERAL PROVISIONS

## Article 3

### Guidelines

1.      In consultation with the Member States and assisted by the Advisory Committee on Safety, Hygiene and Health Protection at Work, the Commission shall draw up guidelines on the assessment of the chemical, physical and biological agents and industrial process considered hazardous for the safety or health of workers within the meaning of Article 2.

The guidelines referred to in the first subparagraph shall also cover movements and postures, mental and physical fatigue and other types of physical and mental stress connected with the work done by workers within the meaning of Article 2.

2.      The purpose of the guidelines referred to in paragraph 1 is to serve as a basis for the assessment referred to in Article 4 (1).

To this end, Member States shall bring these guidelines to the attention of all employers and all female workers and/or their representatives in the respective Member State.

## Article 4

### Assessment and information

1.      For all activities liable to involve a specific risk of exposure to the agents, processes or working conditions of which a non-exhaustive list is given in Annex 1,

the employer shall assess the nature, degree and duration of exposure, in the undertaking and/or establishment concerned, or workers within the meaning of Article 2, either directly or by way of the protective and preventative services referred to in Article 7 of Directive 89/391/EEC, in order to—

    — assess any risks to the safety or health and any possible effect on the pregnancies or breastfeeding of workers within the meaning of Article 2,

    — decide what measures should be taken.

2.    Without prejudice to Article 10 of Directive 89/391/EEC, workers within the meaning of Article 2 and workers likely to be in one of the situations referred to in Article 2 in the undertaking and/or establishment concerned and/or their representatives shall be informed of the results of the assessment referred to in paragraph 1 and of all measures to be taken concerning health and safety at work.

## Article 5

### Action further to the results of the assessment

1.    Without prejudice to Article 6 of Directive 89/391/EEC, if the results of the assessment referred to in Article 4(1) reveal a risk to the safety or health or an effect on the pregnancy or breastfeeding of a worker within the meaning of Article 2, the employer shall take the necessary measures to ensure that, by temporarily adjusting the working conditions and/or the working hours of the worker concerned, the exposure of that worker to such risks is avoided.

2.    If the adjustment of her working conditions and/or working hours is not technically and/or objectively feasible, or cannot reasonably be required on duly substantiated grounds, the employer shall take the necessary measures to move the worker concerned to another job.

3.    If moving her to another job is not technically and/or objectively feasible or cannot reasonably be required on duly substantiated grounds, the worker concerned shall be granted leave in accordance with national legislation and/or national practice for the whole of the period necessary to protect her safety or health.

4.    The provisions of this Article shall apply *mutatis mutandis* to the case where a worker pursuing an activity which is forbidden pursuant to Article 6 becomes pregnant or starts breastfeeding and informs her employer thereof.

## Article 6

### Cases in which exposure is prohibited

In addition to the general provisions concerning the protection of workers, in particular those relating to the limit values for occupational exposure—

    1.  pregnant workers within the meaning of Article 2(a) may under no circumstances be obliged to perform duties for which the assessment has revealed a risk of exposure, which would jeopardise safety or health, to the agents and working conditions listed in Annex II, Section A;

    2.  workers who are breastfeeding, within the meaning of Article 2 (c), may under no circumstances be obliged to perform duties for which the assessment has revealed a risk of exposure, which would jeopardise safety or health, to the agents and working conditions listed in Annex II, Section B.

## Article 7

### Night work

1.     Member States shall take the necessary measures to ensure that workers referred to in Article 2 are not obliged to perform night work during their pregnancy and for a period following childbirth which shall be determined by the national authority competent for safety and health, subject to submission, in accordance with the procedures laid down by the Member States, of a medical certificate stating that this is necessary for the safety or health of the worker concerned.

2.     The measures referred to in paragraph 1 must entail the possibility, in accordance with national legislation and/or national practice, of—
   (a)  transfer to daytime work; or
   (b)  leave from work or extension of maternity leave where such a transfer is not technically and/or objectively feasible or cannot reasonably be required on duly substantiated grounds.

## Article 8

### Maternity leave

1.     Member States shall take the necessary measures to ensure that workers within the meaning of Article 2 are entitled to a continuous period of maternity leave of at least 14 weeks allocated before and/or after confinement in accordance with national legislation and/or practice.

2.     The maternity leave stipulated in paragraph 1 must include compulsory maternity leave of at least two weeks allocated before and/or after confinement in accordance with national legislation and/or practice.

## Article 9

### Time off for ante-natal examinations

Member States shall take the necessary measures to ensure that pregnant workers within the meaning of Article 2(a) are entitled to, in accordance with national legislation and/or practice, time off, without loss of pay, in order to attend ante-natal examinations, if such examinations have to take place during working hours.

## Article 10

### Prohibition of dismissal

In order to guarantee workers, within the meaning of Article 2, the exercise of their health and safety protection rights as recognised under this Article, it shall be provided that—
   1.  Member States shall take the necessary measures to prohibit the dismissal of workers, within the meaning of Article 2, during the period from the beginning of their pregnancy to the end of the maternity leave referred to in Article 8(1) save in exceptional cases not connected with their condition which are permitted under national legislation and/or practice and, where applicable, provided that the competent authority has given its consent;
   2.  if a worker, within the meaning of Article 2, is dismissed during the period referred to in point 1, the employer must cite duly substantiated grounds for her dismissal in writing;

3. Member States shall take the necessary measures to protect workers, within the meaning of Article 2, from consequences of dismissal which is unlawful by virtue of point 1.

## Article 11

### Employment rights

In order to guarantee workers within the meaning of Article 2 the exercise of their health and safety protection rights as recognised in this Article, it shall be provided that—

1. in the cases referred to in Articles 5, 6 and 7, the employment rights relating to the employment contract, including the maintenance of a payment to, and/or entitlement to an adequate allowance for, workers within the meaning of Article 2, must be ensured in accordance with national legislation and/or national practice;

2. in the case referred to in Article 8, the following must be ensured—
    (a) the rights connected with the employment contract of workers within the meaning of Article 2, other than those referred to in point (b) below;
    (b) maintenance of a payment to, and/or entitlement to an adequate allowance for, workers within the meaning of Article 2;

3. the allowance referred to in point 2 (b) shall be deemed adequate if it guarantees income at least equivalent to that which the worker concerned would receive in the event of a break in her activities on grounds connected with her state of health, subject to any ceiling laid down under national legislation;

4. Member States may make entitlement to pay or the allowance referred to in points 1 and 2(b) conditional upon the worker concerned fulfilling the conditions of eligibility for such benefits laid down under national legislation.

These conditions may under no circumstances provide for periods of previous employment in excess of 12 months immediately prior to the presumed date of confinement.

NOTE
See further the Statement set out in the Notes at the end of this Directive.

## Article 12

### Defence of rights

Member States shall introduce into their national legal systems such measures as are necessary to enable all workers who should themselves wronged by failure to comply with the obligations arising from this Directive to pursue their claims by judicial process (and/or, in accordance with national laws and/or practices) by recourse to other competent authorities.

NOTES
This Article is printed as in the *Official Journal*: it is thought that the word "consider" ought to have been inserted after the word "should".

## Article 13

### Amendments to the Annexes

1.    Strictly technical adjustments to Annex I as a result of technical progress, changes in international regulations or specifications and new findings in the area covered by this Directive shall be adopted in accordance with the procedure laid down in Article 17 of Directive 89/391/EEC.

2.    Annex II may be amended only in accordance with the procedure laid down in Article 118a of the Treaty.

## Article 14

### Final provisions

1.    Member States shall bring into force the laws, regulations and administrative provisions necessary to comply with this Directive not later than two years after the adoption thereof or ensure, at the latest two years after the adoption of this Directive, that the two sides of industry introduce the requisite provisions by means of collective agreements, with Member States being required to make all the necessary provisions to enable them at all times to guarantee the results laid down by this Directive. They shall forthwith inform the Commission thereof.

2.    When Member States adopt the measure referred to in paragraph 1, they shall contain a reference of this Directive or shall be accompanied by such reference on the occasion of their official publication. The methods of making such a reference shall be laid down by the Member States.

3.    Member States shall communicate to the Commission the texts of the essential provisions of national law which they have already adopted or adopt in the field governed by this Directive.

4.    Member States shall report to the Commission every five years on the practical implementation of the provisions of this Directive, indicating the points of view of the two sides of industry.

However, Member States shall report for the first time to the Commission on the practical implementation of the provisions of this Directive, indicating the points of view of the two sides of industry, four years after its adoption.

The Commission shall inform the European Parliament, the Council, the Economic and Social Committee and the Advisory Committee on Safety, Hygiene and Health Protection at Work.

5.    The Commission shall periodically submit to the European Parliament, the Council and the Economic and Social Committee a report on the implementation of this Directive, taking into account paragraphs 1, 2 and 3.

6.    The Council will re-examine this Directive, on the basis of an assessment carried out on the basis of the reports referred to in the second subparagraph of paragraph 4 and, should the need arise, of a proposal, to be submitted by the Commission at the latest five years after adoption of the Directive.

## Article 15

The Directive is addressed to the Member States.

# ANNEX I
# NON-EXHAUSTIVE LIST OF AGENTS, PROCESSES AND WORKING CONDITIONS

(referred to in Article 4(1))

A. *Agents*

1      *Physical agents* where these are regarded as agents causing foetal lesions and/or likely to disrupt placental attachment, and in particular—
   (a)  shocks, vibration or movement;
   (b)  handling of loads entailing risks, particularly of a dorsolumbar nature;
   (c)  noise;
   (d)  ionising radiation;
   (e)  non-ionising radiation;
   (f)  extremes of cold or heat;
   (g)  movements and postures, travelling—either inside or outside the establishment—mental and physical fatigue and other physical burdens connected with the activity of the worker within the meaning of Article 2 of the Directive.

2.     *Biological agents*

Biological agents of risk groups 2, 3 and 3 [*] within the meaning of Article 2(d) numbers 2, 3 and 4 of Directive 90/679/EEC, in so far as it is known that these agents or the therapeutic measures necessitated by such agents endanger the health of pregnant women and the unborn child and in so far as they do not yet appear in Annex II.

---

NOTES
   * text printed as in the *Official Journal*.

---

3.     *Chemical agents*

The following chemical agents in so far as it is known that they endanger the health of pregnant women and the unborn child and in so far as they do not yet appear in Annex II—
   (a)  substances labelled R 40, R 45, R 46, and R 47 under Directive 67/548/EEC in so far as they do not yet appear in Annex II;
   (b)  chemical agents in Annex I to Directive 90/394/EEC;
   (c)  mercury and mercury derivatives;
   (d)  antimitotic drugs;
   (e)  carbon monoxide;
   (f)  chemical agents of known and dangerous percutaneous absorption.

B. *Processes*

Industrial processes listed in Annex I to Directive 90/394/EEC.

C. *Working conditions*

Underground mining work.

# ANNEX II
# NON-EXHAUSTIVE LIST OF AGENTS AND WORKING CONDITIONS

(referred to in Article 6)

## A. PREGNANT WORKERS WITHIN THE MEANING OF ARTICLE 2(a)

1. *Agents*
   (a) Physical agents
   Work in hyperbaric atmosphere, eg pressurised enclosures and underwater diving.
   (b) Biological agents
   The following biological agents—
   — toxoplasma,
   — rubella virus,
   unless the pregnant workers are proved to be adequately protected against such agents by immunisation.
   (c) Chemical agents
   Lead and lead derivatives in so far as these agents are capable of being absorbed by the human organism.

2. *Working conditions*

Underground mining work.

## B. WORKERS WHO ARE BREASTFEEDING WITHIN THE MEANING OF ARTICLE 2(c)

1. *Agents*
   (a) Chemical agents
   Lead and lead derivatives in so far as these agents are capable of being absorbed by the human organism.

2. *Working conditions*

Underground mining work.

---

NOTES
  As to the scope and interpretation inter alia of Article 11(3) of the Directive, the Council and Commission issued the following formal statement at the 1608th meeting of the Council on 19 October 1992 (OJ(L) 348/92, p 8)—
  THE COUNCIL AND THE COMMISSION stated that—
  "In determining the level of the allowances referred to in Article 11(2) (b) and (3), reference shall be made, for purely technical reasons, to the allowance which a worker would receive in the event of a break in her activities on grounds connected with her state of health. Such a reference is not intended in any way to imply that pregnancy and childbirth be equated with sickness. The national social security legislation of all Member States provides for an allowance to be paid during an absence from work due to sickness. The link with such allowance in the chosen formulation is simply intended to serve as a concrete, fixed reference amount in all Member States for the determination of the minimum amount of maternity allowance payable. In so far as allowances are paid in individual Member States which exceed those provided for in the Directive, such allowances are, of course, retained. This is clear from Article 1(3) of the Directive.".

---

# UK LEGISLATION

# EUROPEAN COMMUNITIES ACT 1972

## (C 68)

*An Act to make provision in connection with the enlargement of the European Communities to include the United Kingdom, together with (for certain purposes) the Channel Islands, the Isle of Man and Gibraltar*

## PART I
## GENERAL PROVISIONS

### 1    Short title and interpretation

(1)    This Act may be cited as the European Communities Act 1972.

(2)    In this Act . . . —

'the Communities' means the European Economic Community, the European Coal and Steel Community and the European Atomic Energy Community;

'the Treaties' or 'the Community Treaties' means, subject to subsection (3) below, the pre-accession treaties, that is to say, those described in Part I of Schedule 1 to this Act, taken with—

(a)    the treaty relating to the accession of the United Kingdom to the European Economic Community and to the European Atomic Energy Community, signed at Brussels on the 22nd January 1972; and

(b)    the decision, of the same date, of the Council of the European Communities relating to the accession of the United Kingdom to the European Coal and Steel Community; [and

(c)    the treaty relating to the accession of the Hellenic Republic to the European Economic Community and to the European Atomic Energy Community, signed at Athens on 28th May 1979; and

(d)    the decision, of 24th May 1979, of the Council relating to the accession of the Hellenic Republic to the European Coal and Steel Community;] [and

(e)    the decisions of the Council of 7th May 1985, 24th June 1988, and 31st October 1994, on the Communities' system of own resources; and]

(g)    the treaty relating to the accession of the Kingdom of Spain and the Portuguese Republic to the European Economic Community and to the European Atomic Energy Community, signed at Lisbon and Madrid on 12th June 1985; and

(h)    the decision, of 11th June 1985, of the Council relating to the accession of the Kingdom of Spain and the Portuguese Republic to the European Coal and Steel Community;] [and

(j)    the following provisions of the Single European Act signed at Luxembourg and The Hague on 17th and 28th February 1986, namely Title II (amendment of the treaties establishing the Communities) and, so far as they relate to any of the Communities or any Community institution, the preamble and Titles I (common provisions) and IV (general and final provisions);] [and

(k)    Titles II, III and IV of the Treaty on European Union signed at Maastricht on 7th February 1992, together with the other provisions of the Treaty so far as they relate to those Titles, and the Protocols adopted at Maastricht on that date and annexed to the Treaty establishing the European Community with the exception of the Protocol on Social Policy on page 117 of Cm 1934] [and

(l)  the decision, of 1st February 1993, of the Council amending the Act concerning the election of the representatives of the European Parliament by direct universal suffrage annexed to Council Decision 76/787/ECSC, EEC, Euratom of 20th September 1976] [and

(m)  the Agreement on the European Economic Area signed at Oporto on 2nd May 1992 together with the Protocol adjusting that Agreement signed at Brussels on 17th March 1993] [and

(n)  the treaty concerning the accession of the Kingdom of Norway, the Republic of Austria, the Republic of Finland and the Kingdom of Sweden to the European Union, signed at Corfu on 24th June 1994;]

and any other treaty entered into by any of the Communities, with or without any of the member States, or entered into, as a treaty ancillary to any of the Treaties, by the United Kingdom;
[and

(o)  the following provisions of the Treaty signed at Amsterdam on 2nd October 1997 amending the Treaty on European Union, the Treaties establishing the European Communities and certain related Acts—
  (i)  Articles 2 to 9,
  (ii)  Article 12, and
  (iii)  the other provisions of the Treaty so far as they relate to those Articles,
and the Protocols adopted on that occasion other than the Protocol on Article J.7 of the Treaty on Europan Union]

and any expression defined in Schedule 1 to this Act has the meaning there given to it.

(3)    If Her Majesty by Order in Council declares that a treaty specified in the Order is to be regarded as one of the Community Treaties as herein defined, the Order shall be conclusive that it is to be so regarded; but a treaty entered into by the United Kingdom after the 22nd January 1972, other than a pre-accession treaty to which the United Kingdom accedes on terms settled on or before that date, shall not be so regarded unless it is so specified, nor be so specified unless a draft of the Order in Council has been approved by resolution of each House of Parliament.

(4)    For purposes of subsections (2) and (3) above, 'treaty' includes any international agreement, and any protocol or annex to a treaty or international agreement.

NOTES

Sub-s (2): words omitted repealed by the Interpretation Act 1978, s 25(1), Sch 3; in definitions 'the Treaties' or the 'Community Treaties' paras (c), (d) added by the European Communities (Greek Accession) Act 1979, s 1, para (e) originally added together with para (f), by the European Communities (Finance) Act 1985, s 1, substituted for paras (e), (f), by the European Communities (Finance) Act 1995, s 1, paras (g), (h) added by the European Communities (Spanish and Portuguese Accession) Act 1985, s 1, para (j) added by the European Communities (Amendment) Act 1986, s 1, para (k) added by the European Communities (Amendment) Act 1993, s 1(1), para (l) added by the European Parliamentary Elections Act 1993, s 3(2), para (m) added by the European Economic Area Act 1993, s 1; para (n) added by the European Union (Accessions) Act 1994, s 1; para (o) added by the European Communities (Amendment) Act 1998, s 1.

No UK legislation has been passed to reflect the fact that Norway did not join the EC.

## 2   General implementation of Treaties

(1)    All such rights, powers, liabilities, obligations and restrictions from time to time created or arising by or under the Treaties, and all such remedies and procedures from time to time provided for by or under the Treaties, as in accordance with the Treaties

are without further enactment to be given legal effect or used in the United Kingdom shall be recognised and available in law, and be enforced, allowed and followed accordingly; and the expression 'enforceable Community right' and similar expressions shall be read as referring to one to which this subsection applies.

(2)     Subject to Schedule 2 to this Act, at any time after its passing Her Majesty may by Order in Council, and any designated Minister or department may by regulations, make provision—

    (a) for the purpose of implementing any Community obligation of the United Kingdom, or enabling any such obligation to be implemented, or of enabling any rights enjoyed or to be enjoyed by the United Kingdom under or by virtue of the Treaties to be exercised; or

    (b) for the purpose of dealing with matters arising out of or related to any such obligation or rights or the coming into force, or the operation from time to time, of subsection (1) above;

and in the exercise of any statutory power or duty, including any power to give directions or to legislate by means of orders, rules, regulations or other subordinate instrument, the person entrusted with the power or duty may have regard to the objects of the Communities and to any such obligation or rights as aforesaid.

In this subsection 'designated Minister or department' means such Minister of the Crown or government department as may from time to time be designated by Order in Council in relation to any matter or for any purpose, but subject to such restrictions or conditions (if any) as may be specified by the Order in Council.

(3)     There shall be charged on and issued out of the Consolidated Fund or, if so determined by the Treasury, the National Loans Fund the amounts required to meet any Community obligation to make payments to any of the Communities or member States, or any Community obligation in respect of contributions to the capital or reserves of the European Investment Bank or in respect of loans to the Bank, or to redeem any notes or obligations issued or created in respect of any such Community obligation; and, except as otherwise provided by or under any enactment,—

    (a) any other expenses incurred under or by virtue of the Treaties or this Act by any Minister of the Crown or government department may be paid out of moneys provided by Parliament; and

    (b) any sums received under or by virtue of the Treaties or this Act by any Minister of the Crown or government department, save for such sums as may be required for disbursements permitted by any other enactment, shall be paid into the Consolidated Fund or, if so determined by the Treasury, the National Loans Fund.

(4)     The provision that may be made under subsection (2) above includes, subject to Schedule 2 to this Act, any such provision (of any such extent) as might be made by Act of Parliament, and any enactment passed or to be passed, other than one contained in this Part of this Act, shall be construed and have effect subject to the foregoing provisions of this section; but, except as may be provided by any Act passed after this Act, Schedule 2 shall have effect in connection with the powers conferred by this and the following sections of this Act to make Orders in Council and regulations.

(5)     . . . and the references in that subsection to a Minister of the Crown or government department and to a statutory power or duty shall include a Minister or department of the Government of Northern Ireland and a power or duty arising under or by virtue of an Act of the Parliament of Northern Ireland.

(6)    A law passed by the legislature of any of the Channel Islands or of the Isle of Man, or a colonial law (within the meaning of the Colonial Laws Validity Act 1865) passed or made for Gibraltar, if expressed to be passed or made in the implementation of the Treaties and of the obligations of the United Kingdom thereunder, shall not be void or inoperative by reason of any inconsistency with or repugnancy to an Act of Parliament, passed or to be passed, that extends to the Island or Gibraltar or any provision having the force and effect of an Act there (but not including this section), nor by reason of its having some operation outside the Island or Gibraltar; and any such Act or provision that extends to the Island or Gibraltar shall be construed and have effect subject to the provisions of any such law.

NOTES
    Sub-s (5): words omitted repealed by the Northern Ireland Constitution Act 1973, s 41(1), Sch 6, Part I.

## 3    Decisions on, and proof of, Treaties and Community instruments, etc

(1)    For the purposes of all legal proceedings any question as to the meaning or effect of any of the Treaties, or as to the validity, meaning or effect of any Community instrument, shall be treated as a question of law (and, if not referred to the European Court, be for determination as such in accordance with the principles laid down by and any relevant [decision of the European Court or any court attached thereto)].

(2)    Judicial notice shall be taken of the Treaties, of the Official Journal of the Communities and of any decision of, or expression of opinion by, the European Court [or any court attached thereto] on any such question as aforesaid; and the Official Journal shall be admissible as evidence of any instrument or other act thereby communicated of any of the Communities or of any Community institution.

(3)    Evidence of any instrument issued by a Community institution, including any judgment or order of the European Court [or any court attached thereto], or of any document in the custody of a Community institution, or any entry in or extract from such a document, may be given in any legal proceedings by production of a copy certified as a true copy by an official of that institution; and any document purporting to be such a copy shall be received in evidence without proof of the official position or handwriting of the person signing the certificate.

(4)    Evidence of any Community instrument may also be given in any legal proceedings—
    (a) by production of a copy purporting to be printed by the Queen's Printer;
    (b) where the instrument is in the custody of a government department (including a department of the Government of Northern Ireland), by production of a copy certified on behalf of the department to be a true copy by an officer of the department generally or specially authorised so to do;

and any document purporting to be such a copy as is mentioned in paragraph (b) above of an instrument in the custody of a department shall be received in evidence without proof of the official position or handwriting of the person signing the certificate, or of his authority to do so, or of the document being in the custody of the department.

NOTES
    Sub-ss (1)–(3): words in square brackets substituted or added by the European Communities (Amendment) Act 1986, s 2.

# SCHEDULE 1
# DEFINITIONS RELATING TO COMMUNITIES

Section 1

PART II
OTHER DEFINITIONS

'Economic Community', 'Coal and Steel Community' and 'Euratom' mean respectively the European Economic Community, the European Coal and Steel Community and the European Atomic Energy Community.

'Community customs duty' means, in relation to any goods, such duty of customs as may from time to time be fixed for those goods by directly applicable Community provision as the duty chargeable on importation into member States.

'Community institution' means any institution of any of the Communities or common to the Communities; and any reference to an institution of a particular Community shall include one common to the Communities when it acts for that Community, and similarly with references to a committee, officer or servant of a particular Community.

'Community instrument' means any instrument issued by a Community institution.

'Community obligation' means any obligation created or arising by or under the Treaties, whether an enforceable Community obligation or not.

'Enforceable Community right' and similar expressions shall be construed in accordance with section 2(1) of this Act.

'Entry date' means the date on which the United Kingdom becomes a member of the Communities.

'European Court' means the Court of Justice of the European Communities.

'Member', in the expression 'member State', refers to membership of the Communities.


# SCHEDULE 2
# PROVISIONS AS TO SUBORDINATE LEGISLATION

Section 2

1.—(1)    The powers conferred by section 2(2) of this Act to make provision for the purposes mentioned in section 2(2)(a) and (b) shall not include power—
  (a)   to make any provision imposing or increasing taxation; or
  (b)   to make any provision taking effect from a date earlier than that of the making of the instrument containing the provision; or
  (c)   to confer any power to legislate by means of orders, rules, regulations or other subordinate instrument, other than rules of procedure for any court or tribunal; or
  (d)   to create any new criminal offence punishable with imprisonment for more than two years or punishable on summary conviction with imprisonment for more than three months or with a fine of more than [level 5 on the standard scale] (if not calculated on a daily basis) or with a fine of more than [#100 a day].

(2)    Sub-paragraph (1)(c) above shall not be taken to preclude the modification of a power to legislate conferred otherwise than under section 2(2), or the extension of any such power to purposes of the like nature as those for which it was conferred; and a power to give directions as to matters of administration is not to be regarded as a power to legislate within the meaning of sub-paragraph (1)(c).

2.—(1)    Subject to paragraph 3 below, where a provision contained in any section of this Act confers power to make regulations (otherwise than by modification or extension of an existing power), the power shall be exercisable by statutory instrument.

(2)    Any statutory instrument containing an Order in Council or regulations made in the exercise of a power so conferred, if made without a draft having been approved by resolution of each House of Parliament, shall be subject to annulment in pursuance of a resolution of either House.

3.   Nothing in paragraph 2 above shall apply to any Order in Council made by the Governor of Northern Ireland or to any regulations made by a Minister or department of the Government of Northern Ireland; but where a provision contained in any section of this Act confers power to make such an Order in Council or regulations, then any Order in Council or regulations made in the exercise of that power, if made without a draft having been approved by resolution of each House of the Parliament of Northern Ireland, shall be subject to negative resolution within the meaning of section 41(6) of the Interpretation Act (Northern Ireland) 1954 as if the Order or regulations were a statutory instrument within the meaning of that Act.

NOTES
   Para 1: first-mentioned maximum fine increased and converted to a level on the standard scale by the Criminal Justice Act 1982, ss 37, 40, 46; second words in square brackets substituted by the Criminal Law Act 1977, ss 32(3), 65(10).

# EUROPEAN COMMUNITIES (AMENDMENT) ACT 1993

## (C 32)

*An Act to make provision consequential on the Treaty on European Union signed at Maastricht on 7th February 1992*

## 1   Treaty on European Union

(1)   . . .

(2)   For the purpose of section 6 of the European Parliamentary Elections Act 1978 (approval of treaties increasing the Parliament's powers) the Treaty on European Union signed at Maastricht on 7th February 1992 is approved.

NOTES
   Sub-s (1): amends the European Communities Act 1972, s 1(2).

## 2   Economic and monetary union

No notification shall be given to the Council of the European Communities that the United Kingdom intends to move to the third stage of economic and monetary union (in accordance with the Protocol on certain provisions relating to the United Kingdom adopted at Maastricht on 7th February 1992) unless a draft of the notification has first been approved by Act of Parliament and unless Her Majesty's Government has reported to Parliament on its proposals for the co-ordination of economic policies, its role in the European Council of Finance Ministers (ECOFIN) in pursuit of the objectives of Article 2 of the Treaty establishing the European Community as provided for in Articles 103 and 102a, and the work of the European Monetary Institute in preparation for economic and monetary union.

## 3   Annual report by Bank of England

In implementing Article 108 of the Treaty establishing the European Community, and ensuring compatibility of the statutes of the national central bank, Her Majesty's Government shall, by order, make provision for the Governor of the Bank of England to make an annual report to Parliament, which shall be subject to approval by a Resolution of each House of Parliament.

## 4    Information for Commission

In implementing the provisions of Article 103(3) of the Treaty establishing the European Community, information shall be submitted to the Commission from the United Kingdom indicating performance on economic growth, industrial investment, employment and balance of trade, together with comparisons with those items of performance from other member States.

## 5    Convergence criteria: assessment of deficits

Before submitting the information required in implementing Article 103(3) of the Treaty establishing the European Community, Her Majesty's Government shall report to Parliament for its approval an assessment of the medium term economic and budgetary position in relation to public investment expenditure and to the social, economic and environmental goals set out in Article 2, which report shall form the basis of any submission to the Council and Commission in pursuit of their responsibilities under Articles 103 and 104c.

## 6    Committee of the Regions

A person may be proposed as a member or alternate member for the United Kingdom of the Committee of the Regions constituted under Article 198a of the Treaty establishing the European Community only if, at the time of the proposal, he is an elected member of a local authority.

## 7    Commencement (Protocol on Social Policy)

This Act shall come into force only when each House of Parliament has come to a Resolution on a motion tabled by a Minister of the Crown considering the question of adopting the Protocol on Social Policy.

## 8    Short title

This Act may be cited as the European Communities (Amendment) Act 1993.

# EC COMPETITION LAW (ARTICLES 88 AND 89) ENFORCEMENT REGULATIONS 1996

**(SI 1996/2199)**

NOTES
Made: 23 August 1996.
Commencement: 28 August 1996.
Authority: European Communities Act 1972, s 2(2).

## 1    Title, commencement and extent

(1)    These Regulations may be cited as the EC Competition Law (Articles 88 and 89) Enforcement Regulations 1996 and shall come into force on the day after the day on which they are laid before Parliament.

(2)    These Regulations extend to Northern Ireland.

## 2    Interpretation

(1)    In these Regulations—

"the 1973 Act" means the Fair Trading Act 1973;

"Commission" means the Commission of the European Communities;

"the Director" means the Director General of Fair Trading;

"the MMC" means the Monopolies and Mergers Commission;

"practice" means any form of conduct or any other matter which may constitute an abuse of a dominant position;

"qualifying undertaking" means an undertaking which is—

    (a)  in the case of an individual, a citizen of the United Kingdom and Colonies, or

    (b)  a body corporate incorporated under the law of the United Kingdom, or of a part of the United Kingdom, or

    (c)  a person carrying on business in the United Kingdom, either alone or in partnership with one or more other persons.

(2)    References in these Regulations to Articles are (except where the contrary intention appears) references to Articles of the treaty establishing the European Community.

(3)    Except in the case of the word "undertaking" in regulations 14, 20, 22 and 24, expressions used in these Regulations and in Article 85, 86, 88 or 89 shall have the meaning they bear in the treaty establishing the European Community.

(4)    Any provision of these Regulations which is expressed to apply to, or in relation to, an agreement is to be read as applying equally to, or in relation to, a decision by an association of undertakings or a concerted practice (but with any necessary modifications).

## 3    Preliminary investigation by the Director

(1)    If it appears to the Secretary of State that the United Kingdom might have a duty under Article 88 to rule on the question—

    (a)  whether or not there is or has been in existence an agreement prohibited by Article 85 to which a qualifying undertaking is a party, or

    (b)  whether or not the carrying on of a practice by a qualifying undertaking constitutes an infringement of Article 86,

he may ask the Director to carry out an investigation (a "preliminary investigation") and to advise the Secretary of State of the outcome.

(2)    In carrying out a preliminary investigation, the Director shall take into account all representations made to him by persons appearing to him to have a substantial interest in the subject matter of the investigation.

## 4    Action by the Secretary of State on an agreement

(1)    This paragraph applies where, following a preliminary investigation by the Director of an agreement, it appears to the Secretary of State—

    (a)  that there is or has been in existence an agreement, to which at least one of the parties is or was a qualifying undertaking, and

    (b)  that the United Kingdom has a duty under Article 88 to rule on the question whether or not the agreement is prohibited by Article 85.

(2)    Where paragraph (1) applies, the Secretary of State may, if it appears to him that the agreement does not or did not fall within Article 85(1), decide to certify that, on

the basis of the facts in his possession, there are no grounds for action on his part in respect of the agreement.

(3)    Where paragraph (1) applies, the Secretary of State may, if it appears to him that the agreement falls within Article 85(1) or did so fall, but that the conditions for application of Article 85(3) are met or were met in respect of the agreement, declare the provisions of Article 85(1) inapplicable to the agreement.

(4)    Where paragraph (1) applies and the Secretary of State has not made a decision under paragraph (2) or a declaration under paragraph (3), he may refer the agreement to the MMC for investigation and report.

(5)    Where, following a preliminary investigation by the Director, it appears to the Secretary of State that there may be, or may have been, in existence an agreement to which at least one of the parties is or was a qualifying undertaking, and that, if so, the United Kingdom would have a duty to rule on the agreement under Article 88, the Secretary of State may refer the suspected agreement to the MMC for investigation and report.

## 5    Action by the Secretary of State on a practice

(1)    This paragraph applies where, following a preliminary investigation by the Director of a practice, it appears to the Secretary of State that—
  (a)  a practice is being, or has been, carried on by a qualifying undertaking, and
  (b)  the United Kingdom has a duty under Article 88 to rule on the question whether or not the practice infringes Article 86.

(2)    Where paragraph (1) applies, the Secretary of State may, if it appears to him that the practice does not infringe Article 86, decide to certify that, on the basis of the facts in his possession, there are no grounds for action on his part in respect of the practice.

(3)    Where paragraph (1) applies and it appears to the Secretary of State that the practice may infringe Article 86, the Secretary of State may refer the practice to the MMC for investigation and report.

(4)    Where, following a preliminary investigation by the Director, it appears to the Secretary of State that a practice may be being or may have been carried on by a qualifying undertaking, and that, if so, the United Kingdom would have a duty to rule on the practice under Article 88, the Secretary of State may refer the suspected practice to the MMC for investigation and report.

## 6    Publication of decisions by Secretary of State

(1)    Subject to paragraphs (3) and (4) below, the Secretary of State shall publish any decision to certify taken by him under regulation 4(2) or 5(2) and any declaration made by him under regulation 4(3) together with such an account of his reasons for making the decision or declaration as in his opinion is expedient for facilitating an understanding of his decision or of his declaration.

(2)    Any publication of a decision or declaration under paragraph (1) shall be in such manner as appears to the Secretary of State to be appropriate.

(3)    If it appears to the Secretary of State that it would be against the public interest to publish a particular matter which he would otherwise include in an account of his

reasons required to be published under paragraph (1), the Secretary of State shall exclude that matter from the account before publishing it.

(4)     Without prejudice to paragraph (3), if the Secretary of State considers that it would not be in the public interest to disclose any matter which he would otherwise include in an account of his reasons required to be published under paragraph (1),

> (a) relating to the private affairs of an individual whose interests would, in the opinion of the Secretary of State, be seriously and prejudicially affected by the publication of that matter, or
> (b) relating specifically to the affairs of a particular person whose interests would, in the opinion of the Secretary of State, be seriously and prejudicially affected by the publication of that matter,

the Secretary of State shall exclude that matter from the account before publishing it.

## 7   Variation of reference

The Secretary of State may at any time vary a reference made by him under these Regulations.

## 8   Publication of references

On making a reference under these Regulations or a variation of such a reference the Secretary of State shall arrange for the reference or variation to be published in such manner as he thinks most suitable for the purpose of bringing it to the attention of persons who, in his opinion, would be affected by it.

## 9   Time limit for report on a reference

(1)     Every reference under regulation 4, 5 or 20 shall specify a period (not being longer than six months beginning with the date of the reference) within which a report on the reference is to be made.

(2)     The Secretary of State may give directions to the MMC allowing such further period for the purpose of reporting on a reference under these Regulations as may be specified in the directions, or, if the period has already been extended once or more than once by directions under this paragraph, allowing to the MMC such further extended period for that purpose as may be so specified.

## 10   Functions of the MMC on a reference of an agreement

(1)     On a reference under regulation 4 the MMC shall investigate and report on the questions—

> (a) whether such an agreement which is the subject of the reference exists or has existed;
> (b) whether any qualifying undertaking is or was a party to it;
> (c) whether the agreement falls within Article 85(1);
> (d) whether the agreement affects or has affected competition within the United Kingdom, and, if so, what are those effects.

(2)     Where, during an investigation on a reference under regulation 4, it appears to the MMC—

> (a) that there may have existed or be in existence an agreement (other than that which is the subject of the reference) to which some or all of the parties to the agreement which is the subject of the reference are party;

    (b)  that the parties to that other agreement include a qualifying undertaking; and

    (c)  that the United Kingdom may have a duty to rule on that agreement under Article 88;

the MMC may investigate and report on that agreement as if it had been the subject of the reference.

(3)    Where a report of the MMC on a reference under regulation 4 includes the conclusions that—

    (a)  the agreement which is the subject of the reference (or is treated as the subject by virtue of the preceding paragraph) exists or has existed;

    (b)  a qualifying undertaking is or was a party to it; and

    (c)  the agreement falls within Article 85(1);

the MMC shall also investigate and report on the question whether in their opinion the conditions for application of Article 85(3) are met.

## 11    Functions of the MMC on reference of a practice

(1)    On a reference under regulation 5 the MMC shall investigate and report on the questions—

    (a)  whether the practice which is the subject of the reference is being carried on or has been carried on;

    (b)  whether that practice infringes or has infringed Article 86;

    (c)  whether any qualifying undertaking is carrying on or has carried on the practice;

    (d)  whether the infringement of Article 86 has had an effect on competition in the United Kingdom and, if so, what are those effects.

(2)    Where, during an investigation on a reference under regulation 5, it appears to the MMC that a practice similar in form and effect to the practice which is the subject of the reference may be being carried on or may have been carried on by a qualifying undertaking and that the United Kingdom may have a duty to rule on that practice under Article 88, the MMC may investigate and report on that practice as if it had been the subject of the reference.

## 12    Report of the MMC

Any report of the MMC shall include definite conclusions on the questions on which the MMC is required to report under regulation 10, 11 or 20 together with such an account of their reasons for those conclusions as in their opinion is expedient for facilitating a proper understanding of their conclusions.

## 13    Recommendations of MMC

Where a report of the MMC—

    (a)  on a reference under regulation 4 includes the conclusions specified in regulation 10(3); or

    (b)  on a reference under regulation 5 includes the conclusions that a qualifying undertaking has infringed Article 86;

the MMC shall, as part of their investigations, consider what action (if any) should be taken in respect of those conclusions by the Secretary of State or any Minister or public authority and may, if they think fit, include in their report recommendations as to such action.

## 14　Undertakings as an alternative to a reference

(1)　Where the Secretary of State has power to make a reference to the MMC under regulation 4, regulation 5 or regulation 20 he may, instead of making a reference, accept from such of the parties concerned as he considers appropriate undertakings to take such specified action as the Secretary of State considers appropriate—

> (a)　to terminate or prevent the recurrence of the infringement of Article 85(1) or Article 86 which it appears to the Secretary of State has occurred or may have occurred, or
>
> (b)　to enable him to make a declaration under paragraph (2).

(2)　Where the Secretary of State has accepted undertakings under this regulation in respect of an agreement, and it appears to him that, if the undertakings are fulfilled, the conditions for application of Article 85(3) will be met in respect of the agreement, he may declare the provisions of Article 85(1) inapplicable to the agreement.

(3)　The Secretary of State shall arrange to publish in such manner as appears to him to be appropriate—

> (a)　any undertakings accepted by him under paragraph (1);
>
> (b)　any declaration made by him under paragraph (2);
>
> (c)　such an account of his reasons for his decision to accept undertakings, and, if it be the case, for making a declaration as in his opinion is expedient for facilitating an understanding of his decision or his declaration;
>
> (d)　any variation or release of such an undertaking.

(4)　Regulation 6(3) and (4) shall apply to the account referred to in paragraph (3)(c) as they apply to an account of the Secretary of State's reasons published under regulation 6(1).

(5)　Where an undertaking has been accepted under paragraph (1), it shall be the duty of the Director—

> (a)　to keep under review the carrying out of that undertaking, and from time to time to consider whether, by reason of any change of circumstances, the undertaking is no longer appropriate and either—
>
> > (i)　one or more of the parties to it can be released from it, or
> >
> > (ii)　it needs to be varied or to be superseded by a new undertaking, and
>
> (b)　if it appears to him that the undertaking has not been or is not being fulfilled, that any person can be so released or that the undertaking needs to be varied or superseded, to give such advice to the Secretary of State as he may think proper in the circumstances.

(6)　Where it appears to the Secretary of State that an undertaking accepted by him under paragraph (1) or which has superseded such an undertaking has not been, is not being, or will not be fulfilled, the Secretary of State may by order made by statutory instrument exercise such one or more of the powers specified in regulation 21 as he may consider it requisite to exercise for the purpose of terminating or preventing the recurrence of the infringement of Article 85 or Article 86 which it appears to the Secretary of State has occurred; and those powers may be so exercised to such extent and in such manner as the Secretary of State considers requisite for that purpose.

(7)　In determining whether, or to what extent or in what manner, to exercise any of those powers, the Secretary of State shall take into account any advice given by the Director under paragraph (5).

(8)    The provisions contained in an order under paragraph (6) may be different from those contained in the undertaking.

(9)    On the making of an order under paragraph (6), the undertaking accepted under paragraph (1) or which has superseded such an undertaking shall be released by virtue of this regulation.

## 15    Duty of Director to assist MMC

It shall be the duty of the Director, for the purpose of assisting the MMC in carrying out an investigation on a reference made to them under these Regulations, to give to the MMC—

(a)    any information which is in his possession and which relates to matters falling within the scope of the investigation and which is either requested by the MMC for that purpose or is information which in his opinion it would be appropriate for that purpose to give to the MMC without any such request, and

(b)    any other assistance which the MMC may require and which it is within his power to give in relation to such matters;

and the MMC shall take account of any information given to them for that purpose under this regulation.

## 16    Procedures of MMC and General Provisions as to Reports

The following provisions of the 1973 Act, namely sections 81 (procedures in carrying out investigations), 82 (general provisions as to reports), 83 (laying before Parliament and publication of reports), 85 (attendance of witnesses and production of documents), and Part II of Schedule 3 (performance of functions of the MMC) shall apply in relation to references under these Regulations and reports of the MMC on such references as if—

(a)    a reference under these Regulations was a reference under the 1973 Act;

(b)    functions of the MMC under these Regulations were functions in relation to an investigation under the 1973 Act;

(c)    a report of the MMC under these Regulations were a report under the 1973 Act;

(d)    in section 83 references to the Minister or Ministers were references to the Secretary of State;

(e)    in section 85(6) the references to a fine on summary conviction were to a fine not exceeding the statutory maximum;

(f)    in paragraph 11 of Schedule 3 the reference to a monopoly reference were to a reference under these Regulations and the reference to section 52 were a reference to regulation 7;

(g)    paragraph 16(2) of Schedule 3 were omitted.

## 17    Laying aside of references

(1)    If, at any time during an investigation by the MMC on a reference under these Regulations, it appears to the Secretary of State that the United Kingdom is not under a duty under Article 88 to rule on the agreement or practice which is the subject of the reference, the Secretary of State may direct the MMC to lay the reference aside.

(2)    The MMC shall comply with any direction under paragraph (1) but shall furnish to the Secretary of State such information as he may require as to the results until then of their investigations.

## 18  Director to receive copies of reports

The MMC shall send a copy of every report on a reference under these Regulations to the Director and the Secretary of State shall take account of any advice given to him by the Director with respect to such a report.

## 19  Exemptions under Article 85(3)

(1)  Where—
   (a)  the report of the MMC on a reference under regulation 4 includes the conclusions specified in regulation 10(3); and
   (b)  it appears to the Secretary of State that the United Kingdom is under a duty under Article 88 to rule on the question whether or not the agreement concerned is prohibited by Article 85;

the Secretary of State may, if it appears to him that the conditions for application of Article 85(3) are met in respect of the agreement, declare the provisions of Article 85(1) inapplicable to the agreement.

(2)  Before deciding whether to make such a declaration the Secretary of State shall have regard to the recommendations of the MMC and to their opinion as to whether the conditions for application of Article 85(3) are met.

(3)  The Secretary of State shall publish any declaration under paragraph (1) in such manner as appears to him to be appropriate.

## 20  General provisions about exemptions

(1)  This regulation applies to any declaration made by the Secretary of State—
   (a)  under regulation 4(3);
   (b)  under regulation 14(2);
   (c)  under regulation 19(1);

and to any renewal of such a declaration under paragraph (3) below.

(2)  A declaration to which this regulation applies—
   (a)  shall have effect from such date as may be stated in the declaration being a date not earlier than the date on which the agreement or these Regulations came into force whichever is the later, and
   (b)  shall have effect for the period stipulated in the declaration.

(3)  The Secretary of State may renew a declaration to which this regulation applies for a further period if it appears to him that the conditions for application of Article 85(3) continue to be met in respect of the agreement at the expiry of the original declaration.

(4)  A declaration to which this regulation applies may be made unconditionally or subject to such conditions as the Secretary of State thinks fit.

(5)  It shall be the duty of the Director to keep under review the operation of any agreement in respect of which the Secretary of State has made a declaration to which this regulation applies and to advise the Secretary of State if at any time, he considers that the conditions for the application of Article 85(3) cease to be satisfied in respect of the agreement.

(6)  If it appears to the Secretary of State in respect of a declaration to which this regulation applies—

(a) that there has been a material change of circumstances since the declaration was made; or

(b) that any information given in respect of the agreement concerned to the Director, to the MMC or to the Secretary of State is or was in any material respect false or misleading; or

(c) that any person who gave an undertaking under regulation 14 or 22 to the Secretary of State as a result of which the Secretary of State was able to make the declaration has not complied with it;

the Secretary of State may revoke or vary the declaration as he thinks fit.

(7)    Before deciding whether to renew, revoke or vary a declaration to which this regulation applies, the Secretary of State may refer the matter to the MMC for investigation and report.

(8)    On a reference under paragraph (7) above, the MMC shall investigate and report on the question whether in their opinion the conditions for application of Article 85(3) are met in respect of the agreement which is the subject of the reference.

(9)    The MMC shall, as part of their investigations on a reference under paragraph (7) above, consider what action (if any) should be taken in respect of their conclusions by the Secretary of State or any Minister or public authority and may, if they think fit, include in their report recommendations as to such action.

## 21    Powers of Secretary of State to make Orders

(1)    Where—
(a) paragraph (2) applies, or
(b) pursuant to Article 89(2), the Commission has taken a reasoned decision relating to an infringement of Article 85 and has authorised the United Kingdom to take measures needed to remedy the situation;

the Secretary of State may by order made by statutory instrument exercise such one or more of the powers specified in Parts I and II of Schedule 8 to the 1973 Act as he considers it requisite to exercise for the purpose of terminating or preventing the recurrence of the infringement of Article 85 concerned or for the purpose of enabling him to make a declaration under regulation 19 or a renewal of such a declaration; and those powers may be so exercised to such extent and in such manner as the Secretary of State considers requisite for that purpose.

(2)    This paragraph applies where—
(a) it appears to the Secretary of State that the United Kingdom has a duty under Article 88 to rule on whether or not an agreement which is the subject of a report of the MMC on a reference under regulation 4 is prohibited under Article 85(1), and
(b) the report includes the conclusions specified in regulation 10(3) and the Secretary of State has not declared Article 85(1) inapplicable to the agreement.

(3)    Where—
(a) the Secretary of State has received a report of the MMC on a reference under regulation 5(3) which concludes that there is or has been an infringement of Article 86 by one or more undertakings at least one of which is a qualifying undertaking and it appears to the Secretary of State that the United Kingdom has a duty under Article 88 to rule on whether or not that infringement has occurred; or

(b) pursuant to Article 89(2), the Commission has taken a reasoned decision under Article 89(2) relating to an infringement of Article 86 and has authorised the United Kingdom to take measures needed to remedy the situation;

the Secretary of State may by order made by statutory instrument exercise any one or more of the powers specified in paragraph (4) for the purpose of terminating or preventing the recurrence of the infringement of Article 86 concerned.

(4)    The powers which may be exercised under paragraph (3) are—

(a) the power to prohibit a person named in the order from carrying on the practice constituting the infringement of Article 86 specified in the report of the MMC or decision of the Commission or from carrying on any other practice which is similar in form and effect to that practice; and

(b) such one or more of the powers specified in Part I or II of Schedule 8 to the 1973 Act as the Secretary of State considers it requisite to exercise for the purpose mentioned in paragraph (3);

and those powers may be so exercised to such extent and in such manner as the Secretary of State considers requisite for the purpose mentioned in paragraph (3).

(5)    In determining whether, or to what extent or in what manner, to exercise any of the powers under this regulation the Secretary of State shall have regard to any recommendations included in the report of the MMC.

(6)    For the purpose of this regulation and of regulation 14(6), Schedule 8 to the 1973 Act shall be construed as if—

(a) an order under section 56 were an order under these Regulations;

(b) paragraph 3 were omitted,

(c) references to the appropriate Minister were references to the Secretary of State.

(7)    It shall be the duty of the Director to keep under review the action (if any) taken in compliance with an order made under regulation 14(6) or under this regulation, and from time to time to consider whether, by reason of any change of circumstances, the order should be varied or revoked or should be superseded by a new order, and—

(a) if it appears to him that the order has in any respect not been complied with, to consider whether any action (by way of proceedings in accordance with section 93 of the 1973 Act as applied by regulation 24 or otherwise) should be taken for the purpose of securing compliance with the order, and (where in his opinion it is appropriate to do so) to take such action himself or give advice to the Secretary of State or other person by whom such action might be taken; or

(b) if it appears to him that the order needs to be varied or revoked, or to be superseded by a new order, to give such advice to the Secretary of State as he may think proper in the circumstances.

## 22    Undertakings following a report

(1)    In any circumstances where the Secretary of State has power to make an order under regulation 21 it shall be the duty of the Director to comply with any request of the Secretary of State to consult with any persons mentioned in the request ("the relevant parties") with a view to obtaining from them undertakings to take action indicated in the request made to the Director as being action requisite in the opinion

of the Secretary of State, for the purpose of terminating or preventing the recurrence of the infringement of Article 85 or 86 concerned, or of enabling the Secretary of State to make a declaration under regulation 19.

(2)     Subsections (2) to (5) of section 88 of the 1973 Act shall apply in relation to consultation under paragraph (1), undertakings given in pursuance of them and orders made under regulation 21, as if—

(a) references to the appropriate Minister were references to the Secretary of State;

(b) references to powers under section 56 were to powers under regulation 21;

(c) references to the "relevant parties" were construed in accordance with paragraph (1) above.

## 23     Procedure relating to orders made under these Regulations

(1)     No order made under these Regulations which exercises any of the powers specified in Part II of Schedule 8 to the 1973 Act and no order varying or revoking any such order shall be made unless a draft of the order has been laid before Parliament and approved by a resolution of each House of Parliament; and the provisions of Schedule 9 to the 1973 Act shall apply with respect to the procedure to be followed before laying before Parliament a draft of any such order as they apply to an order such as is mentioned in section 91(1) of the 1973 Act.

(2)     Any statutory instrument whereby any order is made under any provision of these Regulations, other than an instrument whereby an order is made to which the preceding paragraph applies, shall be subject to annulment in pursuance of a resolution of either House of Parliament.

(3)     Section 91(2) of the 1973 Act shall apply to an order made under these Regulations (other than an order to which paragraph (1) applies) as it applies to an order made under section 56 of the 1973 Act other than an order such as is mentioned in section 91(1) of the 1973 Act.

## 24     Provisions as to orders and enforcement

Sections 90 (general provisions to orders), 92 (investigation of company), 93 (enforcement of orders), and 93A (enforcement of undertakings) of the 1973 Act shall apply in relation to orders made under these Regulations as if—

(a) references to orders made under section 56 of the 1973 Act were references to orders made under these Regulations;

(b) the words "either for all persons or" in subsection (2) of section 90 were omitted;

(c) subsections (5) and (6) of section 90 were omitted;

(d) references to the Minister were references to the Secretary of State;

(e) references to an order to which section 90 of the 1973 Act applies were references to an order made under these Regulations; and

(f) references to undertakings accepted by the Secretary of State under section 75G of the 1973 Act were to undertakings accepted by the Secretary of State under regulation 14 or regulation 22.

## 25     False or misleading information

Section 93B (false or misleading information) of the 1973 Act shall apply in relation to information furnished by any person to the Secretary of State, the Director or the MMC in connection with any of their functions under these Regulations as it applies to information furnished to the Secretary of State in connection with any of his functions under Parts IV, V or VI of the 1973 Act.

**26**

Section 129 of the 1973 Act (time limit for prosecutions) shall apply in relation to offences under these Regulations as it applies to offences under the 1973 Act.

**27**

Section 132 of the 1973 Act (offences by bodies corporate) shall apply in relation to offences under these Regulations as if—

    (a)   the reference to section 85(6) were a reference to that subsection as it is applied by regulation 16, and

    (b)   the reference to section 93(B) were a reference to that section as it is applied by regulation 25.

**28    Restrictions on disclosure of information**

(1)    Subject to paragraphs (2) to (4), no information with respect to any particular business which has been obtained under or by virtue of the provisions of these Regulations shall, so long as that business continues to be carried on, be disclosed without the consent of the person for the time being carrying on that business.

(2)    Paragraph (1) does not apply to any disclosure of information which is made—

    (a)   for the purpose of facilitating the performance of any functions of the Director, the Civil Aviation Authority, the MMC, or the Secretary of State under these Regulations, or the Fair Trading Act 1973, or the Restrictive Trade Practices Act 1976, or the Resale Prices Act 1976, or the Competition Act 1980, or the Civil Aviation Act 1982, or the Airports Act 1986; or the Licensing of Air Carriers Regulations 1992, or Part IV of the Airports (Northern Ireland) Order 1994, or

    (b)   for facilitating the performance by the Commission of its functions under Article 89, or

    (c)   in pursuance of a Community obligation within the meaning of the European Communities Act 1972.

(3)    Paragraph (1) does not apply to any disclosure of information which is made for the purpose of any proceedings before the Restrictive Practices Court or of any other legal proceedings, whether civil or criminal under these Regulations, the 1973 Act or the Restrictive Trade Practices Act 1976.

(4)    Nothing in paragraph (1) shall be construed—

    (a)   as limiting the matters which may be included in, or made public as part of, a report of the MMC; or

    (b)   as applying to any information which has been made public as part of such a report or of a decision or declaration made by the Secretary of State under these Regulations or as part of an account published with such a decision or declaration.

(5)    Any person who discloses any information in contravention of this regulation shall be guilty of an offence and shall be liable—

    (a)   on summary conviction, to a fine not exceeding the statutory maximum;

    (b)   on conviction on indictment, to imprisonment for a term not exceeding two years or to a fine or to both.

**29    Amendments to other enactments**

(1)    In paragraph (a) of section 133(2) of the 1973 Act (exceptions from the general restriction on the disclosure of information obtained under or by virtue of certain provisions of that Act), after "or the Coal Industry Act 1994" there shall be inserted the words "or the EC Competition Law (Articles 88 and 89) Enforcement Regulations 1996".

(2)    In paragraph (a) of section 41(1) of the Restrictive Trade Practices Act 1976 (exceptions from the general restriction on the disclosure of information obtained under or by virtue of that Act), after "or the Coal Industry Act 1994" there shall be inserted the words "or the EC Competition Law (Articles 88 and 89) Enforcement Regulations 1996".

(3)    In section 19(3) of the Competition Act 1980, (exceptions from the general restriction on the disclosure of information obtained under or by virtue of that Act) there shall be inserted at the end the following sub-paragraph—

>   "(q) the EC Competition Law (Articles 88 and 89) Enforcement Regulations 1996;".

(4)    In section 74(3) of the Airports Act 1986 (exceptions from the general restriction on the disclosure of information obtained under or by virtue of that Act) there shall be inserted at the end the following sub-paragraph—

>   "(o) the EC Competition Law (Articles 88 and 89) Enforcement Regulations 1996.".

(5)    In article 49(3) of the Airports (Northern Ireland) Order 1994 (exceptions from the general restriction on the disclosure of information obtained under or by virtue of that Order) there shall be inserted at the end the following sub-paragraph—

>   "(r) the EC Competition Law (Articles 88 and 89) Enforcement Regulations 1996.".

**30    Past agreements and infringements**

Nothing in these Regulations shall enable or require the Director or the MMC to investigate or report on an agreement which was determined, or on a practice which has ceased, before these regulations came into force.